THE LIVING LIGHT DIALOGUE

Volume 17

Reproduction of the cover image of the
1972 edition of *The Living Light*

[See the appendix for a discussion of the image's symbolism.]

THE LIVING LIGHT DIALOGUE

Volume 17

Through the mediumship of
Richard P. Goodwin

Living Light Books

The Living Light Dialogue Volume 17
Copyright © 2022 Serenity Association
Through the mediumship of Richard P. Goodwin.

All rights reserved. No portion of this book may be reproduced—electronically, mechanically, or via internet transmission—without advance, express written permission of the publisher except in the case of brief quotations embodied in critical articles and reviews. No derivative work—games, supplemental material, video—may be created without advance, express written permission of the publisher. For information address Living Light Books, P.O. Box 4187, San Rafael, CA 94913-4187.

Cover design copyright © 2022 by Serenity Association.
Cover photograph by Serenity Association, 2022; copyright © 2022 by Serenity Association.

www.livinglight.org

Library of Congress Control Number 2007929762
ISBN: 978-1-947199-44-6

FIRST EDITION

This volume of teachings is dedicated to the spirit friends who brought to Earth the Living Light Philosophy. With eternal gratitude, we pray that we may demonstrate these principles and continue to bring to publication these teachings.

CONTENTS

Acknowledgment ix
Preface xi
Introduction xv
A/V Class Private 51 3
A/V Class Private 52 29
A/V Class Private 53 53
A/V Class Private 54 79
A/V Class Private 55 103
A/V Class Private 56 125
A/V Class Private 57 149
A/V Class Private 58 173
A/V Class Private 59 197
A/V Class Private 60 199
A/V Class Private 61 221
A/V Class Private 62 243
A/V Class Private 63 275
A/V Class Private 64 297
A/V Class Private 65 321
A/V Class Private 66 347
A/V Class Private 67 371
A/V Class Private 68 393
A/V Class Private 69 415
A/V Class Private 70 439
A/V Class Private 71 457
Appendix 481

ACKNOWLEDGMENT

Grateful acknowledgment is made to the many friends and associates for invaluable aid in compiling this book, for their helpful suggestions, for their loyal interest and encouragement.

Special acknowledgment is due to those who painstakingly and selflessly transcribed and proofread the text.

PREFACE

It was through the mediumship of the Serenity Association founder, Mr. Richard P. Goodwin, that a philosophy known as the Living Light was given in more than 700 classes over a twenty-five-year period.

To be specific, the philosophy was imparted through Mr. Goodwin by a magistrate who had lived on Earth some 8,000 years ago. The former magistrate is known to Living Light students as "the Wise One," and he narrated the journey of his soul on the other side of life, the experiences—especially the difficulties—he encountered in having to face himself, as well as the teachings he earned to help himself through the realms in which he traveled. It was his decision to share the teachings with souls on both sides of "the curtain."

Prior to the advent of the Wise One, Mr. Goodwin had prayed for a teacher from the realms of light. Mr. Goodwin, since age fourteen, had been the instrument through which spirit was able to communicate with those seeking help. But he saw that his mediumship brought only temporary solace, because the people he was trying to help soon became fascinated with the phenomena and ignored the help that spirit was imparting. He prayed for someone who would bring forth teachings that would benefit any soul seeking a path to a greater awareness of himself and of God.

His prayers were answered in 1964 when the Wise One came through for the first time. Mr. Goodwin, at first apprehensive about what this new teacher would impart, was taken into deep trance and not able to control what was being revealed through him. Upon hearing the recorded classes afterward, however, he became convinced of the goodness of the teacher and of the value of the simple, beautiful teachings. This, then, was the beginning of the Living Light Philosophy given to Earth through the mediumship of Richard P. Goodwin.

In carrying out the request of the Wise One and Mr. Goodwin, students of the Serenity Association transcribed from audiotape the classes that had been brought through. Because most are in the form of teacher-student interaction, the classes became known as *The Living Light Dialogue*; and the students were instructed to publish the classes as a multi-volume set of the Living Light Philosophy. *Volume 1* was published in the autumn of 2007.

The present book, *Volume 17,* continues the A/V Class Private series. As their name suggests, these classes were originally given as private classes and were to be shared and discussed only with those who were in attendance. The instructions from Mr. Goodwin regarding publication of these teachings included guidance that even the private classes be published after he had passed on to the higher life; and so, these private classes are now becoming more widely available. In many ways, these classes are of a more personal nature. The teacher frequently addressed the students by name and the students would often interact with each other. Many of the teacher's responses include references to the individual experiences of the questioner, and although this helps the student to better relate to the teaching, his responses also reveal the principle involved. Thus, in this series the names of the students are included, but have been replaced with more generic terms of identification in order to respect their privacy.

These classes were held Sunday mornings at the Serenity temple. This particular volume includes twenty classes, from A/V Class Private 51 through A/V Class Private 71, and cover the period of time from June 15, 1986, until December 21, 1986.

The foundation of the classes—the foundation of the Living Light Philosophy itself—is the Law of Personal Responsibility which states, in part, that we are responsible for all our experiences, and that our experiences are the return of the laws that we have established with our thoughts, acts, and deeds. Through greater awareness of our thoughts and by exercising our divine right of choice, we may choose to establish laws of greater harmony and goodness.

The Living Light Philosophy teaches that we have come to Earth to learn the lessons that are necessary to free us from the dictates and limits of our own thoughts and judgments, which are the mental patterns that we follow through our own lack of awareness and are so very potent, forceful, and limiting. These teachings guide us in making the necessary changes in our thinking in order to free ourselves from those patterns and to express our soul consciousness.

The choice of guiding the direction of our life, as stated by the Wise One when he speaks of being with a person, place, or thing, is, in essence, of being in this world and not a part of this world. He further explains that no matter what experiences we encounter, no matter what we do or do not do, we—our spirit—may view the experience in objectivity from a soul level of consciousness where peace reigns supreme.

The teachings of this volume help us to restore harmony or balance in our life by flooding the consciousness with spiritual affirmations and prayers, a few of which can be found in the appendix. When reason is restored, by balancing our sense functions with our soul faculties, we will consciously experience peace. Without annihilating our ego or our sense functions, we will find a pathway of expression for our soul. Where there was once disturbance, now there is acceptance. Where there was disease, now there is poise. And where there was hopelessness and despair, now there is reason, divine neutrality; and peace shows the way.

If you make the effort to apply these laws, such as, "If man is a law unto himself, what are you doing with the law that you are?", and demonstrate the wisdom of patience, the truth of this philosophy will be your living demonstration.

As the teacher states in CC 130, "My journey of many centuries and much experience has brought me here to Earth to share with you these simple teachings that have come as the effect of a long, long, long journey. Let not your journey be so long in the realms of illusion. For it is not necessary for you. For in your evolution, you have earned an awakening. But it is up to you to do something that is constructive and worthwhile."

INTRODUCTION

[This introduction was written by Mr. Goodwin and originally appeared in *The Living Light,* which were the first teachings of the Living Light Philosophy published in book form. The entire text of The Living Light was republished in *The Living Light Dialogue, Volume 1.*]

"Think, children. Think more often and think more deeply."

The teachings in this book were given as a progressive series of lessons to a group of four students who were sitting for spiritual unfoldment with me beginning in January of 1964. The communications were regular until October of that year, when nearly a seven-year silence ensued, and resumed in 1971 to the present. They were received in three ways by me as a channel. The main text was taped from a direct control of my voice in deep trance at special sittings of our group, during which I had no experience of the voice or what was being transmitted. A few scattered verses were given independently when I was privileged to see and hear our teacher clairvoyantly. I have also been a channel for this communicant when speaking from the podium at church and in answering difficult questions at our public seminars.

Nearly all we know about our teacher is contained in the lectures. He reports that he had tried for sixteen years to break through an interference barrier that the channel had to deep trance. When our conditions were in resonance with his patient wisdom, he came through ready to teach his understanding. I have seen him as an old man dressed in white with long flowing white hair. He has blue eyes, slightly smiling and deeply compassionate. I have always called him the Old Man. The students liked to call him the Wise One. He is surely one of those often called a Teacher of Light. I do not know his country, although he indicated at one time that he was from 6000 B.C., and a form of a judge in his time.

The text is often difficult, but it is complete, having been transcribed word for word from the original tapes recording the trance voice. It is presented with a minimum of punctuation to be freer for the individual interpretation of each reader. The lessons given before the long silence are phrased with many allegories often paradoxical. There are repetitions and renewals of theme, but it is explained that if an understanding is not perceived, compassion dictates that it be said again. Some of the topics have but a simple mention with little development but all are revealed, we are told, according to merit.

The Old Man is a fine teacher. He has in a hundred ways intertwined his allegory, progressive explanations, unfolding exercises, and timely references to reach a multitude of levels of individual understanding. A notable change is his more direct style of presentation beginning in 1971.

There is an endearing intimacy of person that can be felt through his lectures, a meaningful and loving encounter with a wise friend. Like an old man, he makes a mistake and conscientiously corrects himself a few paragraphs later. He listens often and carefully to our earnest discussions of his words. He consults with a group of experts on evolution and cites their learning in his lesson. His use of the direct address "children" or "my children" is not patronizing but infinitely loving and supportive.

A word must be said about the teachings. The Old Man makes clear that his lessons are not dogma, a creed or a narrow way, but simply his own understanding offered to us as a form of instruction to aid us in our own individual progression. When he speaks of Laws, he does not refer to man-made rules or moral traditions but to the cosmic and atomic way-things-are, the natural world of what-is, the universal laws of life, part of the original creative design and through which creation is fulfilled. These laws are beyond the possibility of being changed, suspended, transcended, or destroyed but they are ever a tool of mankind, not his master. First, through our awareness of the universal laws and then slowly through our developed understanding, the powers of creation are accessible to us. Not power over men's minds or circumstances, but power over whatever is selfish and imperfect in ourselves is the way up the eternal ladder of progression. When the Old Man cautions us concerning the Law of Responsibility or gives us a thinking exercise to explore the Law of Identity in a dynamic manner, he prepares us to take another step. And all move in accordance with the Law of What Can Be Borne.

Our teacher shows us how the two worlds are drawn together. In his realm, he describes, there is a great diversity of thought, many schools of understanding; but the Light is always known by the Light. Because of the interdependence of the two realms, listening to our discussions helped to clarify his teaching to others on his side of the curtain. His love and gratitude he humbly equates with ours.

The lessons to be perceived are not new, they are very old, but they are new to certain levels of our being. I would personally advise the reader, after reading this volume of discourses in full, to make a daily habit (or when there is a feeling or need) to sit quietly with the book. Open it at random and be guided to the Light by the passage that is there for the day. This technique is still used by the original students who were given the lessons and by many students after them who have studied in unfolding classes with me through these teachings.

Go beyond the words into feeling, into the immediate meanings for you. Touch into the inspiration that flows into the form of this book. It is from the Divine.

RICHARD P. GOODWIN
San Geronimo, California
June, 1972

A/V Class Private

A/V Class Private 51

[This class was recorded outdoors in the garden of the temple, near the east pond with the waterfall on. The sound of the waterfall often masked the questions asked by the students.]

Good morning, good morning, class.

Today, as you know, marks the ending of our first year of these particular classes and the beginning, of course, of our second year. It is not a graduation. I'm sure you will agree with that. However, it is a celebration. There is a vast difference between [a] celebration and a graduation. Our little friend, here, is thirsty, as usual. *[The teacher offers his glass of water to Mr. Red, the temple's dog.]* So we'll give him a moment to quench his thirst, considering my other students have so many moments quenching theirs. There. Is it quenched? *[The teacher addresses Mr. Red, when he paused in lapping water from the glass.]* Not yet. This mustn't get to be a habit here. All right now. Well, it doesn't want to sit there. *[The teacher refers to replacing his glass of water on the stone retaining wall.]* We'll sit it right there.

And so we'll begin this class today, a celebration of our survival and one year in the jungle of creation while attending weekly class. That's something, really, I think you will all agree, is worth celebrating. And so I know that many of you have had your ups and downs. Usually you think they're down. Well, down to one level, of course, is up to another. And so it's a matter of perspective whether you're up or down—your evolution and your perspective. So when you feel down, you're usually rising up. And when you're rising up, you usually feel the opposite way. So [if] you understand what that's all about, then you've come a long ways in your year here of survival.

Now let's get on here right away in these classes today with these questions that you have. Yes, [Student H].

I'd greatly appreciate hearing your definition of the difference between graduation *and* celebration.

Oh, yes. We celebrate many things and graduate from few. Yes, I'm glad you appreciate that. I appreciate it myself. Ofttimes we think we're graduating and we celebrate and there's no graduation at all. Hmm? Remember that whenever you want to remain in any endeavor, you must accept that which is necessary to remain in any endeavor. And what is necessary to remain in any endeavor? To refrain from every endeavor that is contrary to the very purpose for which you have decided to remain in one endeavor. So a house divided cannot, cannot stand. Therefore, if you want to remain in something you must accept refrain. And I'm not speaking about a song that some sing. *[Some students laugh.]* Yes. So remain and refrain are inseparable. Yes, [Student Y].

Is the Light within us projecting out as the lesser light that is dependent upon the source?

Is the Light within us projecting out on the lesser light?

As the lesser light.

As the lesser light. And so that's what—what I'm trying to follow with your question is that when you look out and see the lesser light, is that an effect of the brighter Light within you project[ing]?

No, no, sir.

Yes, I want to clarify that.

Yes, sir. The Light that's within us, it's, the Light that—

Is—the Light that flows through us, yes, that's the Light within us.

Since it's—is that dependent—that is dependent upon the source as the moon to the sun?

That is dependent upon the true Source. That is what we are.

OK. Does, does that project outside? As—is that a lesser light—

I—

—or is that a symbol?

The Light that you are projects through your being and is censored only by that which covers it. For example, if you have thoughts that are created in realms of consciousness that are in the earth, fire, water centers of consciousness, those forms are very dense. So the Light that you are, which is projecting, must pass through the density of those forms that have been created. And so the intensity of one's density is then, of course, measured by their own acceptance. So if one only accepts forms created in the earth, fire, water centers, in earth, fire, water, and air centers, then try to understand that the projection of that which you are into the world is dimmed by the density of the forms created by your own acceptance. Does that help to clarify that, [Student Y]?

Yes, it does. Thank you.

Yes. That's very, very important. And I remember that one of my students, how pleased they were when they received that wonderful law: The intensity of density is measured by acceptance. You see. And it brought such a lovely happiness to their soul and a smile to their face. Not a grin, of course. Yes. Yes.

In the beginning—

Yes, [Student M].

Thank you. Last week you spoke of Adam and Eve in that Eve was a part of Adam, being the rib, which was necessary for the breathing, thus, survival. And he created something to which he was dependent upon. Now was that the beginning of the separation of creation of believing in the form, therefore, extending it outside as the illusion?

Yes, I'm watching the movement of these forms here. *[The teacher may be referring to the non-physical forms.]* Now if you will accept that Adam and Eve are within your own consciousness and you are choosing within your own consciousness Adam or Eve, then you will have a greater understanding, and you will not be able to support limit and form by the justification of the sustenance of the Light that you are. Did that help with your question, [Student M]?

I think so.

Well, in simple terms *[The teacher laughs as he responds.]* it's a matter using the Light by the limit—it's a tempt of the mind to use the limitless by the limit, when the law reveals that the limit is sustained by the limitless and the limit does not in any way, nor can it, control that which is limitless. Now I think if you will listen to your little video today, you will really understand that better: that the beginning of one thing is the ending of another. And so the beginning of the separation was the ending of the whole. And therefore, we are ever returning to that which we are.

Thank you.

It's very, very important. Yes, [Student L].

Is there a contract signed in the Rotunda for all species entering form, including the amoeba, or only self-aware species?

The individualized soul is the—the form which has the conscious awareness of the individualization or the separation are those who are subject to contract in the Rotunda. Yes. *[After a short pause, the teacher continues.]* After all, you know, the little animal does not, does not and is not aware of this conscious choice of separation from the Source of which it is an inseparable part, you see. Only the form known as the human form has that self-awareness. Yes.

Thank you.

You're welcome. Now [Student U] has a question, please.

Are Adam and Lucifer related?

Are Adam and Lucifer—Are Adam and Lucifer related?

Yes.

Well, if you're speaking of Adam, then you're speaking of Eve, for without Adam there is no Eve, and without Eve, in that respect, there is no Adam. So if you're speaking in that respect, then, yes. Yes, definitely. Which came first, the chicken or the egg? Now the Eves insist they were first. The Adams justify and have all of the necessary reasons in their minds why Adam was first. When Adam and Eve is in the consciousness of the being, and that's where the separation took place.

Whenever you choose that which you are not, known as belief and bondage, then you're Eve. And when you make an intelligent decision to accept what you are, then you are Adam. So if you want to be an Eve, that, of course, is part of the evolutionary process that through the laws established you have chosen. And if you want to be an Adam, then accept what is. Yes. I do hope that's helped with your question.

And [Student D] is waiting. [Student Y] and [Student S]. Yes, [Student D].

The Indians believe that all form evolves from small beings all the way through man.

Yes?

There is life even in the rock.

Correct. There is.

Does—have we evolved from the very smallest form through to what we are now?

All things you are, can do and be, for you have been and the law is established. Does that help you with your question, [Student D]?

Thank you.

Now [Student Y] is waiting.

Without the Adam and Eve, how would one view oneself?

Without the Adam and the Eve, they could not view themselves. It's not possible. The separation exists only under the Law of Duality, which is the Law of Creation. Limitless does not see limit. Limitless sustains limit. Limit sees separation, for it is limit that looks out to see what it is not and wishes to become. That's Lucifer. Yes.

So then is it not, is it not possible to view oneself without the Adam and the Eve? Is that it?

Truth is individually perceived. When you perceive truth, you do not perceive form. Do you understand that, [Student Y]? In other words, if you awaken to what you are, then you no longer, in that awareness, are the vehicle that you are restricted by. You see? *[After a short pause, the teacher continues.]* Do you have another question, [Student Y]?

Ahh . . .

[I'll be] right with you, [Student S].

Well, I think I understand what you just said. Yes, that's all. And it answered another thing.

Well, if you understand that it is not [Student Y] that is asking the question, [but] it is the form that [Student Y] is using. And the question, the participation, is important in order that the form that [Student Y] (what you truly are) is using may expand through a broader horizon, a greater acceptance and that broader horizon and greater acceptance permits that which you are to express itself with less obstruction or densities of form. All right?

Yes, now [Student S] here has a question. And I'll be right with you, [Student M].

Yes, in our world we have a word for the setting of the sun and the oncoming of darkness that we call evening. *Did that come from the Eve and the Eve principle?*

Well, as far as Adam and Eve, if you look to the Light, and all teachings will teach you that, that's understood as Adam. And if you look to the lesser light, that's understood as Eve. And so if you understand the story that has been given—that Eve tempted Adam—well, first of all, you cannot grant what you do not have. One cannot grant what they do not already have. And so it was Eve that already had the denial from the demonstration that she was qualified to tempt. So she offered her denial to the weakness of Adam.

Now I think where you're confused [is that] you take Adam and Eve as a limited form instead of a principle of Light and lesser light within your own consciousness. And when you do that, you have problems with the very basic understanding of the Light and the lesser light. So as I said at one of our other classes, people who are overidentified with limit, known as self, are people who are more easily influenced by the laws of creation. And so the moon and the sun and the planets, the macrocosm, of which you are a microcosm, are more in control of one's being ever in keeping with one's overidentification with limit or self.

You see, the more overidentification there is with limit, the more denial there is of what one truly is, the more need they experience. A person who experiences need is a person who is overidentified with limit, you see. And being overidentified with limit, they deny the limitless, the abundant good, that they truly are. So the more one thinks of one's so-called self, considering that they have considered self a limited form, the more they think of self, the more destructive they are to self, the more, in time, the suffering becomes so unbearable that they no longer can endure it. They [in time] choose not to overidentify with limit. Do you understand that, [Student S]?

So, you see, when you are affected by these laws of creation, you are affected ever in keeping with your insistence that you are limit; therefore, you are subject to the laws of limit. You see? And one who overidentifies with limit is one who is in a constant process of the need of something. Hmm? Yes. Go ahead.

So the word evening is—when they coined that word, did they have any understanding of this? That it was the evening instead of . . .

Well, they were aware that it was a descent. Yes. Anytime you experience lesser light, you are descending from what you are, and you are entering what you are not. You are tempting yourself to believe what you are not, and in so believing what you are not, you experience the functions at the expense of the temporary loss of the faculties. Hmm? You see? Does that help with your questions?

Now [Student M] is waiting, [then Student L] and [Student U]. Yes.

Thank you. Last week you spoke about the law of involvement and receiving— [Student M begins her question.]

In reference to participation. I do feel that that is what I was discussing. Participation?

Yes.

Yes, that's very important. You see, because participation means one thing to the mental world and involvement means something entirely different and depending on each one's experiences. Go ahead with your question on participation. Yes.

Yes. Well, because I was wondering what the understanding was of involve—the law, what is the law of involvement?

Well, I think if my students will understand that we discussed the Law of Participation, did we not, students?

Yes. [Student M responds.]

Participation. Have you had the, have you established the opportunity to study last week's class?

Yes.

Tell me how many times the word *participation* was mentioned, and how many times the word *involvement* was mentioned.

More of participation.

Oh, well, then let's discuss what there was more of. There's no shortage. *[The teacher laughs joyfully.]* Go right ahead, [Student M]. Let us discuss what there is more of. Hmm?

OK.

And so we won't experience this foolishness known as denial and need. Let us discuss what there's an abundance of. Fresh air, beauty, and life. Yes, go ahead.

OK.

Participation? Yes, please participate.

And you were talking about receiving and giving.
Yes. Yes, certainly.
Then I must—
Mostly about giving.
Yes.
[The teacher again laughs joyously.] Yes. And you would like to know how you can give more?
Yes. And I was, I think I had, I listened wrong then.
You listened wrong?
Yeah. Just—
Well, no, one doesn't listen wrong. One hears what one wants to hear.
Right.
What is it that—what was the question, [Student M]?
The question—
To solve your personal problem, there, yes. Involvement. Because I understand that's what you're interested in. Please go ahead. Such a lovely day. Yes.
It was in regards to receiving and giving.
You would like him to give more. I understand. Well, if you want him to give more, then you're going to have to learn that you're going—[if] you want to receive more, you're going to have to learn to give more. And if, if you think you're giving all that you've got, then you're not giving at all. And if you're giving is not, you are not experiencing the harvest of your giving, then you best make some honest viewing inside and change the way you're giving. Hmm?

You know, ofttimes we think we give a great deal and the centuries pass and we find out, "Why, I never realized that. That was all a loan. Look how much I've got out on loan! No wonder I feel such a terrible debt." Yes, go ahead.

That's it. [Student M and a few students laugh.]

You know, I like to get [to]—what do you call it?—the bottom line, because I find the bottoms are so important to my students. So I want to get right to the bottom line. *[The teacher and several students laugh.]*

And, you know, sometimes, I understand, it's difficult; you seem to have difficult[ies], some of you, with the way I answer your questions. But then again, some of you are not looking at the forms that are asking the questions. And it's important. Yes. Yes, I understand that your forms want to find a way to get your husband to give you more. Because they've already decided and made the judgment they've given him plenty.

Well, it's important that when we ask our questions that we have an awareness of what inside of us has prompted us to ask the question. So when I answer your questions I must first take a look at these many different realms to see where they're trying to lead all of my students from some slip that I may be tempted into by not checking that all out first, you see. And then because that means that more than one student, one soul—there's a responsibility, there's a responsibility to all of the other souls, you see.

Yes.

I'm very, very interested in how the human mind—and always [have] been—how it uses the beautiful Light in order to justify why someone else has got to make a change. [The mind says,] "But I have already done what I need to do. But someone else has got to change." And that someone else being someone we want something from. I want to help you to look to what you are, and you won't have to be so frustrated with getting something from someone else that you think that they owe you something. Do you understand that?

I do.

Yes.

Thank you.

Don't you feel better that way?

Yeah, I do.

Well, yes, I think so. *[The teacher laughs joyfully.]* Oh, my, my. I've spent too many, too many centuries working with the—they're very clever. I want you to awaken, as students, to how cunning and how clever they really are. You see? I know that's not you, but I want you to be aware of how they use whatever is in your mind to get what they want. You will never make him make a change.

Right.

Why don't you tell them that? And you will have no problem. *[The teacher laughs again.]* Yes.

Thank you.

[Student L] has a question. *[The teacher continues laughing.]* Oh, he will change. The law says we grow or go. But not from your perspiration, no. Not in that respect. Yes, [Student L], go right ahead.

Last week you spoke of the test-tube babies in the way they—

Oh, isn't it wonderful, a nice little glass test tube. Yes. Thank you.

Yes. Would they—during their period of gestation would they require a host mother or will there be a way—

Mother!? Oh, no, no, no. Music. Unless you want to call music and harmony mother, that's all that's necessary. Yes. Music.

Oh, wonderful.

Let there be music. Without music, there is no peace. Yes.

Then they'd be free from any of the forms that they'd get from the parents that way. That's wonderful.

Yes, it certainly is. And evolution is wonderful. It's a wonderful step that's being made in that respect. So your technology, you see, can be put to some very good use. Very, very good use. Yes. Why, certainly. Absolutely. It will certainly help the human mind to accept that it's not king or queen of the universe; that the laws of creation can come together inside of a little glass tube. Why, certainly, it's a wonderful step that's being made. A wonderful step.

Then women, of course, some women will say, "Well, what's the need of me being around?" Well, you know they have to take that, you see, in the laboratory and put that together. There's a purpose. Of course. It isn't the way that you're used to, perhaps, but then again, you'll be free. Just go in, take a couple of moments. That's all it takes, you know. And then they put that in a test tube and everything works fine. Yes. It's wonderful. Just wonderful. It'll save you a lot of time, a lot of energy, and a lot of money and a lot of grief. I can assure you of that.

Well, now save some for me here! *[The teacher addresses Mr. Red, the church's dog, who is lapping from the teacher's glass of water.]* Thank you. *[The teacher picks up his glass of water, laughs, and pats Mr. Red on the head.]* Yes, someone else had a question. [Student N] back there, yes. My! Just a little bit greedy there. *[The teacher again addresses Mr. Red.]* Yes.

I was wondering if the planets revolve around the sun at the same distance all the time or if they—

Oh, they do?

No, I'm asking if they—

No, they don't. You should do your homework. But go right ahead, yes. Yes. They have their orbits, yes. But if you are saying exactly the same distance, that is not correct. That is not true. Yes, go ahead.

So would it be, would it be an eight, a figure eight at all? . . . would it revolve— [A few words are difficult to transcribe.]

They will not cross over their source; no, they're not that great. No. They can only go around it.

Yeah.

Yes, they cannot cross over that which is. You see, no matter what your mind says and no matter what you think and no matter what you do, you cannot cross over what you are. Oh, you can get close to it, but you can't cross over it. Because the minute you tempt to, there's nothing. You see? There's nothing. Yes. "The father is ever greater than the son." You cannot cross over what you truly are. You can only temporarily believe that you have, but you cannot cross over. Does that help you?

Thank you.

Yes, [Student Y], please.

Are there other planets that are maternal like the moon for our solar system?

In our solar system? Well, if you want to say maternal, it depends on the level of consciousness you believe that you are, then you might consider Venus. That seems to be one of the most popular maternal ones. Mars is another one. Yes.

Mars is maternal?

Yes, to some people it is. When you're angry and upset and you're in service to the forms of the planet Mars, why, certainly, to that person at that time, they would consider that Mars [is] a maternal planet for them. After all, it's supplying them with all that fire they are expressing. Yes, certainly. And there are other experiences, too. Yes.

So if—well, I guess the question I'm having [is], Are the planets male, are the planets male and female, like the sun and the moon?

The forms upon the planets—try to understand that anything that is limit has a negative and positive pole in order to have that which is limit. All right? The only thing that is neutral is formless and free. That which is limit is subject to, by the laws of limit, is subject to the laws of creation, which is duality. And duality, as you understand it, of course, is positive and negative, and male and female. So in that respect, they are limit; in that respect, they contain forms that are both positive and negative, male and female, yes.

After all, the moon isn't all bad, you know. I say, the moon isn't all bad. I don't want you to think that the moon is nothing but bad because, after all, it does service the water center. And if [it] wasn't for water, you would not have form on your planet as you know it. All right? Yes. And although your scientists have not yet explained it in your world, that your Earth planet and several other planets could not remain on their axis if the moon no longer existed. All right. Yes. Yes, [Student U], please.

Eve was the effect of Adam's denial. Does—

Eve is the effect of Adam's denials. Yes. So whenever you deny anything, you know, like you say, for example, "Oh, I'm so upset I don't have enough money," well, that's when you're Eve. In fact, I think I'll instruct my channel to call people Eve when they're in those denials. Yes. You see, and you want to be Adam, correct?

Well, wouldn't—yes.

Well, when you're in denial, you're Eve.

Correct.

All right? So I have to call you Eve, if you're in denial. Now hopefully you're Adam. Yes.

So Adam became Eve in consciousness . . .

Yes.

. . . before Eve actually manifested.

That's the descent and the fall of Lucifer, isn't it?

Yes.

Hmm? Ah, now we're getting there. Now where's Adam located in your physical vehicle that you're walking around in on your planet? Where's Adam located? Yes.

The neck?

Uh-huh. Now where's Eve located? *[After a short pause, the teacher continues.]* Well, if you don't know by now, I'm not going to tell you. *[The teacher laughs.]* You already know where Adam is located. What does the neck represent?

The will.

Fine. All right. Now I think we've said enough on that. And I think you ought to do some homework. I've given it to you so many times in so many different ways. *[The teacher laughs again.]* Does everyone have an Adam's apple?

[The students' responses, if any, are difficult to transcribe.]

They don't? Who doesn't have an Adam's apple?

[Again, any responses are difficult to transcribe.]

[Student S] doesn't have—you don't have an Adam's apple? Pardon?

Yes, I have one. [Student S responds.]

Well, she has one. So she's Adam. Does [Student M] have one?

Yes, I do. [Student M responds.]

Well, there's Adam. But you see, so, you see, everyone has Adam. Right?

Right. [Student U responds.]

Well, if everyone has Adam, who is it that has no Eve? Hmm? Do you have no Eve?

I must, but I don't know where it's represented in the body. [Student U continues.]

Ohh. *[The teacher sighs and then laughs.]* Yes, [Student D].

Denial is the water center. So would it be the area of the solar plexus?

Well, the solar plexus is actually the seat of the solar system; so it could not be the solar plexus, [Student D]. Yes. But it is there. It is there. Eve is located there. Is she so hard to find in your consciousness? Is Eve so difficult to find? Hmm? Evidently. Let's stick to Adam then. We all know where Adam is. He's located in the will. Right?

Right. [Student U responds.]

Yes.

If Adam was tempted by Eve with the apple, why do we call it Adam's apple? [Student S asks.]

Why do you call it Adam's apple? Well, what did Adam do with his will? Did he eat the apple?

Yep. Yes. [Student S responds.]

And he's got a lump in his throat, hasn't he? And he's never been without it since, has he?

Thank you.

Do you know of anyone that's without a lump in their throat? I think it's a very appropriate place to have put it. I mean, it's in keeping with the divine laws of demonstration of evolution. Well, my good children, stop and think. Stop and think. Hmm? I'm here to help you to help yourself to think. Yes, someone else has a question here? [Student L] has a question this morning.

Is the planet—

Has my red-headed student gone to rest? I'll save a little water there. *[The teacher looks around for Mr. Red and when the teacher sees that the dog is not present, he puts down the glass of water that he had been holding. There wasn't much water remaining in the glass. The teacher concludes class with a drink of water.]* Yes, [Student L].

Is the planet we're related to at birth, like, such as Venus or Mars or whatever on our, on our astrology chart—

Is what related to what, [Student L]?

I believe . . . is related to Venus according to the astrology that we know. [Her complete comment is difficult to transcribe.]

Well, yes, you're speaking of the Babylonian astrology. Yes.

Is there any relationship between the supposedly ruling planet and the place we have just come from?

Well, there's all kinds of—you must be a Libra.

Yes.

But, of course. Well, we're going to discuss that this fall. I think I spoke—that's what you all decided. Yes. I don't think it's fall. Is it fall today? *[Many students laugh.]* [It] looks more like early summer to me. Beautiful day, isn't it? Yes. But I don't think it's fall at all. Yes. Yes, [Student Y], please.

Will some type of reunion take place as we return to the Source?

Well, there's no other way to return to the Source. Yes, there's no other way. You see, first of all, you're here from a separation from the Source in consciousness. And the only way to return to the Source is a unification within the consciousness and back to the Source. You see, that's something that happens, can happen at any moment. It is not subject to the passing of the physical vehicle. You understand? That can happen at any moment. Hmm? When you, through control of your mind, you accept the demonstrable truth of what you are in all centers of consciousness, in that moment you're free. Then you are what you are. Yes, [Student Y].

I was thinking in terms of, let's say . . . the Earth. [Her comment is difficult to completely transcribe.]

Earth?

[Again, Student Y's words are difficult to transcribe.]

The planet itself? It will return—oh certainly, they all return to the source from whence they have come. All children return unto their parents. All children.

What occurs then, I mean, what occurs—does it, does the planet have, like, a consciousness or . . .

Consciousness is God. Even [in] the stone, there's consciousness. Conscious awareness is something different. Consciousness is the Principle of Good, God. That is consciousness. So there is nothing [that] exists without the sustenance and the sustaining power of the Consciousness, the Light, the Truth, that which is. Whether it's the ant or the angel, there is no difference. There's no difference in the power that is sustaining it. There is no difference in the intelligence. You see, the flower here *[The teacher reaches out and gently holds a Shasta daisy by its stem.]* is sustained with the same Consciousness that is sustaining you at this very moment. The limit is in the form through which the Consciousness is expressing. It's only the form that is limited. It does not speak in language that you understand. It does, however, speak. And it doesn't want me to break its neck. So

I won't. But the Consciousness, you see, is limited by the form through which the Consciousness or God is expressing at any moment. Hmm?

You see, as long as you believe that you are the limit, then you cannot communicate with the consciousness that's expressing through the flower. You see? And your belief will not permit you to believe that you are the flower; so therefore, you cannot communicate. That's not the wise way of doing it. The wise way is to free yourself from the belief that you are the limit that you are; then in so doing, you are aware of everything that is; that you are inseparably [a part of all]. That which you are, is in the flower, sustaining the flower, you see? That's when you communicate. Hmm? Yes.

But you say, you know, when you're trying to make changes and I share with you an understanding, well, look at the cloud and see the beautiful ships that sail through the sky, the airships, you see. You call them clouds in your world. You see, you take a look and see what is really going on. But then again, when it comes to your limited identification with your form, you imprison yourself and, therefore, cannot communicate in that respect. Hmm?

You see, it's like in your concentration and your meditation, you enter the void. It's void. The void is ever in keeping with your insistence and belief that you are the limited form that you identify with, you see. To pass through the void, you must pass through that judgment wall you have created in your consciousness. See, that which the mind cannot control, therefore, cannot exist; therefore, it states it's void. Do you understand that?

And so your belief that you are your mind restricts you from the expression of what you truly are. It's only your belief that does that. Nothing else does it to you. Your belief does that to you. Hmm? And your belief is ever tempted—that's the Eve within us, you see—your belief is ever tempted by your experiences that you have already had. And then those shadows come up to get even stronger and stronger and stronger. Does that help with that question there, [Student Y]?

Thank you.

Certainly. Time's passing quickly in your world. Yes, [Student D].

In meditation, the breath in creates forms. Then we pause, it's—there is nothing there. And then we release the forms. I was—

We have to stop at that point. You inhale and create a form, correct?

Right.

When you pause, you're pausing with something in there, correct?

That's what I thought.

When you pause, you pause with what's in there.

Yes.

With what you have inhaled. All right?

Yes.

So that's when you've sustained it. Now you exhale it and it's released out into the world, correct?

Yes.

Yes. Go ahead with your question.

Yes. I have a difficult time controlling the flow of breath out. Is that because the forms are in . . . to get out? [A few words are difficult to transcribe.]

Well, all this, of course, [is] from practice, you know. You haven't practiced a long time in the exhale of the breath. You see, try to understand the human mind. We have no problem gathering it, do we?

Right.

But we do allow our self to have great difficulty in letting it go. It's like—it's the breath of life, you see. We let it go at Huh! Huh! Huh! *[The teacher demonstrates three short, quick exhales of his breath.]* In spurts. Is that correct?

Yes.

But we have no problem taking it in one great big gulp. *[Several students laugh.]* No problem at all. But just try letting it out. It only gets out very jerky, when it gets out, isn't it?

Yes.

You see, there is no Law of Harmony governing release.

Ahh.

Do you understand? Because it's controlled by the forms that we are servicing. All right?

Yes.

You see?

Thank you. Thank you.

You see, it's like a person, now, you cut your finger. Well, you tell the bleeding to slow down and it [doesn't] slow down. It shows that your breath of life, the practice has not been made to control your breath of life, you see? Otherwise, you could look at your cut finger; you could concentrate and slow down the pulsebeat, slow it down until the little blood got to coagulate. Do you understand?

Yes,

But you must learn to control your breath, for your breath *is* life, you see?

Yes.

You see? So everything begins with the breath, you see? In so—even in your books that have been left to your world, in the beginning, God, the Principle of Good, breathed into the nostrils the breath of life, and man became a living being. See? So the most precious thing that you have, the most precious thing is not being wisely used. And it's telling you everything when you go to do your concentration and your meditation: it's telling you how much control you are gaining over your mental world, you see? Hmm?

Thank you very much.

You're welcome, [Student D]. You're very welcome, yes. The breath of life. [Student N] and [then Student S]. Yes, [Student N].

If we're working toward an endeavor and we're continually having to let go of the way we thought it should—if you don't know that you're putting up obstructions and yet you never really get anywhere with it, what's the best way to continue to let go, I guess, and have acceptance?

Yes, because, you see, it is the levels of consciousness that we believe at any time that we are that are telling us we're growing or not growing. So if they haven't been fed for a while and they take a look in your mind and see, well, your energy's been going to something else, then they will tell your mind, "Well, you're not growing spiritually at all. You're not growing at all." Because, you see, they take a look in your mind—they have access to your mind, having been created there, you understand, in your water center in your mental world—and they look into your mind and see what's been taking the energy or the feeding. And if it hasn't been going to them, they'll tell you all kinds of things. Well, they'll tell you you're getting old; you need to retire. They'll tell you, you need a vacation. They'll tell you, you work too hard. That's the reason you don't have any money because you've been working so hard. And then if you do work hard and you do make money, they'll tell you, you have no play time. You have to understand how they work, [Student N].

Thank you.

You can relate to that, can't you? Oh, they'll tell you all those kinds of things. Remember, whatever you choose as an endeavor to remain in, you must pay the price of refraining from that which is contrary to it and detrimental to your endeavor. Hmm? *[After a short pause, the teacher continues.]* Hello?

Yes.

That helps with the question, doesn't it, [Student N]? Now [Student S] here has a question.

It's when—

[Student S] east and [Student N] west. *[Student S and Student N have the same first name.]* Yes, [Student S] east.

When the Earth returns to its source, I understand that it retrospun out.

Yes.

So it has to reverse its spin to go back.

Why, certainly.

And it—

And what is the reverse of retrospin?

I—

Yes.

Well, I had a prior—

Well, either you spin or you retrospin, don't you?

Right.

Yes.

What's going to cause it to change?

What's going to cause it to change? Human beings, just like planets, they'll go so far out from their source to the limit, and then it returns. It always does. It's just like the wandering child. It'll wander out into the desert, and when it finally reaches, it finally reaches the demarcation line of personal survival—I speak to all mothers and fathers today—it will return to its parent. Would you not agree, [Student B]? There is no time in all creation that that law hasn't fulfilled itself. When personal survival is at stake, it shall return unto its source. As long as it believes it is the limit, it'll search for its parent to get whatever it judges it must have for its own survival. You see, that is the Law of Creation. And so as the planets move and go to the very extreme of the distance from their source and when they go into that area where they're going to lose their survival, they will start the spin. And once that spin is started, there is no stopping it. They're right back to their parent. Hmm? Yes.

A moment ago, you said our axis is dependent on the moons?

Why, of course, it's—no, I didn't say "moons." I said, "the moon."

The moon.

I said if there isn't a moon, if you remove the moon, which has an effect upon the waters and the life of your planet Earth, [if] you remove that, you have no life as you know life. So why would you—I was speaking in respect to seeing the good in all things, because it definitely serves a good purpose. You see? If you don't have water, you don't have life as you know it. Yes.

In a prior class you said when we, inside, change from a spin to a retrospin—

Yes.

—that we must increase the rate of vibration.

Yes.

With the planets, would then—because the axis has so much to do with the spin—

Yes.

—would this change of spin have anything to do with the moon then?

Definitely. Absolutely. Try to understand—

How—

Well, [Student S], I'll tell you. And I'll tell you exactly in a way that you would understand, I am sure. Whenever you make the effort to return to that which you are, then prepare yourself for great thirst of the senses. *[The teacher raises his glass of water and then takes a small drink.]* And this is why greater effort must be made in your concentration and your meditation. For when you begin the spin to return to what you truly are, if you do not make that effort, in that tenacity of believing you are the limited form, then the thirst of the limited form shall become unbearable. Do you understand that?

Yes.

You know, it's like a person waking up and suddenly deciding, "Well, I spent all those times now drowning myself, and now it's time, I think, to be celibate." And they just make the decision. And tell me how thirsty they get.

Well, now, are you watching—don't you have a responsibility there? How many fingers do we have there? Ten? *[The teacher addresses the cameraman who is recording this class.]*

Ah, yeah, ten. Actually, it's eight. [The cameraman responds.]

Well, that's better to be honest. Took two minutes to get your attention. Does that help with your question? *[The teacher laughs.]*

Very much. [Student S responds.]

Yes, my time is a little bit different than yours. Good.

Thank you.

All right. So how thirsty do you want to be? And how long do you want to remain thirsty? So that's always the question, you see. You see, a fast growth is not a healthy growth. A slow growth is a healthy growth, you see. Otherwise, these fast growths, you see—it's a hothouse flower. It cannot weather the storm. And this is why I recommend a slow growth, an intelligent growth. A little thirst every day is better than a drought for a month, wouldn't you all agree? *[After a short pause, the teacher continues.]* [Student O], would you rather have a drought?

Not necessarily.

Good. How are you feeling this morning? Is the light too bright there in that spot?

No, the light is just fine. I'm just absorbing it.

You're what, [Student O]?

I'm absorbing it.

Absorbing?

Yes.

Good! Be a good sponge. Not one that falls apart now. Because, you see, if you're a real good sponge, then you can hold it, you see. If not, you move the sponge and whoosh! It drips all over the place. Yes. [Student B] has a question.

So much of our planet is water. And our bodies are made up of—

Water. Correct.

[It is difficult to transcribe the student's short remark.]

Correct. And we find more problems with our emotions, don't we?

Right.

And our judgments.

Right.

Because those are the forms that we have merited, the planet Earth, here, the fifth planet. Faith. Hmm?

I was wondering if this is a water planet and we're water people.

Why, yes. You are water people. Certainly. Absolutely.

And Neptune is also a water planet?

Yes, Neptune is a water planet.

Could that be our ancestor?

The what?

Our—could that have been where we came from?

Well, no, that is not guaranteed because, you see, there is the evolution and those who have not passed their lessons coming from other planets—because there are other planets, also, that offer experiences in the water center, though not as abundant as this. You see, the souls entering the planet Earth, as I stated long ago, the planet Earth is the fifth planet to which you have come to demonstrate faith. Hmm?

Yes.

All right. Now faith, you understand, overrides all emotions, all judgments. That's faith.

Fear, however, is the servant of the water center. We all agree to that, don't we? We create judgments and forms based upon fear, survival. Fear. And so the planet Earth is a planet, the fifth planet, for you to make intelligent choices—all inhabitants—to demonstrate faith. For it is a planet be—yes, thank you *[The teacher acknowledges a signal from the cameraman.]*—it is a planet which offers the water center and offers fear.

So if you want to learn something, you go where the lesson is the most difficult and it has the most to offer. Would you not agree? You do not grow by hiding from your temptations in life, correct? See, one doesn't strengthen themselves by running from their weaknesses. One faces their weaknesses. And so your soul has entered the evolution into the planet Earth in order that you may face the fullness of the weaknesses of the form, and it offers you a form known as the water people.

Yes. Yes, you are the water people. That doesn't mean you're all Pisceans. You come from various planets. But when the judgment is made by the human mind to choose the lesser light over the brighter Light, which they truly are, then in their evolution they are destined to be water people at some time in their evolution. You see, you see, we always get what we really want. And so we've come to the Earth planet totally drowned in the water because we chose that fear over our faith in what we truly are. Does that help with it, [Student B]? That's very, very, very, very important.

And so although the path is straight and narrow, it is thirsty, but there is always those moments to rest and have refreshments, you see? So, you know, I spoke to you so long ago: a drink not a flood, a wise person follows. Hmm?

And I must say good day. Time is up. And have a nice celebration—I know you will today—of your survival on this lovely water planet. One year in the Light where it's a little bit dry and thirsty at times. *[The teacher holds up his glass of water, which has very, very little water.]* See, that's all I—don't need more than that. My friend around here somewhere—there he is—he needed some. *[The teacher refers to Mr. Red, the church's dog. The teacher drinks the last sip of water.]* All right. Thank you very much. You have a good day.

JUNE 15, 1986

A/V Class Private 52

[This class was recorded outdoors in the garden of the temple, near the east pond with the waterfall on. The sound of the waterfall often masked the questions asked by the students.]

Good morning, class. Another beautiful day in your world as it always is in ours.

So this morning in keeping with review of the classes and the work, your homework and your studies, we will discuss what was discussed long ago in one of these classes, and that is the necessity of educating desire and how it is accomplished. Some time ago I discussed with you the ways of accomplishing the education of desire and the necessity for it. And now we will clarify that even more, for some of you.

Uneducated desire is the open door to possession from entities who have left their physical form. The education of desire is simply accomplished by separating what you are from what you believe that you are. Without accomplishing that, you are subject to and victims of the many forms that you cannot see with your physical sight nor can you hear or sense with your physical being. You can and do, however, experience the effect of their possession of your vehicle. You can and do, however, experience an awareness that you have lost control of that [which], by divine law, you are responsible for.

And so each moment, as we make that effort to be aware, we know beyond a shadow of all doubt whether or not we are in control of that which, by divine Law of Evolution, we have earned.

Now we'll pause for questions on this particular subject this morning. *[After a short pause, the teacher continues.]* Oh, that's so encouraging: no questions, no possession.

Yes, [Student Y], please. Or is it the other way? Yes. Yes, [Student Y].

When you speak of the—is that the same as when you lose, one loses one's temper in anger.

When one—and we're always aware and we're always filled with regret after the fact, that is when, in that regret, we are experiencing that something else, something that we did not consciously choose, has used what is rightfully ours, yes. Now we, of course, can use any of the senses that we have earned and when we do so, we're not filled with regret after we have used them. For example, if you use your hand to take a glass of water. *[The teacher picks up his glass of water and takes a drink.]* And after having done so, you do not feel regret because you have done so, that reveals that you have made a conscious choice. A conscious choice. You're at home; you've made a conscious choice to have a sip of water to quench what you, your senses, have told you: you're a bit thirsty and what to do. That is vastly different than taking a drink and then, after having done so, be filled with regret because you had done what you had done and your mind tells you [that] you had no control. Well, your mind is telling you correctly someone else had control, yes.

You see, a person does not free themselves from addictions by freeing themselves from a physical body. The physical body only registers the addiction in a physical world with physical effects. Yes, [Student Y].

OK. So, speaking of anger, I'm interested in anger.

Yes. If you consciously choose to use that function, and when you have finished using that function, you consciously choose how long you're going to use it and when that time is up, you no longer have any experience of it, that reveals to you that you are in control of that function. Yes.

So if you don't—if one doesn't feel they're capable of controlling anger, then what is the best . . .

What that reveals is that that function has been given, you understand, through lack of education of the desire to anger, has been given to other forms in other dimensions who enter when they choose to have that experience. Do you understand? Yes. And so without the education of desire, one must accept the reality of possession: something they cannot control. For only through the education of desire can one consciously, consciously choose the function and to use it and how long to use it and how much of it to use. Yes, go ahead, [Student Y].

So what if you feel that it's appropriate, in some given situations, to use anger and yet, you know that you don't have a lot of control over that part of . . .

Then it is necessary to make the effort to educate the desire until you gain control over it and may use the function wisely under the guidance of the light of reason, which, of course, everyone has available to them. Yes. [Does] that help with your question?

Yes. Thank you.

Yes. You see, in these private classes that you are receiving, the time has come for you to be aware, truly aware of when you are at home and when you are not at home and to consciously choose whether or not you want to leave home after becoming aware of who will enter the home, your home, that you are leaving, you see. You see, because if that is not accomplished prior to your leaving your earth experience, it is much more difficult to accomplish once you have left the physical substance. Yes, it is much more difficult. Yes, [Student M],

The law—while you're in blind desire . . .

No, just in uneducated desire. Yes.

Is uneducated desire and blind desire—is that the same?

Well, blind in the sense that someone has control of your form and your mind, and you don't know who that form or what that form is and that form is simply fulfilling its earthly addiction that it never made the effort to educate and to overcome. Yes.

Now that's different than the forms that we have created.

Why, certainly. Certainly. One creates their forms until they believe that they are their forms. Then after they have firmly convinced themselves that they are the forms that they have created, then the door is open to total possession, yes.

I see.

First, one must establish those laws of conviction that that is what they are. Once those laws of conviction are established, then the door may be opened by any form in any of those dimensions, yes.

Thank you.

Yes, [Student N].

We're always—our mind is always creating forms.

Correct.

And—

Until we make the effort to properly breathe, so that it's at a neutral state of consciousness, yes.

So there is the possibility of not having forms at all. Or do we need them for anything? Can we can use them for—

Well, yes, we use them all the time. We use them to walk down a stairway. We use them to stand up or to sit down. We use them to eat. We use them to speak. Certainly, we use the forms, the ones we have created. Now, however, the danger is if you convince yourself that you are the forms that you have created, then you open the door to total possession from decarnate forms as you know them, decarnate. Yes.

So when is it that our, that our soul is the one speaking through our forms and our—and who are using and who are working through our . . .

When the soul is at home in the house that it has earned in its evolution.

So then we don't use forms, then, at all.

When your soul is at home, the soul—it's a conscious choice of using the forms that have been created by the mind in order for the inspiration to express in your world of creation.

So our soul uses our forms.

Yes, the soul can and does all things create. Yes, certainly it does.

And those forms—

You see, I think the problem—perhaps if I interrupt here and speak—is that we are confused on the souls creating of all things, which it can and it does. The problem is that we permit the mind, which is the experiencing of those forms—you follow me, [Student N]?

Yes.

We permit the mind, the forms of the mind to convince us that that is what we are. Do you understand that, [Student N]?

Right.

The moment we permit our mind, the mental world, to convince us that we are the forms that have been created and are being experienced by the mental world, the moment that happens, we establish the law which opens the door to those realms to possess our form. When our form is possessed, our soul is not in that form at that time.

Now because a soul is necessary, you understand, to activate the form—now, you follow me carefully—that reveals to you that a decarnate soul, one who has been in a form, now residing in a world without physical form, is now using the physical being. So when you permit yourself that conviction that you are that which you have created—and that is revealed through attachment to the fruits of action. Now attachment to the fruits of action reveals a person who has convinced themselves, by their mind, that they are the forms that they have created. So you can readily tell whether or not you have convinced yourself that you are the forms you have created by being aware of whether or not you are attached to your efforts. Yes.

So when we create a form and it's just created and it's something that we consciously created to do in this world, do we keep evolving it? Do we keep evolving and expanding that form?

Yes, well, you refine it and you strengthen it as long as you remember that it is something you have created and it has been designed by you to serve a purpose for you in your evolution. Do you understand that?

Yes, I'm beginning to—

Well, you see, you see, take, for example, a singer. Perhaps they've been a singer for many of their evolutions and incarnations, you see. And so ever in keeping with their conviction that they are the singer and not that which is causing the form to sing, you understand, express itself, as long as they have that conviction that they are that which they have created, then they will continue on to control the mind until it awakens that they are not the form created. They are the power, the source that is behind the form that has been created. You see?

So does, like—does the soul sing?

The soul expresses. And so the form is created by the soul in keeping with its evolution for the finest possible expression of the soul, yes. That's the same as speaking. Does the soul speak? The form that has been created by mental substance is that that you know as speaking, all right? However, without the soul, the very source, then you're not aware of any speaking.

So if the soul wanted to communicate to another soul without the form, it is on a totally different . . .

Well, it's an entirely different expression. You would perhaps best relate to it as various color emanations.

Color emanations.

That's what it is. That's what all sound is. That's what all music—everything is, is a vibration, which is color. You see, vibration is color; color is vibration, and vibration is sound and sound is color. Everything is color. So communication from soul to soul is [an] emanation of the Light. And so as you understand communication as speaking, you would see varying shades of color, for, you see, all color is in truth white, and that is the great, white Spirit or the great, white Light. That's what it is. Yes.

So if we really saw the plants as they are instead of the form that they're, they're in . . .

Instead of the form that we have created for them.

For them.

Yes, we created that, and so that's how we say, well, we see it that way or that way. We have created that. Yes.

They're just a beautiful array of colors.

Correct. Correct. Everything is light and the emanation thereof.

And that tells the story of everything.

Well, everything. Everything that you know as form. Now, for example, I'm sure you are aware that there are times a person will say, "Oh, my, that singer was off-color tonight." Off-color, I think you even use that term in your world, you see. Uh-huh. Well, they were off-color. The colors were probably brown instead of pink and some of those lovely lighter colors. You see, the lighter the color, the more expression of the truth. Because, you see, the lighter colors are an emanation of the white, the white Light of eternal truth. And so, as you are in the pastels and the very light colors, you have less obstructions to the emanation of the Light itself. Does that help with your question?

A lot. Thank you.

You see? So whenever you sing—you are a singer—when you sing, you see, you are releasing from your being varying colors, you see. If those colors are closer to the expression of that which is—you understand that?—if there is less mental substance (shadow) in the way, then the colors and what you understand as sound is very beautiful. Yes.

So the subject matter of the song—sometimes I have trouble with my judgments about the subject—

Well, yes, because then you put—you darken the color of the emanation of what you understand as the voice.

So if I just sang that song and didn't think about it in that particular way . . .

That's correct. If you were neutral, in reference to what the words were, then they would come out beautiful. Of course. Yes.

Thank you very much.

Yes. It isn't what we say; it's how we say it. So it isn't what we sing; it's how we sing it. Does that help you with your question?

Yes.

Yes. So, you see, it's like here, our little class. We have this lovely little choir. The color has been terrible. I have already instructed my assistants to see that that changes immediately. The reason that it's off-color is because the mental substance and the forms are in the way of the emanation, you see. *[Although Serenity was no longer holding devotional services, the choir still performed at the Serenity temple.]*

Yes, [does] someone else have a question? See, whether it's singing or it's work or it's business or pleasure, whatever it is, it's all color. Yes, [Student U].

What is regret? Is that the recognition that the soul has reentered the body?

Well, regret—you have a regret over something that you have done?

Yes.

Yes. And so a regret is a registration in the conscience that you were not at home. And, you see, no one likes to leave their house and return and find somebody else in it or somebody's just left it and left it in a terrible mess. So you are aware, you understand—that is an inner knowing—that you left your house. You didn't have proper security. And because you didn't have—that little plant is very thirsty there. See that it's taken care of after class—and you didn't have a—that one right there in the corner—and you didn't have [or] make proper effort for security and you come back and your place is a mess. So you're experiencing the mess and you have regret. You see, you have regret.

You know, that's like a person that falls in love with someone. And they fall in, and after they fall out, they're filled with regret, you see. They wasted so much energy, ofttimes so much money, yes, yes. Did that help with your question?

Yes, sir.

Anyway, they judge they're wasting something. Yes, [Student B].

Does the decarnate spirit or entity or form that comes in when we are attached to something, does it—

If you believe you are the attachment.

Yes, so . . . [It is difficult to transcribe her complete response.]

Oh, yes, if you believe, which is the bondage, you understand, if you believe, [that is,] totally convince yourself, that you are that attachment, if you really believe that, then the door is wide-open for the possession. In fact, here just weeks ago, I instructed my assistants to see that certain—you know, you have regular movie night. I have instructed my assistants to see that certain movies will be brought to you that are available in your world to help you understand more about possession. Yes, and in fact, you have some coming up on your movie schedule. Pay attention. Particular attention to it. All of your movies are chosen for the spiritual truths they reveal in a way of entertainment and in keeping with the classes that you are receiving. *[Thursday evenings, when spiritual class was not being held, was movie night. See A/V Class Private 21 for an example of one movie night.]*

Yes, [Student B]. Go ahead with your question.

Well, I'm wondering if crimes are committed, then, by people who believe their own thoughts are them.

That is correct.

They're really not in their own house; so they do criminal acts.

That is correct, yes. You see, what happens, you have the worst possible system in your country of taking care of this very real, serious problem. You send over to the other world so-called criminals and murderers and people of that nature, instead of permitting them to be educated through a proper process in an institution. Do you understand? So what you do, you send more of them over to the astral realms in the mental worlds who remain earth-bound and now [are] stronger than they were before they left the form in the sense of their desire and their vengeance and their revenge. And therefore, you make the situation worse by sending them out of their form, you see. Do you understand that? So the worst possible system is what your world has developed. It's the worst possible system. Causes more grief, more crime than, than anything else in your world. Yes.

There's a difference between a form here that has to have revenge in their minds in order to attract that . . .

Oh, yes, but it would only have to be in principle. They may have revenge in some other entirely different area. But if they have established the Law of Revenge in any area, then, you see, through the Law of Attachment to their fruits of action, conviction that they are the form they have created, convinced that all of their experiences are caused by something they cannot control, those are the necessary ingredients to establish the law through which unfulfilled desire opens the door of total possession. Yes, does that help, [Student B]? Yes. Yes, [Student L] has a question.

I'm wondering whether those who . . . entities possess, who possess the forms— [It is difficult to transcribe one word.]

Yes.

—when we're out to lunch, have to be—

Usually, it's dinner. It takes longer. Thank you. Go ahead, [Student L].

—whether there has to be a rapport in consciousness and like attracts like.

That is the law. Like attracts like [and] becomes the Law of Attachment. That's, of course, in keeping with that law, certainly.

So depending upon what level you are on when you go out to lunch, you can attract different entities at different times.

Well, you will attract them ever in keeping with believing that you are the forms you have created, the attachment to the fruits of action. So it isn't necessary at that moment that you have done such and such, for you have established the law. And any of those forms who wish to once again express in a physical world will do so. And they do so frequently. Frequently, yes. Yes, [Student O], please.

Yes, are any of these forms that inhabit our body present at the time we signed our contract?

They are ever in keeping with the contract that has been signed. For example, you see, you have to establish that law; the contract has been signed and you enter evolution. Now you are not helpless and certainly not hopeless. And so you have, moment by moment, [an opportunity] that you can make [an] intelligent choice. Now those particular forms aren't there, but their representative is. Their representative is there, yes. Well, say, for example, say that you have a Kool-Aid form, and that you believe that you are Kool-Aid, you see. And so at the time of signing the contract, there wasn't a Kool-Aid form sitting there. However, the representative that represents that whole realm in principle was there. Did that help?

Yes.

You see, it could have been an ice-cream cone or a Kool-Aid, you know, or a lollipop! It could have been a lollipop, don't you see? Yes. Did that help, [Student O]?

Yes.

Yes, certainly. Now, was it—[Student D] had a question this morning.

Sometimes I say something that I immediately regret. Now if we pause, is that a vehicle which brings us back into our body that—

It certainly is. It absolutely and positively is. First of all, the first step is to pause, the lion's strength. Now once you have paused, from that point on you start communication—communication with the forms within. You see, if you will make the effort to pause, then you can start talking to those forms and say, "Now just a moment here, every time that I let you in, you do me in. Now I have a track record here of many years of my life that you do me in every single time. So I'm not going to let you convince me this time that you are me or that I am you. So get thee behind me." All right?

Thank you.

Yes, the sense to pause, the lion's strength. Yes, [Student H].

Yes, can a soul use color to get back into its home?

Can a soul use color to get back into its home?

Yes.

Well, first of all, color is established for it to be exited; yes, you know, to get booted out. Yes.

And would the soul then have to use retrospin to emanate the pastel tones?

Well, the soul is going to have to use a retrospin, certainly. First of all, they spun themselves out by convincing themselves that they are the form they have created and the attachment thereto. And so they have to use retrospin, certainly, and awaken to that is what they've created, but that is not what they are. So if more time is spent with a person reminding themselves, "All right, this is what I am. This is what I have created. I'm responsible for what I have created, but that is not what I am," you see? See, you draw a picture; you paint a picture. That is not what you are. If you believe that is what you are, then you've got a serious problem. If you are aware, "This is what I have done through the forms that I have created"—you understand?—"I am not attached to it and I do not feel that it's good, bad, or indifferent; it just is. That's what I have created. That is not me; therefore, whatever happens to this that I have created will not affect my life for it is not me." You see?

Yes.

"It is not me. It is what I have created and I am responsible for, but it is not what I am. Therefore, it cannot have an effect upon me for it is not what I am." Does that help with your question, [Student H]?

Yes. Thank you.

Yes. [Student S] has a question here this morning.

I'd like to know if there is a difference between being possessed by a decarnate spirit and being possessed by a soulless creature or form.

Yes, there is a difference. There certainly is a difference. Obsession and possession—there's all the difference. Yes, indeed, there is. For example, try to understand, try to feel you are a soul; without form, you're in limbo; aware of everything that's happening to your body, to your vehicle. And you're there in limbo, what you may well relate to as limbo, a state of seeming nothingness, a state of seeing everything happen and not being able to do anything about it, yet responsible for its happening—spiritually responsible. Try to understand a condition like that for centuries and centuries and centuries. Once the possibility of entering a vehicle, any vehicle—so that you don't have to keep seeing it, you can do something with the form. Try to understand that a form, which is a decarnate soul that has left form from the laws that it has established is much, by far, more tenacious than the soulless creatures. They've got much more at stake.

Now it is true, the soulless creatures have to face annihilation. That is true, but annihilation is certainly not as painful as the continuity of eons of suffering by watching all these things happen and only being able to see it happen and to do nothing about it and knowing that in some century you shall return into form and be responsible for all that has happened. Did that help with your question? Yes.

And is there any difference in how we work with them—the soulless creatures versus the decarnate spirits?

Why, certainly, the decarnate ones are much more difficult to remove from the vehicle. They're much, much more difficult. You see, [they are] much more difficult than the soulless creatures created by the mental worlds because they are an actual soul who has been residing in limbo for some time, either in limbo or sent up from below from old Lucifer himself, you see.

You see, now, the soul goes into what you understand as a state of limbo, and in a state of limbo, they are called and tempted below limbo, below purgatory, into service to the king of creation, all right? And so a soul is more easily tempted to go below and dedicate themselves, until they finally learn through centuries what it's really like, you see, and then be sent back up to possess a physical form that is still on a planet. Yes.

You see, the ones who are tempted from the states of purification, what you understand as states of purification, the states of limbo, the ones who are tempted down into those forms, they dedicate themselves and then are sent back up and they are absolutely dedicated to enter physical form, to possess it. And if they are not successful, then, of course, they have to return to the king of creation and all the justifications and excuses only cause more pain and suffering for them. Yes.

Is there any way we can help them so that, so that there is another way for them to evolve rather than by possessing another form?

We would, then, have to return Lucifer to the right hand of God. And we are not, I don't think, any of us, in that position as yet. You see, he made a conscious choice and descended and became king of form, of limit, you see? And he has all that limit has to offer, all of the thrills and sensations; and only someone greater than that could return him. He's not ready to return. He's not about to return, no. Yes, [Student J], you had a question this morning.

One of my questions, sir, was, What method could we consciously use to stay within our self and not lose control?

The breathing exercises. Holding the breath and doing the exercises that you have will help you to reside in your home and not be controlled by those other things, you see. Now try to understand that these laws, these laws of possession, are initially caused from the moment the soul enters into form. Now I'm talking about the moment of conception, not the nine-month time after. For, you see, the mind[s] of the parents, you understand, are overidentified and convinced and believe that they are the forms they have created. And so they are convinced and believe they have created this little child. Do you understand that, [Student J]? Now that is the wide-open door for possession of the parents. And so a soul entering, at the moment of conception enters and no one can be sure, you understand, except the Light itself, whether or not those parents, their soul was in the form at that moment or it was a decarnate entity. Do you understand that?

And so, you see, not that it is impossible, for nothing is impossible to the Light, but it does mean that great effort should be made by anyone who wishes to remain free from that type of possession, you see. Great effort daily should be made to be aware of one's thoughts so that they are not overidentifying with form or limit because then the next step is belief that they are that. And the next step is, from those convictions, you understand, the door opens wide, and they experience unfulfilled desires. Do you see?

You see, I taught you so long ago, and I remind you again: do not suppress desire, for when one does that, they suppress it; it goes to work inside. The pot boils over. It goes to work inside and opens the door wide open to the possession, you see. And the education of desire—for desire is the expression of the Divinity. It belongs to the Divinity; it is the Divinity. And so it is the education of it, not the suppression of it in any way, the education of it: the education of it being separating truth from creation. Separating what you are from the constant process of believing that you are what you've created, you see.

So a person should make great effort, through their breathing, through their exercises and especially to refrain, as much as possible, from thinking about what they judge as the self. To refrain from thinking about the self helps to keep a person free from possession, you see, and obsession.

See, in your world today, you don't have the workers, you don't have the workers. And there are so few that are even aware of how to remove these possessions: to send these decarnate souls that are in mental worlds and astral bodies—they don't have physical substance. There are so few left in your world that know how to exorcise them, to remove them from the form so that the soul who has earned that physical form may return. And then—I don't want to say too much, yet, in your growing processes here—but then sometimes they don't stay out for half an hour.

And it takes quite a bit of energy. You've got to understand desire is a phenomenal force, and force is energy. And so when you have a decarnate soul that has waited five or six centuries to get into a form, you understand, a physical form—to return to it—you have phenomenal force. And it takes a great deal of energy to exorcise that type of a being, do you understand? It takes [a] phenomenal amount of energy. And you don't, as I say, you do not have the qualified workers in your world. There are few, and very few there are.

Does that help with your question, [Student J]? And so not thinking about the self isn't something that one [says,] "Well,

I don't want to think about myself." No, no, no. It's one's own survival. It's one's own survival, yes. Yes, [Student O].

Are there just decarnated forms that serve, that serve the sense functions? Or are there decarnated forms that serve the soul faculties?

Oh, no, no, no, no, no. No, a decarnated form that is serving the soul faculty has no need, want, nor desire to experience, you understand, that which they have already evolved through. Oh, yes, yes. No, no, no. No. Decarnate souls [who are evolved] do not enter the forms for the purpose of experiencing sensation. They have moved beyond sensation. They enter forms in keeping with their service, if they are evolved souls—you understand that?—

Right.

–to the Light that they serve.

Oh, good.

Yes. And if they do that, they have something that is worthwhile and something that can be tried and tested. Does that help you?

Yes, sir.

Yes, [Student M], please.

Yes, on our planet—last week you said we are the water people.

Yes, yes.

And we believe that we are our forms, you know, and—

That are created in the water center. You believe you are the judgments; and therefore, the door is wide-open, certainly.

And we attract these decarnated spirits when we believe those forms very strongly to open those doors.

Yes, that is correct. That is a process. It doesn't just happen in five minutes. It's a lifetime process. Yes.

Right. Now, there are other planets in the solar system. Do they also have decarnated spirits that have gone on and because of their—what I'm trying to—

Unfulfilled desires? Do they have—

Yes.

Certainly, they do. The law is not exclusive to the planet Earth.

No, but I'm—we are the water people. Now, is each planet like a fire people and an air people?

Correct. Correct.

And they have denied their source and to—the air center, you know, and they become the air people and, therefore, decarnated—

Why, certainly. Absolutely. Certainly, yes. When you are under the influence of the air people, the mental world, you are convinced that you are the thoughts that your mind creates and there's nothing else. There can't possibly be. You're absolutely dedicated to it.

But aren't all, like, all are concentrated to the water center?

For this planet, you're water people. It is my understanding you were talking about other planets that represent other centers of consciousness.

OK.

Yes.

Thank you.

You're welcome. [Student Y], please.

Wasn't the original choice of the—we had choice of freedom that Lucifer was allowed to believe that he was form?

Yes, that choice is with us moment by moment. The original choice is still with us. We choose at any moment to believe we're form. Yes, [Student Y].

Was that, was that set up that way so, for the conversion process?

In keeping with the formless, free Spirit, the Light that is—do you understand that?—expresses through limit for the awareness of itself. In other words, without form, there is not self-awareness. There is not—without form, there is not awareness of form. Does that help with your question? So you have to have some kind of limit in order to have what you understand as the awareness of self, all right?

Now where the choice is, moment by moment, is whether a person wants to make that effort to pause to intelligently consider, "This is limit. This is form. This is what I create. This is not what I am." So if you, as students, will remind yourself of that more frequently in the course of a day and evening, "This is what I have decided to do; it is not what I am. It is what I have chosen to create, but it is not what I am. Therefore, not being what I truly am, I am responsible for what I am creating, but I will not identify"—you understand—"to the point with what I have created that I am affected by the limit of my own creation." Did that help with that question? Yes, [Student Y].

Yes, it does. Just one more small question.

Certainly.

Did the divine, neutral Intelligence know—was there a knowing what would happen? That the fallen angel—that that split would occur?

Why, certainly. You see, that gave unto man, that gave unto a mental world a conscious choice, you see? To choose to fall and to conquer or to choose to rise and be free. It is only through division that you can experience the thrill of conquest. And so anyone who believes they have a need to be thrilled is a person who is dividing in consciousness in order to conquer and, from the conquering, experience the thrill. It's a registration to the senses only. Yes. Thrills register in the senses only, yes. And the senses are the forms. So if you believe you are the senses, then you've established the law to be possessed. Did that help you there, [Student Y]? Yes, now [Student D] has been waiting.

When a spirit merits being in limbo—

Yes, the soul, yes.

The soul. Do they go beyond limbo by becoming neutral to what they see?

All right, now let me follow you here. First of all, they're in a state of limbo where they're able to see and not able to do.

Yes, right.

Only to see—

Right.

—what's happening to their form. Now, you're understanding from that was, do they what?

Do they—is the way they get out of that to become neutral to reactions to what they see?

Oh, definitely. To be neutral, therefore, not to have any registration or reaction and the awakening you are responsible and how you got into that situation in order that you may evolve and get back out of it.

So when they become neutral and aware, they are able to transcend that limbo state.

Correct. Because they are no longer affected by that realm; that means that they no longer serve it. That which you are not affected by you are not in service to. You see, if you are affected by your emotions, then you are in service to that realm and those forms that are created, you see. That which you are not affected by you are not in service to. That's very important to understand that; just that one statement alone, you see. "For that which affects me is in truth controlling me. So that which does not affect me does not control me." All right?

Thank you.

Now, [Student M] is waiting and [Student N] is waiting.

Thank you.

You're welcome.

Within—when Adam was created—and he represents within us all what we are and Eve represents what we believe we are.

Oh, yes. We did discuss where they put Adam's apple, didn't we?

Yes.

Yes. Did you take a bite? We never found out the rest. Go right ahead, [Student M].

Within Adam, he had—he has both—he's in form. He has electromagnetic within in his own consciousness.

That's what you are.

Right.

All right. Fine.

Well, at the beginning, then why was it necessary for Eve, if he had within him—

Well, isn't that a wonderful question? Why was it necessary for Lucifer to descend into creation and become king of it? When he had everything sitting at the right hand of the Principle of Goodness. [Student B, do] you have an answer for that?

I think he wanted to be God. [Student B responds.]

That's right! Therefore, he had to look outside and compare, you see. You see, the moment you look outside and convince yourself that what you want is out there, then you've entered his realm. And Adam is no longer Adam. We now have the chasing for Eve. Do you understand? See, Adam and Eve is in the consciousness. And when you understand more about the rib, you'll see how Eve was created out of the rib. Not the toe, not the finger, not the elbow, certainly not the nose or the ear or the eye, but out of the rib. Go [ahead.]

Thank you.

Does somebody else have a question here?

Yes, [Student N]. I did promise to come back to you, yes.

I have a question about—last week you were speaking about a desire or a goal that you have and not—and it's a fine line not to be distracted by opportunities or . . .

That which we create—that's what opportunity is. [It] is something we've created. [We] don't recognize we've made the effort to create the opportunity and then we say, "Oh, that's good luck." Yes, I don't want to tell you about good luck. I think

I spoke about luck once a long time ago, what luck really is. Yes, I think [Student J] remembers that one. Yes, go ahead, [Student N].

So if you have a desire and we're creating things along the way, our opportunities along the way, what do we, what do we follow if we don't follow the opportunity? If you don't—

I didn't say you shouldn't follow the opportunity. I'm simply saying that you should not convince yourself that you are that which you have created, whether you call it opportunity or anything else.

So how do we—

Use it; don't abuse it. You see, you abuse that which you have created by believing what you have created you are. That's how you abuse the law. You abuse the very law and the principle of design. See, the moment that you—you design something with your mind and you create it and you manufacture it. And you've designed and created and manufactured it to serve a purpose for you, that which you are, in expressing in creation. The moment that you permit yourself to believe that you are what you have created, you no longer use the Law of Creation; you abuse the Law of Creation. And whoever abuses anything must pay the price for the abuse. Does that help you, [Student N]?

Yes. And I was wondering, [since] you create many opportunities, which one do you know to follow? Do you decide, looking at the design—

The lion knows. The lion knows. The lion, the sense to pause. You want to use the lion's strength. You have the lion within you. Of all of the planets, what symbol does the lion represent? Of all the planets, which one does it represent? [Student M.]

The sun.

Does anyone not understand that it represents the Light? Yes, that's what that symbol [represents]. That's what I've been talking about for years. The sense to pause is the lion's strength. That's when the Light, that which you are, enters into the consciousness. So [if] you have question, [if] you have doubt in all of that, [then] use the lion's strength. The sense to pause is what turns you, in your consciousness, back to the Light, you see. And the Light will guide you, the Light within. It never faileth. It never has.

However, the Light within doesn't register in the senses, you understand. That's the problem I find: most of my students, when they tempt to go by the Light, the Light that they are, it's a temptation. It's not a conscious effort. It's a temptation. You cannot tempt the Light that you are. Temptation only affects the lesser light. It has no registration upon the Light that is. So when you feel that you're tempted to turn to the Light, try to understand and realize which Light you're turning to: it's the lesser one. For temptation does not register in the Light. Only the lesser light. Yes, [Student Y].

Do you mean temptation in the sense of like greed and pride and—

Well, temptation is temptation. What is temptation? Yes, thank you. *[The teacher acknowledges a signal from the cameraman that the videotape is about to come to an end.]* What is temptation? What is, what is the cause of temptation? [Student Y.]

Love of, love of oneself. Thinking of oneself.

Denying what you are. The moment you deny what you are, you are tempted by everything that you believe someone else has. *[The teacher laughs.]* You see, you must first deny what you are in order to be tempted, you see? You see, you look out and you start servicing that realm: compare and judgment. You're tempted. You've established that law. You deny what you are and are tempted by what you are not, hmm? Yes. And besides, ofttimes a person entering that, they are tempted by what they are not and after they get it, they wish they'd never in the world ever experienced it. Because, you see, temptation is absolutely blind. Now, you see, our time is passing. Perhaps one more. We have time for [Student J], here.

Am I correct in assuming, sir, that the affirmation "Not mine, O God, but Thine" should be used at the time that we accomplish something and that affirmation prevents it from entering into the ego?

Definitely. Absolutely. Because if it doesn't enter into that realm, then you won't have all those experiences that follow in that realm.

Should we always use that affirmation?

Always. Always.

Not mine, but Thine. And whenever you are tempted, declare the truth: not mine, but Thine, because then it will return unto the source and you will evolve free from that stuff.

Thank you.

Absolutely. And don't forget, children, the lion's strength.

Beautiful day. How quickly classes pass. But they pass so quickly in all worlds. Thank you. We look forward to seeing you again, then, next Sunday. And don't forget our wonderful celebration coming up in your world on—oh, I took it off, didn't I?—on the Fourth of July. *[The teacher refers to the microphone that he just removed, which had been clipped to his shirt.]*

Thank you and good day.

JUNE 22, 1986

A/V Class Private 53

[This class was recorded outdoors in the garden of the temple, near the east pond with the waterfall on. The sound of the waterfall often masked the questions asked by the students.]

Good morning, class.

Through denial of the right of ownership we destine ourselves to indebtedness of creation. You might want to take note of that, although it is recorded on your tape for you.

Now in continuing on with these classes and especially this week as we face this celebration of freedom—and as I mentioned to my channel here the other day, we all have a great many things we would like to be freed from. So if we apply that law that was just mentioned and respect the right of loan and refrain from the denial of that, we will not experience so many things that we desire to be freed from, for we will not have claimed so many things that cannot be ours by ownership, only by temporary loan.

Now we'll go right on with our questions this morning so that you may reveal to yourself how well you've been doing with your homework. Yes, [Student U], please.

In the last class, reference was made to breathing in such a way that the mind was left in a neutral state, not creating any forms.

That's correct.

Could you share with us—or do we already have understanding of that breathing method?

Yes, you already have the cleansing breath, don't you?

Yes, sir.

Yes, I don't think there's anyone present that doesn't have the cleansing breath. If there are, please raise your hands, because that will tell me that you've been out to breakfast, lunch, and dinner and certainly haven't been present over these many, many months in your world. Yes. You have the—you have all of the tools that are necessary for you to remain free from those things.

Now as I mentioned here last week in class, I have left instructions and you are receiving more and more entertainment in your world that is revealing what these things are really like and to understand, through an inner awakening, the difference between obsessions and possessions and to nip the things in the bud while they're in the state of obsession before they advance into possession. Because once they've reached those final states, it is not impossible, but it is indeed difficult and takes much time and effort to free yourselves from them.

You see, so many students believe that it's just impossible for them to change what they've spent a lifetime believing. Well, so I have instructed you students over these years, you don't try to leap before you crawl. You refrain from thinking about the very thing that offers to you these obsessions and possessions. You refrain from thinking about what you think is yourself. Because when you think about what you think is yourself, you are identifying with that which you have created. And those creations compose what you understand as your image, your self-image. Your self-image is a combination of all of the things that you are in debt to in your days of ignorance. So when you think of what you think is your self-image, what you are actually doing [is] you are serving that which you have created in times past and believe that you are.

When you do that, you establish the law for that which has passed, which is no longer under your control, in that sense—consciously—and having established that law, you establish the rapport—like attracts like—that is necessary and indispensable for those forms, those souls who have once been on your planet who have denied the right of nature to reclaim the physical vehicle, which is, by law, the right of nature, which has been loaned for the soul's expression in its evolution. So when you establish that law, you open the doors wide to be possessed by those forms who continue to deny the right of the law of nature: that physical form is loaned to the soul, in keeping with the laws of evolution and service, and is reclaimed by the laws of nature to what you understand as Mother Earth. Therefore, they are attracted by that law into your physical form and take control of you.

And this is why when you make the effort to refrain from thinking of what you understand as self—which is, as I said a moment ago, a combination of all the things you have created that you believe that are you, that are past events [that] have been justly reclaimed by the mental substance law through which you have borrowed it. And I do hope that's helped with your question, [Student U].

Thank you.

So if you do not make the effort to start with the very law that, in ignorance, has been established, there cannot be a cure. You do not battle those forms that you have created, that move from obsession and into possession. You accept the divine, just law. And you stop thinking about what you call self-image.

Does that help you, [Student O]?

Yes, sir. [Student O responds.]

Yes. Any other questions on that? Yes, [Student U].

Is there anything that signals that you are on the verge of becoming obsessed? We learned last class that regret lets us know that the soul has returned and we are experiencing that something other than ourselves was in control.

Correct.

Is there some warning sign that lets us—

Why, certainly. There's a change in attitude. There's a change in vibration. There is a change that you have not consciously chosen to make the change to. When a change in attitude comes over—you become aware that, you become aware that you don't feel this way or you feel that way, there appears to be a sudden change of attitude, and you have not and you cannot recall consciously making a choice to move from that vibration over to that vibration, then it is a very good indicator that by making no effort to be on guard—to be awake, aware, and alert to where you are—that something else is using what has justly, by the law, temporarily been loaned to you, known as your form and your mind. Yes.

Thank you.

Yes. Sudden changes of attitude reveal it very quickly. Yes, [Student M].

With these decarnated souls, from last class I have, they can see and not view.

Correct.

And when they see another form to go into that is totally identified and their soul has left, they go into that particular form for the length of time until that, until that . . . I'm not sure [of] the process. After it goes into another form, as it sees and it says, "I can go into this form. They're out to lunch." Or, you know, they've left. Their particular soul has left, that incarnated soul—

Yes. The house is empty, to be used.

When they're in this particular realm, does our soul go to that same realm that these souls are coming from?

Your soul goes into a state of limbo where it cannot do anything. It can only, it can only see everything.

Our soul also.

It watches what's happening to the form. That is correct. To your form. It watches it.

It watches. So our soul—

It cannot, it cannot do anything because you have transgressed the law and you have left the form. You see, you have transgressed the law to be aware, awake, and alert, which is the necessary things to be on guard, you see.

Right.

You see, you cannot [not] be on guard. And so over the years you've understood "You're out to lunch," or "You're out to breakfast," or "You're out to dinner," or "You're out all day and evening," whichever, you know. You see, you want to look at the positive side of the law and not just look at the law as something negative. For example, it is necessary in order for me, here, to be present to share this Light with you for the soul of the form, that justly belongs to my channel, [to be] in another area and is not in a state of limbo. But you are dealing with laws: the laws of self and the laws of selflessness. There is a vast difference, you see: one is controlled by the desire of the functions, and another is controlled by the awareness and the aspirations of the soul.

So it depends on whether or not you are consciously making a choice, and in so doing, through that law that you have established, that like attracts like, that's what enters your form and takes control, you see.

Yes.

Now, in speaking on the positive side of the same law, for all laws, depending on their application, you see—the law is neutral. So it is the application of the law that's either seeming good or seeming bad. Surely, we all understand that law is absolutely neutral, you see.

Law is not good and law is not bad. Law just is. Like truth, law *is*, you see. Now the use of law is what makes the law constructive or destructive. Law itself just is. Your application of the law, your perspective and your use or abuse of the law, that's what makes it good and bad. The law in and of itself is absolutely impartial. The law is neutral. Yes. Applicable to all.

So when a person leaves their form, the form that has been loaned to them by the divine laws of evolution—which it truly is the ownership of nature, creation, and the elements that control creation, you see. When a person consciously, through their effort, chooses to leave their form, they must stay on guard, they must stay on duty. Because if, in that process of leaving or returning—when it is necessary, an identification with self [is required] in order to enter the form. Do you understand it?

Yes.

So it is very critical that they have that awareness without becoming trapped in it. In other words, you must have the awareness of form without the belief that you are the form. You see?

Yes.

You see, for without the awareness of form, you don't have the identification to form. So the separation is the awareness of form minus the belief that you are the form. You must have the awareness of form in order to animate it and to move it, you see. In order to enter it, you must have the awareness of it. It is the belief that you are it [that] is your great danger, not your awareness of it. Yes.

Thank you.

Yes, [Student Y] has a [question], and [Student D] there.

So are you saying that when it's seemingly, [when] the law is seemingly bad, that it's just our minds that . . .

It is our own, it is our own perspective; it is our own view of the law. See, the law in and of itself—divine law is not good and is not bad. Divine law, like divine truth, it just is. It is how you use the law, how you see the law that makes the law good or bad. Now like attracts like and becomes the Law of Attachment. The only way that attachment, the Law of Attachment, is bad is when a person believes that they are that which they are attached to, instead of aware. You see, you can be attached and be aware of your attachment, all right? The moment that you believe that you are that attachment, that's where your problem begins. The Law of Attachment is not a bad law. It is not a good law. It's what you do with the Law of Attachment. Yes. Yes, [Student Y].

So, so what you're saying is that the suffering comes from when it moves up or down.

Correct. Correct. You see, because when you believe that you are the attachment, that is when the functions are over 51 percent in control of your own view. Do you understand that, [Student Y]? You see? So if they're in balance, then you don't have that problem. Therefore, the Law of Attachment is not bad. Yes.

So it really—knowing that, if you could put that into practice in your life, then you could . . . [Student Y pauses for a moment.]

Yes?

. . . but my mind has a lot of weight—it puts a lot of weight into where my spiritual being is. Like, I'm noticing that.

Yes. Well, you see, when you put a lot of attention to that, you increase the identification with the functions to the point you believe that you are the function. That's where the problems are. Do you understand? You see, that's like becoming what you're using. That's when the tools, the functions, which are tools, no longer serve what you are. You begin to serve what you are not. Do you see that, [Student Y]?

You see, it's not a matter of—you have functions. That is a part of the process of form. You have functions and you have faculties. When each and every function is brought into balance with each and every soul faculty, you have a neutrality. That's when you have, you gain the perspective of the Light itself. You use that which you have earned, but you no longer believe that you are that which you use. Yes.

So could you do that with any—you could apply that to anything in your life.

It must apply to everything. That's the separation of truth from creation. That's what our classes and our teachings are all about. The separation of truth from creation does not state that truth in its expression through form—in order for recognition, that does not mean that it becomes creation. It uses creation. You learn to, once again, regain that which you are, to use that which you have earned and refrain from believing what you are using is you.

You see, when you begin, through overidentification with the functions of the form, when you begin to believe that you are that which you are using, that which you think you are using is in truth using you. You see, that's the difference. Without that daily, constant effort to separate what you are from what you are using (or what you are not), then you fall into the trap: you believe that you are what you are using, you see?

Yes, that help you there, [Student Y]? I'll be right with you, [Student N]. [Student D] had a question waiting.

Animals have awareness of form, but they don't have belief in their form. Is that true?

Yes. They do not have, in the sense—they do not have belief that they are the form in the sense that the human form or the human animal believes they are their form. They don't. They register pain. They register pleasure. You understand that? But you also understand that they are in a different state of evolution than the human animal. Yes.

So when they die, they don't—it doesn't bother them, passing, like it does—

Oh, no. No, certainly not. Certainly not. Absolutely not. Because, you see, it's like, with the animals, if the food is food—if it's good food—if it's food and they're hungry, they'll eat it.

Right.

Now you take the human animal, if it's food and they're hungry, they may or may not eat it because they are controlled by forms they have created, you see. Now the human animal offers that to domesticated animals, unfortunately. And unfortunately, many domesticated animals, they will not eat because they are hungry. They will eat because some form that they've been educated to by the human animal says eat. Do you understand the difference?

Do they—

And they may or may not eat what's given to them as good food. It depends on the human: on what the human animal has trained them to do. And they call that "education," you see. Yes.

Do the animals create forms or do the humans create the forms that control the animals?

The animals create forms in keeping with their education by the human animals. I hope that that's clear to you. You see, for example, say you take and domesticate an animal. Well, in your world, you call that that you train or you educate them. You offer to them—see, they have the ability to do so. Oh, yes, they have that just like the human animal. And so the human animal offers them these various forms. They can learn very quickly, if they want to. You understand?

Yes.

You see, if they are tempted to by their senses. You see, you train an animal, or what you call "educate" them, by first becoming aware of their weakness, you see. That's how you control them. So you study them; as human animals, you study these other animals, and you see that they're fond of this and that. And you start the programming process to weaken them. So that when you offer them some of that, they are weakened—what you know as temptation—and you have control over them. If you want them to come here, you see, you offer them something to the weakness that you have been able to see that you can work with.

You see, human animals do that to other human animals, and they also offer it to the rest of nature. I think you're aware of that, you see. Yes. You see, instead of making the effort to understand through—of course, the human animal would have to refrain from this overidentification that they are that limited form in order to communicate with what the human animal looks like is an inferior state of evolution. Do you understand? Because the Intelligence is identical.

This is the one thing, I think, that most people become confused [with]: the Intelligence, the Infinite Intelligence that is available, expressing through the animal, you see, the non-human animal, so-called, is identically the same and has the same potential as the human animal. The Intelligence has the same potential. It is a matter of the form through which it is expressing, you see. Now you say, well, that the dog cannot count. That is very ignorant thinking. The dog can count; the dog can do an algebra problem just as well as a human animal. If you make the effort to communicate with the animal, the Intelligence is as capable of anything that you are capable of. The limit is only in the form that the Intelligence is expressing through. There's the only limit. Yes.

So if a rock or a tree had our form—

Yes?

... be developing into ... [It is difficult to transcribe a few words.]

Why, certainly. For example, you can't move your arms, you say, and fly like the eagle or even like the robin. You see? And yet your mind tells you, you are a more evolved animal. Well now, in that respect, no one could ever say that they are more evolved than the eagle that soars in the sky of your world, you see? You see, you can do the same thing. It is not aerodynamics that's the problem. The problem exists in what the human mind is in service to.

So the human mind is not in service to the understanding of the necessary movement to fly. Now it won't fly like the eagle. It won't even fly like the robin. But it will fly in its way. Do you understand that?

Yes.

You see? But those changes have to come about in the consciousness of the human being. Yes.

Thank you.

You're welcome. Now [Student N] has a question, please.

I'd like to know what's the effect of having continuous difficulties at the beginnings of things. And—

At the beginning of what, [Student N]?

The beginning of anything. Beginning—

Oh, yes, yes. That's most understandable. Yes, yes. That's what you might call in your world a common problem. Yes, anyone [who has difficulties], if there's anything different than what they are used to, reveals they're in total service and absolutely bound by what is known as the self-image. Yes. The greater difficulty you have in making a change, the more you will awaken of how controlled you are in overidentifying with your form. Yes. That which you have created. Yes. Yes, [Student N].

So how do you, how do you break from that?

Well, [there's] no problem at all: stop thinking about what you call self. When you stop thinking about self, you'd be amazed how you evolve. You see? You see, the more you think about self, which is a combination of all of the forms you have created, [the more difficulties]; the less you think about self, the more graciously you make change, the more graciously you evolve. Do you understand that? *[After a short pause, the teacher continues.]* [When] you think about yourself, you have problems making changes. Because you have to understand what you have created has been solidified.

Does that go back to just having the—when you have the desire, giving it up and then just following whatever—

Get yourself out of [it]; get yourself out of it. Get what you think is you out of it, and then you will see the change come in a more harmonious way. The difficulty is in your identifying with forms you have created which take a look at the change as annihilation to them. Do you understand that, [Student N]?

Yes.

And so they rise up in your water center—the very center in which they have been created (your judgments)—and you believe that that's you: that you have great difficulty making changes. You have difficulty being aware of anything that, in their limited, little world, has been created and you believe that that is you.

Well, it's a little better, but I want to see it have more water, that poor, little thing. *[The teacher refers to a plant in the garden that, in the previous class, he requested it be given more water. It was the responsibility of the students to care for and to maintain all the indoor and outdoor plants of the temple.]* Have some compassion, you people responsible for the gardens around here.

Yes, [Student N].

So, what can be done—

I'll see you thirstier than that. *[The teacher may be inspiring his students who are responsible for the care of the plants by offering to them the same consideration (or lack thereof) that they have offered the plants.]* Yes.

—if you've already begun and you've already made mistakes.

Well, you let that go. Those are forms, the effect of what you've already created.

And just continue on?

Well, you start anew.

And so—

Why, certainly. Let go of what you think you have and you'll be amazed at what you'll receive. But you got to first let go of what you think you have. You see, your cup overfloweth. Your cup overfloweth. And if you stop thinking about it, then you will be able to experience it, you see?

Thank you.

Yes, you see. You see, it is the nature of the human mind to try to manipulate everything. Do you know why? Because it believes it's the things that is manipulating it. *[The teacher laughs joyfully.]* I don't like to be manipulated. Not after the eons that I spent behind the wall. No thank you. Not in the closet. Behind the wall. *[Please refer to Volume 5 of* The Living Light Dialogue.*]*

Yes, [Student Y], please. *[The teacher laughs again.]* Yes.

So until you make this change in consciousness, you'll experience that very thing everywhere you go.

Oh, why, certainly.

So if, if I—

In all worlds at all times, you'll just continue to experience it. And when you [have] had enough, it'll go. That's when it goes, when you've had enough. And then you—because then you start thinking, "Oh, this is it. This is it. This is no way to live. There has to be something better." And you stop thinking about what you think is yourself. Yes.

So first—the first step, then, would be to make the change in one's consciousness and not keep hopping around the universe.

That's correct. Absolutely. Absolutely. Because you'll only encounter the same thing everywhere you go. Because you are taking it with you. You see? And so all you can see is what you take with you because you believe that you are it. So how can one see anything else? No matter where you go. It doesn't matter where you go; you'll have the same so-called problem. Hmm? You see? Oh, yes, yes.

You know, it's like a person—you know, so many times some of my students, they always cry they don't have enough affection, they don't have enough this, they don't have enough that. Well, if they would only accept the demonstrable truth: they don't give any. You see, you can't, you can't experience what you don't give. I mean, I know that some of my students, they think they give plenty. They're giving nothing, because, you see, they cry they're not getting any. You see, the law is very clear. It tells you very clearly: those who are getting nothing aren't giving anything, you see?

So you can cry until hell itself freezes over—God forbid—but I can assure you, you're giving nothing. *[A few students laugh.]* That's why you're getting nothing, don't you see. So don't cry, please, to my channel about you don't have any love and you don't have any affection and nobody really cares about you, because you're only telling him—and I have reminded him several times—that you're not giving one bit of love, not one bit of care, not one bit of consideration. All you're doing is crying about it, feeding that *thing* that you believe that you are. No. People who don't get any don't give any.

Yes. Someone else had a question. Yes, yes, yes, [Student N]. I'll be right with you, [Student O].

What would be a pure—I—what would be a pure sense of affection or care or love? What would that—

Stop needing it because every time you allow yourself to tell you that you need it, it shows very well that what you're doing is feeding your unbelievable greed and selfishness. That's all it's telling you. Ridiculous. Stop thinking about that thing you call yourself, [then] you won't have to worry about affection and love and care because you'll start releasing some, don't you see? Yes. You see, as it is now, with all this whining and crying and that foolishness, it only shows that the identification with that self-created image, why, it is so bombed-out in delusion, it doesn't know what it's doing. Yes, does that help you? Why, my goodness sakes alive, let's be honest with our self and enjoy this beautiful day. You see, and stop all that foolish selfishness. That just shows how selfish, you know, a human mind can be. My!

I have instructed my channel very strictly not to listen to that foolishness. That selfishness is unrealistic. I ought to know. I had to pay plenty for that. Yes, [Student O] has a question, please.

Yes.

[Such] foolishness.

Would you explain what is going on in the mind in one's being when this seeming fog or sleep comes over them and they're really not consciously trying to go to sleep or drift off?

Yes, something else has got control of them.

Yes.

That's very obvious. Yes. Yes, that's very, very obvious. You know, and so, it just shows that whoever that person is, they're going to have to start making a little bit of effort. A little bit of effort. And stop thinking about [yourself]. As I just got through telling my student here, [Student Y], you know, and this cry-of-affection foolishness that has been in this atmosphere around here on these beautiful, beautiful days here. Just beautiful. Stop thinking about yourself.

Just try [to] stop thinking about what you think of as yourself for five minutes and you'll experience the great goodness of life itself, you see. Life is beautiful. Your planet is beautiful. But all you see—unless you make that little bit of effort each day to think of something besides yourself, you're not going to experience that wonderful goodness. You're going to end up crying that you don't have enough. Do you understand that, [Student O]? And you don't want to end up that way, do you?

No, I don't.

Well, I don't think so at all. Think about something besides yourself. Think about a little ant down there. See, underneath of there. The little lizards crawling around there. Take a look and see those things. You see, [when] you open your eyes, you can see them. You see, when you're thinking about what you think of as yourself all the time, you can't see anything that's around you. How can you experience the beauty that surrounds you when you're thinking about something that is far from beautiful? Something *you* have created, you see, with your mind, you see.

The laws of nature do a greater job at creation than the laws of the mental world; I can assure you. Take a look at the flowers, the atmosphere and see the colors and things. You say you cannot see it? The only thing that stands in your way—there's nothing that stands in your way but your insistence on believing that you are that image that you have created. There is no other veil between you and the Light. That's the only veil there is. Nothing else exists. It is a self-created veil between *you* and what you are. So [if] you do not see those beautiful things in the atmosphere and you do not experience them, it is because you insist, from lack of effort—do you understand that, [Student O]?—

Yes, sir.

—you insist, from lack of effort to refrain from thinking about what *you* have created, you see. And in that sleepiness—it's not like a sleepiness; it's more like a narcotic comes over a person. Do you understand?

Yes.

Oh, yes. Do your breathing and experience that great goodness that *is*, that which you are, you see. It's so beautiful. And once you experience [it], you won't be tempted with this other foolishness, you see. Hmm?

Yes, sir. Thank you.

You have everything, everything necessary to experience what you are, the goodness of life. Everything else is something you have created that is past, that you are transgressing the very natural laws by trying to possess and own it. Those who are tempted to possess shall be possessed. Hmm?

Thank you.

Possess not and be not possessed. Hmm? Accept in gratitude. "Thank you, God, you have loaned this to me. How many moments, days, or hours, I know not. That, however, is not important." And when it has served its purpose and it is time to go, it shall go. Even though you have feelings of attachment for it, you are aware that you are not the attachment, you see? You see? All right.

And don't take license with that great law and use it as a justification of why you didn't care for something that was brought, by the law, under your responsibility in life. Don't say, "Oh, well, it's going anyway," and abuse it. For by abusing things, you shall be abused by them, yes.

Someone else—[Student D] has a question there.

So a walk in nature takes you out of self because you are observing and being around forms that you did not create.

That's right. Take a look at the, at this bamboo, there. Yes, that bamboo. Oh, this grows hundreds of feet, you know. This is really, really miniature. The stuff I see you have here. But anyway, take a look at that beautiful bamboo and its potential. You see, there's an Intelligence expressing through it. It doesn't appreciate it if it doesn't get a drink of water when it's thirsty, you understand, because it has senses. You see, it has sensation. It senses a thirst; it senses a drought, you know. I mean, you sense a drought, and you scream and open your mouth and get a drink of water. Well, it senses drought and all it can do is to show you wilted leaves, you see. Where's your compassion for life? You see?

You see, get out there—unfortunately, you know, people come out [into the garden] to look after a little plant. There, look at that, you see. It got bent over and it's still trying to grow there. *[The teacher gently examines a Shasta daisy with a bent stem.]* You see, people go out to take care of things, but they're not taking care of what they're seeing. They're taking care of what they're thinking. Oh, there's a vast difference, my children. *[The teacher laughs.]* Oh, yes. This is why I say, "Well, did you water that plant?" Like that one there. It's had a little water. Better make sure it gets more. Or someone won't get a drink of water that's responsible for doing it, [Student O].

Anyway, you see, you [have] got to think of something besides what you're used to thinking about to experience that goodness. Yes.

Thank you.

Yes, [Student B].

Are self-thoughts magnetic?

Self-thoughts are absolutely magnetic. And the only thing they serve is the destruction of one's own being. That's what they serve. Self-thoughts are extremely magnetic. And, you see, a magnet attracts like unto itself. Hmm? So all you [have] got to do is think of self, and you'll pull—because that's magnetic, you see—you'll pull all that like-stuff into your universe. And the next thing you know, if you're in self-pity and you feel miserable, you'll talk on the telephone and you [have] got somebody miserable; somebody comes to the door and they're miserable. Every place you go, it turns to you know what. Because that is what you're pulling into your universe. Sure. Well, as [Student J] here said, and several others, what goes around comes around. Keep spreading it around; it will only come back again. Sure, they're very, very magnetic. Hmm?

So if you want to pull things to you, well, start thinking and feeling how good life is, how great you feel, and you'd be amazed because the only thing that will be able to get to you is all that goodness, you see. Like attracts like and becomes the Law of Attachment. So is that necessarily bad? It depends on how you view it, you see. Don't believe you are the goodness in life and take great pride in such, then you will not have to believe that you are the suffering misery of life and take such you know what in the experience. Yes.

Yes, [Student B]. I'll be right with you, [Student N].

Does that explain, then, the possession of, actually of those forms, those magnetic forms?

Yes, definitely. Because you transgress the law. You see, you are electromagnetic by the laws of nature. You do understand that? All right. Now, between the electric and the magnetic is the flow of what you truly are: the divine Neutrality. Do you understand that, [Student B]? See, that's what you are. So when you permit—now remember, here's this divine, intelligent

Energy, the very source, that which you are in truth—when you permit that to be expressed out of balance into the magnetic or out of balance into the electric—do you understand that?—but especially into the magnetic, then you overidentify [and] establish that law. You no longer have this balance of the electric to keep about that Intelligence that you truly are. So you go out to lunch. Magnetically you're pulled right out to lunch. You understand that? You're pulled out to lunch. Something else comes in. And how do you get back in? It's a little difficult, right? Yes.

Do you use the electric to get back?

Absolutely. Definitely. Because you went out by a total imbalance, you see, right into the magnetic. You see, if you tip the scale and you go more into the magnetic than into the electric, you're walking in very dangerous waters. Because you start to believe everything you have created while in the magnetic center of consciousness. Does that help you, [Student B]? Now once you've done that, then you've totally overidentified; you do not have the light of reason and the other centers working. You're now locked right into the functions. You understand?

Yes.

That's where possession takes place. That is where possession—first, it's obsession. You become obsessed with it. You understand? The next step is the possession. Yes.

Thank you.

It's an over-imbalance. You are the divine, neutral, intelligent Light, known as Energy. That is what you are. The expression of it is a delicate balance between the electromagnetic of the form—hmm?—in which you are expressing. Yes.

Are we always either the electric or the magnetic in experience?

You're moving constantly. There's a very delicate balance between the two, you see. You see, you [have] got that 10 percent. That's where your 40—the 40 percent of your faculties, 40 percent of your functions. All right?

Yes.

All right? Now, that's 80, right? Your totality is the 10 percent will that you have. You see? So in every thought, in every expression, in every movement is the electromagnetic.

Now I've taught you to put God into your effort or forget it. You can't get God in, which is the divine, neutral Power, until you balance out that electromagnetic. Hmm? That must be kept balanced. When that's balanced, you see, then God gets into the endeavor. This is like we're speaking over here to [Student N] and the difficulty of making changes; how difficult it is. It's because that energy, that which she is, is overidentified—you understand?—to the point of belief that she is the experiences that she creates. Do you understand that? And then those forms rise up and you don't want to make changes. *You* want to make changes, of course. That's the Law of Evolution. But the forms that you temporarily believe that you are, by being overidentified in the magnetic field, they're not about to. That means their annihilation. Absolutely. They're not about to. Yes.

Yes, [Student N]. And I'll be right with you, [Student M]. Go right ahead, [Student N].

What—why is it—is that the push-pull of the, to the future? You've created something and then you resist it.

Why, you don't resist it. Yes, you identify with something of the past which your new creation represents a total, total annihilation to that which you have created which you temporarily believe that you are. So you fluctuate back and forth.

So you identify the new with the old.

That's correct.

And shove it away because you don't want the old?

Well, you don't want the—the old doesn't want to go and you believe you are the old, because you created it. That's really attachment to the fruits of action. Certainly. You can say it in a thousand words, but it is an overidentification with self that offers it to us, you see?

You see, you put God in it or forget it. Whatever it is. That means that you must have a balance of the electromagnetic until that divine—God is the divine, neutral Intelligence. God can get into nothing that isn't a balance, so that God can get into it. You either put the magnet in or you put the electric in it.

Now, [Student M] has a question. Do you understand that, [Student N]? Why, certainly. Encourage yourself. What is encouragement? Hmm? What is encouragement? *[After a short pause, the teacher continues.]* When you're encouraged in something, how do you feel?

Good. [Student O and others respond.]

You feel good, don't you, [Student O]?

Yes.

Well, certainly, it's a faculty, not a function. Wouldn't you agree?

Yes.

Why, surely you feel good. You feel good. At the very thought of encouraging yourself in anything, you begin to feel good. You start to move into those centers of consciousness, into the faculties, you see. You feel good. You especially feel good if it is something you don't have to depend on someone else for. Right, [Student D]?

Yes.

You see, that's when you truly feel good. You see, when you feel encouraged, you think you're feeling encouraged and you're depending on someone that you have no right to control, that's when you're stimulated, tempted. That's not encouragement. No, no, no, no, no. A lot of people, a lot of people, unfortunately, they confuse temptation with encouragement, you see. Yes. No, no, no. No. There's all the difference in the world.

Encouragement that, "Oh, I'm able to breathe fresh air. Oh, isn't that encouraging!" You see? Well, put yourself inside of a chimney that's smoking and see how much you'll value fresh air. Otherwise, you see, you don't think about it. Think about the water that you drink. How much thought do you give to it? You don't think about the food that you eat. You don't think about all of the beauty that surrounds you, you see?

Stop and think what you haven't been thinking about and then you'll answer your own question [on] why you've been feeling miserable, some of you. Huh! Just pause for a moment and ask yourself, "Now let's see, what haven't I been thinking about?" "Well, I didn't think if the pine tree had any water. Is it happy today? Let me see, that one looks rather happy, satisfied a bit. *[The teacher looks at one of the pine trees in the garden.]* Has that one had any water today? How is that looking? How does that flower look over there?" Look around the world and think of something besides what you think is yourself, so you can experience the goodness of life for a change.

Yes, [Student M] has been waiting. Yes, I'll be with you in a moment, [Student L].

Yes.

Time is passing quickly.

This balance between the electro and magnetic, you're saying that the soul leaves when we identify magnetically because it leaves—

When you overidentify.

Overidentify.

Yes.

And we bring it back electrically through moving our will to the higher centers. Is that the process with which we bring our soul back from limbo?

Well, first of all, if you're shoved out into limbo, you're out there as long as the form that is possessing your form (the entity) is able to stay in there. Now the entity has to use will, you know, to stay in there, don't you see.

I see.

So, you know, like attracts like and his or her will is just as strong as yours. I mean, I would like to see that some people would spend less time being possessed and more time being awake, but you have to understand that like attracts like and the will is the lord of the universe, their universe, you see. Yes.

Thank you.

I hope that's helped with your question.

Yes.

Now, [Student L] has been waiting.

Well, you know, you see, stop thinking about how many times you've been possessed and start thinking about all of the times, from this instant on, you're not going to be. Why don't you think something positive for a change, children? My goodness sakes! You know, what can you do about those moments and hours and times gone that you've been possessed? All you can do is think about it and feel sorry for yourself and have the thing come back in again. That's all you can do. Do something with what you can do something with. [From] this instant on! You make your intelligent decision. And you accept the demonstrable truth: "That's what it's offered me every single time. Every single time that [I say] 'Oh, I don't have any love. I don't have'"—isn't that the problem? The thing you created—isn't that [the] form? I see that form right in front of you. "I don't have any affection. Nobody really cares about me. I don't have this. I don't have that." Stop thinking that way and you won't be possessed so frequently. You see?

That's terribly selfish, you see. Face the truth of what it offers you.

It's true.

You see? There is no way that you're going to force anyone beyond your right of control to satisfy your selfishness of what you call love and affection.

Correct.

You know? When you turn to God, you won't have any concern or interest about love and affection. God's an overabundance of it. Even takes care of the little bamboo there. Now that's love: to consider. Consideration is love. So stop looking to man to fill what you judge is your lack of consideration in your life. And start looking to God, the only place that you can be considered. Thank you.

Go ahead, [Student L].

Wake up [to this] beautiful world here. Yes.

Yes. Thank you. Can you have encouragement without gratitude?

Have encouragement without gratitude?

I don't think—

Well, I think you ought to talk to [Student M], while I answer someone else's question. That's something for private discussion: to be encouraged without any gratitude. You know, I don't know—is that a statement or is that a question? I think I should spend—I don't know. I think you all should discuss that on your time. Yes, [Student Y], please.

Should we consider this, like this particular tree here . . . in having the same divine, that same Intelligence, as a student? [It is difficult to transcribe a few words.]

Why, of course!

At this very moment.

Well, that's what you are. Why, certainly. That has the same Intelligence. The same Intelligence flows through it. Why, certainly. You think—it knows when it's thirsty. It knows what it requires for the survival of its form. Why, certainly. It hears and it sees and it knows. It has personality. Oh my, oh my, yes, indeed. Why, even the daisy has that. Of course it does, yes. There's only one Life and one Truth.

And are you watching the time? *[The teacher addresses the cameraman.]* You are?

[It is difficult to transcribe the cameraman's response.]

Good. Because I think it's very important for my students to ask themselves—and [Student L] brought up this wonderful statement. You know, a way to have encouragement with no gratitude. And I think that all of you should work on that to see what your understanding is, inside of you, as [Student L] has presented that for your benefit, you see: encouragement [in the] absence of gratitude. Because, you see, to have gratitude means one must recognize a greater authority than themselves. And so to be encouraged without the recognition of a greater authority than your own ego, well, that's something that would require a lot of discussion. I would think. What do you think, [Student B]? Hmm? *[After a short pause, the teacher continues.]* Yes. Because, you see, the self, what you know as self, would love to find a way to be encourage[d] without recognizing that there's anything greater than it. And I think that's a most important discussion for you students. You know, discuss that this week.

Someone else have a different question? I'm—yes, go ahead, [Student J].

Is work related to disassociation?

It certainly is. And this is why work is God's love; it is the manifestation of goodness in a person's life. You see, when a person is really working, they must give some thought to the job they have to do or the job don't [doesn't] last at all, you see. You see, people who don't work always have a mountain of justifications and problems in their life. And life is just totally miserable. So work is not a luxury for a person; it's indispensable for experiencing the abundant goodness and joy of life itself. And a person who turns to God is never short of work. You see, there is—because it is the very principle of God, you see?

So there is no such thing as no work. It doesn't exist, you see? No work, no job, no good only exists for people who turn to that which is opposite the Principle of Goodness, which is overidentification with the human ego, called self. So there is no shortage of work in any world because the only shortage of work you can possibly experience in life, in any planet in any universe, is an overidentification with what you are not, which is opposite to the Principle of Good.

So God's—work is God's love made manifest. So one who wants to experience the goodness of life must turn to the Light within, where there's work for everyone. There is no shortage of work for those who turn to the Principle of Good. So if you're ever working with anyone and they tell you there's no work for them, there's a shortage of work, you want to really try to help that which they are. Tell them the truth: there is no work for those who deny the existence of the Principle of Good, known as God. You see? You see, you don't have to have a religious person and talk about God. Just talk about the Principle of Good. They all want the Principle of Good! You see? And so—Yes. *[The teacher acknowledges a signal from the cameraman.]* That's very important that you understand the only shortage of work in any world is the absolute, blatant refusal of the human uneducated ego to recognize and accept a greater authority, known as the Principle of Goodness. Hmm? Yes. And, of course, that all takes place inside.

I always look to my students in all of my classes; I have all of them working, whether it's the little squirrels or the deer or what you call the dogs or my two-legged dogs—I mean, my two-legged animals. *[Many students laugh.]* All of those, you see, they're all workers! Yes! Because that's the goodness of life.

Thank you. I look forward to celebrating this wonderful day of freedom of all of my students constantly working so they can experience the goodness of life. Thank you. And good day.

JUNE 29, 1986

A/V Class Private 54

Good morning, class.

Today we will discuss the act of good.

Now the experiencing of need is dependent upon the denial of the human mind. Therefore, whoever accepts the possibility cannot experience the need. And so we find in our life that whenever we experience need of anything, we are, at those times, denying the possibility.

Some time ago I spoke to you on the detriment and the dangers of the thought of I. Not upon the I that you are, but the thought or the form, the limit of what you are.

You may pick up your pencil cap, [Student O].

It is when you permit your mind to limit what you are that you experience, of course, what you are not. And when you experience what you are not, then you experience what you understand as need. It is what we create with our mind. For example, you say in your mind that you are this and you are that; you are capable of accomplishing this and you are not capable of accomplishing that. What is speaking to you is the limit, the thought of I and not the I that you are. By placing your attention upon the limit, by placing your attention upon your mind's own effort to limit or control what you are, you experience these needs, these turmoils, and these upsets.

And aren't you happy that my assistants asked that the [water]falls be turned off this morning? Or you would have had a nice little shower during our lovely class here, which is known, in our world, as the faculty of consideration. For the breeze is not coming this way; it is going that-a-way. *[It was rather windy that day and the sound of the wind in the trees is clearly audible on the recording.]*

Now it's time for your questions. *[After a short pause, the teacher continues.]* Attention is being placed on the limit of what you are. Yes.

Is this possible or is it so that animals can also be possessed by disincarnated . . .

Well, yes, you understand, of course, that the minds of men have created forms and, in so doing, tempted what they call their domesticated [animals] or their pets to be receptive to the forms that have been created. For example, if you wish to control an animal, you first program the animal to a certain type of food. And then the animal, in keeping with that mental programming, slowly but surely begins to believe that in his loyalty to you as a master—and remember that an animal looks to you, once you have domesticated them, what you call domesticated them, then the animal looks to you as his god. For what we look to for our survival—you understand that?—becomes, in our mind, our god. So if you take an animal and you make the effort, the conscious effort to program them to certain foods or certain patterns, as the animal looks to you for his or her survival, looking to you in that respect, in a mental world, as their god, then the animal, of course, is receptive to the forms in a mental world that you have created for him or for her. Do you understand that, [Student Y]?

And so a person who has a strong desire to control another, either human animal or four-legged animal or winged animal, makes great effort, conscious effort, to establish that type of programming in order that they may be worshipped as a god. Yes, [Student Y].

OK. Thank you. And along with that, is it—in Indian mythology, there were those who entered as spirit into animals. Is that possible? Like into a bird or a wolf?

No, the form of the animal rejects the lower evolution of the human animal. Yes, [go ahead].

Is—did that have a—

You see—I might like to say one thing at this moment. The human animal, the mental world, has deluded itself that it is higher evolved spiritually. Well, now let us gain a little perspective on evolution. The animals that you view on your planet that [are] yet waiting to be contaminated, unfortunately, you call them "born free." In fact, you even have songs and music in your world of "born free." The animal, you understand, its primary objective is the continuity of the species in its own duty to its own evolution. So its primary responsibility is its duty and its survival.

The animal does not destroy to survive. Now you look and you think, "Well, they are predators of this and they are predators of that." The greatest predator on your planet is the human animal, for it is a predator not for simple survival and the duty of the continuity of the species; it is a predator for the whims of an uneducated mental world.

Does that help you, [Student Y]? Yes, go ahead with your question.

I would—that does help. And I'm interested in, in the Indian mythology of human taking animal form, was that merely symbolic?

Well, there are attributes in the human animal that are— there are attributes that are revealed in the various species of other animals of your planet. And so, for example, you see, you have animals who are predators and express in a certain way, as a predator, for their own continuity and for their own survival. Try to understand the main difference between the human animal and the animal that you are speaking of that is supposedly non-human in that respect, the main difference is there is no animal in the universe, outside of the human animal, that is a predator for the purpose of controlling another form. You see, an animal will be a predator to another animal for its survival, but not for the control of another animal. Do you understand that?

You see, it is like, for example, you have various animals; they have what—you look at [and] you [say], "Well, that animal is king and is in charge of this whole group of animals." That animal is expressing his or her responsibility and duty for the survival of the species. That animal, from its own demonstration, has proven to be the most qualified, and by being the most qualified for the survival of the species, your mind looks at him and says that animal is king of that particular group of gorillas or tigers or whatever. That animal has simply proven that it is superior in its efforts and its demonstration for its duty for the survival of the species that it represents. Does that help you with your question?

Yes.

So, you see, that animal is the one who looks out to see that the predators don't come and destroy the continuity of the species. That is its sole purpose, you see. And their society is very intelligent. It is indeed considerate of the whole. For example, the animals, the non-human animals will drive one of their kind out of their pack rather than the whole being contaminated, for the duty of the head of the pack is to see that there is continuity of the species. Does that help you with the question?

Yes. Thank you.

You're welcome. Yes, [Student O] has a question.

Yes. Would, would you speak on the basis, the basis of retaliation and the logic that the mind offers for it?

Yes. The reason for retaliation and the logic that the mind offers for it is very well presented. For example, the basis of retaliation and the logic that the mind offers for the retaliation simply reveals a human animal—for the other animals don't do that—a human animal granting control over their life to another human animal, for they are dependent not to what they are, but to what they have created. For example, a man retaliates against his wife because a man has sold out and denied the personal responsibility of his own continuity. Do you understand that, [Student O]?

So, you see, as you depend on something that is beyond the boundaries of the law of which you have created, then you become dependent upon that which is beyond your divine right. And having done so, you have denied what you are. By denying what you are, you experience need; and whoever experiences need is a dependent person, for they have first denied what they are. You see? You see, a person says, "Well, I can't live without her. I can't live with her. I can't live without her." And, you see, that's the in-between stage of a boy who grows into manhood. You see, at the stage of a boy, you listen to a mind that says, "Well, I can't live without her. I can't live with her." That's the in-between stage as a boy is growing into manhood. Does that help with your question?

And so we find boys at that stage of their evolution filled with resentment, filled with frustration, filled with retaliation, for they are dependent upon that which is beyond their control by divine law. Yes, and vice versa, of course, you see. So a girl depends upon a boy for what she has denied herself. And by denying it, she expects to get it from someone else. And so she must pay the price of selling out what she is, you see. Did that help you, [Student O]?

For sure.

Yes. Well, for example, if you live in a little shelter and accept in your mind the possibility that you're going home to your shelter; you're the only one there. You have to feed yourself. You have to clothe yourself. You have to wash your clothes. You got to take care of your things. Why, you even have to brush your own teeth yourself. And visualize something like that and you'll experience a wonderful freedom. You see? You see? Because it won't matter—you're no longer dependent on something beyond your control—so it won't matter whether they're there or not, you'll still brush your teeth. Do you understand that?

Yes, sir.

And if you don't have a toothbrush, then you use your finger. Does that help you?

Yes, sir.

Yes, now [Student J] has a question here.

With respect to your opening remarks, what is the best method to disassociate from need?

Yes. Well, it's most difficult because, first of all, acceptance is not only the will of the flow of goodness and the will of God, accepting the possibility establishes within the consciousness very clearly the law that you are what you are and not what you have believed that you are. And so, you see, a person, they believe they are the hand and they suffer with what the hand does. They believe they are the eyes and suffer with what the eyes do. They believe they are the foot and suffer with what the foot does. You see, for example, the moment you believe that you are your foot, then you are dependent on what the foot is dependent upon. Do you understand that?

Yes.

So the moment that you believe you are your hand, you are dependent, believing you are your hand, upon your wrist, upon your arm, your elbow, and all other parts of your body. So if you believe you are one part, you are bound by all parts. Do you understand that, [Student J]?

So, you see, I find so much in that stage of evolution. A person—when you believe you are one part, you are the victim of all parts. Now a person, like, you see—I've had some of you students in this particular class—not in my other classes—you know, consider they want to be freed from a certain part of their body. And so they want to go celibate. Well, when they do go celibate, you see, because they do not understand that that part of their body is dependent upon all of the rest of their body, they have phenomenal problems. And so it lasts for so long a time and the next thing I see, I see them being drowned by the flood. Because, you see, you must understand whenever you permit your mind to believe you are one part, you are therefore the victim of all parts. You see?

And so the best way to work on what you understand as need is to refrain from denial. Now one can only refrain from denial by accepting the whole. Accepting the possibility. You cannot experience need when you accept the possibility.

Now what happens to the human mind in the early stages, one says, "I accept the possibility"—now try to understand you're dealing with m, e, and s. Because that's the only thing where the restriction is, where the limit and the problem is. So now the reason that you're dealing with m, e, and s, is because the e, what you understand as the ego, the uneducated ego, the form of the I, the thought of the I, is expressed in two ways. Here, it is expressed in what you call money, in survival, security, you see. And over here it is expressed in its expression and its glory of itself. Well, a person must first truly establish the Law of the Thought of I in order to experience the so-called need of the glory. The moment you permit your mind to limit what you are by creating the form, the limit, or the thought of the I, the moment you do that, you experience need, for you have denied what you are. So each moment you deny what you are, you establish the law of experiencing need.

Now, when you experience need, your energy is siphoned off to the forms that you have created with your mind. And you have created those forms to serve your own denial. Do you understand that, [Student J]? And so when you permit yourself to think of "I", that is, to form what you are, when you permit that—and I've told you in many other ways, the thought of self, well, you see, which is the limit of the I—the moment that you do that, you are in service to the forms you have created that, in your mind, have satisfied or temporarily filled the vacuum known as need.

So what happens is you then are under the dependence of the forms that have been created and the feeding thereof, you see. Now no one wants to spend their life feeding forms they have created, for that establishes the first law known as obsession. So the form they've created in their mind comes in and obsesses them, and they just have to have it. Do you understand, [Student J]?

Yes, sir.

Now after they have spent some time in servicing that which possesses them, a thought form they have created, the next advanced stage is a decarnate being, who is yet to grow out of that, fills that form for them, you see, and lives off of their life energy, you see. And so we find a pathetic situation, in the advanced cases, which does take eons of time to grow through. If you recall, I think I related to this class, some time ago, the years I spent behind the wall of the forms that I had to face in my own evolution that I alone had created. So one wants to be free from those things and must establish that law, what is known as personal responsibility: "I am what I am. I am not the form and the limit that I am creating of what I am." You see?

You see, look in the mirror. It is a reflector. When you look in the mirror, you are experiencing what you have created. And so you look in the mirror and your mind says to you, "You look pretty good today." You look in the mirror and your mind says, "You're getting old. Look at those lines and everything." That is how it works, you see. You see, you have created forms when you were young. Now those forms do not change. They take a nap. They go to sleep. And they wake up very hungry and when they do, they really, really go to town. So when you were 16, you created forms and they served you well. And then you get to be 36 and 46 and 56. And, like my cameraman over here, he has these forms; they're closing his eyes. And he better look out, because he won't have eyes to close when we're finished. *[The teacher laughs as he speaks.]*

And so, you see, you look in the mirror and you look with—through the eyes of many forms. You see, you look through the mist. And so you look there and you have the 16-year-old [Student

J] looking in the mirror. You have the 36-year-old [Student J] looking in the mirror. You have the 46-year-old [Student J]—go on down the list. And so they're all looking through. Now depending upon your need of the moment will depend on which one you are servicing and is telling you what it's telling you in your mind. Do you understand that, [Student J]?

You see? So, for example, perhaps say, the 16-year-old one is looking through your eyes into the mirror. And it says, "Oh, this is terrible! I [have] got to do something about this grey hair of mine! Oh, this is awful! Look at these lines here!" That's the 16-year-old one or 20-year-old one that's looking and seeing that. [It] doesn't like it at all. Because that one was created, you understand, that you're just so: such and such. And that's the way it remains. You see, the forms created do not change. They are created to serve a purpose. They don't grow when you grow, you see. They don't grow.

So the moment that you permit yourself to limit the I that you are, then you have to service them, you see. And the sadness is, so many people in their dedicated service to the forms they have created really do believe that when they enter their mind, that's them. And so you want to be free from that. You'll be freed from that—the very first thing is, you see—without the personal responsibility declaration, the cleansing breath cannot serve its purpose. You see, you must declare the truth. You must declare the truth: that very principle of personal responsibility. "This is what I use. It is not what I am. This is what I use. Let me use it well." You see, "for the goodness of my life." You see, declare [that] truth and refrain from what so many of us fall into: what someone else did. It doesn't matter what *they* do because they're doing it takes place in your mind. You see? You see?

You see, we look to see what another does depending on which form wants to look at it, you see. And so we talk to a person, and we think we're talking to the person. And as we talk to them, if we're not on guard, different forms rise up. And if the person that we're talking to is a weak person, as far as effort in personal responsibility, the next thing you know you have these forms passing back and forth. And someone's going to end up with a house full, you see, a full house. Now not all full houses, you know, are like poker. Oh, no. Truly, you like—I know you people say life is a gamble. Well, it certainly is. And when you [have] got a full house, forget poker; it's full of something else. Now, does that help with your question, [Student J]?

So, you see, personal—you see, I know I've said it to you all so many times. Personal responsibility, you see. "This is a beautiful day," you see. You declare that. Now, the moment you declare, "This is a beautiful day," the moment your mind declares that, you must prepare yourself. Because you have all the forms that have told you "This is a beautiful day" when you've been to the beach, when you've been out with a young lady, you know, one that is not passed on the rose bush, you know, one of the new buds. And, you see, you've got to, you've got to consider all of that, you see. You've got to consider the moment you declare "What a beautiful day this is. There is good in everything," the moment you declare that, all those forms rush in to take control of that goodness that you have just declared. And if you are not doing (your form) what you did when you created them, then the next second, you know, you have a miserable day. Do you understand that, [Student J]?

Yes.

You see, because they only have a good day in keeping with the purpose of their design. So if they were designed while you were on vacation in Waikiki or Tahiti, then when you declare "It's such a good day," they come in immediately for their slice, you see, for their—for the energy. They have awakened. The moment you declare "It's a good day," they wake up, you see, if they were forms that were created at the time you were feeling good. Does that help you, [Student J]?

Yes, sir.

So prepare yourself in your declaration. "Life is beautiful. It's such a good day." And, you see, then you prepare yourself, because they all come in. They're going to get a part of that. Don't you understand that?

Yes, sir.

You see. So, well, I find that most people say, "Oh, it's so miserable and that one did it and that one . . ." You see, those are only forms. Those are things they have created. That's not what they are, you see.

You see, it's like a person, a form comes in and says, "Oh, I'm going to have this wonderful time. Let me see what time it is here. Oh, I must be there at that certain time." And if that time comes and passes and they're not there, they will know immediately whether or not they're at home or a form they created [is at home]. You see how simple that is? You see, how—you see, the moment you declare you're going to get something, something good and something you waited for—you understand?—the moment you do that and the time comes and goes and you're not there to get it, you will know right away whether you're at home or a form you've created on how upset you are. Oh, you'll know right away, [Student J]. You'll know right away.

That's like—you know, how you wine and dine, you know, in your world, you wine and dine the girls and everything. And the girls wine and dine the boys nowadays and give them flowers and everything. And you know when you're just about to move in, and she says no and takes a taxi and goes home. Well, you know how you feel. Well, then, that tells you right away whether or not you were in service to a form you have created, you see? Or you'll say, "Great! I didn't want to waste the energy anyway." Like you say, "I'd rather have the cash." So, you see, it depends on what you're doing with the forms that you have created, you see. Does that help you?

Yes, sir.

You see, you work on that consciously. "This is such a beautiful day." Now when you declare that goodness, you see—you see, the moment you declare that to the mind, they all rush in. All of those [forms] you have created and that you would only allow that goodness in, in keeping with serving them. See, it is the law that you experience the goodness of life without servicing the mental things you've created. Do you understand that? You see, it is the law that you can pause and say, "What a beautiful moment," without service to forms you have created who only gave you a tidbit. Do you understand that? Just a little tidbit. Just a little tidbit of all of your energy spent, you see. Hmm? Did that help you? Yes, go ahead, [Student J].

In keeping with what you just [said], did I understand you to say that the cleansing breath is more effective by saying a verbal affirmation prior to doing it?

Personal—Yes. Personal responsibility. "I accept the divine right of the control of my form."

And then do the cleansing breath?

Yes. "And all that it has created. I accept the divine right of that control. I am the master by divine law. It is [in] service to me. It shall not tell me what to do." You see, like this moment when you say to yourself, "I feel real good," you must stay on guard. Because I see all the forms rushing in; they want that, you see. Because they are the ones, in keeping with their purpose of design in the days of ignorance, who allowed you a tidbit of that goodness. Do you understand that, [Student J]?

Yes, sir.

So you declare the truth. You see, when you declare that truth, they look at you and they get a little scared, you see. Those mental forms get a little bit scared, because they know you, once again, are declaring your right. *You* are their father. You and you alone. And they will either obey you or get out. And they don't want to get out. Yes.

Should we do this affirmation every time we, we—prior to the cleansing breath?

Yes. Definitely. Definitely. Declare that truth every single time. Declare that truth.

Thank you.

Declare that truth and prepare yourself. Declare it and prepare yourself. Because they'll come in a-screaming, you see. You see. You see, we find—and I found—well, to most of you, you would say it was the hard way because it did take me centuries to get through the wall of forms. It did. You will find that when you declare that wonderful goodness, you will experience, for a split second, that wonderful goodness, and then they'll all rush in. And if you don't do what they tell you to do, they will take it away from you. They will take it away in the sense that you believe you are that which you've created. Now if you don't believe you are that which you have created, they can't touch that goodness at all, you see. Yes.

Could you give us a more structured affirmation to use prior to the cleansing breath, please?

Prior to the cleansing breath. Let me pause a moment to see which ones you've all had and which one that you could use as the most effective for your present stage of evolution. [*The teacher pauses for approximately thirty seconds and then continues.*] Declare the simple truth that will help you most. "I am the captain of my ship. I am the master of my destiny. I am the captain of my ship. I am the master of my destiny. I accept the possibility of goodness without dependence." Declare that truth. "I am the captain of the ship. I am the master of my destiny. I accept the possibility of goodness without dependence." For you're free. In that moment you're freed. And do your cleansing breath.

Thank you, sir.

In that moment you're actually free. Declare it all the time. Declare it *all* the time. All the time. Until you can—it finally gets through that you feel it in your heart. Declare it all the time. It doesn't matter what time comes or time goes. That is meaningless. For if it matters, then that [that] matters is your god, and you are its slave. Do you see?

Yes, sir.

Understand that, you see. It only reveals to us our gods. Our gods are not something that, once established, there they are. Oh, they come and go. There's all kinds of gods we're in service to, you see. The clay-footed gods. You see? You see, when we're upset and we're not experiencing the goodness, that which we truly are, well, we're in service to one of the gods we've created. You see? And what do they offer us in return? It's a very poor deal. It's a very, very poor bargain. You couldn't even consider it [a] bargain. It's so poor. No, no, no. That's what you consider a bum deal. A bad rap or a bum deal. Believe me, that's what that stuff is. Surely, that's what it is. It kept me behind the wall long enough. I kept myself behind there long enough to learn that lesson, children. Yes. Does that help you?

Thank you, sir.

Declare that, but do it from your heart. Do it all the time, you see. And you will be amazed how good you'll feel [and] how that'll continue to increase. Why should you, as a[n] individualized, evolving soul, be dependent on the little morsels the forms you have created will allow you? When you can pause at any moment and experience the goodness, that which you truly are? You see? What does it matter whether someone does this or someone does that? For you alone are captain of the ship. They're not steering your ship, unless you want them to. And the moment they disturb you, that reveals you want them to control you. Oh!

There's our little friends over there. Are you—What's the matter there? Are you asleep? Look at our little friends all over here. *[The teacher refers to the birds in the garden.]* Aren't you the boy I heard whining there's no birds and little creatures around? *[The teacher addresses the cameraman.]* I see untold numbers of them all over. And I wasn't even looking over that way. But [what] God granted is, you see. You see, you don't have to see to know. You got ears, also.

Yes, [Student Y].

When you were speaking earlier of need in regards to celibacy and you said "Accept the possibility," is that in relation to the goodness?

Why, absolutely. You see, you see, your mind has created the goodness from a certain form you have created. And you only experience the goodness, unfortunately, some students, when that form—when you're in service to that form. You, by the very purpose of your evolution, are not, you understand, are not designed to serve created forms for the goodness that you are. It's, indeed, a very stupid way of thinking, you see. Your goodness is not dependent upon forms your mind has created until you make it so. But it isn't very intelligent to make your goodness and your God and your joy of living and your abundant happiness dependent on some form your mind has created, when your mind is changing forms all the time. They're going to sleep [and] waking up hungry and wild. That's, that's very foolish. It's very foolish.

You see, we have everything that is necessary for the fullness of our life. We don't have to do anything outside of our consciousness to experience it. *[Birds have been singing and chirping throughout the class. The teacher now refers to one of their songs.]* There's a little friend up there. He's very happy there. He's come to say hello this morning. Yes, [Student Y].

Does that include, does that—so if we have everything we need for the fullness of life within ourselves—

That is correct.

Then—

You already are full.

So then we really, in terms of—well, I'm interested in celibacy. So that's what I'm going toward. You—so if you, if you work on that, then you could—could you successfully practice celibacy?

Well, yes, but you have to practice the laws revealed, and you must free that energy through higher centers of consciousness. And that is not something that happens overnight. Suppression is a very destructive force. I find too many people suppressing and very few people exposing and educating and evolving. Yes.

So what do you in the meantime if you know that that—

Decrease the frequency. *[With the index of his right hand, the teacher points to his right temple, indicating his mind.]* Rather than total abstinence, decrease the frequency. It's the most difficult way of freeing oneself from the forms, you know. The most difficult way.

Do you mean the actual practice up here? [As the student speaks, the teacher again points to his mind.]

Why, certainly. It's up here before it's there. *[He continues to point to his mind.]* You see, a person who does not decrease the frequency in a mental world is only suppressing the physical. You see, of what good is it to refrain from physical rape when mental rape is constant? Does it help with your question? You see, it—you see, you see, it only reveals that you suppress the physical. So what are you doing with the mental, where the cause is? You see, you're working on the effect, and therefore there can be no cure. You're not working on the cause. You see?

You see, the cause is a form that has been created that allows you a tidbit of feeling good only in that way. You see, that's where the cause is. So of what benefit could it possibly be to abstain physically when the cause is a mental form that is created that is expressing through a physical vehicle? Does that help with your question?

It does, and I just need a bit more clarification.

Yes.

So if you work on it, if you abstain from it mentally, is it possible—

Yes, lust is in the mind. That is correct.

OK. So if you start there, is it possible that you could successfully not have to . . .

Express it physically?

Yes.

Well, yes, because then the energy will go up into other centers of consciousness and express there. The physical energy. You see, by it not being siphoned off by the form you have created, it has to go someplace else, you see. You see, as I said here to you all, perhaps several classes ago, in these private classes here, you are exposed to more Light, which is more energy, a higher degree of energy, a refinement of the energy, you understand? Now you're exposed to more of that. You can't be exposed to something without receiving it. Some of it rubs off on you.

Now, if you do not make changes in consciousness, through the declaration and the demonstration of personal responsibility, the forms that you believe that you are, are now strengthened, for you have more energy, which they siphon off. Does that help with your question? So, you see, it isn't a matter of choosing to be celibate. It's an inevitable path for you. Because otherwise, it will blow you apart. It'll just blow you apart. Yes.

So it would be wise—if you know that that action could take you out of the Light, that it is such a strong form within you . . .

Yes?

. . . then it would be wise not to . . .

It's not advisable to just say "Pssst!" and shut it off like that. *[The teacher makes a sound that is difficult to transcribe.]* You see, that's not advisable. Because it's not shut off here. *[The teacher may have gestured toward his mind, but the camera is pointed away from him toward the garden at this moment.]* You can refrain for a time. And then you find yourself going back again. You see, usually I find with celibacy, what usually happens, a person gets so tired of servicing someone else, they get so weary of what they call the trips, that they mentally make a judgment: "That's enough!" You see?

But you must understand that's another mental form they have created that is telling them "That's enough." So you [have] got this mental battle going on. That's not evolution spiritually. That becomes very detrimental. You see, it's like having—well, what do you call it?—a bad rap or a bum deal, I think you call it, love affair. And so when you don't get your own way, you say, "That's it. I'm finished with that. I'm celibate." Well, that's like a child! And if the fire engine don't [doesn't] do what he judges the fire engine's to do, he jumps up, he stomps on it, and he destroys it. Do you understand that, [Student Y]?

So, you see, what is the motive of making this change? That's very, very important. If the motive is that some guy gave you—what you judge—that some guy gave you a bum rap, you have a terrible motivation; you're going to pay a terrible price. Or if your motive is, for some fellow, that some girl, she went and chose someone else, well, you've got a terrible time. You see, that's not evolution; that's not spiritual evolution. Yes.

Well . . .

The question is, you must ask yourself, "Why do I want to be celibate?"

OK.

You ask yourself honestly why you want to be.

OK.

Is it because some great love gave you a bum rap, in your mind? If it is, forget it. You're not ready. Is it, for a man—that his wife—he went home and found out she was with somebody else? Forget it. You're not ready.

You see, it depends on what your motive is, you see. You see, is it a wife who is tired of listening to her husband's raving or what she considers violence because she gives him a little bit and he doesn't do what she tells him to [until] two days later?

Forget it. You're nowheres near close to celibacy. It's a waste of time, a waste of energy. You see? That's not the way. That's not the way, you see?

And if you think you're giving it up because—well, I'd rather say—because you're getting old physically, that's not the way, because you make it worse here. *[The teacher again gestures toward his mind and then laughs joyfully.]* No, no, no, that's not the way at all. No.

Yes. *[The teacher laughs again.]*

If one knows that it, that there's the possibility that if one doesn't practice it, that it has all these other colors to it and it could pull you out of the Light, what should one do then?

One should declare the truth: you are greater than that that you have created. You declare the truth, you see. You see, for example, be objective. You have a physical exercise that you're interested in refraining from. So you just don't refrain from it just like that. *[The teacher snaps his fingers.]* You just make— you see, you cannot come from a mental world and make a decision like that. You don't come in from a mental world. Do you understand that? You see, you must first take a look at the form that has allowed you this tidbit of goodness in your life only through that way. And then you've got to take a look at that and you [have] got to say—declare the truth, "Is that me? Well, I've believed that's me for all of my life. I don't believe in anything else." Some of my students have told my channel very clearly that's the only thing they believe in; that's the only god they ever knew. And they're not interested in knowing any other god. Well, they are nowheres near close to celibacy, but nature takes her toll. And so physically, you could say they are celibate. Mentally? Forget it. They're worse than they ever [were] before.

Do you understand? Does that help you with your question? *[Again, the teacher laughs joyfully.]*

This is very important. You, you see, you see, you are not a physical body. You *use* a physical body. You are not a mental body. You *create* a mental body. So let's understand what we truly are. See? And now if you insist on believing you are what you create, then you've got a problem.

You see, what you can no longer—it's like a person, say, oh, say they're a jogger. And they get what they call is a—what do you call those things? They call it "high." They don't call it "low." But some kind of a high. And they get it because there are certain chemical reactions in their body if they keep on running and running and running. Well, at a certain point, the interpretation of the mind, you understand, of this chemical change—you see?—a form is created. Do you understand that? All right. Now the form is created by the mind. They are experiencing chemical changes in their body; the interpretation by the mind is that this is coming to them from their constant running. Do you understand that?

Now time passes on. The form is created that lets them have this good feeling, what they call a high, this feeling of goodness from moving their physical body, you see, like a machine. And the day comes [when] their physical body won't move like that anymore. So what do they—what happens to them? So physically, they've become a celibate jogger, right? They refrain from jogging physically. So they're now a celibate jogger. So they're now a celibate jogger, but are they a mentally celibate jogger? No, no, no, no. They're only a physically celibate jogger. Mentally, they keep racing every single day so that form will let them have that good feeling. Do you understand that? You see?

You see, that's like people—they watch a movie. And they're sitting there and they see this beautiful, lovely lady on the film there. And they say, "Oh . . ." And the next thing you know, they're inside [the film]. That's them! I mean, they do believe it, those forms, you see? [The forms say,] "There, that's what you really are." See?

Well, it's the same thing. It's all created by the mind. You see? You know, it's like your money or your sex or whatever the forms want to tell you that you are so you can feel good, they're all created by the mind. That's the mental world. That's how they trap you. The minute you believe you are what you create in your mind, you're trapped. Do you understand that, [Student Y]?

Yes, I do.

Now how do you suppose that form that lets you have a tidbit of goodness is going to let you do on this celibacy foolishness? You move very slowly there, see? Very slowly.

Now I have an experience here. Some of my female students have felt, for spiritual growth and evolution, they've told themselves, that they'll be celibate so they can get even with their husbands. *[The teacher laughs.]* That's when we try to use the Light, you know, we try, you know—creation uses the Light against us. Do you understand that? You see? No, no, no, no. Slow steps are sure steps under the guidance of the angels that are in charge of your soul, you see.

Or that's like a man, you know, he finds a little extra on the side and he comes home to his wife and she says, "Well, I'm not feeling very well. It's been six months since I've had it." And he says, "Well, that's fine." He says, "You know I'm working on celibacy." Oh no, no. *[The teacher laughs again.]* That's just foolishness. As my student [Student J] says, "I'd rather have the cash."

Now where was that other question here. [Student D] has a question. *[The teacher continues laughing.]* "I'd rather have the cash! The cash, I can go do something with!" Yes, [Student D].

If one is attempting to work beyond the physical exercise . . .

Yes?

. . . could one focus that energy into another form of physical exercise that doesn't include another person?

Oh, it should always be one that doesn't include another person. Yes. *[The teacher laughs.]*

Is that better than doing it with another person to find another form of expression of that—

Well, the moment that you permit your mind to create another person, that is the very moment you're in service to their whims and all their forms and whatever they want to do with you, you see. That's the open door to total license. Yes. This is why, you know—I know my channel has always said he's so grateful that he's managed to be freed from—what [do] you call that institution? What do you call that? Marriage? He was just so grateful for that, you see. Because that's what it offers; that's what man makes of it, don't you understand. Yes, go ahead, [Student D].

Now, then when you have a relationship with another person, you're in service to them and to the forms, also?

And to—you're in service to your forms in order to have a relationship with their forms.

Right. So—

See? Form to form, don't you see? Bondage to bondage. Yes. Slavery to slavery. Yes?

So if you focus that energy into another form—

Yes. Yes, I know. An hour has passed already. *[The teacher responds to a signal from the cameraman.]* Go ahead. I got four minutes. Go right ahead. A full hour! *[The teacher laughs again.]*

[The student continues her question while the teacher is speaking; so it is difficult to transcribe some of her words.] . . . *another form of exercise that does not include that person, then you're only working with your forms, right?*

That's correct! And, you see, a person has got a much better chance working with their own forms because, being honest with themselves, they know their own. They have no possible idea what that other person's are. They're only deluded by their own forms, you see? So if you understand, you have less to work with and you know what you [have] got to work with. You know a person knows what they've created, you know? But when they go for another person, you know, all they can do is say, "Well, he told me that's what he created." *[The teacher laughs joyfully.]* But you don't know for sure. No.

What did you say about your timing over there? *[The teacher addresses the cameraman, who does not verbally respond.]* Is that three minutes [left on the videotape]? You mean to tell me you've gobbled up a whole hour already! Well, I have time for one, quick question. Who would ever dream that an hour has passed?

Yes, yes, I think—yes, [Student B]. We have to be real quick. Yes.

I'm wondering if, when, when we create a form, then, do we hop out of our body when we place our attention on the form itself? I mean, are we like—

Oh yes, definitely. Because, you see, the energy to sustain you in the vehicle is now going to the form that you believe that you are. You see, that's a—[we will] carry on with that again next week. You see, the first step of possession is obsession. Obsession is the belief you are the form you've created. That's the first step of leaving home.

I do hope that's helped you [with] all your questions. And an hour has passed. I best say good day. Have a lovely day. I know you will. Thank you.

JULY 6, 1986

A/V Class Private 55

Good morning, students.

Let us pause for a moment and enjoy the tranquility of the morning. *[After a short pause, the teacher continues.]*

Today I will speak to you on peace and force. I like to speak to you on subject matters that are, what you might consider, current events, for I find them to be most beneficial, as you will find them to be most beneficial in your evolution. And so today, our subject matter is peace and force.

Violence is an effort of the human mind to protect and to defend by force whatever it is attached to. Therefore, one finds that which is gained by force can only be maintained by force.

Some time ago I spoke to you on the power of peace. Those who make the effort, through their cleansing breath and their various exercises they have been given, will find that victors are those who demonstrate the power of peace. Victims are those who demonstrate the force of violence. And so we find and we know the way to be the victor in any endeavor. We know that peace, in the final analysis, is the power of God. It is the expression of goodness.

No one wants to be the victim, for to the human mind, victimization reveals to the mind that something is controlling it. And so in working with these realms of consciousness, the reason that those realms, in the final analysis, are never victorious is for they have only one, only one ingredient for their battlefields. And that's the ingredient of force. For they are composed of mental substance, which is force.

And so whenever you find yourselves mentally upset [or] frustrated, pause. Take control of your mind through your breathing exercises. For you shall be the victim of the force that you express. And that is why the Light is the sustainer. The force is the container. So it is better, in anything in life, to be the sustainer rather than the container, for a container never knows who's going to put the lid on it. And that certainly is not freedom. It is not truth. And, as I have stated long ago, truth needs no defense. Truth does not contain need. Force contains need, for force is denial of that which sustains it. So we see now in our evolution: either be the container or be that which sustains the container.

I spoke also to you years ago, a bit, about my own personal evolution. I have refrained over these many years from revealing much over it for the simple reason that the interest in my evolution was, let us say, not as broadened as the principle of interest reveals. However, now that we have progressed to this day and this moment, I will, once again, perhaps broaden the horizons on the wall that I spent so many eons behind.

Now to all of us the wall represents, of course, an obstruction. A wall represents an obstruction because we cannot do with the wall what we want to do with the wall. A wall is an obstruction. It is an obstruction to anyone who believes they are force and mental substance. It is not an obstruction to what you are. A wall is only an obstruction to what you believe you are. And so the wall, the obstruction, we find our self behind and know it not. But we do not know it not forever, for the moment comes when we clearly see the wall of our obstruction. And we clearly see through the wall, but cannot move through the wall. We see through the wall and see the many forms that we alone have created. We must pass through the wall in order to be free from the obstruction to our own evolution.

As I spoke to you at that time in our classes, the forms behind the wall you peer through are the forms you have created. The wall is an obstruction, an effect of your own denial. So though it took me some time to awaken to that truth, when you spend as much time as I have spent behind a wall, you finally awaken and demonstrate, to some degree, acceptance, the divine will. "Not mine, but Thine" *is* the divine will. Now, when you accept "Not mine, but Thine," when you accept that, this wall of denial, that you have created, you will pass through.

Be, however, not deceived. For when you pass through the wall of your own denials in life, awaiting on the other side of the wall are all of the forms, all the children that you have created. Now they wait for you. They wait. They look at you, like you, perhaps, in your world look at one of our little creatures behind bars in what you call your zoos. They look at you and they examine you. And they study you and they stare at you, waiting for the moment when you will awaken and pass through the wall. They wait, very hungry for you. So once you have accepted the divine law: personal responsibility—for there is no acceptance in any world without a demonstration of personal responsibility. Once you have accepted [and] you demonstrate personal responsibility, the wall created by your own denial disappears.

You pass through the wall and the forms grab you to tempt you. And you experience what you understand as fear, for you, once again, permit yourself to believe you are that which you have created. And in believing you are that which you have created, you experience what you know as fear when you try to go against what you have created and believe that you are. And so the wall rises in keeping with the Law of Denial, in keeping with the law of not accepting personal responsibility.

Fear is a force. Those who fear are those who are attached to all they have created. That's the only thing fear is: the mind's control over the eternal being that you are. You know that as fear. Fear is force. You cannot experience fear without an absolute conviction that you are what you have created and are therefore attached to it. It is not possible to experience fear without that deception of your mind: that you are that which you have created.

And so those who permit themselves the luxury of believing they are that which they have created are people who experience fear and express it in what is known as violence, an expression of force. And it's very important that you understand the payments that are offered by believing you are the thoughts that you create.

Now, we'll pause for the questions that we have this morning. You may raise your hands. Yes, [Student N].

So once we pass through the wall and all these forms greet us and we don't take responsibility, we just build another wall and keep going through that process?

That is correct. You see, if you permit your mind, if you permit [yourself] to believe that you are your mind, that which you have created, if you permit yourself that luxury, you deny the truth of personal responsibility. For example, in your world if you say you feel a certain way because of what someone did, then you have denied the Law of Freedom and cannot experience the goodness that you seek. Yes. Yes, [Student B].

On the other side of the wall, are those forms the same as the forms we're aware of now? Do they go to sleep if we tell them to go to sleep?

No, not those forms. Those forms do not sleep. Those are the forms that have been created—those are known as universal forms. Those are mass forms. Those are forms that have been created by human minds over eons of time. They combine and amalgamate as like attracts like. And those forms exist and are servants of the realms below. Those forms don't go to sleep by the speaking of one individual's declaration. Do you understand that? For, you see, you have passed through the wall and there you meet the forms that are the combined forms of all mental substance and all force. Yes, yes. Did that help there?

Yes.

Yes, [Student L].

Is the wall itself built of your forms?

No. The wall itself is built of your denials. Your denials are your destinies. The destiny is the wall of obstruction. The wall, you see, the wall is a transparent wall, which you cannot move through. You can see through it and you are constantly being monitored by the forms who wait for you, as you would—as a flashlight, a bulb would wait for its battery, for the charge. They wait for you for the charge, you see. Yes. Yes, [Student Y], please.

Are there diff—as you pass—as you evolve, after you leave form as you awaken—

Yes.

—to the personal responsibility, does it get—does it become, like, I don't want to use the word refined, *but does that—is it like, is that how the wall is? It's like a, like a degree of it? One being thicker than . . .*

Yes, in the sense that the wall is as thick as your own denials, your denials, your denial of the truth. You see, when you deny, you destine yourself to strengthening or thickening the wall. Yes, each and every denial in your mind. Yes. Yes, [Student Y].

How do you know when you have—when you are coming out of it? How does one know?

Oh, you have no problem there whatsoever, because when you pass through the wall, you'll experience all the temptations and everything that those forms have to offer that are strengthened by like attracts like. For example, let's put in reference to an army: you can compare the buck private, as a buck private, your own forms and temptations, as an individual, in rank. Those forms on the other side of the wall, you would consider those generals. Yes. As far as their strength is concerned and their position in service to the lesser light. Yes, those are generals. They wait for you. They wait for every soul. Yes, [Student Y].

So every soul must go through this wall.

All souls do go through the wall. Some go through many, many times. And some wait for a long time, like I did myself, to even reach the point of accepting the divine will; that that is the [divine] will: the only thing that will free us. There's nothing else that will free us. Yes.

Force binds; power frees. It's that simple. And violence is the expression of force. Yes. Yes, [Student Y].

So was this created for this very purpose? Are we creating this wall?

Oh, yes, yes. The mental world has been creating it for eons of time, yes. Yes, [Student Y].

So it's, it is, it serves a high purpose.

Indeed, indeed, it does. As you would put it in your words, as you said, a refining process. Indeed, it does serve a very fine purpose. Yes. It is not something that any mind looks forward to. No one looks forward to the obstructions in their life, you see. However, by constantly denying, the obstruction just increases. Yes.

Yes, now [Student L] has been waiting. Yes.

I think I remember from years past that you said the wall parted. Is that what happened?

It opens; just like a hole suddenly opens up in the wall and you pass through it, yes. But how long will you be through the wall before the next one? You decide to create the next one from your denials in life, you see. Hopefully not too long.

Now [Student O] is waiting with a question here.

Yes. Is objectivity to a greater degree as you get closer or beyond the wall or do you—is objectivity, I guess it would be conceived on earth, but then perceived before you go through the wall?

Yes, yes. You see, the purpose of your exercises—you see, what takes place in your spiritual exercises, to those of you who are working daily with your proper meditations, your exercises, your cleansing breaths, etc., you are saving yourself centuries of time, is what you're doing.

Now, you know, when you have a distasteful experience to go through in life, it's best to call it all forth in keeping with your strength and go through it, for you're never going to get more than you're capable of bearing. Now if you have something distasteful to go through, it is better to call it forth in one day rather than stretch it out over a hundred years. Wouldn't you all agree to that? You see? If it's something inevitable, well, let's face it and get it over with. So what you are doing as you do your part spiritually, you call forth all of that that you have created and believe that you are; you call it forth into your experiences, you see. You see, as the Light of your soul shines brighter, as you are exposed to more and more Light here in your little temple, in your school, the more you are exposed, the more alert, the stronger you must become spiritually. For, you see, as I spoke to you before, the mind cannot cope with that, you see. Therefore, you must turn to the Light, for the Light is the power; the mind is the force.

And, you see, if you will try to visualize, you, as one person, on a battlefield with 500,000 other soldiers and you are using force—you're using the same weapons that they are using—you shall be defeated; you shall be the victim. For the odds are against everyone. And force and violence is an expression of the very composition of the soldiers from below, you see. You see, the soldiers of those realms—remember this: the reason that they serve is because they fear, you see. They believe they are that which they create. Therefore, they experience fear. And so they do what they are told to do from fear because they believe they are the forms they have created and their very survival is at stake. They believe that, you see. Does that help you, [Student O]?

Yes, it does.

Yes. And so, you see, even in your physical world here, you have had the greatest of your spiritual leaders demonstrate there's only one way to victory: it is known as the path of peace. Passive resistance is the only victory. There is no victory without the power of peace.

Power is greater than force for power sustains force. That which sustains anything is greater than that which is sustained, you see? And so when man believes he is a thought that he has created, what man is doing is he is consciously choosing to be the victim; he's constantly choosing force over that which he is. Man, the soul, that which we are is power. That which we are not is force, you see. And whatever is force can only be contained and sustained by force, you see. Does that help, [Student O], with that question?

Yes, sir.

Yes, now [Student S] here had a question, yes. Good morning.

Yes, I'd like to know if you had any help, spiritually or anything, when you were behind the wall in order to get to—

Well, I'd like to pause right there. The only help that I had—and I look here in your classes and see how fortunate you are. How fortunate that you have merited guidance. I had no one at the time behind the wall. I had a voice whisper to me as I wandered and wandered and wandered. You see, you must understand that you have someone that—here you have my channel to speak with all the time and to relate with and to communicate with and to talk with. Well, when you have a guardian angel—which you all have guardian angels—when you're all upset, you have no way of knowing or guaranteeing (your guardian angel) you'll be able to hear them, you see. But I find you, as my students, very upset frequently. And my channel hears you loud and clear. You see? So there is quite a difference in that respect. Yes. Yes, go ahead, [Student S].

And I'd also like to ask—

He shouldn't hear you, but he does. Yes.

Once we pass through the wall and we're faced with all these general-type forms—

Well, you understand, for example, if a person believes they are a certain form, that's fine. They have that form in their consciousness. They have created it. Now those forms behind the wall are all of those forms that have been created by the minds of men over eons of time who have now amalgamated.

You know, there's one that represents a certain need of this. Another represents a certain need of that. There's one that represents affection. There's one that represents money. There's one that represents all of those different senses, you see. Yes. They are composed of un[told], [numberless] number[s] of ones that have been created by human minds. Yes.

Is there anything that we should know as far as establishing the law to ask for help or do whatever is necessary to get through those forms?

Why, certainly. Stop denying. You see, all you have to do is to refrain from denying. You see, when you permit your mind, for example, when you permit your mind—oh, yes!—when you permit your mind to use your mouth to say and to declare a defeatist attitude or to say, "I can't take anymore," then what you are doing at those moments [is] you are in service to force, you see. Now try to understand when you reach that point in your mind, as many of you have, "Well, I just can't take anymore," what is using your mind and your mouth is declaring the truth. It is speaking the truth. It can't take anymore, for it won't survive. If you believe you are that form you have created, you (the eternal being), if you have entered into that consciousness, then it moves you right away from the Light because it is a form that has been created by your own mind that you temporarily believe that you are.

And take a look at the living demonstration. That which is formless is free. It is non-destructible, you see. You see, force destroys. You see, force is a destructive, very destructive—it destroys anything it touches. Now power is constructive. Power builds; force destroys. So you look at any people or any nation and you will find those who are guided by force self-destruct. It may take varying times for them to self-destruct, but all force, the expression of it being violence, is self-destructive. Do you understand that?

So when you allow your mind to say, "I can't take anymore," and you believe what your mind is saying, then what it is, you believe you are the forms that you have created and they're telling you that you can't take anymore. Because *you* (what you truly are), being formless and free, the power, is not subject to destruction. You cannot destroy what you are. You can only destroy by force what you believe you are. Yes. And so if you, in your evolution, can only allow yourself to awaken by self-destruction, then self-destruction is what you shall experience. But that self-destruction is only by your believing the forms, the thought patterns that you have created. Yes. Did that help you with your question?

Yes.

And [Student Y] has a question this morning.

I know you've given us this before. And you've spoke, you just spoke that your channel can hear us in our upsets—

Yes, what I'm saying is he can hear you physically and emotionally, unfortunately. But he is receiving much help in that respect. Yes.

What can, what would be—I know you've given us this before, but could you, again, say what our part would be in helping that?

Well, yes, an application—a greater effort in application of these wonderful classes that you are receiving. You see, you must try to understand that my channel is as human as any of you. And he's just as human as I am. And he doesn't, yet, have that much separation. He's still in a physical form, you understand. And so you must realize when you choose force over peace, you must realize that you are instruments only to tempt his own mind, for he is tempted to return to the public arena, because his mind experiences, painful as it was, his mind experienced less constant upset than it has over this past year. So it is—I have spoken to him many times, but he has the divine right, you understand, of his growth. It isn't an absolute that he cannot return to the public arena. There is no law that has been revealed to us by the Light that my channel cannot return to the public arena. And you can make greater effort with your violence and your choosing force over what you are, because you'll only shorten the day when his divine right shall be permitted by the Light and he shall return to the public arena.

[Serenity first held public devotional services on May 2, 1971, and they were held weekly through June 9, 1985, at the American Legion log cabin in San Anselmo, California. On Saturday, June 15, 1985, at a Serenity dinner social held at the log cabin, Mr. Goodwin announced that church services had ended and that private classes were beginning the very next day at the temple. He invited all those who were present to apply. The classes published in Volumes 14 through 17 are transcriptions of those Sunday morning classes. It is unlikely that these classes would have continued if Mr. Goodwin returned to work in the public arena.]

Yes. Did that you help with your question?

Thank you.

Yes. Yes, [Student B].

When we get to the other side of the wall, are the forms that— do they have souls?

No, those are the soulless ones of which we now speak. Those are the soulless ones. Remember that obsession precedes possession, you see. You see, obsession is the soulless forms. We choose to become obsessed with them. And after once we have become obsessed, then there is no problem to move into the possession of the decarnate or the astral forms that are soul creatures, yes, that have spent time on the planet. Yes, [Student B].

And is our experience there in keeping with the amount of violence that we demonstrated during our time on this planet?

Oh, yes, because, you see, well, if you understand, there's much violence. There's the violence of the mind. Sometimes it gets through the physical body and ofttimes it doesn't. But the violence is there, you see. The violence, as I explained earlier, is an expression of the force. It is a person who believes and is completely attached and convinced to what they have created with their mind, with the force, you see. Yes. Yes, indeed. Yes, [Student N].

Are those forms that we—that come to us after we pass through the wall the same as the ones when we pass—leave this physical body?

Oh, no, no, no. Now we're speaking of a different phase in our evolution. [When] you leave the physical body, you have all of those things calling you and tempting you to go off here and go off there. And they take on the garments of those that you are attached to in form.

Oh.

You see? And so you want to follow the Light. But then, you see, you follow the Light and then you must go through all of the processes. You get into, if you're fortunate, in keeping with the laws you've established, you go into the Halls of Repose. You are awakened. You get so much time in school, those of you who have earned that and merited that. And we're speaking of this wall of obstruction is the evolution to the final Light, what you truly are and your return unto it. Oh, yes, yes.

Yes, you see, there's all these different phases, you see, as you go through all of these different experiences on earth. You must realize what you're going through each day here in your physical world, you're going through over there, you see. You see, I find difficulty in your relating to what's taking place because you're so overidentified with flesh and bone that you are not opening your eyes to see that the experiences that you are encountering in your physical world is taking place in realms that you do not see. It is your movement through these realms. Yes, yes. Well, when you allow yourself to say, "Well, I'm not about to change. I'm stubborn. I'm this. I'm that. I'm not going to make effort to demonstrate the divine Law of Total Acceptance," you see, you are in realms. And those realms and those forms use your mouth, for they use your mind. You see, most people do not make any effort to know what they're thinking. And therefore, why, they're wide-open freeways for all the forms to come in and think for them. Yes. You see, there's a vast difference between self-discipline and violence. Yes, [Student L].

Do our families not come, truly, to greet us when we're passing through to the other side?

Well now, you've been in private class long enough and I think we've discussed enough that you're going to have to know who you are in order to know who they are and not be deceived by your senses.

OK.

Hmm? You see?

Yes.

I mean, many philosophies and religions have taught you to test the spirit from whence they cometh. Yes. For your minds create many things for you, because if you do not make the effort through your proper breathing and your cleansing [breath] and your exercises to create what you choose to create, then something else creates it for you. Yes.

Yes, [Student Y] has a question, please.

When you speak of—you speak in terms of direction. Sometimes you say up there and sometimes you say down there.

Yes. I indeed do. I do that because your minds cannot relate to another dimension. They can only relate up and down, back and forth.

So—

And because they've so overidentified to up and down and back and forth that I must use the terminology in which I may relate to your minds, which you believe, temporarily, that you are. Yes, [Student Y].

OK.

Hmm.

Ah—

I find no problem in your relating to up and down and back and forth. Yes. Hmm.

Does—so I'm just trying to get a better sense of what you're speaking of.

Well, it's not up and it's not down in that sense. But, you see, if I don't say up and down [and] I don't say back and forth, then I [have] got to say in and out. You see, you see, you are two dimensional in the belief; overidentification and creating the belief and the attachment places you two dimensional. So I've got to offer you these alternatives—in and out, up and down, back and forth—in order to relate to what you believe you are. Yes, [Student Y].

OK. Would it be likened to a constellation in the sky where there are points and you, like, you may see a configuration of three stars—

Yes.

—and you can image, like, the fourth point. Is it like that, in a sense?

Well, I think it perhaps best—I tried to do what I could to draw on a board there, on a blackboard one time for you to try to get you to perceive another dimension. Let's take a look, for example, let's choose something that you can look—look at the trunk of the lovely tree there. Now look at the trunk. All right? Just let your eyes—don't stare at it. Just look at it. Now experience what is happening as you look at the trunk of the tree. Now, you see what you call bark, right?

Right.

Now you keep looking at that very speck of bark until it becomes totally pinpointed for you. Now, move with that inside. What do you see now?

Now I can actually see the inside.

All right. Now you must go right inside and on through. You see?

Yes.

However, your mind doesn't know what is on through it. Now you reach a point at which your mind tells you "It's blank." Do you understand? See? You see, there's no reference. There's nothing for the two dimension—you see, to move beyond two dimension, you must pass through that which does not relate to two dimension. You see, two dimension is dependent on reference. Do you understand that? Two dimension exists because of reference. Now you will have to pass beyond reference in order to enter the fourth dimension. Yes.

So that, that lines up with what you said, you must let go of what you do know to . . .

Experience what you don't know. Yes. You must let go; you see, you must let go of the two dimension, which is dependent on reference. What is reference dependent upon? Experience. What is experience dependent upon? What you have denied. Do you understand? For denial is the destiny. So in order to move beyond two dimension, the two dimensional world, you must let go of what you know in order to experience what you do not know. For the moment that you have reference, you are bound. Do you understand that?

See, reference is an indispensable ingredient for bondage and slavery, you see? So to move through that, you'll come against what you'll—you'll either—what you'll do [is] you'll come up against what you understand as an obstruction. You'll come up against a blank wall. Now that wall may be black—you see, it depends on your mind—if black is what you fear the most. You know, it's all darkness, you understand, which comes from reference of childhood.

You see, a person who, on a spiritual path, whenever I hear them say, "Well, there's nothing there." All right then, I will say to them, "There is no thing. Then, tell me your experience of no thing." They will then tell me, "Well, it's all black. It's all dark." Now I know why they tell me it's all dark. You understand? They are telling me they cannot control what they cannot see.

You see? So, you see, you will find in your spiritual evolution that when you are working, as you are—many of you are coming along, but you have to go through all of these things of reference of your two dimensions—when you make that effort through your meditation, you see, and you start to have experience: you go beyond the forms and you'll enter this, this darkness, you see. This black. It's all dark. It is whatever color that is recorded in your mind in the two dimension that represents to your mind you can't control it. So if, to your mind, [in] black or darkness, you can't see anything—therefore, you can't control what you can't see—then you will experience fear. For the forms will stimulate your senses and you understand that as fear. See, fear (the sensation) is a stimulation of the senses. Does that help you?

Time is passing quickly this morning. So go right ahead. Yes. Now you have those lovely flowers to take care of. *[The teacher may be addressing a bee that flies very close to his face.]* Yes, [Student M].

Yes. As we go through the wall and the thought or the belief in any kind of fear brings the wall back up. So . . .

Your denial of personal responsibility puts the wall back. The wall is composed of denial. Correct. Yes.

OK. And when we pass out of the form and are aware of these truths that you are teaching us, do the same, the same things apply—the affirmations, the meditations? It's a similar world as it is today only the forms are visible there waiting for us? I'm trying to get a—

Well, you see, I would like to have you understand that the forms are visible waiting for you this moment. They're always present, you see. And the walls—I don't recall any of you telling me you're totally freed from obstruction. You see? So this obstruction is the wall, and the forms wait for you on the other side. So as you make the effort to pass through the wall (the obstruction), what you do in truth, don't you see, you call all of that forth, and you face personal responsibility. And you accept that divine law. You pass through and they all scream at you.

You see, I can tell easily when any of my students have passed through the wall because all those forms are after them as never before. Now you pass through the wall a little bit and then you create another wall with your next denial and your next one and your next one. Yes. This is happening in a world in which you are moving at this moment and always has happened in that world. The only reason you are not aware of that world is because the effort is not being made sufficiently to move beyond the two dimension, you see. You see, when pride falls, you let go of all you know. And when you let go of all you know, you experience all you don't know. You see?

Yes. Thank you.

You see? And so, you see, pride, of course, is an expression of one's attachment to what a wonderful job they've done with themselves. Yes.

Did [Student Y] have a—[Student N] has a question. Yes. I don't find any shortage of pride. Yes. Of course, it can serve a good purpose, like if you take pride that you brush your teeth each day, then it serves a good purpose for your teeth, if you believe you are your teeth. Yes, [Student N].

In principle, passing through the wall, would it be the same as seeing through the trees?

Well, no, because it's much easier for you to see through the tree than it is to pass through the wall. Because, after all, the tree, you don't believe you are. The wall, you believe you are. So it's much easier for you to pass through the tree, you see? You see, the tree, in your mind, doesn't represent something that you are. Your forms that you have created by the Law of Denial represent something you believe you are. Now the tree, you don't believe you are. It would be much easier for you to pass right on through that tree than to go through the wall of your own creations, oh, yes, your own denials. [It would] be much easier. [It would be] much easier for you physically to pass through the tree. Definitely. Because, you see, you don't believe you are the tree.

OK.

So, believing that you are *not* the tree, you have no problem with attachment to it, do you? Well, I find some people have no problem with not believing they're a tree at all because they just saw them and chew them up. And they have no consideration at all for anything. They don't even speak to it when they go to cut its arms off. Yes. Yes, [Student D].

So the forms here that create the walls here—

They're creating walls in the third and fourth dimensions. Certainly, they are.

We—our personal responsibility is in accepting the forms we have created and accepting them as forms and not as our, our self.

Correct. Correct.

When we get to that great wall that has the universal forms on the other side—

Oh, yes indeed.

—is it the same process: we accept that we have contributed to the formation of those forms?

Why, certainly. *[The student speaks a few words simultaneously with the teacher, but they are difficult to transcribe.]* That's personal responsibility.

And then that frees us—

Well, what happens is—and when you do that, you attract, through the law that like attracts like, the soldiers of Light on the battlefield, for it's a battlefield you pass through. And it's very well mined. Yes. That's called temptations.

Yes.

Yes. Yes, indeed.

Thank you.

I think, also, in your world they call temptations booby traps, don't they? Yes.

Yes. So, you see, if you want to continue to experience the walls of obstruction, continue on with discouragement and you can't take anymore and all that type of thing. That's all you have to do is let those forms in and tell your mind that kind of stuff; and then, you, through overidentification with self-glory, you know, romancing the stone, you know—why, my channel was instructed here just the other day to make it clear to the students, by his own mother, that the students shall stop romancing the stones and polishing the jewels here in the school, you see. Yes. But that is why you have the boundaries beyond the school. You see, that's what that's for: to romance the stone and polish the jewel, you see. And I think—I don't think there's anyone here, except our little student Mr. Red, that can't relate to romancing the stone and polishing the jewel. *[Mr. Red is the church's dog and he was neutered.]* Yes.

Yes, [Student Y]. Perhaps [Student E, also], but he won't be long before he romances. *[Student E was the youngest student, and he was not quite two years old at the time.]* Yes, thank you. Go ahead, please.

So is it, is it good to say—if you're experiencing discouragement—

Experiencing discouragement? Yes, you are permitting energy to one of those forms. Yes. That's all it is. Yes.

All right. OK, how do I . . .

Yes, go right ahead, [Student Y].

So at that point, to remind oneself that there is no power greater than God—

Why, of course! That's the declaration of truth. Oh, all of this other is just, is just a temporary delusion of the mind, of the realms of force. That's all that it is. That's all it ever was. That's all it ever can be. It is nothing else.

Yes. I think we should close class here. My students, some of them, are falling asleep. Yes. Yes, [Student Y].

So when you're faced with the wall, would that be—is it possible, when you're out of form and you're in—you're up against the wall and all these forms, if you can—is it possible to say that to oneself?

Yes, one declares that truth. Yes. Absolutely. You declare the truth. You are captain of your ship. You are master of your destiny. You have all the affirmations and breathing exercises necessary that will free you. For in that instant, you accept personal responsibility. You see, you free yourself from the destiny. You see, you must relate that destiny is the effect of denial. And so when you free yourself from denial, you free yourself from the destiny of the obstruction. You see? Acceptance is the will of God. Don't tell yourself—[don't] let those forms tell you what you don't have. Let your mind declare the truth of all you do have that you may distribute it in balance and reason, you see?

You see, it's nothing more nor less than a form in your mind that you have created. If you insist on allowing yourself to believe you are the form using your energy to declare your discouragement or how bad things are, they get worse because the very form calls in all of the others of like kind. Yes. And that's known as experience. Yes, [Student Y].

So when you're out of your body, when you—let's say—
You're out of your physical body.
Physical body.
You still have identities; therefore, you have some form.
OK.
Oh, yes. Yes.
I think you answered this, but I just want to make sure.
Yes.
So you, you can remind yourself that God is the great—that there is no greater power than God—

That is, that is correct.

—when faced with whatever—

Absolutely and positively. In your being you declare that truth. You declare your truth. "God is the power. This is the force." You see? God is greater. You see, declare the truth. God sustains the force. So God is who you turn to. Do you understand? [If] you turn to force, you turn to limit. You see, it's our ego, uneducated, and our pride that uses force.

Force is not an instrument of the soul, you see. It's an instrument of the realm of the mind, for those who take pride in their accomplishments, you see? You know, in your world—and it's so interesting. Perhaps you can better relate to this. Some of you students, over times, you know, (and I won't be mentioning any names) have said, "Well," you know, in their process of romancing their stone and polishing the jewel, have said "Well, I sure put a smile on her face." Well, you know, what they're really saying is they [were] able to get the poor, pathetic thing to grin for a short time. *[A few students laugh.]* There's a vast difference between a grin and a smile, you know.

Are you checking your time over there? What's your time say? *[The teacher addresses the cameraman.]*

Fifty-three.

Well, that gives us seven minutes—doesn't it?—maximum. It takes seven minutes—oh, if you could only get through romancing the stone and polishing the jewel and putting a grin on someone's face in seven minutes, you'd be in heaven. *[More students laugh.]*

And I think I'll call it a day. Thank you. It's been such a lovely day and so [will be] the rest of it. Yes. Thank you. Don't worry about a rocket to the moon. Just take a rocket to heaven. It's called a seven-minute trip, I think.

Good day.

JULY 13, 1986

A/V Class Private 56

Good morning, class.

This morning we'll spend some time on discussing application of the teachings that you are receiving.

And before we start on the application of what you are receiving, let me share with you this morning [the] answer to those of you who have been questioning in your minds how long I shall remain in this particular class, as your teacher. The duration of my stay in any of my classes is in keeping with the law of the application of what is given, for those laws of giving and receiving cannot be transgressed without, of course, severe payment or penalty. Therefore, I have been encouraged that the percentage of this particular class has been making effort in applying the laws and the teachings that they are receiving. However, it is time to help you in applying more of what you are receiving, not just that I remain as your teacher, but that you benefit from the efforts that you make in your presence.

Now, we'll go through some of the teachings that you have received and whether or not you have been applying them. The spoken word is life-giving energy. What words do you speak? What experiences do you encounter? Now if you are speaking forth a word knowing that it is giving life energy to forms which are responsible for returning to you what you have created them to do, and the returning to you is known as experiences, then you must relate, in applying these teachings, you must relate to what you are giving life-giving energy to.

If you say, for example, that life is miserable, then you create those forms to return to you an experience of what you understand as misery. If you say, "I don't have enough of this. I don't have enough of that. Someone else is causing my problems. This is what I can do. This is what I can't do," then experience returns to you; those forms come back to you as experiences. So you must ask yourself the question this morning, "What am I experienc[ing]? What is returning to me?" And by applying the law of the spoken word—for, you see, before you speak a word, you must first create the form. So whatever word you speak forth, the form has been created. The form goes out and brings back to you what you have created it for. So you think the form; you speak the word; you have the experience.

Now are you applying what you understand in your world as a positive vibration of constructive good? Positive is constructive; negative is destructive in speaking on this particular subject. Do you constantly doubt? Do you constantly worry? Do you constantly wonder? Are you filling your minds with fear, which return to you those type of experiences? Therefore, you know beyond a shadow of all doubt whether or not you are applying what you are receiving.

Now if you are applying what you are receiving—and no one in form, that is, in limit, being perfect, for that which is formed cannot be perfect, for it is missing that which is formless. You see, it is limiting that which it is; so therefore, that which limits that which it is cannot be perfect, whole, or complete. That which is perfect is whole and complete. Therefore, that which is form cannot possibly be perfect, and it is foolhardy and is foolish to even seek perfection in that which is limit, for it is contrary to that which is.

Now, there are times in your life, in everyone's life, when you slip, when you make the effort and then you fall in other ways, in the applying of what you're receiving. You have experiences. Once again you awaken. You establish new thoughts, new forms, and you have new experiences. And then you move on to the next step. The question is, How long will you take in applying the laws you are receiving? How much do you think your mind needs to suffer sufficiently to make the changes that are necessary for you to enjoy life?

Now, [I'll] pause now for your hands to raise. Yes, [Student N].

Is peace—does it have a form?

No. Peace is power. Power is formless. Therefore, power is free.

So when you have this thought of peace and you feel the essence of it, there is no form that goes with that.

No, the moment there's form, you've entered force.

OK.

You see, peace, power is the sustainer of form. Force is the expression of form. So that which is force is contained and, as I spoke to you in one of our other classes, it's time for you to move from being the container to that which is containing the container—to that which sustains, rather, the container. I also spoke to you that those who insist on being the container must accept what goes with the container: it's known as a lid. And it's under someone's control besides your own, because you have given that control to someone else in order to deceive yourself that you are the container.

Did that help you, [Student N], this morning, with the question? Yes. Yes, [Student Y] has a question, too.

Do you or your channel ever see us without forms around us?

Why, cer—without forms?

Yes.

Seeing what you are, viewing what you are, is formless and free, and therefore if you would like a description of it, the best description can be is rays of light. Varying colors and shades of light, yes. Yes, [Student Y].

So there—now that's when we aren't creating negative forms.

Well, you, regardless of the negative forms—you see, for example, you are, you are Light. That is what you are. Light is intelligent Energy; intelligent Energy is what you truly are. So when one looks through the fog of forms created by what one deceives themselves and believes they are, then one views the Light that they are, yes. So the Light shines ever in keeping with how much fog is covering it. Yes, [Student Y].

Thank you. So do you ever, do you see us—so they're always moving around us, these forms we've created?

Yes, because, you see, you are the only one that sustains them. Whereas you are the mother or father of them, they have no one else to go to for their feeding. Do you understand that? Now if you have someone who you are in rapport with, and you are in rapport with them in keeping with a vibration of harmony on certain beliefs—we're now speaking of the realms of forms—then, of course, they could go to your neighbors for their feeding. That's crossing the bridge. And we view that all the time in our experiences, you see. [If] you talk to a person to help them through a certain situation that you've had experiences with, when you do that you face instantly the forms that have created that experience for you in your own consciousness. And you must be aware and alert of that, you see.

So if you are working with someone, for example, and you have not moved into the soul faculties, where there is duty, gratitude, tolerance, compassion, patience, and wisdom, etc., and understanding, if you do not move into the soul faculties, then, of course, you trap yourself in the very forms that are shadows that you, at times, believe that you are. Does that help with your question? Yes, [Student Y].

It does. And the question that I had in my—the question that I had was, are we ever without these forms around, I mean, are we ever in a state of harmony where we don't have them lingering about us?

Not as long as you believe that you are them. As long as you believe you are the container, then you are contained, and the forms are there, you see. You see, whenever you make the effort to free yourself from the belief that you are the limit, that you are the form, which is the limit, in those moments, you are freed from them, yes.

Now in reference to that question, there are many times, through effort, that a person, the forms that they have created are having their nap, yes. Oh, yes, there are many times. That's what we should all strive for in creation or in form, is for that which we have created with our minds to take a nap, to just stop and take a nap. That, you see, that is when the Light that we are shines most beautifully; it shines clearly, you see. And when a person—you're working with someone and you tell them to stop it, you are speaking to the forms that their little soul is trapped in. Now when the person stops it, that reveals a person who is making effort, you see. And that effort is experienced in a much happier life, as long as that effort is made. Do you understand? And they're freed from those forms that they used to believe that they were. Do you understand that?

Yes.

You see? And so we must discern; whenever you are working with yourself—for one is always working [with] oneself when they're working with another, you know. You see, you can't work with another without working with oneself. So whenever you work with another, you see, God, the Principle of Good, is experience[d]; the one helps themselves by helping another. See, by helping another, you are actually helping yourself. That is the law. For, you see, in order to be an instrument for another to be helped, you must first free yourself from that which they are trapped in. Therefore, you must face those very forms inside of yourself, and order them to rest, to take a nap, and in so doing, you have helped yourself and are now an instrument to order those forms in another to speak to the soul. You see, soul speaks to soul; spirit to spirit, and mind to mind. If you are working with someone and do not feel that you have an experience (that's there's been no effect), that reveals that you are not in the soul faculties, where wisdom and patience reigns supreme. And therefore, you are being deceived by your own forms. In other words, their forms have not done what your forms have ordered them to do. Hmm?

Yes, go ahead, [Student Y].

OK. That, that helps a lot.

Yes, thank you. Now [Student N] has a question.

I was wondering when you—last week you were saying when you look through the trees—you used the tree as an example—

Uh-huh.

—on the other side, if you can do that, do you see . . . [The teacher laughs and the student who is asking the questions laughs also.]

I understand the limited vocabulary of your world. Go ahead, please.

If you . . . [The student continues laughing.]

Yes?

If you can do that, which eye do you—do you see through the other side with your physical eyes as well or with your inner eye?

Well, I'm trying to get your question into perspective. Do you mean by "you," do you mean [Student S] or [Student J] or [Student P], or do you mean my channel, myself, or [Student R] or [Student O] or [Student M] or [Student B] or [Student D] or [Student L] or [Student U] or do you mean [Student N]?

Form. When you look through form. [The teacher laughs again.] *Me, I guess.*

Well, [*The teacher continues to laugh.*] it is true that which is speaking cannot accomplish piercing the veil, for it believes it is the veil. You see, the container cannot, you understand, be what it is not. It shall always be a container. So what you are saying is, Can *you*—you mean "[Student N]," you see—can *you* look through the tree and move from a two-dimensional world into a three-dimensional world? Do you understand that, [Student N]?

Yes.

All right. Now that which is speaking and using your mouth cannot accomplish that, for it is a two-dimensional world that is speaking.

OK.

For, you see, first of all, in the statement is the question. You see, the statement says, in the form of a question, which is a statement, "If you can etc., etc., etc." Now what that does, it is making a statement that, "If *you* can do that, how is it that I cannot?" And so it is trying to justify remaining as a two-dimensional entity to enter a [third]- and fourth-dimensional world. Do you understand that, [Student N]?

I'm trying. [Student N spoke at the same time as the teacher.]

You see, a two-dimensional world is subject to the laws governing—a two-dimensional entity (an object) is subject to the laws governing a two-dimensional world. So you cannot move two dimension into four dimension, for it is restricted and limited by the dimension in which it has been created. So when you move in your consciousness from a two-dimensional thinking, from the flat thinking to round thinking, you see, then you will not have that question. You will not make that statement. You see, the question is a statement. Do you understand that? And it's from a two-dimensional form. No, it is not possible. It is contrary to the Law of the Dimensions for a two-dimensional form to pierce the veil into a third- (or three) dimensional or fourth-dimensional realm, yes. Yes.

So to start thinking in a more round—it's just more of an expanded way? Or do I think about circles?

No, no, no, no. You're back into two dimensions.

I'm back into two dimensions.

No, no. All right, you want to move from two-dimensional thinking. What moves a person? Say that you're climbing up a stairway. How is it possible for you to climb the stairway?

By lifting one leg in front of the other.

How do you know to lift one leg and then the other?

Through experience.

How did you get that experience?

By just doing it.

Well, how did you first get inspired to do it?

I wanted to get from one place to the other.

You wanted to get from one place to another. All right. And in your desire to get from one place to another, did you depend on anything?

No.

You didn't? In other words, you just knew instinctively that you should lift your legs and you would move up those steps since you [were] a baby.

Trial and error. Right?

Trial and error? Well, did you depend on anyone through your trial and error?

Probably, yes. Probably.

Well, it's either yes or it is no. Did anyone teach you to lift your foot?

I don't, I don't remember. I don't think so.

Well, have you ever had any experience with any baby that was born and automatically lifts its foot and walked up a stairway?

No.

What happens with a baby? Does someone they depend on begin to train them and teach them? Pardon?

Yes, they do.

Is that person two-dimensional in their thinking or three?

I don't know.

Well, is that person dependent on a certain process to lift the leg and move it and walk up a stairway to get to the top of the stairs?

The person teaching?

Yes. For the child that is learning, dependent on the person who is teaching, establishes the law of whatever that teacher and that person is teaching them. [Student Y], perhaps you are following me. Are you following me?

Yes, I am. [Student Y responds.]

Yes. Well, now do you understand that when you are a child, even before you leave the womb, you are already dependent on a two-dimensional world? That two-dimensional world is increased, and as you grow up, you depend on two-dimensional thinking, because two-dimensional minds offer that to you, and that's what you depend upon. Do you understand that?

Yes.

All right. So, you see, you want to move from there to the top of the stairway. You have accepted and established the Law of Acceptance and Denial; there's one way to get there. Correct?

Correct. [Student N responds.]

You must move your physical body.

Right.

Is that correct?

Correct.

Well, it is your belief, you understand, it is your belief that that is the only way you can get to the top of the stairway that establishes the law and binds you to the dependence of a two-dimensional world. Do you understand that?

Yes.

You see? So, you see, what you must understand is, the only way to move beyond that intelligently is to refrain from the dependence on the two-dimensional world, which is the belief that you are mental substance, for the belief that you are mental substance is a two-dimensional world, in which you have become completely addicted. You see, you deny the possibility of moving from this spot—your physical being—to the top of the stairway without a certain process of certain movements. Do you understand that?

Yes.

And through your denial, you are destined to that limit and that bondage of a two-dimensional world. Do you see that, [Student Y]?

Yes, I do. [Student Y responds.]

You see? So the slow process, over eons of time, is the gradual reeducation, you hear? Now the wisest path in your physical world is to refrain from identification with that two-dimensional limit, which is known as self, you see. You see, self, the identification with self, self-thought, form, is the most destructive force you can ever experience, for it limits you; it limits you from moving from there to there without certain things that *it* dictates you must do. You have accepted that since your entrance to Earth because you believe you are a mental being. You create a thought; you believe that it is you, and because you believe that it is you, you experience all kinds of trauma in your life. You convince yourself that that is you. Your experiences are ever in keeping with your insistence and tenacity upon believing you are the form that you create.

Thank you.

That's what keeps you in a two-dimensional world, yes. Now there are people in your world, many people, many scientists and many artistic people, who, at times, free themselves from the two-dimensional bondage. And you get to experience what they, you understand, what you believe they have created. Now those who are honest will tell you immediately—scientists included—they did not create that. They received that somehow. They cannot explain how they received that, because to tempt to explain it they must enter, for your world, for your mind, a two-dimensional world. And it did not come from a two-dimensional world. Therefore, it cannot be explained fully or justly or accurately in two-dimensional terms. Now does that help you, [Student N]?

Yes. Thank you very much.

You see? You see, that's like trying to define inspiration. That's like trying to define God. The moment you define it, you put it into a two-dimensional world, and you bring it from what it is to what it is not, in order that you may accept it in keeping with your belief that you are the forms that you create, you see. I spoke to you, this class, before about this flat thinking, you see. Flat thinking. Flat thinking is a person who is absolutely convinced. They are so overidentified with the forms they create they believe they are those forms. They firmly believe that they are the children that they create, you see? And so when you believe that you are the form that you create, the thought form, when you convince yourself of that, then you must realize that you are no longer there: that which you have created, a soulless creature, is using your body, using your mind, and bringing to you like kind, you see?

You see, when a form you have created—and then you believe that you are the form you have created, the first thing it does in your house is have a party. It opens up your doors of your house to all of its buddies and all of its friends, and it has a regular party. Like you could best relate to a group of teenagers, you see, that just found themselves, and they're in your house. So let's consider that because that's what, that's what really goes on, you see. And it's only because, first of all, you overidentify with what you have created, to the point that you believe that *you* are what you've created. And when you believe that you are the thought that you have created, that's when what you truly are goes out to breakfast, lunch, and dinner. And what you have created comes in and takes over. And then, what you have created, using your mouth, using your mind and your body, goes to work to convince everyone else that's the way it is. Don't you see that?

So when you're working with people, try to understand, and in understanding, first make sure your own soul is at home, in its house. And by so doing, you will awaken to accept the demonstrable truth of what you are speaking to. You are speaking to a form, which you believe is a person, which is a hollow form, that by their convincing themselves that they are what they have created, what they truly are is gone. So your work is to work with that soulless creature that they have believed that they are, and takes over the house, so that you can bring back—be an instrument for the soul to return home. Do you see?

And the forms, when they're in charge, I can assure you they are most convincing. You must realize they convince the most intelligent minds of your planet. Why, they certainly do. You see, for they have access to all the intelligence that you have earned in evolution.

And so, you see, that intelligence—now remember this: infinite, intelligent Energy, your soul in expression of that, try to remember that the intelligence of your mind is a created thing. The mind knows much, and the soul always knows better, you see. So all of that intelligence, when you give way and believe in a form of your mind that you have created is you, that's when your little soul goes out. It leaves that form, you see? And that form that has taken over that house of yours, I can assure you, it is very difficult to perceive the difference between the person, what they truly are, and what they are trying to convince you they are. You must first awaken your own soul and make sure it's home in order to see the difference, you see?

Now, are there any other questions here this morning? Yes, [Student J].

What method would one use to awaken one's soul, prior to trying to help another?

Yes. Well, before one makes that effort, you see, and they're called to help another, first of all, one should go into their exercises inside themselves. They can do that immediately without disturbing anything around them. And immediately turn to the Light that they are, you see, and declare the truth: "I am here, that what I truly am, as a servant of the whole, for without the whole, I am not." See, we do not exist without the whole.

So in that declaration inside oneself, honestly, you have no personal feelings in working with another person, whether they make changes or they don't make changes; that doesn't even enter your consciousness. The only thing in your consciousness is that you are now appealing to a part of yourself. For, you see, that which you truly are is not limited to your form. See, that which you are is in everything and everyone.

So to communicate with that other part of you, you see—for you are a part of a whole, as all of these other students and myself are. So when that is accepted within your own consciousness, there will be no obstruction to speaking directly to that part, you see. And you will not be deceived by the hollow forms that try to convince your mind that that person is the person you think they are, because you won't even be working in that realm of consciousness. You see, you will be, now, in another dimension, a third dimension of consciousness. There, you see the Light of which everything is. All of the shadows disappear. You are then free to speak from the Light that you are, without the slightest thought of any offense to the person, for you have not the slightest need of anything that you may think that they have, for your mind doesn't think they have anything, because your mind isn't even there, you see? Something else is working, [Student J].

Now, so it's important to practice that with oneself. "This is what I'm experiencing, for I'm temporarily believing that I am the thoughts I have created." One talks to themselves that way daily, you see. So you feel real good. And you take a look and say, "All right. Yes, well, I'm happy I did create something that makes me feel good. And I am not going to be deceived by this other one that's coming in that makes me feel bad, because my feeling good or bad is only a two-dimensional world that I am not. That's a world I use." And so when one allows themselves to feel good or bad because of some experience, then one must remember that they now, through overidentification, believe they are a two-dimensional world, which you are not.

See, you, in your entrance to your planet, have come to your planet into a two-dimensional world to use the two-dimensional world for its own expansion, evolution, growth, and refinement. That's your purpose of entering the planet Earth, you see, and many other planets. Now that is your purpose. Now when you create a thought form and you allow yourself, by playing with the thought form—because that's what happens. Overidentification is playing with the toy, you see. You create a little toy, and you play with it long enough, and before you know it, you believe you are the toy. And after believing you are the toy, that which you are is gone; and that which you have created is using the toy. All right?

So your purpose—you've come to the planet, to a two-dimensional world, as I said, to expand and to refine and evolve the forms that you create. How does one evolve a form? It is very simple. If you want to help a person—and that includes a form—you don't constantly feed it because you know if you constantly feed it, the day will come [when] it can't move without you. You'll have to lift it. You'll have to carry it, you see, because its legs and all of it parts will not function properly, correct? Now we can all relate to that, can't we? All right.

So your purpose is: the forms you have created, to keep them on a rigid diet. Well, you call that discipline. You keep them on a diet. "This is the time you can express to do this which I have created you for. Now it's time for your nap." And it takes a nap. Do you understand that? And then you consciously, you call them up and say, "All right. It's time for you to go to work. You get the job done, and then I feed you." Do you understand that? You see, you must use these things intelligently. As above, so below. So as a person believes they're the hands, they believe they're the different parts of their vehicle, so these forms you create, temporarily you believe that you are them only because you have created them and have played with what you have created to the point that they control you, you see?

You see, a child cannot play with something without becoming identified with it. Do you understand that? So the more you play with something, the more you become identified with it until you reach the point where it tells you, you can't live without it. Haven't you had that ex—oh, I know you've had that experience. That you just can't live without it. Well, that's when you know the form is inside, using your mind. You see, you're gone, and it's telling your mind, "Well, you can't live without me." Because, as it convinces your mind, it builds its security, and then the next thing you know, it's in all the time. Correct? And then sometime, finally, your little soul tries to get back in, and you're all upset and you're furious. And then we have these other forms that they go through, I guess they call it reformation. May God save you from the reformists. Because, you see, that's not the way. That only makes them stronger; education [is the way.]

So be very choosy in what you put your attention on, you see. And so when you put your attention on any form, be awake, aware, and alert. "Now, has this form, which I have created, has it been on a diet long enough? I mean, is it doing what I designed it for?" Well, if it isn't, get rid of it. Put it to sleep. Let it sleep for a long time until it wakes up so hungry, and it will come to you and say, "I'll do the job you created me for and I won't do any more of these games." You understand that? You must learn to work with the forms that you have created, for if you don't work with them, they certainly work with you. Oh, yes, they do whatever they want. They do whatever they want.

You see, they're nothing—how can one fear what they have created? You see, to permit a form to use your mind and to tell you, "Well, I just can't live without it. Why, I just can't help it. And everything's wrong out there. This experience is not something I created. It's what someone else did," it's foolhardy. It's foolish thinking. Because the experience is an effect of the forms doing what they wanted to do, contrary to what you designed them to do. Do you understand that, you see? You see, you design it to do a thing, and they're only supposed to do it when you consciously tell them to do it. You see, that's the purpose of their design, you understand?

So if you don't monitor them, if you don't monitor them, then they're going to do what they're going to do, when they want to do it, to the point that they've actually convinced your mind that you just can't do without it. Hmm? You see, when they tell you, you can't do without it, say, "Oh, you can't? Oh, isn't that interesting. Well, now we'll just time you and see what you do, that you can't do without it." And then go through the experience. Do you understand that, you see? And that experience will reveal to you how much you have allowed them to convince you that you are them. Hmm? You see? You tell them, "Stop it!" You see? [When] they tell you, you've got to have something and you [have] got to have it real bad, you say, "You stop it! I'm going to watch just what you think you're trying to do to me." And watch what they try to do to you.

You see, that's the Law of Disassociation. See how they use your emotions. Now remember, they always use your water center because that's where they [had their] birth, right? Oh, they can't use your electrical center. No, no, no, no. And your air center, you see, they'll try. But it's your water center, because that's where they had birth. That's where the judgment gave them birth. Do you understand that? That's where denial gave birth to them, you see. We deny and experience our judgments and give birth to those forms. Yes, does that help you, [Student J]?

Yes, sir.

Why, certainly. Absolutely. Now you've had a little experience here in this past thirty-six hours where some of the other forms you created are starting to do their job. Well, those are the ones, you keep them working.

Yes, sir.

Those other ones, tell them, say, "Listen. Oh, no! I know your games. Out!" And you watch how they treat you. Oh yes, [you are] coming along, [Student J], very well. You see, the ones that do the job, that you've created, do a fine job; well, those, you keep feeding them. Don't pay any attention to those other ones because the moment you give them attention, you give them energy, all right?

Yes, sir.

Yes, did that help with your question?

Yes, sir. Thank you very much.

Look at that lovely—the birds are having a nice time today. Yes, you're welcome. Someone else? Yes. [Student M] has a question here.

Yes, communication—since communication is so very important in, it seems, in every sphere, is that a soul faculty or is that a function?

Well, without communication, there is no understanding. It's a soul faculty. Yes, yes, indeed. Yes, well, I know that through communication or the lack thereof we express many different functions, but that in no way establishes a law that communication or understanding is a function. Yes.

Thank you.

Yes, you're welcome. Time [is] passing quickly. A short class today? Yes, [Student D].

You spoke last week on interest and the principle of interest. Could you explain—

Interest and the principle on interest, is that what we were speaking on?

Of interest. You were speaking about students in the past being interested in your experiences and—

Oh, yes. Well, they were interested in [that] for motivations that [were] not in the best interest of them. So we didn't speak too much on that, just a little bit. I was—yes, yes, I see your question. I do think I see your question.

Has there been any interest in the principle of—

Why, there most certainly is. Ofttimes our minds are interested in many things in order to do us in. And I think we can go to that and see very clearly that our minds tempt us, rather frequently sometimes, to use the Light of our own eternal being against us, you see? And they're very cunning, these forms.

Understand that here, even in this class, you see, I speak to your soul, and your mind records it. Well, not that your soul is not listening, but I'm talking about what you believe you are now. You see? So we, you know, speak to our soul, and our mind records it. Our soul, it's there in our soul, of course, but as long as we believe our mind—now, say, here you have these lovely teachings. The mind is recording it all. Whatever is recorded in the mind is available to the forms we've created, all right? All right. So if you don't give them their way and if you weaken, they will use everything that's in your mind, including this lovely class, against you. Oh, yes. And then, not only that, they'll tell you that it's your divine right. Oh, yes, yes. Yes, indeed. Definitely. Oh, absolutely. In fact, if you really believe you are those forms that you've created, you will totally declare that, yes, it is your divine right to kill yourself. It is your divine right to make your life miserable. It is your divine right to destroy your life. Yes, they are certainly capable of that. Yes, absolutely.

In fact, even here in this little class here, my nice little class here on Earth, I have some of my students temporarily on the self-destruct train, you know. Trying to kill themselves, you know. Not enjoying the beautiful life and not having the abundant good, which is their true right, you see; their divine right, [which is] not what the forms are trying to convince them, that they believe they are. Yes, I have my own students, some of them, at times, demonstrating a blatant transgression of the application of this wonderful truth. Blatant transgression. And not only that, those forms using this wonderful teaching to justify why they are blatantly going against it. But it is a temporary thing. It's the forms they have allowed in. When a person plays with themselves, I think I've spoken to my channel several times, it's known as mental masturbation. And when a person is masturbating, that's the experiences that they have. And they go totally against the Light of demonstrable truth. Yes, yes.

And so we slip down there, and, of course, all of you bear the spiritual responsibility. All of you bear that responsibility, when one of my students here—I'm not to be here with you constantly, twenty-four hours. One of my students temporarily, through a mental masturbation process, lets one of those things take control of their mind, their mouth, and their body, then you bear a responsibility to discern the difference between who they are and the forms that are using their body at the moment. You see? Souls are welcome; bodies I can do without. Does that help with your question?

Thank you.

Certainly, yes. Not that I didn't spend my time with bodies. Certainly. Absolutely. We all have our evolution. But as I've informed my channel, your souls are always welcome, but your bodies, they're going to go back to where they came from. You know, I've never been overly fond of worms for my lunch or breakfast or dinner. Yes, someone else have a question? Yes, [Student L], please, yes.

You spoke to [Student J] a few days ago about becoming the light of reason before you talk to the soulless creature.

Well, I don't think I told him to become it. He already is it. Yes, yes, I do want to clarify becoming and what we are, you see. You see, permitting the light of reason to rise into our consciousness. Certainly, certainly, yes.

At the times one is— [Student L speaks softly.]

I'm sorry, [Student L] . . .

At the time one is— [She speaks more loudly.]

Did you have breakfast this morning?

Yes!

Oh, just speak right up. Could you hear me?

Yes.

Well, then, speak up; let me hear you.

At the time one is speaking to the soulless creature that's in the body...

Yes?

... is the little soul nearby hearing it, too?

Well, it depends on how long that soulless form has been in the form, you see. You see, the longer we permit the soulless creature to use our body, the farther out our soul goes, if I can say farther out in order to express in your two-dimensional world, yes. And so they always hear. Sometimes it's just a little whisper that they can hear because they're so far out, you see. They've been gone so long. So, you see, that's why I've taught you whatever it is, nip it in the bud; because the longer you permit, in speaking in your two-dimensional terms, mental masturbation there, the longer you permit that, the farther out your little soul is. So when you start to play with those forms, and you're getting close to the point of believing that you are them, you know—you're in the playpen in the sandbox playing; the longer you're in the sandbox, the more difficult it is to get out.

You're a mother. You know how a little child is out playing in his sandbox. He doesn't want to leave his sandbox, even though it's time to go to bed or take his nap or to have his dinner. Isn't that correct, [Student B]? No! So the longer you allow yourself to play in the sandbox, the more difficult it is, you see, and the farther out the soul has to return home. Does that help you with your question?

Yes. So, you see, when you find yourself—God helps those who help themselves by helping others. God works through man, not to man. And when God is helping you and perhaps using someone to say, "Say, [Student L], you've been in the sandbox too long, way too long," you want to look to God, and thank

God, that the message is getting through, you see. Do you understand that? Yes. And then you'll be amazed how much better you will feel. Did that help you, [Student L], with your question?

Thank you.

Certainly, yes. Yes, [Student S] here has a question.

Yes, you've said that it's our responsibility to help evolve the forms that we create.

Why, certainly. A mother's responsible for her children, yes. And a Father his.

I'd like to ask, on this planet then, in the past you've said that we are more evolved and responsible for the forms. Then, am I presently to understand with these present teachings that that doesn't necessarily mean that we're the most evolved animals spiritually on the planet. Is that correct?

Well, I don't think I said you [were] the most spiritually evolved. I did say you [were] the most evolved of form. I think if you'll study the teachings—[Student B], have I stated you were the most spiritually evolved on the planet? *[After a short pause, the teacher continues.]* I have stated that you are the most evolved in form and are responsible [to] care for the other forms, beginning with one's own. And so I think it's a very delicate thing to discuss the patience, the loyalty, the wisdom of the elephant, because, then again, some of my students might be tempted to say they want to come back as an elephant, and there's no possibility whatsoever. *[A few students laugh and the teacher does as well.]*

Let's be grateful. Sometimes we think we're a dog, and we feel terrible. When I look at the dogs, they have a wonderful life. So I don't know. The human mind is most interesting, those forms. They say, "Oh, I feel like a dog," meaning that they're miserable. And yet in another moment, they look at a dog lying around eating, enjoying life, basking in the sun, and they say, "Oh, what a life! They got a dog's life! It's just wonderful. They don't have to work. They don't have to do anything. They sleep in as long as they want. Why, they've got a real dog's life!" So, you see, one moment with one of the forms they believe they are, a dog's life is a life of misery. And in another moment, another form they have created—the same mind has created it and the same person believes they're both things, you see—it says, "Look at that. [That dog] doesn't even have to get up. [He] could even have breakfast in bed, if he wants it. Why, this is ridiculous! Why couldn't I have been a dog?" Do you understand that?

Yes.

Now, that's—think of that, children. That's what you tempt yourself to believe that you are. Absolute, blatant contradiction. And not just in your view of a dog's life, meaning that's a real dog. [If] you got a car, you say, "That was a real dog. How did I merit that?" Or you had another experience and you look out and say, "Oh, I don't feel like getting up. I wish I was a dog!" So, you see, that doesn't make any—there's no reason there at all. So one moment you believe—the same mind, by overidentification, believes in two things that are absolutely contrary. Does that help with your question, [Student S]?

Yes.

Do you have another question?

Not at this time.

All right, fine. [Student Y] has a question. I think we're going to move [Student Y] a little bit to the left. Can you move a little bit to left there? See—there! I know you and I were discussing the pine tree, but there's no reason why you should sit [behind one]. *[The teacher laughs joyfully.]* Yes, that was last week. Yes.

Is there as much—I know this is from—it's two-dimensional thinking.

I understand.

I want—I'm looking for direction.

Yes.

Is there as much space in the fourth, third or fourth dimension as there is . . .

As much space? Space doesn't exist in a fourth dimension. Space does not exist. You see, try to understand—space—you see, you understand space. Space is necessary for you in order for reference. You see, you get your time from reference. Well, if you don't have space, then you don't have reference and you don't have time. Time and space do not exist in a fourth dimension. They're nonexistent. You see?

You see, for a two dimension, for a mental world to tempt to place itself into a fourth dimension and still contain a two dimension, [that] cannot exist, for a two dimension is dependent upon time, which is dependent upon space, which is dependent upon reference. You see, they're all combined, you see? You see, you lose depth, you lose dimension, for depth and dimension, for a two-dimensional world is dependent on reference. Yes, [Student Y]. And we [have] got two minutes left.

So there's no distance, like—

Distance doesn't exist. Distance exists—we'll have to reserve [Student S]'s question for next class. We've got one and a half minutes left. We'll have to reserve your question. Distance does not exist beyond a two-dimensional world. Time does not exist. Where time—look, where there is no space, there is no time, there is no distance, there is no reference. So let us continue on with time, distance, reference, and space, which doesn't exist in a fourth-dimensional world, at our next class.

Thank you and have a very good week.

JULY 20, 1986

A/V Class Private 57

Good morning, students.

Everything we desire *is*. When we are what is, there is nothing to desire, for when we are what we are, there is no denial. And no denial, there is no need. Where there's no need, there is no desire.

In my centuries of experience through the various realms, I finally awakened to that demonstrable truth: everything is reflecting what you think you are—all obstructions and all ways.

Now in awakening to that truth, one must be alert that they do not justify making no effort to evolve the forms they have created in their evolution, for that would be a denial of personal responsibility for your children. And the purpose of entering form would therefore not be served. The human mind can and does all things justify. There is no limit to the excuses that mental substance is capable of using.

You will find in these teachings and classes, when you feel discouraged, pause, and you will see the form that you believe you are. And indeed, it is discouraged. It's losing the battle of control over your life. We always experience what we know as discouragement when we are being wrenched free from what we have believed that we are. As my assistants told my channel as recent as yesterday, we have no problem ever looking and seeking the arrivals. It's the departures in our life that sadden us. We're always discouraged and saddened by the departing (the departures) because something that we thought for a time that we possessed is leaving. That's known as a departure.

And so when you feel discouraged, you can be rest assured that, temporarily, you believe that the form that is departing from your universe you are. And as long as you believe you are it, you will experience what you understand as discouragement. Now at the same moment, you could think of an arrival and you'd be amazed how your minds would be encouraged: the possibility of a new conquest. The mind always feels encouraged at the possibility of conquering something that it has not already conquered. It's a stimulation to the human ego.

We'll pause for a few moments for your questions. Yes, [Student B], please.

We're taught that when we have a desire, we should release it and give it to God.

Yes.

And today you said that we should work on evolving our forms.

Correct.

How do we give it to God and yet evolve our forms?

God, the divine Principle of Good, is the principle of refinement or evolution of the return to the source from whence anything has wandered, including a created form. Therefore, when one has a desire and they give it to God, they are serving the purpose for their evolution in form, for they're giving it to the only source that can evolve it.

You see, so often, you know, we find our self discouraged in making great effort to bring about changes. And when we release it from our mind and we truly give it to the source from whence we have stolen it, we find the change has taken place. For that which is limitless, of course, is greater than that which is limited. That which sustains a thing is greater than the thing that is being sustained. And so when we have a desire, what we have done [is] we have formed the divine expression, known as desire; we have limited it by creating a form or a boundary for it. And so when we do everything that we can (our minds) to try to get it fulfilled and it doesn't work, when we give it to the Source from whence we have temporarily stolen it, as a principle, then it returns unto us, and the desire is fulfilled, but not in the limit in which we have placed it. Did that help with that question with you, [Student B]?

Thank you.

Yes, certainly. Yes, [Student U], please.

If, in making changes, we do everything that our mind suggests we do and the change does not occur because we have not given that to God, is then the discouragement that we experience a step in the process or is it more of a trap that we sometimes and regularly fall into?

Well, what you want [to do is] take a look at a person who says and believes that they are discouraged in anything. Does their infinite intelligent Energy flowing through them go to that which they have judged they have not received or does it go to something more expanded that they are moving to? Yes, [Student U], which does the, which does the attention or the energy go to: the obstruction or the way?

The obstruction.

It goes to the obstruction. Now how does that answer your question?

We have a tendency to become that which we place our attention on.

Yes, well now you asked the question—repeat your question and see if you have found the answer.

Does discouragement—is discouragement a step in making changes or is it a trap that we sometimes fall in?

Now what do you think it is?

It's a trap.

And why is it a trap?

Because it's placing our attention upon the obstruction, when we have the choice to place our attention upon what we want to become.

Absolutely. So we find, of course, that discouragement is a trap and increases the obstruction that we are discouraged over. Hmm? Would you not say?

Yes, sir.

You see? And so you have a person who says, "Well, I am discouraged about this. I'm discouraged that changes haven't come about. I am discouraged over my years of effort." Then you have a person that has trapped themselves. Hmm?

Yes, sir.

And so one discouragement breeds another one. And the next thing you know—that it is really, in truth, an instrument and a vehicle through which the pity of the self can be increased. You know, you take a person who is an encouraging person and their self-pity forms get very little energy. You take a person who is discouraged, and you have a person who is increasingly thinking of themselves and their own limit. And so the more you think of limit, the more limit that you experience. The more you think of lack, the more lack you experience. Do you understand?

Yes, sir.

So if you want to enjoy the suffering of limit and lack, then all you have to do is to continue to feed intelligent energy to that which you have created, in this particular instance, lack. Yes, I would consider that a trap of traps. Yes.

Thank you.

Certainly. And why—you know, people ask why is it easier to think of the negative and to be discouraged and seemingly so difficult to think of the positive and to be encouraged. Why is it—why does the human mind say it's easier? *[The teacher pauses a few moments to allow the students to respond.]* Yes?

The forms of lack are so much greater. [Student U responds.]

Why are they greater? Are they greater through a lack of directing energy to them? Or are they greater from an increase of energy being directed to them? Who controls the mind?

We are—we have the choice.

Yes. Who controls it? *[After a short pause, the teacher continues.]* Oh, I don't deny the choice. I wouldn't deny it for myself. *[The teacher laughs.]* Who controls the human mind?

Lucifer.

Yes, and does he control the limitless or the limit?

The limit.

And so whenever you think of yourself, then prepare yourself for the limit, prepare yourself for the obstructions, prepare yourself for the lack, and prepare yourself, of course, for discouragement.

Yes, [Student Y] has a question on that. Yes, [Student Y].

When one says "can't," what are they really saying?

When one says "can't"?

[An airplane flies overhead, which makes it difficult to transcribe the student's response.]

That's very important, because you can.

And I would like [Student L] to move over and [Student Y] to move over. I don't see why they keeping sitting you behind the tree, although you were interested in looking through it, weren't you? *[The teacher's preferred seating arrangement was to be able to have an unobstructed line of sight to all of his students.]*

That must have been it. [Student Y responds.]

[The teacher laughs joyfully.] Well, let's move these chairs over. Let's move [Student B] over. She can see me through [Student P] and [Student H]. And let's move these chairs over here. So we don't have someone directly behind the pine tree. Well, you see—there! Now, don't you see, isn't that better?

It's much better. [Student Y responds.]

Don't you feel better? All right. Now the question is, Why does a person say they can't?

What does that really mean?

What does it mean? When a person says they can't—they can't do this; they can't do that—that is a person who truly believes that they are the limit. You see, a person who believes that they are the limit has all the forms of limit using their mind. Now the forms of limit are created to serve the purpose of the limit for which they have been created. Do you understand that? So when a person says, "Well, I can't do this and I can't do that. And this is not possible and that is not possible," the forms that have been created for specific jobs are telling you for them it is not possible. And you believe that you are those forms. Do you understand that, [Student Y]?

Yes.

So, you see, you will find, however, that there are times when an experience comes into your life, through the law, and you say, "I can do this. And I will do this." Well, that's in keeping with the form that one believes they are at the time that has been designed to do that specific job. And so you find people that say, "Yes, I can do this. No, I can't do that." You see? It depends whether they have a form created for that which they are expressing at that time. Do you understand?

Yes.

You see, a person has forms created and they—those forms—they are convinced they are those forms, and therefore that person says, "I can see." Another person has forms created for the purpose of driving a car. And someone says, "Would you drive the car?" And you say, "Yes, I can." Correct? So, you see, a person believes they are the mind and it depends on which forms are in control of their mind at that time through their overidentification with them. You see?

And so you have a singer say, "I can sing. Right now, I can sing." And then you have another moment with the singer when he or she will say, "Why, I can't sing now." Because, you see, the forms are created, limited forms. They have certain requirements. If those requirements aren't fulfilled, then the singer who can sing cannot sing. Do you understand that, students? You see?

And so that's one of the prices, of course, that we all pay in believing that we are the human mind. Do you understand that? Hmm? So you know in your life's experiences there are times when you say you can do something—and have demonstrated that to yourself. Then, there are other times, the opportunity presents itself again [and] you say, "I can't do that." And then if someone says, "Well, why can't you do it? You have done it before," then you say to them, "Well, because it was this and that and that and that. And under these conditions I cannot do that." Is that not correct? You see? So, you see, what you are revealing is that the forms that you have created, that have their limit and very specific requirements, are in charge, and their requirements are not being fully met. You understand that? Therefore, you cannot do what you have done. Hmm? Does that help with your question there, [Student Y]?

Yes. Thank you.

Yes. That's how the human mind [works]. So you take a person, an artist or someone, or a performer or something, and depending on what they have created with their forms will depend on what conditions that those forms will allow them to sing or to perform under. Do you understand that?

Yes. [Student Y speaks very softly.]

Pardon?

Yes. [Student Y speaks more loudly.]

Oh, all right. Good. Yes. You're welcome. [Student D] has a question here this morning.

When children say "I can't," the response of parents, quite often, is "You can," but it's [with] a sense of force. How can they approach that with a spiritual principle?

Why, certainly. When you're dealing with a child and the child says that "I can't," then you must first recognize and realize that the child has learned that from someone. Therefore, by your child learning that from someone, you cannot deny personal responsibility: you permitted your child to learn that, either from you or from someone; that doesn't exempt you from the personal responsibility that you have. So you accept the personal responsibility that your child, that you are responsible for, has been taught and trained by either you in moments of ignorance or by someone else that they cannot do something. Therefore, facing the personal responsibility that is yours, you use the faculty of consideration: you sit down with the child and you go through all the time and energy that is necessary to show him how he can. Hmm? For you are then facing personal responsibility.

And whoever faces personal responsibility and demonstrates it is free. And being free, they offer that freedom, of course, to whoever they are offering it to. But a person must first face personal responsibility: no matter who taught the child that he can't, they are responsible as the parent.

[Thank you.]

Yes. You're welcome. And now [Student M] has a question this morning. I don't get many questions from over here, but I'll find out why in a moment. Yes, go ahead, [Student M]. *[The teacher laughs.]*

You were just speaking this morning on desire and evolving the forms.

Yes?

Now it's my understanding when—it could be just my image—but with desire, it's one and the same as all of our thought forms because it also is a form and a soulless creature that has to be evolved and refined.

Correct. In other words, we have limited the divine expression. Correct. Yes.

It seems to me or appears to me that desire seems to be like a whole—it's like a different sphere than our other thought forms. Is it because we are so filled with need and desire where it's different than another thought form?

No, it's not different than another thought form, only in the sense that it receives more energy and it's much stronger. That's the only difference. In the sense, you see, that if you have what you call a desire for something, you have first created a form and you have established the law of believing that you are the form you have created, and that form is created with certain requirements and contains the ingredient of need, for you cannot desire that which you already have, you see. So first you must—you must first establish that law that, through comparison, you look out there and say, "Now, I would like to have that." And the more you think about it, the stronger your feelings get. Would you not—

It's true.

You would understand that, wouldn't you, [Student M]?

Yes.

You know, as you look at a form and you look at it, and the more you look at it, the more you want it. And then you soon pass the state of wanting it. The next step is you have to have it.

It's true.

And after you've spent some time in having to have it, in your mind, the next step is no matter what you're going to get it.

Sure.

Well, now you would call that desire, right?

Right.

But, you see, you have created that form.

Right.

You see? Yes. And so you can take any thought form that your mind creates and the more attention or energy that you feed and direct to it, then you experience it as a desire. Would you not understand that? I mean, for example, you can take and you can think of—perhaps you think of an ice cream. Hmm? Or a sundae or something like that. And the more you think about it, the more you think you want it. Is that not true?

That's true.

And so if you think about it long enough, you'll want it even more. And then it moves to the state where you have to have it. And then to the next step: no matter what, you're going to get it. Is that not true?

That's true.

Then after you get it, you wonder how come it came into your life. And then you want to know how to get rid of it. *[Some students laugh.]* Well, the way to get rid of it is the way you got it. You see? You see, you gave it a lot of energy to get it.

Yes.

Well, now you must remove all of that energy to get rid of it. You see, people say—like, they get a cold. And, oh, they'd like to get rid of that. Well, if they would stop thinking about it, it wouldn't stay so long. You see, it can only stay as long as it has energy to stay. So the more you think about it— *[The teacher coughs.]* Excuse me. The more you think about it, the longer it's in your life. So if you have something distasteful in your life and you are enjoying the experience of it and the suffering of it, just think about it more. It'll stay very, very long. Because its length of duration is dependent on how strong it is from energy that you are directing to it.

So, for example, like a married person, you know, who seems to enjoy—what do you call it?—picking the bone, well, the more you enjoy and think about picking the bone, you'll find you have nothing to pick but bone, you see?

True.

Nothing left.

True.

You see? You see, we have to understand that these forms, you know, sometimes whether it's picking a bone or filing a nail, it doesn't matter, the more you think about it, the more you have it. Because you are sustaining it with life-giving energy. It is a soulless form that you have created. So think about it, think about it, and think about it, and it'll be with you day and night in your consciousness, you see.

[Do] you like to pick bones, do you?

No.

You don't like to pick bones? Well, stop thinking about it and you won't have no bones to pick. Do you like to pick bones, [Student O]?

Not really. [Student O replies.]

You don't? Oh, well, don't think about picking bones and there won't be any bones to pick. Now someone else—yes, now [Student Y] has a question.

When one takes experiences in life personally . . .

Personally?

Yes.

Yes. You mean when one is so totally in love with themselves that everything's personal. Yes, thank you, [Student Y].

That was my question.

Yes. Yes.

. . . frustration. [Student Y speaks simultaneously with the teacher; so it is difficult to transcribe a few words of her response.]

Well, you have a wonderful affirmation there that's been used in many of my classes: the romance of self-love. *[The teacher may be referring to "The Laws Be" affirmation, which can be found in the appendix.]* You see, it's a romancing. And so if you love yourself (your image) to that extent, you have no problem at all: you have that with you all the time. Yes, everything will be personal. Oh, yes. Yes. If you walk along the walkway and you step on one of these lovely, little creatures going all over the place there, well, you will take it personal that that was in the way and didn't get out of the way when you were walking by. You take it all personally. And if the sun—it comes out and it's too warm, you'll take it personal. "What's God doing to me to make the day so hot and I'm miserable?" See, everything will be personal. For a person who loves themselves, you know, even the breeze, you see, there's too much, there's not enough. No matter what it is. "Hasn't rained today? Well, why hasn't it rained today. I'd like it to rain today." And you take it personally because God didn't make it rain. Forget the seasons and everything else, you understand, and considering anything else, but it's a personal thing. You go to apply for a job, you don't get the job, well, you take it personal. You had a little wrinkle there that you didn't notice and didn't get it covered up just right, don't you see, or there was something in your eye there—everything is personal, you see.

Somebody says hello to you, you take it personal. "How come they're saying hello to me? What do they want out of me?" The next person doesn't speak to you, [then you think,] "Well, how come they don't speak to me? What are they trying to do to me?" You see? You see, no, that's one of the many ways that you can see how much a person loves themselves. Yes. Yes, [Student Y].

So that would be looking at the—on the outside all the time from—it's like looking at life from too much from within oneself? Is that—

Well, I'd like to say this. A person who spends their life thinking about what they consider is themselves—which is, in truth, thinking about the forms they have created and the forms they have created tell them what they are. I think we'll all agree with that. [It] depends on what form is using the mouth. And then the person says, "Well, this is what I am." Only in a minute later or a few seconds, another form gets in, and then the person says, "No, this is what I am." So a person ends up they don't know what they are. That's a person, you see—a person who loves the fruit of their womb—in other words, that which they have created, you see.

Now don't misunderstand, men have the fruit of their womb as well as women have the fruit of their womb. So let's get that understanding. It takes two to tango. I think it's what you call it in your world. So a man that has a total attachment to the fruit of his womb, don't you see, even though it requires a female to finally produce it, but regardless, a man that has a total attachment to the fruit of his womb is a man (or a woman) who is so overidentified, through a love of what they create, of what they're able to accomplish—do you understand?

You see, it is a very natural thing for a being to accomplish. The dog accomplish[es]; he [is] lying down there resting. That's an accomplishment. This one over here is lying there rest[ing]. That's an accomplishment. A little bird up there is chirping away. That's an accomplishment, you see. So everyone is accomplishing something. Hmm? You see?

Now a person who, in accomplishing a created form in their mind, limits themselves to believing, you understand— and takes great pride in, "This is my accomplishment"—is a person who traps themselves. Instead of thinking in a broader aspect: "I got up out of bed this morning. I actually took a shower. I brushed my teeth. I managed to go to work." That's an accomplishment. You see, gratitude for the crumbs, instead of this overidentification with this form you've created and that form you've created. And then, those things coming in; you're so overidentified with them you believe that you're them. Thinking about something accomplished that is not solely, wholly, and completely dependent upon you. Hmm? You see?

Yes.

And so—because it's natural for a person to experience the good. In fact, it's a necessity. But why limit it to forms you're creating? Like, you go to look for a job or something and you take it personal when a person says, "No, not today," or "Come back in a month." Do you see? Everything is personal, which reveals the effort [is] not being made to work with your affirmations, especially your breathing, especially your breathing, you see.

You see, I've taught you for years, as I teach my other students, no new thought can arrive in the consciousness when, through proper breathing exercises, you take control. Everything that has ever been, everything that is, everything that will be already exists and is available in consciousness to those who take control of the forms they have created by refraining from overidentifying with them. Everything *is*, you see. Everything *is*. Your tomorrows already exist. They already exist. They already are. The centuries yet to be already are. You go to it in consciousness. You believe you go to it in the movement of limit. That's not how you get to it. To go to it that way, you have to wait centuries. You go to it in consciousness for it exists in consciousness.

Now don't misunderstand and say, "Oh, well, what can I do? It's predestined." Now this is a real cop-out. That's using the Light—attempting to use the Light against the Light. Everything that is to be, that has been, *is*. There is no future. There is no past. For everything *is*. Everything *is*.

And so when you make the effort, through your proper exercises, to refrain from overidentification with the limits you have made, then you will experience that which is. And that which is, is everything.

Yes. Does someone else have a question? Yes, [Student S]. Ah, we are getting some questions over from this side. I'm going to move you over closer here if I don't get any questions from this end. Yes.

Since there's no time and distance—

Time, space, and distance can only exist to limit. Without limit, there is no reference, there is no existence. All right? Yes. It's very important that we understand that. There is no time and there is no space. That exists only if you believe you are that which you create. Yes, go ahead, [Student S].

I'd like to know if, if in the fourth dimension—

Yes?

—if you can be in what we call two places at once, like when you come to our class?

Yes?

Or does that change it because now you've entered the second and third dimensions?

No. No, it only changes it if I change it through an error of my own ignorance. For example, that which you are, that which I am, is everything and everywhere. Do you understand that?

Yes.

Now if, in that awakening, you permit yourself to identify with limit, then you can only be one place in that sense. Do you follow that?

Yes.

You see? You see, identification, the indentation of the principle, is the only thing that makes the boundary. Yes.

And do you have to identify to be in your channel's form?

Yes. You must identify in order to be in to form [and] to use the form. However, it depends on your degree of identification. You can identify with your form [and] still be aware, awake, and alert to what is happening in the other dimensions and classes for which you are responsible. For example, you all demonstrate that you can listen to a radio, be aware of what's being said while you're writing something down. Is that not correct?

Yes.

Now some are more proficient with it than others. Some can listen to a radio, write a letter, and read a book. You see? But that takes a little control of one's mind. But that's the principle that's involved. So, you see, you can be there doing that and aware of the other, you see.

Thank you.

You're welcome. Yes, [Student Y].

When you say there's no—in the fourth dimension, you say there is no distance or space.

That's correct.

I was, I was trying to picture how you could be there—another vibration if—how would one, like yourself—

Yes?

—move through—

Yes? Yes?

—different dimensions? How then are the consciousnesses together?

Because they're never separated. You see, the separation in consciousness is ever in keeping with the identification with limit. So, you see, if you are fully identified with the form that is an effect of your creation, to the degree of the identification, you are not aware of that which you are. You see, that depends upon degree of identification. You find that when you're overidentified with what you believe you are, you do not have awareness of what you are. Is that not correct? You see?

Now, say you go to sleep and sometimes you'll remember a dream or this or that. And you don't remember all that is taking place. In other words, you have dreams and you are the victim of those dreams. Correct? In other words—especially if they're ones not to your liking, then you say, "Well, I am the victim. It just happened." Yet it is your responsibility to take control before you lose conscious awareness so you may dream what you consciously choose to dream when you say you are sleeping. Because through your conscious choice the dream manifests itself. As I said long ago, "Dreamer, dream a life of beauty before your dream starts dreaming you." Those who believe they are the dream are those who are the victim of their own creations. Yes.

You see, it's like the automobile. If it does what it wants to do, then it is not serving you. Would you not agree, [Student J]?

Yes, sir.

You see, it is designed to do what *you* choose for it to do. Your dreams are designed as vehicles for you to drive. But if you don't drive them, they drive themselves. And then you wake up in the morning or during the night and say you had a nightmare. I say you're having daymares. *[A few students laugh.]* You see? You see, it's designed—those are all vehicles. Your hand is designed to serve you. When it does not serve you, then remove it. For of what benefit is it, if it does not serve you? Of what benefit can your hand be if it does not serve you the way you choose it to serve you? Of what benefit is your foot if it does not serve you the way you choose it to serve you? Does your foot just jump all around? You tell it to stop jumping and it won't stop jumping. Then of what benefit is it to you? Remove it. Cut it off. Yes. Yes, [Student Y].

So in—so since you're together because you don't—you're not overiden—so, in the fourth dimension—

Yes?

—you're together because you don't experience the separation.

That is correct. Because, you see, if you identify 100 percent, you are separated from the Source. If you identify less than that—90 percent or less—then you are not separated from the Source that you are. In other words, you are aware that you are using the vehicle. You are aware that it is registering (the vehicle) certain experiences. You know, consciously—that's objectivity, you see. You're objective when you are not separated from the Source that you are. Yes, [Student Y].

So would it be vibration that brings—so in the fourth dimension, you mentioned a while back that it was vibration or—that brought beings together of like kind.

That is correct. The frequencies.

The frequencies.

Yes. Or vibration. Yes.

That's what would bring it together.

Absolutely. Definitely. You see, when you overidentify with limit, then the only thing you can experience is limit. You can't experience anything but limit. So if you identify with limit 90 percent, then you have 10 percent of experiencing the limitless. If you identify 20 percent with limit, you have 80 percent of your consciousness experiencing the Source that you are. Does that help with that, [Student Y]? So it depends on what you consciously choose to do.

Now let us not forget that we consciously choose each form—you understand?—to use our physical being. We make that conscious choice. Now the thing is, from repeating a conscious choice to a particular form, you get to understand that as a habit. The thing automatically comes up and uses your mouth. Well, it's your responsibility to put it in its place until it remembers what you have designed it for. You see, the moment that you do not continue your effort, that which you have created does what it is going to do. Do you understand that? Whether you call it up or not. Because you have granted it, consciously, that license. For example, the longer you do something, the more difficult it is for you to change doing it, dependent upon your belief that you are the limit. Hmm? You see? See, it's not difficult for a person to make changes no matter how long they have done something if they are not overidentified with themselves. People who have difficulty in making changes are people who are overidentified with themselves.

And if you want to help a person to make a change, then you must help them to stop thinking about themselves because they have forms they have created that have had their way for such a long time. The one thing you must help them to do is to stop thinking about themselves, for that's the terrible trap, you see.

Yes, you're welcome, [Student Y]. Someone else—[Student L] has a question, please.

Yes. Is the fourth dimension the wholeness?

Well, the wholeness is that which is, and that includes the fourth dimension. Thank you. Yes. I mean, not just because I spent much of my earth life as a magistrate—in fact, my entire life on Earth. The thing is that we must—I do hope that you are alert, some of you students, to how questions are presented, [Student B] or [Student S]. You see, not—I think, in fact, it's very, very important—communication. Without communication, there is no understanding. It's very important how we speak: the words we use, the traps we present for our self. For example, if we ask the question—I do want to help all of you this morning in that respect. If we ask the question—and what was the question? So that you can repeat it. The fourth dimension.

Is the fourth dimension the wholeness?

Good. Now I want you to be alert, aware, and awake of how questions are asked. Because, you see, you're asking inside of yourself. The question is asked, "Is the fourth dimension the wholeness?" Do you understand the question—the statement? You see, the question is a statement. And it supports limit.

Now, is the fourth dimension the wholeness? I answered your question: The wholeness includes the fourth dimension. Now had I responded to the form, I would have said to the statement-question, "Is the fourth dimension the wholeness?" I could have—and I know better—said "Yes." You're trapped. You have trapped your soul. You see, to say that the fourth dimension is the wholeness denies the inclusiveness of all other dimensions in existence. Do you understand that? So you must ask yourself, when you make the question-statement, "What is this that I am saying? What is this?" It is so important, you see.

You see, certainly it is my responsibility to correct this in the class. And I correct it as many times as the Light allows it to be corrected. But it is very important to you, as students, to understand and see the difference between a question-statement that says, "Is the fourth dimension the wholeness?" and an answer. For someone asks you that and you tell them yes, you have immediately established the law of denial of what you are working for, the very freedom, Light, and Truth.

Do you understand that, [Student B]? Or don't you understand that?

I don't think I do. [Student B responds.]

No. If a person says to you, "Is the fourth dimension the wholeness?" and you say, "Yes"—all right? You're saying yes. Do you understand that? *[After a short pause, the teacher continues.]* All right. When you say, "Yes, the fourth dimension is the wholeness," you open the door of denying the third dimension, the first dimension, the second dimension, and all other dimensions that you're not aware of. So to say that the fourth dimension is the wholeness is to establish the law of the possibility of denial. Do you understand that?

Yes.

Now to speak the truth and say the fourth dimension is included in the wholeness—in other words, I'm trying to help you with perspective. The fourth dimension is a specific. Do you understand that? The wholeness is not. Would you understand that? So to place priority on the specific or the letter of the law at the sacrifice of the spirit of the law [means] you cannot experience truth and freedom. Would you relate to that?

Yes.

So what I'm trying to help you students with—and with [Student L] this morning, who so clearly demonstrated it for us—[is] the letter of the law must be recognized and perceived within our being before the form is allowed to use our mouth to speak it forth. The letter of the law killeth. So, you see, [Student L] and any other student, that which you desire is not fulfilling itself because it is controlled by the letter of the law. And the spirit of the law that giveth life is not present. Does that help you, [Student L]?

Yes.

You see? You see, form is the priority. I can tell the moment you open your mouth. You don't have to open your mouth, but open your mouth—I want *you* to recognize, through the forms that you use, whether or not limit and form is the priority: the letter of the law or the spirit of the law. Be it the spirit of the law, you shall be free and remain free. Can you see the difference, [Student L]? *[After a short pause, the teacher continues.]* Not yet.

Not quite. [Student L responds.]

[Student R], could you see the difference between the question-statement. Now what is the difference to you? This has been going on so long. And I am so happy I am permitted by the Light to, once again, speak to that because I know what it's doing to your life personally. Yes, go ahead, [Student R].

It revealed to me the mind's insistence on putting the wholeness into limit.

Very, very good. Very, very good. [Student N], you had something on that. What did you want to say?

I don't know the question.

You don't know the question?

No, I—no.

You had another question. Well, you be patient then. Now we are discussing the mind's insistence on the Light serving creation, instead of creation serving the Light. You see, when I speak to you on the letter of the law killeth, that is insistence that the Light serve creation. The spirit of the law giveth life for creation, then, serves the Light. Now there is the difference right there and it's very, very clear. The mind insists on that which is limitless to be subject to limit. Hmm? Does that help you, [Student L]?

Yes.

Yes. All right. Now someone else—[Student N] has a question this morning. A most disturbing question. Please ask it. *[The teacher laughs joyfully.]* Disturbing for her. I didn't say for me. For you, you'll have to wait and hear it. Yes.

So every time that you evolve a form or you create a new form that's more expanded than the other form going in the same direction—

Same direction? Yes.

Well . . .

Yes, yes, that's all right. Go right ahead, [Student N].

You're always going to go through the death or the, putting the other one aside, the previous form.

Well, it is disturbing when we recognize and finally realize and accept that we can't have our cake and eat it, too. Yes, it does; it becomes very disturbing for some of us. Hmm? Can't have both. Which would you like?

You can't have all, all of the . . .

It won't all fit into a container.

Right. [Student N responds and then laughs.]

I mean, no matter how much you might want and desire it, I can assure you it won't all fit.

Why, why does the—

Why won't it fit?

No—

It's your container. I'm not disturbed. *[The teacher laughs joyfully.]* Yes, yes, [Student N] Container. *[Student N, the teacher, and many students laugh.]* Well, I told you it was disturbing for you and anyone else who believes they're a container. Didn't we talk about the lids last week? Or was it the week before? Yes, [Student N] Container, please. Yes, do, please, speak.

Why, why does the mind want to hold on to all the forms instead of just moving on to the next one? You know, there's—

Well now, let us, let us understand what we're speaking about here. Why does your mind want to hold on to all the forms it creates? Is that the question? That is the statement, isn't it?

Yeah, I—

Well, isn't that what you said?

Yes.

Yes. Well now, let us stop and think. A queen's glory is dependent on the number and loyalty of her subjects. So if you're a queen that only has ten subjects, and you look over there and see a queen who has a hundred subjects, and you look over there and see, "Why, there's a queen with ten thousand subjects bowing and worshiping the throne I sit on. Oh, I want that one of ten thousand!" So, you see, if you understand the human mind, [to the human mind] bigger is better; more is desirable. You see, the human mind in that realm, it's a vacuum. It's empty. You see, you keep filling and it never fills up. It never ever fills up.

So, you see, you look around the world and say, "Well now, I've worked for that one. That one's got to stay there. Why should I let that one go to get that? No, no, no. I just set that one in the back of me just in case I want to pull it through at some time in the future." Don't you [understand]? That's how the mind works, you know.

Haven't you in creation experienced people who have a little book—I think they call them a little black book there—and they have all the names, addresses, and phone numbers written down there? And some of them have to have a suitcase just to carry the address book. You see, they don't let go of anything just in case the possibil—you see, that's a very insecure person. An insecure person must gather and garner ever more and more and more and more. I mean, in your world I think they call them pack rats. You see? They can't let go of anything just in case. It shows a person who's emotionally most insecure.

Yes, I know. Time has passed so quickly. *[The teacher addresses the cameraman.]*

It shows a person that's so insecure, emotionally insecure. Do you understand that?

Yes.

You don't have to be insecure. And I can guarantee you bigger isn't necessarily better. And more is certainly not desirable because there's a lot of things we wouldn't want more of. Wouldn't you agree?

I agree.

And, you see, when you are secure in the Principle of Good, you don't have to have all those forms tucked back there, just to be called up just in case. Because there won't be any "just in case," because you'll never be without. You don't have to have a list of all those things. Do you understand that, [Student N]? *[After a short pause, the teacher continues.]* Pardon?

Thank you.

You see, God, that which you are, is your security. You don't have to sit on a throne with more subjects than everyone else has. Do you understand that? Yes. Because, you see, it's a lot of weight of responsibility. And the only way to get free is to turn to God. Can you imagine a hundred thousand subjects screaming your name? "[Student N], [Student N] Container, where are you?" You see? *[Many students laugh.]* They always have— *[The teacher laughs.]* they always have something that they want or desire, and it always has to be right now. Why, no, no, no, you'll ruin your life.

Thank you. The time has passed, believe it or not. And I'll see you next week. Good day. *[The teacher takes a sip of water and continues.]* I prefer small classes myself. I never did believe that bigger was better. Thank you very much.

JULY 27, 1986

A/V Class Private 58

Good morning, class.

For today's discussion, we will discuss a law revealed to you some time ago: the lack of use is abuse. Suffering is the effect or experience that we have from believing that we are that which we have created.

The fall of the spiritual being is simply a belief that the angel, in creating form, through overidentification, attachment became belief. And so we find the freedom from these limits and this suffering that we encounter is dependent upon our perspective. For example, we have a thought; we are responsible as the creator of the thought. When we permit our self to believe that we are the thought that we have formed or created, then we descend and we are used by that which we have created. We go contrary to the purpose of the design. A person, creating a thought in their mind and not maintaining the faculty of reason, permits that which they have created to use them. And so we experience what we understand as suffering from our lack of effort to control that which we have designed to serve a purpose in our life.

And now we'll pause on discussion of this most important law. Whoever does not use what they have created shall be used by that which they have created. And we understand that experience as pain and suffering. Either we use or we must pay. From that lack of effort to use what we create, we must pay the price of being used by it.

Yes, [Student Y has a question] this morning.

. . . you say that we [are] abusing that which we have . . . [The noise of an airplane flying overhead prevents a complete transcription of student's question.]

Yes?

Does that mean to educate that which we create?

Correct. For that which is not used—for example, you create a thought. That thought you create for a purpose to serve you. If you do not make the effort to monitor what you have created [to ensure] that it continues to serve you for the purpose [for] which you have designed it, it shall use you (your energy) to do what it chooses to do. Yes, does that help you, [Student Y]?

Yes.

Yes.

Is there another step? Is the first step that one educate— so you have a thought. And you're saying that we create these thoughts to serve us.

Correct. You are responsible for the thought you have created. You cannot be that which you have created. You see, that which you are responsible for is not what you are. It cannot be. For what you are is the intelligent Energy and Power that has the ability to create the limit or the boundary. You cannot be that which you have created. That is the deception. That is the delusion. You can and only be, by the law, responsible for what you have created. You cannot be what you have created. To permit yourself, from lack of effort, to think that you are that which you have created places you under the form that you have created, and forms are subject to the realm of Lucifer. Go ahead, [Student Y].

OK. So—but some—the thoughts, they may be created to serve us in, in the form of a lesson.

That is—

Something with more light.

That is the only reason—you see, for example, the creating of a thought, which you are responsible for, which is limit, the limit of the substance. You have taken and limited it to create a form to serve you for a certain purpose in your evolution. Now if you do not make the effort to monitor that which you have created that it continue to serve the purpose of its design and when the purpose of its design, for which you have created it, no longer is serving you in your evolution, it is your responsibility to see that which you have created is placed in what you understand as limbo or sleep. Now if you do not do that, if you permit yourself to be tempted, from lack of effort, to believe that you are the thought or form, which is a form that you have created, then you are not using it for what you have created it. It, however, does not lie in limbo or go to sleep. It begins to use you. Yes, [Student Y].

So you're saying that it's, there's a necessity to—the monitoring comes in that one must always—that you're continually creating—

Correct.

—these forms to serve you—

Correct.

—for a purpose in your life.

Correct.

If one doesn't set about in a constant, continual effort to monitor those forms—

Correct.

—they take you over.

Correct. Look at the thoughts that you create. Look at them as workers in a garden. You have designed them to do specific jobs for you. If you do not monitor them, they do whatever they want to do, for they are created from your intelligence.

For example, if you make the effort to be awake and aware and alert, if you make the effort to monitor that which you are creating in your mind (to be aware of what you, your mind, is doing), if you make that effort, then the thought forms which you create have, as an indispensable part of their own form, they have that effort contained within them. Do you understand that? So, you see, we find that, at times, a person makes great effort, once they register in their consciousness denial or need, to bring about some changes. But they have already created many forms [and they] have not monitored them. And they are not disciplined. We do not make the effort consciously, frequent effort, to discipline what we understand is our self. So that which we understand is our self, that creates the workers to do the job for us, they [those workers] are not disciplined either. Do you understand that?

So, you see, it's time to move in our evolution to that awakening that that which we create, either we use it or it uses us. However, when it uses us, we must understand that the realm that has descended from the Light—you understand that?—that realm and the king of that realm uses all forms that do not make the effort to serve the purpose of their original design.

So whatever thought that you have or have ever had, if you have not made that effort and do not make that effort, then they are out in the universe working, doing what they want to do, surviving on your life energy. Hmm? You see? You see, some people like to liken the mind to, perhaps, a book that when you were in your formative years that you programmed. There is certain information in it. There are certain restrictions and certain limits, certain denials and certain acceptances. Well, your purpose in this school is to broaden your horizon to reprogram what has been programmed. And how you do that is: the first step is to separate yourself. Stop believing you are the thoughts you have created, for by so doing, [by believing], you suffer and experience an effect of that lack of effort, what you understand as pain and suffering.

You see, ask yourself the question, "Well, I feel this way" or "I feel that way,"—be aware of how you feel at any moment. Then ask yourself the next question, "Why do I feel good?" Or "Why do I feel bad?" "Why do I feel? What is it inside of me that's telling me this is how I feel, this is how I don't feel?" Moment to moment. When you have a certain experience and your mind tells you you're feeling good, is that you or is that a form that you have created? And if it is a form that you have created, which 99 percent of the time it is, then you must ask yourself, "Is this form serving the purpose for which I, originally, have designed and created it or is it using me?" If you are not using it, it definitely is using you. You see?

So in the course of any day, if you say to yourself, "Let me see, this is a thought. I consciously choose to use this thought. This is something that I have created. This is a very strong form. I have designed it long, long ago in my life to serve a specific purpose. Now I have an experience of this in my mind. Am I consciously in charge of this? Am I using it, for I have created it, or is it using me?" You see?

You see, whenever you permit yourself to defend—try to understand, truth not only needs no defense [and] requires no defense, truth is not defendable. You see? You see, truth, that which you are, cannot be defended, you see. Only that which you create can be defended. So if you permit your mind to say, "Well, I must defend this and I must defend that," then you must understand that that is a form that you have created that is using you. You are not using it. You see?

See, truth is not something that can be defended, you see? Truth cannot be annihilated. You can only annihilate that which is limited, that which has been created. Only that which is limit, that which is created can have birth and death. You see, the only thing that can die is that which is born. Well, you have not been born and you cannot die. You awaken to various things in your evolution, you see.

You see, it's like the intelligences that monitor your planet. They are responsible for your planet. They know, however, that they are not that which they are responsible for. That is how they're able to intelligently monitor their responsibilities.

To permit yourself to believe that you are that which you are responsible for is to deceive yourself and permit a realm of limit and destruction to control your life. To deny personal responsibility is not only foolhardy but it is a very great suffering. However, to accept personal responsibility and from that acceptance to believe that you are that which you are responsible for is just as foolhardy and just as destructive, yes.

Do you have any further question on that, [Student Y]?

Thank you.

Certainly. And [Student D] has a question this morning.

Are all thoughts judgments?

All thoughts become judgments in keeping with energy that is directed to them.

So—

See, many people have a thought that it's a beautiful day. But I have few people that have a judgment that it's a beautiful day that is constantly using them. No, no. Because they have all kinds of days from moment to moment. Yes, a thought becomes a judgment ever in keeping with the attention or energy that it receives. That's how a thought form solidifies into a judgment.

So—

And through the bondage that you believe that you're it. If you have a thought and you want it to be a judgment very quickly, all you have to do is believe that you are what you've created. The moment that you believe [you are] what you have created, all your energy flows to it, and before your very eyes it is solidified and known as a judgment. Yes. Go ahead, [Student D].

So when we find ourselves with a judgment that doesn't fit, that's actually a thought that we've solidified.

Correct.

At that point, we should, when it doesn't fit, we should look at it and put it to sleep if it isn't appropriate.

That is correct. That is correct. Because, you see, through your effort what you will do, you will direct intelligent energy; through the soul faculty of reason, you will direct it to that which you have created, and it shall obey you, you see? You see, shadows disappear when the Light is turned on in the consciousness. Now there's more to just a little saying that a shadow disappears in a light. Remember that an obstruction to the Light is that which creates a shadow. A shadow does not exist without an obstruction to the Light. So all shadows, all thoughts, thought forms—try to understand—are obstructions to what you are if you do not monitor them—what you understand as educate them—and place them in their perspective in your life so that they do not obstruct what you are. You see, the moment a thought form that you have created, the thought that you have created, the moment it uses you, you know that as an obstruction to the goodness which is your divine right, you see. You see, you have permitted yourself to believe you are that which you have created. By so doing, you not only solidify the form into a judgment, through a direction of a phenomenal amount of your own energy, but that is when you allow it, from that moment on, to use you and obstruct what you are. It's not serving the purpose of its design.

[Thank you.]

You're welcome, [Student D]. Yes, [Student M].

I mean, yes. When we have a thought form that we wish to put to sleep and do not want to suppress it, we want to—

Well, may I say one thing, [Student M], at this time?

Yes.

To permit yourself to be tempted to suppress that which you are responsible for only guarantees its continued use of your life. Yes, go ahead.

Yes. Is communication the difference and the awareness of how to not suppress it and how to educate it? So communication—and yet you do not want to direct too much energy to it to feed it. So there's like a—

Well, yes, that's very important. Very important, [Student M]. First of all, without communication, there is no understanding. And without understanding, there is no exposure. And exposure is the law through which that which you are is freed.

Yes.

All right? Therefore, it—repetition is the law through which change is made possible. We evolve through the Law of Evolution. All right?

Yes.

Now, so when you want to bring about a change of that which you have created, you want to remove it as an obstruction to what you are—

Yes.

That's what you're speaking of, correct?

Yes.

You must communicate in order to gain understanding. From understanding the Light that you are exposes it for what it is. Now, you see, most people will quit midstream, you see. What you find in communication, in working with these things that we are responsible for, for we have created them—that we are not and cannot be—you understand?

Yes, I do.

What you will find is that most all minds quit before the victory. Now they will quit before the victory because of the repetition necessary and the tenacity of that which we have created that we believe that we are. So, you see, when you're working with yourself or with a person, you must separate yourself from what you have created. You must separate yourself from believing that you are what you have created. You must—first of all, you must accept that you are responsible for that which you have created. And most important: that you are not, nor have you ever been, what you have created. You see. Because if you don't do that, you cannot clearly communicate, you cannot gain understanding, and you certainly cannot free yourself—you understand?—

Yes.

—from that which you have permitted to use you.

Yes.

You see?

Yes.

You see, when we understand, truly understand that these things that we are responsible for, that they are using us—that's what they're doing. We are responsible because they are using us. It is from our own lack of understanding. It's from our own error of ignorance. And when we awaken that we are being used by them—[and] not consciously making a choice—that we are being used by them, then we begin to make some drastic changes in our daily efforts. Yes. You see?

Yes.

You see, what happens to a form once you have created it and believe that you are it? It enters the realm for which the archangel who fell from the right hand of the divine Principle of Goodness is in control. Then it does whatever that king tells it to do. So your energy for the goodness of life is being used; the salt is being mined for old creation. Yes.

Thank you.

And the chemicals—physical chemicals—make changes within your body. You see, a thought that you form in your mind utilizes chemicals, physical chemicals of your body. Now physical chemicals of your body create a tendency to certain type[s] of forms created by your mind. So there's an interaction, you see. The mind affects the physical body; the chemicals of the physical body have an effect upon the mind, you see. Now certain type—we will get to that, be it in divine order, in [these] classes. I've been [discussing] it for—many, many times in my other classes. Someday, be it in order, divine order, we will get to that [in these classes]: which chemicals, physical chemicals, are used by what type of thought forms, you see. Certain physical chemicals are used in order to form certain types of thoughts, you see. Thought forms, they utilize physical chemicals. Yes.

For example, now you have people—you've had some experiences—where they have to have a certain, you know—perhaps you can best relate to when a woman is going through a pregnancy stage: she has certain cravings for this or that. There are certain cravings at other times in a person's life because, you see, the forms being created by the mind use a certain chemical. And someday we'll get to all of that as we get to different parts of the vehicle. Yes.

Thank you.

Yes. Yes, [Student B].

Strictly, what is belief? Is . . .

Belief is an overidentification and an attachment to that which you create, you see. You see, take a look. A person believes in what they create. Hmm? Now a person has great difficulty believing what someone else creates unless there's a similarity with *[The teacher begins to laugh, which makes transcription a bit difficult.]* another form. You take a look. You tell a person, you say, "Oh," you know, your forms are up and they're very happy and say, "Oh, what a beautiful day! It's so nice and comfortable outside and everything." Well, if you tell that to another person and they don't have similar forms, well, they don't believe you at all. Hmm? So, you see, belief is ever in keeping to what you have created.

It's an overidentification with what you have created. And through that overidentification, you experience an attachment. Now you have people, you can look at them and talk to them and they, perhaps, have a similar attachment that you have, you see, or a similar overidentification, in principle. Then they will certainly agree with you. But if they don't have that, they won't agree with you at all. In fact, they can ofttimes become very obstinate about it, you see. Hmm? Yes. It is an overidentification, which moves to an attachment.

You see, you can't be attached to what you don't overidentify with, [Student B], you see, through your attention, your energy directed to it. And from the overidentification, you experience an attachment. From the attachment, you guarantee belief that you are it. From your guarantee of belief that you are it, you have your bondage. That's when it uses you. Faith is freedom. Belief is bondage. Yes, [Student B].

Is it possible to have a belief that you don't think is you? [Student B speaks very quietly.]

That you don't think is?

That you don't believe is you. I mean, without belief—

Well, that's objectivity. You don't have the belief; you have the acceptance. "There is a belief there. I know this is not me. I know I am responsible for it. I know that I have created it. It is what I have created. It is not what I am." This is the phase that we're moving to, you see. So that we can move, someday, be it in divine order, to the actual physical chemicals that are used by certain types of what you would understand as thought patterns. They all require—they have their own specific chemicals that they use, you see. And those chemicals, of course, are available in the foods that you eat and the things that you drink, you see. Yes.

You see, you can tell what type of forms that you are feeding (that are using you, your energies) by the things that you eat, the things that you crave to eat, you see. They reveal that. Yes. Hmm? And even the physical sciences in your world are, slowly but surely, moving to that understanding. Yes. Definitely.

You are what you eat only if you believe that you are this, this uneducated ego, this thing called self. That's when you are what you eat. That is very true, you see. You are what you eat if you believe that you are that limit. Then, you are what you eat because those are the forms that are using you. And in that respect, yes, of course, you are what you eat, in that respect, definitely. Yes.

Yes. Someone—did—yes, [Student J]. Good morning.

Is an interrelationship, sir, between people a rapport of forms?

Oh definitely. Absolutely. They feed off each other. Oh, yes, they feed off each other, and they literally dissipate the physical chemicals. Oh, yes, yes, indeed. For example, when you have a rapport of forms with another person, the forms that are living off of you take a look at that other person, you see? And if there's any rapport and you're not awakened and you're not consciously making the effort at the time—you see, they may have physically drained the person you're talking to and they're still hungry; they're always hungry, you see—and so they start using your chemicals. Oh, yes indeed, you see. Definitely. Absolutely. Yes. Yes, that's how we're known by the company we keep. Definitely. Why, certainly, if you look in that realm, you say, "Oh yes, I know that person very well." *[The teacher laughs joyfully.]* Yes.

Thank you.

You're welcome. [Student S] has a question this morning.

Yes. You said that to monitor these forms that we create for a purpose. And it seems that by the time that we believe we are them, they're already in service below.

Well, they're already using you.

OK. I'd like to know—

You have to get—you have to make the effort prior to the belief that you are them. Because the moment you believe that you are that which you have created, you are no longer using those forms. They are using you. Yes.

And I'd like to know what is the earlier warning signs, then, when you're monitoring these forms to show that we're beginning to cross over that line of belief and be used by the form.

Oh, definitely. Yes. The very early warning sign is the awakening inside—and we always know—when we start to think of our self. The very moment that we start to think of that we believe is our self, at that moment, if the effort is not made, then it's too late. Then, we are used. Yes.

To make it clear, could you give us an example of a thought form that we create for a specific purpose and the process that we—

Why, certainly. For example—yes, I will speak to all of you on that. Say, for example, at a time in one's life they created a certain form which said that they needed affection. You see? Now that form is a long time created [and is] a very strong soldier. Now when you create a form that tells your mind—you see, you've created it in order to experience being affected. All right? Now a person creates a thought in their mind that they would feel good if they were affected. You understand? It's known as an affection form, you see.

However, it doesn't stop there. Because, you see, you don't just create a form and say, "I feel good if I'm affected." You have to, in the programming, like you would program a computer, you have to program it—affection, what does *affection* mean? Well, then the mind says that it means having this and having that, and it also means another person affecting me, doing this and doing that under these various conditions. Now the form affection is created. All right? Fine. And it's very restrictive and it has—you see, it's very detailed and very specific, ever in keeping with the person's mind who created the affection form.

Now some people create an affection form and if somebody slaps them on the face, they accept that as affection. And they're not really that specific. It doesn't matter, don't you see. But then you have affection forms created by minds that are very detailed, very specific, more like a virgin mind or a Virgo mind. And so you have an affection form, all right?

Now when you experience affection, the form gives you what you understand as a goodness or a sensation, more like what you would understand as a thrill, an excitement. And then, you say, "Ah! Now I have affection." All right. When you do not have that, if you are being used by that which you have created by believing that you are that which you have created, when you are being used by the form you have created and you don't have what this form—you don't have this thrill or sensation that this form gives to you as a little payment for servicing him—you understand?—then you feel terrible. So you can only feel good as long as he is allowed to use you. Do you understand that?

Now how does he get to use you or any person? He uses you when you think of what you understand as self. Because he was only created while you were under that control. You see, the forms created are created to serve the senses. You can't experience the senses until you permit yourself to believe you are the limit. Sensation, excitement, thrill is something that is the exclusive domain of limit or creation. So when you believe that you are limit, you see—you see, a person believes that they are limit when they have an obstruction to their desire. When a person has [an] obstruction to their desire, they say they're limited. "What is this?" You see? "I want this and, of course, something out there is stopping me from getting it." But you must realize that tells you when you are being used by that which you have created, you see.

You see, you could not have the desire to be affected, in the beginning, until you denied what you are. You see, a person who has what they understand as a need to be affected is a person who has first denied what they are. By denying what you are, you need to be affected by what you are not. Yes. Yes, [Student S]. *[After a short pause, the teacher continues.]*

And so they use you. They use your form. They use the chemicals of your body. And they work you like a slave in a salt mine. Yes, that's what they do.

So if we see the obstruction to our desire, then we have—

It is not you that's seeing the obstruction to desire. It's the form that's using you.

Right. But—

Yes.

—if we don't see the obstruction and we're experiencing, say, the satisfaction of desire, we're still in it because—

Well, you will only experience what you understand as the satisfaction for a short time.

Right.

Oh, yes. Because the need will rise again. That's how they work to get more. You see, for example, if you have satisfaction from what you understand as a fulfillment of a desire, at first, of course, the way the process works, you'll have it, perhaps, for, say, [it] might even be for an hour you feel satisfied. But as time progresses, you'll feel the hour becomes 50 minutes, 40 minutes, 30 minutes, 20 minutes. And so it has to be more and more and more. That's how they get more workers for the salt mines. Yes.

So there's really no way to experience the forms or monitor or use them for the purpose of their design—it's my understanding, then, that the whole thing, even when you're using them for the purpose of design, you're still in it. Either you're using them or they're using you, but it's—

Yes, but you created them. You see, you see, if a person creates something—say a person hires a worker. Now, I hire you, for example, let's see, to put a nice sprinkler here on this lovely garden here, you see. And so that it works just fine. Now I work hard. I earn my money. I'm paying you top dollar. This is the way you do the job. All right? Now you are using that which you have earned, which you are not, but that which you have earned in creation. You're using your money to pay a worker to do a job specifically the way you want it done. Now if that worker does not do the job the way you have contracted that worker to do the job, then that worker is using you; you are not using them.

Now you have called them forth, you understand, in keeping with the law, and you have contracted to pay them that which they require that they may be used for X-number of hours to do a job a certain way. You understand that. Now they understand, by their desire for what they want, they will allow you to use them in keeping with that contract and that price and that payment. So if they do not do the job in keeping with your payment for using them, then you are not happy when they have finished. Correct?

Correct.

So there's a vast difference between using that which you have created consciously to do what you want it to do—if you consciously use that which you have created to do a certain job, you experience the effect of it: what you call satisfaction. That's a conscious choice. You know that is not you. You have, however, given your senses a little tidbit, you see? You have consciously chose[n] to do that. That's a vast difference than having that which you have contracted and created using you to do what it wants to do, because then you end up not satisfied. And that can be quite frustrating: to work hard and pay for a form—you understand?—to do a specific job and so you can be satisfied. You see?

Right.

And then, you end up—you've paid for the job and you're not satisfied after paying to be satisfied. You see, it's a very practical world. You create and you pay. And you say, "My reward for this effort is to feel a sensation that I call satisfaction." You see? Do you see the difference between "using" and "being used"?

Yes.

You see, by using, you are consciously aware. "I'm going to use this that I have already created, called my affection form, to do this job. I call it up to use it. It's certainly used me for enough years. It's time that it paid me back." You understand that? You see, it's time that it pays you back. It can only pay you back by your absolute disassociation from it; your conscious choice that it will service you. You see? Now what is it getting out [of it]? It's getting from you the opportunity—you understand?—to do its number under your guidance and control. Otherwise, it's just using you.

Thank you.

[If] you believe you are it, then it's using you. That's not the separation of truth from creation. Creation is here to be used. And in the process of using it, it is refined and evolved. If you do not use creation, accept the demonstrable truth: creation is using you. You therefore are not fulfilling the purpose of your evolution through limit. You are not serving the purpose and, therefore, only guarantee a continuity of service again. You see?

Thank you.

Yes. And [Student N] and then [Student Y]. Yes. [Student N] has a question, please.

If you experience obstructions, then that—is that meaning that the form is using you?

Correct. Because, you see, if you're experiencing obstructions, then the form is using you. Why, certainly it's using you. It's standing in the way of your evolution. Yes. You have not consciously called it up and said, for example, "Now, affection form, I have created you. Come in and stand in my way." Do you—you see, for example—and I have tried to share with you for many years [that] creation is here to serve a purpose. Do not look at it as something bad or something good. If you look at it as bad, you are destined to look at it as good. And in that perspective, you lose God. You lose the goodness. It is there. It is there to be used. Its use is your control over it. When you permit yourself to believe that you are it, it is controlling you, [which is] totally contrary to your evolution. Yes. Totally contrary. Yes.

Yes, now [Student Y] has a question, please.

Would the wisest path be to—now I know you just said that creation is here for us to use.

Definitely.

And it not use us.

Correct.

But you have also said that to seek anything outside of yourself, like affection, for instance—

That's correct. That's to deny what you are.

—is within yourself. Like—

Correct.

—affection lies within yourself.

That's where it is.

So if you are truly who you—what you are, then, would one have an—there would be no need to seek the affection.

Well, no, but we're not there yet, are we?

No.

Well, see, *[The teacher laughs joyfully.]* that's why I've come here. So we can help all of us, you see. I've spent eons in those realms and I would like to say, well, we're all there. Then what are we doing here? You see. *[Many students laugh.]* No, that isn't what—no. You see, the Law of Disassociation, use it, for if you don't use it, it will use you. It will use you because you are in it, you see. You are in it and believe you are a part of it.

We have not, you see, in this limit, reached the stage in evolution to be in it and not a part of it. We allow our self the luxury of that temptation to believe that we're it, while we're in it, you see. Be in the world and not a part of the world. There are only moments when we accomplish that. Be with a person, place, or thing and not a part of a person, place, or thing. There are only moments when we accomplish that. Usually at the moment in the divorce court when you sign the paper, from what I see. Yes, [Student Y].

Well, are there degrees? Can there be degrees of this use?

Oh, definitely. Why, certainly. In some areas in our consciousness, we very clearly are using the forms we have created.

We don't have to jump completely into the pot.

Oh no, no, no, no, no, no, no, no. Only in certain areas people jump completely into the pot. And then it starts boiling. *[Many students laugh.]* Yes, it does. Yes, yes, I agree. Yes, yes. Yes, definitely. Positively. Yes. But, however, in other areas, oh, no, no, no: no pot exists at all, let alone a fire. You see, I'd like to have a little fire burning under some of these other areas of consciousness, you see. *[Students continue to laugh.]* You see. Whoever has the ability to light one fire can light another. And there are some areas that could use the fire, you see. Yes. Have to transfer some of the fuel. *[After a short pause, the teacher continues.]*

Well, it's a nice day, lovely day today. Always a lovely day. It always is. Yes, [Student Y].

You spoke, a couple of weeks ago, on frequency.

Yes.

And I wanted to know that—is the refining process—is the, is the higher realm a higher frequency?

It is. Absolutely. Yes. Definitely. You see, it's a higher frequency. It's what you—it's much more accelerated. Do you understand? Now I think that my channel has spoken to you—we have certainly spoken to him—on the deafness of some of you students. You know you have noted that there's been an increasing deafness to certain frequencies. Well, a lot of people are under the delusion and deception that as you get older, physically, you don't hear the higher frequencies because of your age. You see? [It] has nothing to with your age, only in the sense of the repetition of believing that you are the lower frequencies. You see?

You see, if you will understand the senses are low frequencies, and the soul faculties are very high frequencies, if you will understand that, on the octave of any keyboard, then you will understand as time progresses—you know, it's just like with your, with your stereo system there, you see. In fact, our channel was instructed to increase, to *increase* by over 80 percent the high frequency equalization in order that you students could hear. Because, you see, you don't want—it isn't a volume increase. It's a frequency increase.

You see, what is happening in your world—and it's happened before—is you will note that there is an increase in the volume of what you understand as music. There's been an increasing desire for increased volume of the sound. What that is revealing is that the higher frequencies no longer are registering by the human ear because of the overidentification with the lower frequencies. So [if] you find yourself not being able to hear music, then you have to increase the musical balance of sound: you must increase the higher frequencies. For the higher frequencies are the first thing a person loses as they overidentify with limit. High frequencies are the frequencies that have the broader, much broader perspective. Your low frequencies are very contained. Low frequencies contract. Do you understand that? High frequencies expand.

You see, it's like color. You see certain very dark, muddy colors. Those are low frequencies. They're actual frequencies. Then you see very light, pastel colors. Those are very high frequencies. Those are expanding frequencies, you see.

You see, it's like your universe. Your universe—the density of anything is in keeping with its own contraction. You see, as I explained to one of my students some time ago, "The intensity of density is measured by acceptance." So the less acceptance a person has, the more density you have or the lower frequencies or the more solidification. For example, you ask here about a thought form. How and when does a thought form become a judgment? Well, as you overidentify with a thought, you decrease or lower the frequencies going to the form you have created. As you lower the frequencies, you increase the density. That's the solidification process, you see.

It's like your little choir. The frequencies have so lowered that we have temporarily discontinued our choir here at the temple. Now what has caused the lowering of those frequencies and the increase of volume? You see, by the lowering of the frequencies, you've noted that the volume has increased. And the discord and disharmony has increased. This is why we have discontinued it for a time. Until the participants or the students understand and apply the Law of Frequencies. Do you understand that? Yes.

So if you want something very dense in your life, all you have to do is to overidentify with it. It will become extremely dense as you lower the frequencies of that which you have created. And through an overidentification, you attach. Through an attachment, you believe you are it. You are bound by lower frequencies and freed by higher frequencies.

Time is passing quickly so go right on with your questions. Yes, [Student Y].

Acceptance expands, then. Acceptance—

Yes! Acceptance is the will of God, the will of Goodness. You see, acceptance expands, you see. The intensity of density is measured by acceptance. So if you have a little acceptance, you have great density, for you have very low frequency. Does that help you with your question? You see? So, you see, anyone who—I've taught you, also, in other ways, in reference to this frequency, "Put God in it or forget it." [When] you put God in it, you have the higher frequencies, which expand and free. You wonder why business or anything doesn't grow? Well, you're in it and the lower frequencies are there and so it contracts. You see? You see, if you want something to progress, you've got to get yourself out of it so higher frequencies can get into it.

You know, it's like working with a person, you see, [who says], "Well, what can I do? I've done all that I can." Well, thank God you've done all that you can. Get out of it and let God in it. *[Several students laugh.]* You see, there's so much low frequencies in. Get the low frequencies out; let the higher frequencies come in, for high frequencies expand; low frequencies contract.

You see, it's like the universe. How are your planets formed? Well, when you're at a point of which you say there is the gaseous stages, etc., that's an expansion, a free movement, you see, of all those chemicals. [Do] you understand that? Well, as they become self-aware—you see, what you must realize [is] that a chemical, an atom, [an] electron, or a molecule has an identification just like you do. They all have identification. They're living—it's living Intelligence in form. This has an identification. *[The teacher cradles the blossom of a Shasta daisy in his hand.]* It even has its personality. It has its emotion, its water center, its air center, and on through. Because, you see, it is Intelligence encased in limit. So divine Intelligence encased in limit—limit has its identification in order to make the limit or form. Yes.

Now someone else here had a question. [Student U] and then [Student N], yes.

Frequency has been associated with rate of vibration, but I'm not—

Why, of course.

—but I'm not really certain what either one of those things are.

Well, rate of vibration, as I've discussed many years ago with many of you students, rate of vibration—you have a thought. [It] becomes a thought pattern. Your thought pattern establishes a rate of vibration. So the more thoughts that you have that you believe that you are, the lower is your rate of vibration, the more dense is the form, and the more tempted you are to believe that you are it. You see? That's why belief is bondage and faith is freedom. You see? You see, why, why—how is that, that—what is the difference between faith, [Student U], and belief that belief binds you and faith frees you? Faith is not belief. What's the difference? How does that work? Why is faith high frequencies on the octave and belief low frequencies?

What you are identified with—

Is a low frequency, yes.

Is what—

Do you identify with what you believe you are or with what you have faith in? You see, there's a fine line there. There's a fine line there. And if so, how do you do that? How do you believe—yes, I know *[The teacher responds to a signal from the cameraman.]*—how do you believe that you are what you create and have faith in something else? You see, you don't have faith in what you create. You know better. All you do is *believe* you are what you create. You don't have faith in it; you always have doubt. Always. You show me a man or anyone that believes something is going to work out and I'll show you a man that will guarantee you, "Well, I'm not so sure now." You see? It doesn't have the wisdom of patience. Faith has the faculties. Belief has the functions. So, you see, faith contains all those faculties, including wisdom and patience and humbleness and all of those faculties. And belief has all of the other. Hmm?

Yes, we've only got a few minutes left. Does that help with your question? Because I've got [Student M] here and all our questions come up quickly in the last four minutes. Yes, [Student M], please.

You were just saying that, that there is a fine line between the belief and the faith.

Why, certainly.

And the, and the . . .

Well, tell me something; let me ask you. Perhaps you can relate best right away. Do you believe in God or do you have faith in God?

I have faith in God.

Why do you have faith in God, instead of believe in God? Many people believe in God, don't they?

Yes.

Don't they? And don't they even describe God for you?

Yes.

Whoever believes in God has a god they've created. And as long as that god does what their mind tells them or does what those forms [that they believe they are] tell them that he's got to do and as long as he does that, they believe in God. And when those forms don't get their way (those forms using you), then that god goes. That's a created god. Whoever believes in god has made Lucifer his king. Whoever has faith in the divine Principle of Goodness is free.

And I look forward to, once again, seeing you next week. As I've always said, in your world, time is only a moment. Thank you.

AUGUST 10, 1986

A/V Class Private 59

[A/V Class Private 59 is missing. Although a recording of it was made, this class was not released to the students. An explanation for this action is given in A/V Class Private 61.]

A/V Class Private 60

Good morning, class.

The expression or movement of whatever is created in mental substance is known as experience. Now experience is not something that you, as a class, are unfamiliar with. The earth, fire, water, and air centers are the centers of consciousness through which you experience mental substance.

As has been said so many times in your world, seeing is believing, for seeing is a vehicle, such as hearing is a vehicle, through which the senses, mental substance expresses itself. Therefore, when you place your attention upon mental substance, you find yourself moving through the four centers of consciousness that are controlled by mental substance: earth, fire, water, and air.

A person who believes that they are is a person who has convinced themselves, through constant use, that they are the senses, the expression of mental substance and, therefore, continue on the wheel of experience. Experience, being an expression of limit, governed and controlled by limit, is not what we are. Therefore, to permit oneself to hope for better experience or experiences is to insist on believing that we are the senses and, therefore, to remain controlled by the first four phases or centers of consciousness, known as earth, fire, water, and air.

We all know, as students, that to create anything requires intelligent energy, directed. So the more that we permit ourselves to seek new or better experiences, the more energy is required for that creating purpose. This is why we have stated that hope is eternal and truth is inevitable. Mental substance is a substance that has always been, for without mental substance there is not form or creation. So in that respect, of course, hope is eternal and truth is inevitable.

Now our little classes here continue on. They do not continue on by sacrificing that which is. They continue on by intelligent choice. Yes, you may take care of him, [Student S], at this moment. *[Student S's dog requires some attention.]* He believes he is the form. And when anyone believes that, be it four-legged or two-, then it is a servant of that which it believes it is.

Does the bird fly without belief? Does the dog walk without belief? Does the ant crawl without belief? That is the question and I wait for your answer. Yes, [Student O], please.

No, they do not.

And why don't they?

Why don't they? Well, if they didn't believe, they wouldn't exist in a material, physical form.

Thank you very much. You're absolutely correct, [Student O]. For belief is the so-called cement used by mental substance to limit form, what it forms. Only what we create in mental substance, in our minds is the obstruction to what we are. There is no obstruction to what we are. Without belief, there's no obstruction. With less belief, there is less obstruction.

Now when we want to remain in, as you say, the full bloom of the senses, then we have many things that we create. They're in the way of what we are. The less we create, the less obstruction in our way. For example, when you have concern, you're not only a poor businessman but you're very poor in living, for concern is not only an overidentification with what one believes that they are but it is a very high[ly] accelerated program of the mind in creating a multitude of forms or obstructions to what you truly are.

Now take, for example, you create something with four wheels. And in the process of creating it, you wonder if the wheels will turn. And so you think and create something to make the wheels turn: a little motor. Then you're concerned with what will power the motor. Then you create something else that the motor will work powered by a certain fluid. Then you're concerned about the type of fluid. Then you're concerned if the motor will wear out or if it'll even start. Then you're concerned whether or not the ignition will work that you have created. And so the more that you are concerned, the less that you have. Be concerned about your desires, be patient with yourself and enjoy the frustration thereof.

The joy of living, of course, is the lack of concern. Do not forget, I never said the lack of personal responsibility. There's a vast difference between concern and personal responsibility. [Do] you know what that vast difference is? Yes, [Student U].

The absence of self.

The absence of self. Absolutely. Concern, filled with self, creates a mountain of forms. Personal responsibility takes a look at what it's created and makes sure that it does what it has created it to do. It's not concerned about it; it is in charge of it. It has created it! And when it doesn't do what it has created it for, it sets it aside, in the old heap of creation, and creates something else. And if it still doesn't do what it has created it for, it sets it aside. And sooner or later, we all wake up that what we have created is not paying attention to us; so something must be wrong in the way and the motive that is being used for what we create.

Now I've told you [in] many ways, "Put God in it or forget it." The problem is [that] you put the mental god in it; you won't forget it; you continue to be concerned about it. Well, show me, whatever thought you might have, what good it's done for you. If it's done some good, then the light of reason reveals, "Now that's a thought, that's a form I have created. It's doing very nicely. Does just exactly what I created it for. It does what I tell it to do in keeping with its purpose of design when I tell it to do it. Therefore, I must have put a pure motive into that form, as pure as my mind will allow me to put in there." You see?

You see, to move on, to move on to—are you all right there with your nails this morning, [Student N]? Yes. Did you have a problem with your fingers? *[It seems that Student N was clipping her fingernails.]*

No.

Yes. Well, you see, we want to remember, children, that when we do those things in class, in any class, that something else is controlling us. You do understand that, don't you? You don't want that something else to control you—do you?—in the short one hour or fifty-five minutes that's allotted to you? Hmm? You see? So you be grateful when you think things don't go your way; that's when you're truly growing. Yes, indeed. Indeed. Because then you have, you have established the Law of Opportunity that "My way is not the best way. For if it was the best way, it would be going that way because I've certainly put a lot of my energy into it." Hmm? And so something else, you see, is working to help you along life's eternal paths.

Now this is a beautiful day in your world, for some of you who choose to look at it. And for those of you who choose to look at something else, why, you have all week to do that. I come to visit with you once a week. Sometimes twice a week when we have our seminars. So let us use the moments that we all have wisely and get something out by putting something in.

And so if you are in need of a manicure—I don't ever recall my channel, as a channel of mine, when it comes to spiritual benefits in classes, deciding to—whatever you call it—manicure his toenails or something.

You see, it's not a matter of disrespect for me. It is a serious state of disrespect for you as students. And I know that you, as students, have come here for something besides a class on manicuring or on a beautician class or something. Because I do know of people in our world that are very qualified in those particular realms. I'm sure we can find a cosmetologist, if you would rather have those classes. And I'm sure that they would be a bit expensive for you, more so than these are.

So let's move on now and get to our questions of why we're here this morning. And we'll begin here with [Student O], who has been meditating there while we've been giving our little class. Yes, [Student O].

Yes, ah . . .

I like to say to my students, when they're looking down in those holes down there, they're "meditating." It's a diplomatic way of helping them to awaken, I have found. Yes, [Student O]. *[The teacher laughs.]*

Yes. Yes, well—

I never saw a hole up. They're always—holes are always down. You know, whatever your perspective may be, they're still down. Yes, [Student O]. Show me an up hole and I'll show you an upside-down world. Yes.

Yes. Thank you.

You're welcome. Holes are always down.

Yes. I was reflecting on what, this—I was reflecting on a statement that you had just made.

Yes. And, you see, if you look up, you will see what a beautiful reflection of the lovely clouds and the beautiful blue there. *[The teacher looks up toward the sky.]* Look up and all around and about you, you see. And if you're inside, you just look up and look right on through the ceiling, through the roof and see. Because that's, that's where your home is. *[The teacher points toward the sky above.]* Yes.

Yes, sir.

Yes.

Thank you.

You're welcome. So that's where reflection should be. *[The teacher again points to the sky above.]* Hmm? Where home is, you see. What does *reflect* mean to you?

Well, ah—

To consider what has been?

Yes, it does.

Well, then isn't it only proper that one, having descended from their true home, would, in reflection, would look up to where it truly is? *[The teacher points yet again to the sky.]*

Yes, sir.

Yes. So contemplation, reflection, meditation, you see— home's up there. *[And again, the teacher points to the sky.]* Yes, go ahead, [Student O].

Yes, sir. I have questions.

Yes?

Ah . . .

Question. Yes. You had a question. I like to have your questions come from above. I've heard plenty from below. And those aren't questions. The ones that come from below are not questions; they are statements under the facade of questions, you see.

Yes, sir.

See, there's a difference, you know. Yes. Questions from there, you see, how to get back home. Those down there are statements. Yes. So let's go ahead with your reflection.

That was the end of it.

Oh, that was the end of the— *[The teacher laughs joyfully.]* Well, I see that your wife had a question here this morning. *[The teacher continues to laugh.]* Yes, yes, yes, [Student M].

Thank you. The soul faculty of care . . .

Care?

Care?

Yes. Yes, it's a faculty. It's not a mental function of gymnastics. That's true, yes, yes.

Right.

Care! Yes.

Care. Is the, is the concern the sense function of care?

[The teacher laughs joyously.] Yes. I'm only smiling because, you see, you're asking a question about a soul faculty known

as care. And in your question is the mental activity of what someone else does and doesn't do. So the question is based upon dependence. And dependence is absolutely a function. It has nothing to do with faculties. And so I'm answering your question as it truly has presented itself. That's why I like to have you look up. Everyone look up, you see.

Yes.

You see? Do you understand?

I—

You see, you see, you're asking about a soul faculty, known as care, based upon experiences of what your husband does or doesn't do in reference to caring for you. Do you understand that, [Student M]?

I do.

Well, I should hope so because you're the one that brought the facade here. And I'm speaking on the soul faculty; you have asked over a soul faculty.

Yes, I have.

So, you see, when a soul faculty presents itself and it's under the facade of all this mental activity of, "Let me see, now in class it says care is a soul faculty and this is what it is." And then goes home and says, "Now *you* are not demonstrating your soul faculty. I will not have that here." See, you see, I see that, you know, very clearly. That's my work. I'm interested in the soul faculty—you understand?

Yes.

As it is.

Yes.

Not to be used by the sense functions as a facade to service something below. I don't—I'm not interested in reflecting on that down there, you see. And so who of us is so illumined to study these beautiful soul faculties and take them in mental substance to serve the sense functions? No, no, no, no. I will not be a part of that. You know, my married days are long, long ago. I am not interested in being a part of that kind of stuff. Yes.

Now if you want to know about concern—what can you ask about concern when you are so well qualified in it, my dear? *[The teacher laughs joyfully.]*

[Student M responds as the teacher laughs, but it is difficult to transcribe.]

Pardon?

It's true.

Yes. And so do you want to find a way for concern, the sense function, to express itself under the guise of the soul faculty of care? Hmm?

Hopefully not the guise. But kind of help to transform it into—

Well, you want to transform it? It's known as—yes. Well, all you got to do is forget concern and experience and open up to care. Yes! Yes, [Student J].

Thank you. [Student M responds.]

You're welcome.

What's the—if one is in the function of concern, how can one convert that to the faculty of care? [Student J asks.]

Yes. Well, first of all, one must accept the possibility of experiencing the goodness that they are. You see, accept that affirmation that has been given to you. *[Please see the appendix for the complete affirmation.]* Do your cleansing breaths. And each time concern rises up [say], "Just a minute. What am I concerned about? Will I continue to live with or without this that I am concerned about?" Hmm? You see? You see, because concern is controlled by the sense functions.

So a person who has permitted themselves, through errors of ignorance, to overidentify with their senses experiences concern. So, "This has come into my life. This has gone from my life. This here is not so great. It's not greater than what I am. So if it works, it works. If it don't, it don't. I have given it to the universe"—you understand?—"and the law shall fulfill itself and I am freed from concern." You see? You see, but you [have] got to work on that. And every time it rises up, declare that truth. You see? Because it will always work to tempt you, to tempt you to service it, you see. To tempt you. And when it does that, then a person ends up in terrible, terrible condition, only to start on the treadmill again of another project, another experience, another relationship, you see? It's always relationship. See, wherever you have concern, you have relationship.

You see, we want to bring this into perspective. Usually, a person thinks of relationship and what some of the students have overidentified with: boy meets girl, girl meets boy, etc. Well, man meets business, business meets man, and go on through the list, you see?

Yes, sir.

So they're all relationships for the person has permitted themselves, through belief, that they are what they have created. And by that belief, they have established a relationship, for they are affected emotionally. This is why a good businessman is freed from concern. For in business, he doesn't have a relationship with his business, where emotion—the judgments are born in the water center. You see, the water center's not in it. You see, to have the water center of self-concern—that's where it comes from; from the judgments, of course—into practical business, practical business is no longer practical. Would you not—certainly, you understand that, don't you?

You see, a businessman cannot afford a relationship with his business, you see. Now by that I mean an emotional involvement. You see? Facts and figures do not, do not harmonize with emotions. You see? You see, there's the figures; there's the facts in a world of creation, a world of business, you see. Now you may *use*, you may *use* objectively a relationship. You understand? You may use it. You cannot afford to become it. Hmm?

Yes, sir.

Does that help you, [Student J], with that?

Yes, sir.

You see, you see, you keep that totally separated. You look at it. Those are the facts. Those are the figures. [And say,] "Now let's see, do I have, do I have in my water center a form which would work practically for this business? Well, if I do, let me pull it up out of the package that I have created and let me not forget that it is not me." And you use that, you see. That's good business. Hmm?

Yes, sir.

Does that help you, [Student J]?

Very much. Thank you, sir.

Oh, certainly, certainly. Nothing is more detrimental than concern. Self-concern is overidentification; it [goes] along with self-pity, you see. See, a person who permits themselves the luxury of concern is a person who is destined to pity and, of course, of themselves. You see? And a person who destines themselves that way is self-destructing. So there's good in all things. And when the self is finally destructed, well, they're off to another world, you see?

Yes. And [Student Y] has a question this morning.

Thank you. [Student J remarks.]

You're welcome.

Rather than to hope for better experiences to come into your life, what would be—

Yes.

—a better way to create the goodness in your life?

Well, I've said it a thousand times: "Put God in it or forget it." But, you see, for example, when you create something, you say, "Well, God, it's in your hands." See, just declare the truth: "It's in your hands." You see? "Class is in your hands. School is in your hands. My life and all of its goodness is in your hands. And because it's in your hands and because you are the law, known as the Principle of Good, I've just—when I think things aren't good, then all I've got to do is pause for a moment. I took them out of your hands."

You see, this business of bad experiences and difficulties and all of that is only when you steal from what you are and, by so doing, believe what you are not. You see? See, all of these things, they're stepping-stones. Declare—pause and declare the truth. When your mind tells you that things are not so good in your life, say, "Why? Oh, no, I took that away from God again. Now I give that right back to God." You see. You see, because you cannot help but face the truth that you are.

You only have this want, need, and desire because you stole it back from God. You see, your mind tells you, you gave it to God. Your heart tells you immediately when you stole it back. Do you understand that, [Student Y]?

Yes.

So, you see, instead of saying, "Oh, well, I'm feeling terrible and this is going that way and everything's going downhill and etc.," well, stop and say, "Ah! God, I give it back to you. In my ignorance I stole it once again." And don't let your mind play these tricks on you and say, "Oh, I'm so discouraged. I keep stealing it back from God, from the goodness that I am." Don't play those games. Do not permit yourself, your mind to use the wonderful Light and simple laws that you are learning against yourself. You see? Don't do that.

The mind is—mental substance is very cunning and very clever, you see. Cunningness is one of its basic functions, you see. So don't allow yourself such foolish luxuries when all you have to do is declare the truth: "In a moment of ignorance I stole it again. Here, God, I give it back to you." Now when, through practice, daily effort, the minute you say that, it happens in your consciousness, then you will know you're well on your way. You see?

You see, what the human mind says, you know, it's like—even working with my channel and he spent most all of his life in seeing the good in all things. Well, it's in his own best interest, as it is in everyone's own best interest. You see, then the mind likes to tell you, you know, "Well, you're just deceiving yourself. Look how terrible this is. Look at this! No matter what you do." No, no, no, no, no. See the good in all things. For, you see, that's what you can do for you. See the good in all things. No matter what comes and no matter what goes, see the good. Then you won't be discouraged. You won't quit before the victory. And you won't have all these other things that the functions, the four centers of consciousness, [offer you,] you see, in phase four. Right there: earth, fire, water, air. You see? And so don't, don't do that to yourself. When you have available to you to see the good in all things.

So what if someone says, in their mind, "Oh, what a stupid fool. Deceiving himself again." Look, if you want to call it "deception," is it better to deceive oneself into goodness or into misery and grief? If you want to call it that. *[Many students laugh.]* If you want to be—[if] you want to remain in belief, well, let's make an intelligent choice. I'm telling you that your world is ever the way you make it. Now you can make your world beautiful and good, but you have to work on that, you see.

You see, if someone else wants to be miserable and can only see the negative and disaster, be patient; you will see them collapse in time, you know. But, you see, you don't have to be a part of [that]. Your energies, which you require to maintain and to sustain that perspective in life of goodness, well, you see, you have your responsibility. Why let someone else who has another conception about life [affect you]? Because functions conceive. They do not perceive. Don't ever delude yourself, as [Student M] here; and I tried to help her this morning: to try to use a function to conceive a spiritual faculty. You don't conceive a soul faculty. You conceive functions and all that functions have to offer. You see, care is not something that is the domain of functions, that you can use to manipulate and control another person, you see.

And so it's up to you, you know. And if you expose yourself, through the laws you have earned, to people who are constantly broadcasting negativity verbally or just mentally in thought, then remove yourself from it in keeping with the law. And experience the goodness of life, you see. Because you have a mind, and so in that mind is experience. You understand that? Well, you also have a choice, you see?

So when you give it to God, don't keep stealing it back, you see. Because it only means you keep loaning it to him. Hmm? See? See, whoever sees the goodness in all things—if you would only understand, you see, that by so doing you consciously make the effort to raise your rate of vibration, your identification. What you do [is] you change what you identify with. When you identify with good, you can only experience the goodness in return. Do you understand that?

Now that doesn't mean, you see, that you're walking around with blinders on. You must be aware of the other and not identify with it. See, that's being in the world and not a part of the world. To be aware of your surroundings and identify with what you are, you see? You see, your world doesn't have to be the world that you observe. You understand? Your world becomes what you identify with. So if you choose, from lack of effort, to identify with disturbance, then so ye shall be disturbed. However, if you choose to observe it and, in keeping with personal responsibility, to be the instrument to correct it—don't identify with it. No matter how tempting. You see, it can only tempt your senses.

You see, a person is tempted by their senses. And when they make effort not to give in to them and not to sell out to their senses, in the early stages, you observe them as people who are frustrated. They are resisting, resisting the temptation or weakness that is their senses. Do you understand that? You see, that is not how I teach the student to evolve. I teach the student to express their senses and to gradually, through daily spiritual exercises, to gradually reduce their frequency, which reduces the identification with them, which is the bondage of believing that you are them. However, when, in their overidentification with mental substance, their mind convinces them they are greater than their senses, after spending a lifetime and eons believing they are their senses and they simply suppress them, then we have, anywhere in the world, all kinds of problems. You see? You see, recognize them for what they are, and treat them accordingly.

No one likes to go on to what you call a diet. And so a person, you know, taking a look at that, they don't want to make the effort to ration it—you understand that—until they can gain some perspective. No, they just want to take their thumb and their big, fat ego and they want to squash it down there, 'til it rises up to destroy them. *[As he speaks, the teacher holds up his thumb and seems to squash something with it just beyond the frame of the video.]* And they start all over again, you see. Hmm? I can always tell a person who has spent their time suppressing their desires, for when the law has been established, they reveal themselves how very weak they are. See? Suppression weakens the faculty of reason and strengthens the selfishness of greed. Hmm? Do you understand that?

Yes.

Why, certainly. Does that help with your question, [Student Y]?

Thank you.

Yes. And [Student N] has a question. Was that question on anything besides manicuring, [Student N]?

Yes.

All right. Then please speak it forth.

I was wondering about, if somebody's made a judgment about you and you said—

About me?

Well, about me. If somebody's made a judgment about me and—

No, no, choose me because I've had a lot of judgments. I've spent eons evolving through my—the job I earned on your planet as a judge. Yes, yes, speak about me. If someone's made a judgment about me—I love working with judgments because I've spent so much of my time in judgment. *[Several students laugh.]*

About—

I feel a bit qualified, yes. Someone's made a judgment about me. Go ahead, please.

Ah—

Well, you'll feel better if it's objective to you: [if] it's me instead of you. Go ahead.

Well, about a person then, about—

Yes, I'm a person. Go ahead. *[The teacher and Student N laugh.]* Well, I don't consider myself a bird, let alone a canary. *[Many students laugh along with the teacher.]* Not even a black crow. Yes. Maybe a peacock. Yes, go ahead, please. *[The teacher laughs again.]*

And you—how can you be more aware of not, not be—not being that judgment that they've made of you?

Oh, I don't have any problem with that. You mean of being—of not being what they judge that I am? *[Mr. Red, the church's dog, approaches the teacher.]*

Yes.

Well, I have no problem with that at all because I don't depend on them for my survival. You see, only if we, only if we want something out of them are we trapped by—oh, here you are, Mr. Red. Hello? There. *[The teacher offers Mr. Red a drink from a glass of water, but Mr. Red is not thirsty.]* Only—you don't want a drink of water this morning?! *[Mr. Red sometimes drinks from the glass of water set out for the teacher.]* See? There you are. Now I could take that personally, couldn't I? *[Some students laugh and then the teacher laughs.]* But I won't. Because I don't want anything out of him, you see, except, you know, as my channel says, "Except on my turf, he has to behave himself." You see, there are rules and regulations there.

Now. So the only reason that you could have any problem with becoming what someone judged that you are is your dependence upon them. And your only reason you could have dependence upon them is that you want something out of them. Yeah. Did that help with your question—your statement, [Student N]?

Statement? [Student N laughs.]

Well, you did ask the question, How can you be something besides what someone else has judged that you are? Isn't that the question that you asked—or the statement?

That's correct.

Isn't that correct?

Yes.

Well, I'm explaining to you. It's quite simple. If you do not want something out of that person that has made that judgment about you; therefore, not wanting something out of them, you are not dependent upon them. Therefore, you have no problem at all.

Well, what if you are dependent upon them in some way?

How could you be dependent upon them in any way, when you know very well what dependence will do to you? Isn't it your purpose of being in class to rely upon the Infinite Intelligent Energy that never faileth? *[After a short pause, the teacher continues.]* Isn't that the purpose of being here? So you wean yourself away from that dependence, which is simply servicing a judgment that you have created, a form you have created. Hmm? Yes.

You know, after all, your life doesn't come from them. You do understand that, don't you? The sustenance of your life is not dependent upon them. Your food, your roof over your head is not dependent upon them. And if you believe that it is dependent upon them in any way, it is something you have created in your mind. And because you have created it in your own mind and because it is your mind, you are not only responsible for your mind, you have the right to control whatever you create with your mind in your domain. So, you see, in the final analysis it goes right to our own mind and what we choose to create and not to create. And once having created it, putting it to sleep, doesn't it?

Correct.

You see, aren't you—don't you feel very encouraged that way?

Yes, I do.

You see? You see, it's not them. "Them" exist in here. *[The teacher points to his temple with index finger of his left hand.]* But that "in here", that's your domain, right?

Right.

That's where you created it, you see. Oh, they reflect it, in keeping with the law. You see, you see, how do we bring people in our life? "How did this person get into my life?" Well, you created that and in their weakness, you see, because they are not at that stage of growing up, they just fell right into the slot, you see. That's how that works. [You] say, "How did this person come into my life? I don't like this person now that I see what they really are." Well, you got to work on that which you have created, because that's how they got in. And, you see, the way to get them out is the way you got them in. Do you understand that? So you got them in a certain way in your thinking and believing that you are your thinking, which is the forms you create. That's how you got them into your life. Knowing how you got them in your life, you know how to get them out.

Knowing how you created a dependence upon them, you have no problem creating a freedom from that dependence. Do you understand that?

Yes.

Yes, because, you see, it's all inside of you. It always was. They are only reflecting what you have created. A person [who] comes into another person's life is simply the reflector of what the person has created. Hmm? Do you understand that?

Both persons.

Why, certainly. As water reaches its own level by its own weight, birds of a feather flock together. Hmm? Isn't that what they say?

Does someone else have a question here this morning? Yes, [Student D].

Could you explain the soul faculty of care?

Oh, the one that we just got through speaking [on]. *[The teacher laughs joyously.]* Yes, you are most concerned about the soul faculty of care? *[Many students laugh.]*

I would like—

Well, when the concern goes, care will come. All right? You see, they both can't occupy the same space at the same time, you see, entirely two diff—in your consciousness. You either got concern or you got care. They don't even mix. Like oil and water won't mix; care and concern won't mix. It has nothing to do with each other. They are two entirely opposite ends of the pole. So as long as you have concern for care, forget care. *[The teacher laughs again.]* Let's move on to the next question. Yes.

So much—it's so interesting how we—you know, it's not—I know that it's not what we are. I want *you* to know it's not what you are. How the human mind takes such a beautiful faculty as care, you understand, and understanding, and takes those beautiful spiritual faculties and tries to yank them back to concern. Look, as long as you are concerned, you're not in the faculties. Whether it's care, faith, poise, humility, duty, gratitude, tolerance, there's no way possible, you see. Concern is the fullness, *the fullness* of self-identification.

If you want to know what a ripe ego looks like: concern. That's a real ripe ego. It's reached the point just before it rots. *[Many students laugh.]* When it rots, we'll know something about care. *[The teacher laughs.]* But not until it goes back to where it came from.

Yes, [Student O], now that you're looking up this morning.
Thank you. Has man always required sleep? If so—
Sleep?
Yes, sir.
The functions require sleep.
The functions.
The functions. Not the faculties. They do not sleep. It's the functions that sleep, you see?
The functions.
So the more, the more you convince yourself that you are your senses, the more sleep you will require. And so, you see, if you start into concern, you see, the next thing you know [is], "Why, I only got ten hours' sleep last night. Oh, my God, what happened? I only got seven hours' sleep." You see—yes, because that is the domain—it is the functions that sleep. The functions require that, not the faculties. No, no, no, no, no. No, no, no. Well, for example, start being concerned about yourself and see how much sleep you require. Have you tried that?
Yes.
You can try that exercise if you want, [but] not around school, please. Yes, [Student Y].
Is instinct the same as belief?
Yes, it's controlled by creation. It is—instinct is designed to preserve the continuity of the species. So if you believe, of course, if you are concerned (overidentified with self), then you will go by your instincts and you will, of course, temporarily act like what you consider an animal acts like. Take it wherever you

can get it, no matter who it belongs to. Or haven't you seen two dogs on the same bone, yet? Hmm?

Yes, I have.

Oh, it's a most interesting experience. So are they good or bad? No, they are controlled by their instincts. The purpose of the instinct is the continuity of the species. Do you understand? Yes, [Student Y].

So you spoke of the ant crawling and the bird flying.

Yes.

That would be the same because they do that for survival.

Of course. They do it solely for survival. It is its only motivation. Their purpose, their instinct is survival. You see, that's impinged into their mental substance. They do that for survival. They are controlled by—well, we haven't got to that in these classes, yet. They are controlled by the governing spirit of that realm. Yes.

Would that be considered a pure motive?

The instinct? Certainly, because its purpose is the continuity of the species in creation, [which] is its only motivation.

You see, try to understand the animals, you see, in [that] respect, they have what you might consider an angel responsible for that species. Do you understand that? And so that angel [has] a hierarchy's responsibility, [which] is the continuity of the species on the particular planet on which it is on, you see. You see, they serve a very useful purpose. And that purpose, in the overall perspective, is a balance so that the planet may fulfill its purpose, for your planets are born and they grow and they grow up and they pass on. And they return to the source from whence they came. And all things on the planet, including the smallest little creature, is a part of that balancing, evolutionary process. And so a particular species on any planet, any particular planet, is, by the laws established by the hierarchy for the balance of the whole solar system, is—they have a responsibility for that, you see. And so the animal, when it comes to the impingement of the instinct for the continuity of the species, that is the animal's highest personal responsibility. Do you understand? You see?

And so for the human mind to observe the animal and to justify the slaughter of anything and everything that is in the way of its selfish desires is a grave ignorance and a grave injustice to the animal species who are controlled by that for population control and balancing of the planets in the universe.

You see, everything is like a chain. It's all interconnected and related, in that respect, in creation. So what affects one animal has an effect upon *everything*, you see. It does. It always has. And so man should make effort to study that.

Have you ever noticed that animals sleep a lot? Has anyone not noticed that animals sleep quite a bit? Now some sleep in seasons and they'll sleep for months. And they'll wake up for a short time and sleep for months again. You understand? They hibernate. Well, then you've got animals, domesticated animals—you know, there's one thing about domesticated animals: they sleep much longer than the so-called wild animals of the same species. Why do they do that? Does anyone know why they do that? Yes, [Student D] wishes speak to that.

Well, they would have more forms that we have contributed to them to—that would need feeding, right?

Correct. In keeping with what you understand as loyalty to their master, they have overidentified. You see, they have become dependent for their survival upon the hand of the human mind. Do you understand that? In that dependence, they have their price to pay. That includes an increased sleeping.

I don't know if any of you have noticed here with our little friend here, Mr. Red—he's up there. Whenever there's an upset of the forms, he will run away and disappear. Perhaps some of you have been aware of that. Because, you see, that's very draining on his energy. And he goes away, as far as he can get away from the forms, and goes to sleep to recover, to rejuvenate, you see. Yes. Does that help with your question?

Yes.

Yes. The more dependent an animal becomes upon the human animal, the more they're going to sleep and the more sleep they will require, depending—Yes. *[The teacher acknowledges a signal from the cameraman.]*—depending on the individual and how selfish they are and how many forms they create, you see. Yes.

And so an animal, you know, it has its instinct and its survival at stake. It has its personal responsibility to what you know as that instinct. The continuity of the species being its basic purpose. And so when it is aware of all of these forms draining all of this energy, it doesn't want its energy drained; so it will just go off someplace. You know, if it's—you know, the animals are awakened to different stages in consciousness, just like in the human animals. And so they'll go off for self-protection, you see.

You see, because the functions, you see, require protection and defense. Of course, the true being, the spirit, does not. But they do require that and they require ever-increasing amounts of sleep when they are exposed to these, all these selfish forms.

My, you know that an hour has passed so quickly. I look forward to seeing you again, then, next Sunday. And you have a real good day. And remember, the more thoughts you have, the more forms to feed. So silence is not only golden, it's indeed the path to go.

Thank you and good day.

AUGUST 24, 1986

A/V Class Private 61

Good morning, class, and student survivors.

The wings of angels are the glory of God. And so the statement judge not that you be not judged, for in so judging, do you experience what you know as need. Need, the denial of what you are, cannot be experienced until you judge. Now through your daily spiritual exercises, you weaken your awareness of what you are not and strengthen your awareness of what you are. The effect of that, of course, is freedom from the bondage of belief.

And so does the bird fly if his wings are clipped? Of course, the bird does not fly if its wings are clipped, for he has been denied the purpose of his own design.

I assure you that you cannot possibly experience need when you are doing your spiritual breathing and spiritual exercises daily, for in doing those exercises, you find less energy directed to what you are not. And so the mind says, "Well, if I experience no need, then where is the joy of living?" Remember that glory is the domain of what you are, your soul. And so you have been given that truth, "Free me from the needs of glory." *[This quote is from the Serenity song "Humble", which was given through Mr. Goodwin's mediumship. Please see appendix.]* It does not state to free you from glory, for that would be denying what you are. "Free me from the needs of glory." Need being an experience of judgment. Whenever we judge, we are in the domain of mental substance. That is where we experience what we understand as need. So for each judgment, we pay the price of the thrill of judgment and experience the excitement of our senses, that which we are not.

The difficulty that I have seen over these many years with students, in their struggle to free themselves from what they are not, is what they understand and know as fear. As long as we permit our self security in what we believe we possess, we will always experience fear, and we will always move to what we know as the void. Void, to our mind, means only something that we cannot control and we cannot manipulate because we cannot understand it with our mind.

We experience our activities, flux and flows, increases and decreases of our vitality. We can, through proper use of the exercises, be rejuvenated. The rejuvenation takes place when the awareness of what we are supersedes the awareness of what we are not.

To see the good in all things is in one's own best interest. For if one does not make the effort to see the good in all things, then one must pay the price of an overidentification with that [which], by its very design, exists and survives as a leach, dependent upon the energy, the vitality that anyone is receptive to at any moment. Understand that that which is soulless has no energy source of its own. It is dependent upon that which is an inseparable part of the whole of the intelligent life Energy. So whatever we form with our thoughts is a soulless creature. Its continuity is entirely dependent upon your awareness and identification with it. So when you form a judgment, you experience need for you have established the Law of Denial. And in establishing those laws, you direct your energy that you, your soul, the true you, are a part of.

Your form is not the source of energy. Your form is the effect of energy directed to limit or form. It is not the Source. This is why it changes. It comes; it goes. It knows so-called birth and death for it is not the Source itself. It is only the effect of energy directed to it. So a fool holds to form; a wise man knows that it is passing.

When, through your spiritual daily exercises, you slow down the rate of speed of the mental world you have created, when, through those exercises, you slow down that frequency, that rate of speed of your mind, as you slow it down, you increase your receptivity, your awareness of what you are and are rejuvenated.

For the accelerated speed of what you know as your mind is the movement of the many forms, soulless creatures, that you have created.

As you move from the darkness of limit or creation to the Light of eternal truth and abundant good that you are, you pass through the mist. If you do not keep your eye single, if you do not, through your daily efforts, become proficient in what you understand as concentration, then you will find that you will get to the border of the Light, but not pass into it. You will ever see the Light, but not return to what you are: the Light.

Concern, one of the realms through which this little class has been moving, the uneducated ego's insistence on manipulating and controlling that which is uncontrollable, like the storms of the seas that come and go, is passing. As I spoke to my channel early in your day this morning, the ship of Serenity has sailed around what you understand as the horn. There are a few storms. They always come and go. But the first voyage for [these] private classes, around the horn, has passed. You will find, as a class group, new, more pleasant experiences while in class. Our days of relationships have come and have gone. So encouraging, of course, to anyone who is interested in living and not just surviving. And that's why I greeted you this morning as my student survivors. For we're moving from that on to living in consciousness, through your daily efforts of your spiritual exercises.

You see, you have been given so many [exercises] and so varied, all in service to what you are, the Light. For we know that at times you identify in your life experiences with one realm, and in that realm there's no way possible, through your overidentification with the realm, that you will permit yourself to use that particular affirmation. We also know that we have given you other affirmations. So for some of you, in checking with you daily, I find this one says that affirmation sometimes. That one over there wouldn't think of saying that affirmation, because that one they are fond of. The affirmations that we are fond of reveal the realm through which we are passing and believe, temporarily, that we are. Therefore, many exercises, all beneficial, all in service to the Light that you are, have been given to you over the years.

I thought, perhaps, here the other week when I gave to you that beautiful little truth there—"Accept the possibility of experiencing the goodness that you are."—and then I spoke to you last week—"Do not hope for better experiences. Do not hope for good experiences."—that you would pause and discern what may appear to the human mind as a contradiction, that you would pause and think. *[Please see the appendix regarding the "I Accept the Possibility" affirmation.]* By thinking that you are perceiving a contradiction, you might think a bit more deeply and understand in your growing there is a vast difference between accepting the possibility of experiencing the goodness that you are and hoping to experience goodness in your life. You see, there's all the difference in the world between manipulating, which is the latter, [and accepting]. Hoping for better experiences; that's the realm of control and manipulation. Accepting the goodness that you are is the realm of truth that is demonstrable. So stop hoping for all these things in your life, and simply start experiencing them.

You're moving, slowly but surely, through the realms of consciousness. As a great man on your planet once said, "To be or not to be." That is a realm that's passing. Stop the foolishness: to be or not to be; that's the Law of Contradiction, which is the Law of Duality, which is the Law of Creation. Whenever you permit yourself contradiction in consciousness, you are directing the great, intelligent Energy that you are to what you are not. You are looking at the pebble and, by so looking at it, direct so much intelligent Energy to it, it becomes the Mount Everest in your world. That's what contradiction offers. Contradiction, the experience of contradiction outside only reveals the entertaining of contradiction inside.

Know what you want. There is no problem knowing what you want. There is no problem getting what you want. Getting what you want is to let go of what you think you are, so that you may be what you are. So when you find yourself fighting and in contradiction, remember, you are the house divided at that moment. And a house divided is not a house that is healthy; it is not whole, it is not complete, it is self-destructive. It is a house—it's like living in a house sound asleep, off in some slumber land in one of the realms, one of the dimmer realms, and the house burns down around you. That's what contradiction offers. It offers it to you individually and collectively.

So you see the goodness in all things; you move beyond the realm of contradiction. That doesn't mean that you sell out principle. For example, here, I spoke to my channel just here yesterday and again this morning. Orders had been left for your spiritual benefit that class number 59 does not exist. And therefore, because it does not exist, it is not recorded in your numerical class system. So your following class is number 60. And so you look at your little library, and you look at number 58, and you look at number 60, and you say, your mind says to you, "Fifty-nine is missing." Why, of course, it's missing! *You* were missing. It is a gentle reminder that on class 59, you were missing. Therefore, when you look at your library, you are reminded, that part of you that you are at times tempted to believe that you are, that, "On 59, I was missing." And so what happens in your consciousness—and this is the reason, that basic reason, you see, for not filling it in with the following class and totally forgetting about a class 59, and making some other class, class 59—you would not have that spiritual benefit.

You can tell each time you look at your little library. "What happened to 59?" Then those things that you have created, they don't like that. You see, the human mind must have things in the order where it judges it has control. So if you have a hundred or more classes—or less—and you look up, [and say,] "Fifty-nine? Where's 59?" And then those forms rise up; you become very frustrated and very upset because something's missing. There's always something missing to the uneducated ego. And what is that something? Remember, there's always something missing to the uneducated ego, and that something is the thing you can't control. So you if you're moving from number 58 to number 60, how are you going to control what doesn't exist? However, you see, it reminds you that that class number, "Oh, yes. I was missing that class. I'm a part of the whole student body. I can't say that [Student H] was missing; [Student Y] was missing; [Student O] was missing; [Student J] here was missing. *I* was missing, for I'm the one without the number." You see?

So let's move on now to your questions. And because there was so much controversy in the atmosphere, after I had given orders to my assistants that that class did not exist, because there was so much controversy in the atmosphere, I was indeed pleased. You see, there are times one can be objective and be pleased to witness the effect and the benefit, a spiritual benefit, for to the mind, it's phenomenal controversy. You see, when we are informed, our little minds say, "Ah, what I know, I have a possibility of controlling," for this is how the mind works, you see. But if it doesn't know why a number is missing, then it is very, very upset, you understand. And so here we have this lovely class today. Missing number, like a missing link, we'll always be reminded. Remember, the missing link was, is, and shall be number 59. And if you've done any study of what I brought to you years ago, you will know what that number reduces to and what it means. So does anyone know what 59 is? Yes, [Student L].

It's a five.

It's a five. And so what is five?

Faith.

Well, it's just the opposite of the thing that's upset—isn't it?—known as fear.

Yes.

Now let's go ahead with your questions. As I've always said, there's a reason for treason. Treason to the mind is absolute loyalty to the soul. Yes, [Student J].

When we do our breathing exercises and the affirmations and our meditation on a daily basis, will that generate more physical energy for us?

Yes, indeed, it will. It will rejuvenate us physically, for our awareness, you understand, is weakening in the support of the soulless creatures created by the human mind. Yes.

Then during the course of the day if we should experience a depletion of energy, would it be in our best interest to go through the breathing exercise and . . .

Absolutely! Absolutely. And, you know, I've always recommended—and still do—the benefits of twenty minutes [of] rest, as long as a person in the twenty-minute rest, that it's rest and not sleep, because if it's sleep, then the energy, you see, goes to more of the soulless creatures, the forms created by the mind, and those other realms, you see, and a person awakens depleted. I've always been a bit hesitant with anyone who does not practice the control of the mind, because I know they're not getting rest, and I know they'll wake up depleted. And how you—a good indicator is when you awaken in the morning, you see, and if you do not feel rejuvenated, then you may be rest assured that the energy, your vitality, was going to feed the forms that one has created, you see.

And so if you'll take, in the reclining position, approximately twenty minutes, and rejuvenate. You will not feel rejuvenated or refreshed unless before losing conscious awareness, you see, you have entered into the realm of what you are, you see. But that is indeed most beneficial. A person becomes extremely depleted when they are exposed to many soulless creatures. Remember that the strongest soulless creatures are the ones created from a person's belief that they are in need. You see, because remember, now, all judgments, you see, all these forms are created in the water center, you see. That's where they're formed, you see.

Yes, sir.

In fact, your planet reveals all of that, whether it's physical or mental. Everything is created in what you understand as the emotional center, in the water center, you see. There [is] earth, fire, water. So, you see, the effect of earth and fire, of flesh and blood, is the birth of the water center. Well, we all know that; same principle, same laws take place in the mental worlds.

And so when you expose yourself to what you understand as controversy and emotional upheaval, then you are dealing with forms that are very strong [and have been] born from judgments and beliefs that a person is in need. You see, the forms of denial are the greatest forms of all in the strength of force, you see, not in power, but in force. And so you have so many of these forms as effects of people's denial of what they are. Yes, does that help you with that question, [Student J]?

Yes. So then we are—when we are depleted of energy, then we just should go right into . . .

We should before the depletion gets to the point that it has a detrimental effect upon our physical body. Yes. There is a certain point, and if one does not pause and stop at that danger point, then one goes over, and their health goes down, you see, yes.

Thank you.

You're welcome. Yes, [Student M], please.

Yes. I would like to have a little more understanding on the border of the Light. And you spoke about the—

Oh, yes, in the border of the Light. Many people go to the border of the Light and they don't go into the Light because, you see, there's something missing that they can't figure out with their mind. And they know they can't control it. And because they believe they are that, then they don't go in. Yes, yes. You see? You see, fear rises up and they believe that they are the fear. And because they believe that they are the fear, they won't make the next step.

You see, that's like walking, for the mind; it's like, in the darkness, walking, [and] you know that there's a cliff. You don't know how close you are to it. You cannot see it. You cannot sense or feel it with the senses, with the mental realm. Will you continue on, knowing that the Light is in front of you, knowing that there is a cliff there? And so you're always faced with your choice between the mind's control (fear) and faith. You will always be faced with that. Everyone is faced with that. That is the step that everyone makes, you see.

See, if you have put it in God's hands, if you are convinced that there's an intelligent Energy of which you are an inseparable part, what could possibly fall? [Only that which] is controlled by the laws of gravity and the laws of creation. If you have grown in consciousness to that step (that you are not creation), therefore you, that which you truly are, cannot be controlled by the laws of creation, then you will continue on following the Light, through the midnight. And how soon or how late the cliff comes and your form steps over and goes down with it, it doesn't matter. You are not concerned, for you know beyond a shadow of all doubt that you are not the limit, which is the Law of Creation. So when you evolve to that state in consciousness, you will move on. There is no obstruction.

Yes.

Yes.

Thank you.

Does that help with your question? [Student Y] has a question, please.

Thank you. When you say—you use the word controversy, *but do you mean difference of opinion?*

Difference of opinion is one thing. Controversy is something entirely different. First of all, controversy—a person entering the realms of controversy is absolutely convinced that they are right, you see? Now when we are convinced that we are right, we are also under the law of conviction of being right, [and] we are equally wrong. And so the mind moves from yes to no. Do it; don't do it. Doubt and fear, that is what it offers. Now that's a vast difference from a discussion of what you call different views. It's entirely different. You see, an opinion is an expression of judgment and is established under the Law of Duality. So when you are absolutely convinced that you are right, you establish and guarantee the law to bring into your life someone who is equally convinced that you are wrong, you see?

Now outward manifestations are revelations of inner attitudes of mind, as my student, [Student J], is so fond of that lovely statement [given] some years ago. And so, you see, when, through your absolute conviction that you are right, you do not permit the Law of Duality, which is governing it, to rise up and tell you, you are wrong equally, as it has told you, you are right. That law comes to you out of the universe in the form of another person and tells you, you are absolutely wrong. Then, through hindsight—you know, when our hindsight becomes our foresight, we gain insight—then, through hindsight, you say, "I never would have believed it, but I really was wrong. The person was really right."

So, you see, this is what takes place. If you are in a realm, an evolution where your mind will not allow the controversy to express itself, in the sense that you are absolutely right [and] there's no room for the possibility of you being wrong on something, then through the law that like attracts like, you will pull that to you so you may—the law may be revealed to you. That's a Law of Duality. That's a Law of Creation. That's not what you are. So therefore, it is not a beneficial vibration or level of consciousness. It cannot be in any way beneficial in your spiritual endeavors, only to serve as a stepping-stone, you understand. But to experience the spiritual realms of consciousness, you will have to move beyond what is known as the realm and the Law of Controversy. Yes, does that help with your question, [Student Y]?

Thank you.

You're welcome. [Student O], yes.

I didn't have a question.

Good. That's good. I'm so happy, [Student O], that you got it all settled in your notebook this morning. That's very good.

Thank you.

You're welcome. Yes, [Student D].

I have a question on retaliation.

Retaliation?

Yes.

Yes.

We have talked about how we retaliate against someone else for things that we judge [have] been done or not done.

Yes?

Do we—does our form sometimes retaliate against us?

Well, they first retaliated against us before we can express it. You see, whatever we express is first taking place inside. There's no way of expressing it until it has taken place inside. So we first retaliate against our self by believing we are the judgment that we have formed, you see, that soulless creature. See, that's what a judgment is: a soulless creature. Thought forms, they're soulless creatures, you see. And so whenever we enter or over-identify and we have a full awareness of self, you know, and this great self, self-awareness, you see, then we just want to be honest with our self. You see, all of those things must be fed. They're hungry. They're always hungry. They always have need. How could they have anything but need, when they're born of denial? You see?

You see, you cannot give birth to a form under the law—and the purpose of its original design is denial. That's how it is born. You see? A judgment is born out of denial. That's how it's created, you see? So whenever we enter into that realm where we've created it, that's what it has to offer us: denial. The effect of denial is need. [It] denies the Light, the Truth, you see. You see, [if] you create a soulless creature, its only survival is energy. Its only continuity is denial, for it is created to serve that purpose. Hmm? And so when you identify with that form you have created, then you experience need, for you are now identifying, whether you're consciously aware of it or not, with a form you have created that is denial.

See, here's the form. You identify with it. Here's a form of denial—right?—the effect of your judgment. Judge not that you not be judged. The payment is so great. Here is, here is the form you have created—all right?—the effect of your judgment. Now that form—and its purpose of design is denial. So when it talks to you, you experience need. That's what it has to offer you because, you see, the effect of denial is need. So here's the form of denial you've created as an effect of your judgment. And you turn around and think of that realm where you have created it, and you have this wonderful experience known as need. And so the more need you have, the more forms that you have created, that you insist on going in there and feeding [them] energy. They have nothing to offer you, except need, for they are the forms of denial, the effects of the judgments that you have taken pride in making, you see.

You see, I spoke to you about the wings of the angels are the glory of God, do you understand? Well now, the forms of denial, they are the thrill of the senses. And you know who controls that. They're his servants, you see, yes. And so you want to understand when you insist on letting one of those forms you have created from your judgments, the form being known as need, the effect—I mean, the form being known as denial, the effect being known as need, when you speak out constantly, need, need, need, you increase these forms of denial and you thrill in your senses. You get this false thrill, you see, to your senses; not to what you are, only to what you are not. And so you feel this excitement and this sensation. That's the payment for judgments, you see. Yes, I do hope you've carried on through that.

Yes, [Student Y] has a question on that—and [Student U].

Would the wings of the angels, would that be thoughts that fly?

Yes. You see, they fly in the sense that that's symbolic of their freedom, you see. You see, when you permit yourself to believe you are the thrill of the senses, you've clipped the wings of the angels of God of your own soul because, you see, from your belief that you are the thrill and the excitement of your senses, you deny what you are. Do you understand that?

You see, it's one thing to be aware that your toe itches; a mosquito or something has bit you. Fine. That could be a thrill or an excitement, depending on what you do with your judgments. Do you understand that? You see? So it's all taking place inside. It always has; it always will, yes. And then, of course, we're always destined to meet someone, like attracts like, becomes the Law of Attachment, 'til we have whole universes of them.

Does that help with your question, [Student Y]? Now [Student U] has been waiting here. And I'll be with you [shortly].

How is it that suppression weakens the faculty of reason? Does that fall under the last—

Suppression? Why, certainly. What happens with suppression? What do you do with it? Say that you have a form that is plaguing you, one, of course, that you have created, an effect of your judgments, and you take and just shove it down, and you don't work and educate it. What happens to it?

It rises again.

Well, does it rise more hungry or less hungry?

More hungry.

It only gets, it only gets fed and it only receives energy when you believe that you are it and let it have its heyday, doesn't it?

Yes.

And the more you let it run wild, the greater feast it has. So when you suppress it, it's like putting it in prison. It hardly gets bread and water. So when it does get a chance to come up, well, then look what happens. So, you see, of what benefit to the light of reason can suppression possibly be?

None.

Did that answer your question?

Yes, sir.

Yes, certainly. [Student N] has a question. Yes, [Student N].

Yes. I was wondering—you said when we go into the Light and step off the cliff, does that mean we lose, well, will we stop identifying with physical form, or can we still function in—

Why, yes, you just can't control what is. *[The teacher laughs joyfully.]* You see, there's no possible way of controlling that which one is. One ever works to control that which they are not; and one is always frustrated in their efforts to control what they are not. One tries to control the aging process of the form. You know, [in] your world, you do all kinds of things and spend a fortune to control what you understand in your mind as an aging process. You do everything to stop it. And yet—well, I don't want to say that. But it doesn't work. *[The teacher and a few students laugh.]* The wind's blowing the other way. Yes, but you do everything to stop it. You see, your hair turns and your skin and your flesh, it all goes through its changing process, you see. Yet you still try to control it and are frustrated in the process. Hmm?

Thank you.

It only shows you who's really in charge of it. That's creation. And he's much greater than you. Hmm? He is the king of creation. You are visiting his realm.

Try to understand that in your awareness of limit, you are in his realm; he has certain established laws. You will abide by his laws in his realm, as long as you insist on believing that you are limit. Do you understand that?

When you say we insist on believing, and yet we have to believe to be here.

Oh, oh, oh, I think if you will, once again, review your class, you will find there are moments when—and that's the point of your spiritual exercises—when you come out of that believing and then you enter that realm with some objectivity.

OK.

You see? You see, you can tell in creation quickly how objective you are [by] how you react to something, you see? If you still depend on the old king below, then you have a lot of problems with your actions; they all turn out to be reactions. Did that help you, [Student N]?

Yes, it does a lot.

Yes, you see? You see, one of the quickest revelations of how much we are in service to that realm, by believing that we are it, and without objectivity, is concern. The more concerned we are, the more we reveal how much we absolutely insist on believing we are that realm. You see, you can be in a thing and not a part of a thing. You can be with the world and not a part of the world. That's known as being objective, you see. "I am in the form. I am not the form. I am not a part of the form. That which is the form is the domain of creation. That is not what I am. That is what I use. The thought that I form is not what I am. It is a form that I am using. For I have temporarily slipped in my consciousness in what is known as need." You see, each time you seek a thrill, you must pay the price. For the experience of the thrill of the excitement is the energy, your vitality, that you are feeding to the form of the judgment you have created, which is the denial of what you are, and what you understand as the fullness of your needs. Do you understand that?

So when you are thinking, "Oh, I need this and I need that. Oh, I need all of these things," well, just remember this, remember what you are doing with your life: those soulless creatures, you're making them even stronger, you see. You cannot need anything when you are in truth everything. Hmm?

So you were saying—

You're that which sustains it. Yes.

So you were saying earlier today to enjoy life, know that you have everything that you desire. So that—

Desire is the divine expression. The limiting of it is the thrill of man's senses. Now do you understand that?

All right. Thank you.

Does that help you?

Yes.

You see? You see, man gets his little tidbit, known as a thrill, from limiting the divine expression, which is known as desire. In other words, based upon the forms he has created, he says, "Well, I'll have this experience or that experience this way, that way," and all of this censorship and all of these conditions, you understand.

Yes.

The difference between conditional and unconditional surrender to what you truly are. Hmm?

Thank you.

So if you want to surrender to what you truly are with a mountain of conditions, then joyously pay the price of the conditions, you see? You know, a person says, "Well, I'd like to sing. I am a singer. Well, I'd like to have more opportunity." They get an opportunity to sing at the corner drugstore at the sundae counter and, oh, that's way beneath them. Do you understand that? So, you see, those are conditions they place on what they want.

You see, the experiencing of the goodness of life and the problems that the human mind says it has with it is all the conditions it places upon it. And each one has their own set of conditions. This one wants to get married. That one [doesn't] want to get married. And someone else wants something else and something else. And then you say, "Oh, is that all you want?" "That's all that I want." So it appears, [and they say,] "Oh, no. They're only 5 feet. I wanted [someone who is] 6 feet 2. And blue eyes? No, no, no, I wanted brown eyes. No, no, no. I wanted but—" Oh, it is ridiculous. It is just totally ridiculous. *[Several students laugh.]* How could we possibly cry at such a beautiful universe? Oh, that foolishness, it's just pure foolishness.

It's like I had my channel say to one of my students some time ago, "Oh, you want, you're in need of affection? I will give you some affection. I'll affect you with my boot. Let me go get them put on." I told them. Definitely. It is ridiculous! Such a, such a total waste of such a beautiful world, you see.

You see, look at it as what you think you want with your mind, you see. [You] say, "All right. That's all I want." And then you get an opportunity to sing at the corner drugstore and see how quickly you take it. Oh, by the way, they're not going to pay you, because it is for the Boy Scout benefit week. *[The teacher laughs joyfully.]* Perhaps the Girl Scouts or whatever. *[The teacher continues to laugh.]* Yes, [Student Y], do you see?

So the spiritual exercises—what—could you say that that's like an, that's like an armor, so to speak, that one can, like a coat of armor to go into the . . .

Why, certainly, because, you see, it weakens what you are not. It weakens this energy flowing from you to the soulless creatures you have created. You find yourself with less belief that you are your judgments. You will find yourself with less need, until it totally disappears from your life. Do you understand that, [Student Y]?

So, you see, you have all of those benefits to reap. Of course, you will not have as much thrill of judgments, you understand. You won't have that wonderful thrill that's so wonderful to the senses. You won't have that excitement and thrill of the senses, you see. You'll have to pay that price, but you will have the peace inside. Yes.

So one could say that it is a protection. These—

Certainly.

—actually do protect you from . . .

From those realms. They most certainly do. You see, they shut off the flow of energy going towards them because it weakens your awareness of them. Whatever you weaken your awareness to, which is dependent upon you for its continuity, sooner or later, it doesn't even have enough energy—the forms, those hollow forms that you have created—to even move, you see? That's when they go to sleep. It's the sleep of starvation, yes. *[The teacher laughs.]*

Time is passing quickly now. If you have any more questions—if my cameraman is awake over here. You know what time it is? Good. That's good.

Yes, [Student P].

Ah . . .

I was in hopes you'd scratch your heart, instead of your head, before you asked the question. *[The teacher and a few students laugh.]* One should not hope for things in creation. *[The teacher and many students laugh again.]*

In relating to the mind visually, well, like you were describing how we get to the border of the Light and we have to go through the mist, and then . . .

Oh, no, we're in the mist. We're already in the mist, yes. We see the Light through the mist, you understand. Oh, we do see that. It's in front of us.

Uh-huh.

You see? It's always in front of us.

Right.

Oh, yes. Don't worry about any lights behind you. It is always in front.

OK.

Right in front. You see, you're in the mist, like a great fog, you see. Yes, go ahead. And you're walking towards the border, where the Light is shining from, yes.

OK. So then the mind has a tremendous fear of letting go of the forms and the attachments of what it thinks it—

Well, the mind—yes, of course, the mind gives you the sensation, the sensation that you call fear.

Uh-huh.

Tell me something, how many of you get excited over faith? *[The teacher laughs joyously.]* Please don't tell me that you do. I know better. Faith is not an excitement or a stimulation of the senses. Only fear stimulates the senses. Hmm? Yes, go ahead. You're in fear now, you said.

OK. So then . . .

Your senses are full[y] stimulated.

Uh-huh.

Well, do you believe you are your senses?

No.

Well, then you have no problem; you step right on.

Uh-huh.

And all those limits and forms you've created, they all fall down, because that's where they came from. Everything returns to its source. All senses return to the source from whence they have risen, you see. All things return to their source. So to permit yourself to believe you are your senses is a terrible losing battle.

Uh-huh.

You know, some people slowly, begrudgingly become aware of it in their sixties and seventies, you know. Some a little earlier, you know. And some, why, even in their forties they're too old to cut the mustard anymore and they have those early experiences, don't you see?

So it's returning to its source. You can't stop it. You see, that's one thing: you cannot control it. To believe that you are something that you desire to control and cannot control, and go through life living that way, well, it's indeed frustrating, wouldn't you say?

Oh, it's definitely frustrating.

Well, there's no possible way you can possibly control what you are not. You are not that. You see, it proves it. It proves itself to you daily. Now you get the thrill and the stimulation, the excitement of what one likes to believe that they are, but then time marches on. And you soon find out it's not there anymore. It was in the head all the time anyway, and even there it's getting less. Hmm?

Yes, it is.

Now what was that with your question, now? You're passing through the mist. The Light's in front of you. And you don't know what second that that which you used to believe that you are is going to disappear. Because it's going back to the source it came from.

Right.

There is no possible way that anyone can go against the divine, immutable laws. Whatever comes from a source shall return unto the source from whence it has come. So all your senses, all the thrills, all the excitement, and all those things go back, for that's where they have come from, by the law.

So it's just separating yourself from the form and—

Certainly. And not permitting the mind to tell you that you need this or that because, in so doing, you [are] still under the control of those things.

Under the law of duality and limit.

Well, not only that, you're still getting the thrill of the judgments because, you see, the judgments, created by the mind, deny the truth. That's what a judgment does: it denies. Now God is total acceptance. The divine will, the will of Goodness is total acceptance. So you create a judgment; you experience the thrill and the charge to the senses—do you understand that?—by denying the truth of what you are, and you experience—they offer you that experience of what you understand as need.

So if you—yes. *[The teacher acknowledges a signal from the cameraman.]* If you do want to continue on to have this, this sensation, if it is your desire to continue to have the thrill and the excitement and the sensation of the senses, continue to judge, and it is guaranteed you will continue to have the thrill and the sensation of the frustration of not getting what you want because you believe you are that which you are not. Hmm? So, you see, it works just beautifully. So that's all you have to do.

And time will march on and then you will gradually see: "Oh, what's the matter with me? I'm not getting as much excitement as I used to." You're getting just as much thrill and just as much excitement, only as you get older and, slowly but surely, cannot manipulate as well, then you are still getting the sensation and the excitement and the thrill: it's known as total frustration, you see. Prior, when you're younger, it's known as something else. But later in life it becomes known as frustration. But it's still the same principle. The same law is working. It still affects you, you know.

You see, what a person calls affection when they're sixteen is a vast different thing when they're sixty. Hmm? Now, however, they're still affected. It just has a different form. That's all, you know? You see? You see, you can boot a person in the butt and they are affected. It's not the same as a honeymoon when you're thirteen, though, is it? But it is still the same because you are still affected. The principle of affection does not change. See, affection is affection. That which affects you is affection. It doesn't mean a kiss. It can mean a boot. Hmm?

Time is up. I must say good day. You have a good week. There's no reason why you shouldn't. And if you don't—any of you don't have a good week, it's simply because your thrill, the effect from judgment, is greater than your love of God and the joy thereof. And I know that's just foolhardy.

Thank you. Good day.

AUGUST 31, 1986

A/V Class Private 62

[This class was recorded outdoors in the garden of the temple, near the east pond and the pump running the waterfall was on, which sometimes made complete transcription of some of the students' remarks difficult.]

A good day, class.

Today marks the class of application.

We cry as we see the obstructions in our path and rejoice when we view the way. And so because we all know the way, we all rejoice. And that marks, this day, our class of application. Application of what we have learned is viewing the way.

Refusal of viewing the way and insistence on seeing the obstruction is not the Law of Application. And today, this class begins its walk on the path of application.

Solution is what you know as the opposite of a problem. So solution is viewing the way. Problem is seeing the obstruction. Now we cannot see the obstruction without identifying with what we know as self, for it is only in our believing in self that we see obstruction, for that is when we separate our self from the whole that we are.

And as I have just stated, you all have been given and all know the way. Therefore, application—it is not something you are waiting to do. It is something you do. It is not something that requires defense. It is not something that requires justification, which is defense. It is something that you do.

Now some of you may say to yourself, having overidentified with yourself, that you cannot view the way; you can only see the obstruction. That is not what you do from this moment on.

Viewing the way is an effect of your daily application of your breathing exercises and your spiritual affirmations. The lack of doing that is seeing the obstruction, the effect of denying the whole that you are.

Now we'll take a few moments for your questions on this beautiful day in your world. Kindly rise, if you have a question. *[After a short pause, the teacher continues.]* It is so nice, if I will only pause and see, instead of view, that you all view the way, for no one seems to have a question. Therefore, that reveals that no one has a problem. No problem, no question. Only solution.

Yes. [Student Y], please.

Thank you. Could you describe more fully when it is said love, the love of one's judgments—like, in terms of if you're having money problems and you . . . There's something in there that I don't understand. I don't understand what you mean.

Yes, and what could that be for you?

It's the, it's the wording that I don't quite know what you mean when you say . . .

Seeing the obstruction?

I understand that.

Viewing the way?

That, I understand.

All right. Now, [Student Y], stop and think. We see with our mind. We view with our soul. We view what we are. We see what we are not. Now we see when we think of what we understand as self. That's when we see. When we no longer think of self, we start to view. Therefore, if a person says they have a problem, that problem exists only because they think of self. When they do their exercises, they move from seeing to viewing. When that takes place, there are no obstructions for they view the way.

Viewing the way has been given to you students for some time, especially in these private classes. So viewing and seeing is only a matter of choice of a human being. For example, when one is seeing, as an effect of overidentifying with themselves, then one has the breathing exercises and the various spiritual affirmations to move them from seeing, the effect of overidentification with self, to viewing.

Now when we view, we see clearly. We view. And we therefore know clearly what the obstruction is. We know the form that exists in the human mental substance that keeps us from what it is that we desire that is within the realm of our rightful, just domain. Go ahead, [Student Y].

So when you say—so it's the seeing the obstruction that causes the love of the judgment. So—

The love—the overidentification with self is the love of the judgment or forms that one has given birth to and has created. Yes. And the judgments are the obstructions when one is seeing, the effect of overidentification with their mind. Yes.

OK. So with the daily exercises, the application of that and the breathing, then whatever is hidden from you will be revealed.

Yes, indeed it will. That which is hidden will be revealed that you may view it clearly. Therefore, in that viewing, you will know beyond a shadow of any doubt which judgment-form, created, exists within the consciousness of mental substance that you must remove by no longer identifying with. Yes.

Yes, for example, you see, the functions are not a problem to the viewer. Functions, undeveloped faculties, are only a problem to he who sees. They are not a problem; they are a solution to the viewer. They are a problem to the seer.

For example, the movement of your hand is a physical—is a movement of a physical being. It's a function. The physical hand is not required by the faculties for expression. The physical hand becomes a problem when one sees it as their hand; one does not view it as a vehicle through which they may express and evolve the functions, which are undeveloped faculties. For the hand can be used as an instrument for inspiration, which is a faculty. From a view, it is a faculty. From a seeing, it is a function. Do you understand that?

Yes.

So, you see, it can be used to evolve the funct[ions], the undeveloped faculties into functions [faculties]. *[The teacher may have misspoken and said "functions" instead of "faculties."]* Or it can be used as the obstruction. It is dependent on your application of the spiritual exercises and affirmations and teachings that you have been given. Should your hand not serve you well, it means that your hand is, to you, an obstruction, not a solution. Therefore, you should remove your hand, which is an obstruction, in order that you may experience the solution.

The functions are not to be considered bad. They are in the domain of mental substance only through your identification with their limit, which is then a servant of the judgments that you have formed. For example, through identification with self, if you say, "My hand—I cannot do this with my hand." Then, your hand is now in service—you understand that?—to the darkness, to the limit. It is only in service to the limit in keeping with its service to the judgment of your mind that you have created, you see.

This is why functions are considered and are in truth undeveloped faculties. It is dependent on what you do with the function whether or not it is in service to creation or it is in service to the Light that you are. It is not the function that is bad; it is your use of the function. You use it to evolve it as an undeveloped faculty or you use it to bind you in service to the need of glory. For all judgments, limits, are servants of the need of glory.

You see, Lucifer, having experienced the glory of God, having sat at the right hand of God, through his own seeing, saw God and saw himself. He moved from viewing the God that he is, the united whole, to the separation of the individual uniqueness. Do you understand that? So when he made that movement, he descended. He earned from that descent a realm of his own—limited. Therefore, when one believes—through overidentification with limit, one believes they are limit; then the vehicle they have, which is an expression of the functions—do you understand?—designed to be a servant of the Light for the evolution of the undeveloped faculties known as functions, then one is limited.

So you speak of money or you speak of anything that you desire. You see, as I've stated so many times, give it to God, that which you have stolen. For example, a person says, "I have money problems." That is the deception of the mind. The problem is quite simple: one has identified with self and that which they have created. Do you understand? The effect of servicing what they have created is known to them as a problem.

Is there any other question there, [Student Y]?

No. Thank you.

Yes, [Student N], please.

After you're viewing and you are inspired—

Yes.

—I have a problem with timing, the timing of events.

Yes, timing is a problem for timing belongs to mental substance. Time does not exist in truth, you see. You see, one who has time consciousness, has time value, is one who has a very limited, very, very short patience.

You see, we always get what we really want. We believe that we don't get what we really want because we have a love of time consciousness which belongs to mental substance. Do you understand that?

Thank you.

You see, if you look over your life, you will see, over your past life and your record, you will see, "Yes, I got what I wanted. It took a long time coming, but I did get, in keeping with the law of my own divine right, I got what I wanted. I got the experience. I didn't like it, but I got it. And I have moved through it." So, you see, if you permit yourself a value of time consciousness, then what you are doing is seeing. And obstructions can only exist in what you understand as time consciousness. For what is an obstruction today to the mind is a solution tomorrow in keeping with the law of the time-consciousness value that one has, through identification with self, created. I'm sure you'll want to listen to our little tape, because there's many things to consider. Is there anything else with the question?

Not at this time. Thank you.

Yes. Thank you. Not at this time because we are in a world of limit in our consciousness in order to have mental expression. That's very wise. You are absolutely correct, [Student N]. Thank you.

Remember, bewilderment is a[n] expression in the human mind, for it does not have, to the mind's satisfaction, the solution. You will not be bewildered for long, for the solution is before you. And as you listen to your little tape, you will understand that. It might take—I don't want to put a limit on it—but fifteen times. But that's all right. It's worth it. Go ahead, [Student N], if you had another question.

You answered it. Thank you.

You're welcome. Yes, [Student S] here.

Yes.

Try a [Student S] east and [Student N] west here. *[The teacher laughs joyfully. Two students in these classes had similar first names; one was seated more to the east, while the other was seated to the west.]* Yes. But remember that those who are in the west are destined to the east, you see. Everything returns unto that which it comes from, [Student S]. Yes, [Student S] east here, yes.

Thank you.

You just go ahead.

Last week you spoke that we have fear at the border before we enter the Light.

Yes?

And in other classes you spoke of, like the cliff before stepping out into the void.

Correct.

Could you please discuss that a little bit more for us?

Yes, that's very appropriate to our class today on application. This is our class: from this moment on, we apply, you see.

And so as we go to make that movement—and this is the day, this is the day we make that movement that we step over that cliff. For some of us, we consider the function money, for other[s], we consider it something else. This is the day that we move on from now on. All right.

We already understand that fear is mental substance's way of controlling that which we are. We already have had that teaching. And we already understand that. Now when we experience fear, it is a sensation in our functions. You understand that, don't you?

Yes.

Now with that sensation, however, there's a form; there's a thought. Usually several. Do we all understand that? You cannot experience the sensation that you know as fear without a form that is in the consciousness, a judgment. And usually there are several. So when you experience fear, be awake, aware, and alert of the form, not just the sensation. You will see that form. That's the purpose of these higher teachings, is for you to see that form. You look at that form, for that is what you have created.

Now that form will tell you several different things. And usually there are several of those forms. "If I do this, that, that, and that may happen." That increases the fear, the sensation of what you call fear. Do you understand that? "Therefore, I must back off into the security of this judgment that I have created and that I have served for so long in my life. For this form I have created offers to me the security of familiarity. I am familiar with them."

It's like a woman who's married, and she goes to face a separation. And she has these experiences that she understands as fear. And she has these judgments rise up, and they tell her,

"Well, what will you do if he leaves?" Do you understand that? "What will life be like?" You do not have the security of familiarity of what your life will be like. It tells you it will be different. It presumes, if it doesn't want to let go of the form you have created, it presumes [and] tells you, through presumption, that it will be miserable. It will be this way. It will be that way. You will have to do this. You will have to do that. You won't get along as well. That's how it keeps control over you.

Now these classes are designed for you to move, to evolve, to change. If you do not make changes, you cannot continue with this type of class and the exposure thereto. For example, we have already—all of you had experience with one of my students being dismissed—who is here today—being dismissed. Because of the increased light of awareness, those forms, judgments created, rose up in phenomenal fear, the sensation of fear. Do you understand? So if you do not apply the Light that you receive, your destiny is you will remove yourself, through an overidentification with mental substance, from the Light that you have earned.

The only thing that stands between you and the Light that you are, are the judgments that you believe that you are.

And so you are moving on and over this. The cliff is before you. If your value for the judgments you have created is greater than your evolution and your desire for freedom and truth, then you will back off, and you will go back to the familiarity and the security of what has been in your life. As I say, it's like a person being married and facing the light of reason that in order to continue with some degree of peace and harmony and goodness in their life, they must separate. At the moment of that awareness, all the judgments rise up and you experience fear.

You see, that which you give is that which you gain. That which you desire is that which you lose. So it is in your giving. When you give your judgments, when you give what you have created, you gain what you are. In other words, you gain the reawakening of what you are when you give what you have created. Now I am speaking of the judgments you have created in your mind; when you give those, you gain what you are and all of the goodness that what you are truly is. You cannot regain that until you give what you have created, for what you have created in the consciousness is a limit. You see, creation is limit. That's what it is. You are that which is greater than creation, for you have created it. As long as you believe that you are what you have created, you will always see problems; you will not experience solutions. Does that help with your question, [Student S]?

Yes. Thank you very much.

Yes. Yes, [Student M].

Yes. In last week's class, it was stated, I believe this is right, that it is, treason to the mind is loyalty to the soul.

Yes, it's very, very good you brought that up at this very moment. Treason to the mind is loyalty to the soul, that which you are. When you face your mind, through thinking of yourself, you face all that you have created. When you choose to no longer have your security in what you have created, when you choose that (to no longer serve what you have created), to what you have created, that is treason; to what you are, that is loyalty. Do you understand?

Yes.

You see? Now remember, what you have created is created in the water center of consciousness. Whenever it is threatened, water flows. You call that tears. You see, you see, that which you have created (a judgment) defends itself in the very realm that it has been created. And so when it is threatened, that which you have created with your mind, from overidentification with your mind, known as self, you see, when it is threatened, you react. You react with the center in which it was created. That center is the water center, you see.

Correct.

Now if that does not serve that created form well—try to understand—it will descend even deeper, into the fire and the earth center[s], you see?

You see, you have all of these classes. Now you must question so that you will have even greater understanding of how it works, you see. Do you understand that? *[After a short pause, the teacher continues.]* Pardon?

Yes, I do.

Have you ever noticed the use of the water center at times that I use it here for my channel? And always use it when, when I am leaving? Why do you think I do that? *[At the end of every class, as the teacher is about to depart from Mr. Goodwin's physical form and Mr. Goodwin is about to return, the teacher drinks from a glass of water.]* Why do you think that I use that water? Why do I use the very element of the substance of judgments? Why do you think I use that?

Well, to identify. Some degree—

Well, I have to leave; he's got to be brought back, through identification, or you won't find his form on your planet very long. *[The teacher laughs joyfully.]* My goodness. Yes. Without water, your form, as you know it on your planet, doesn't exist.

That's true.

Do you think that the creatures on your deserts exist without water? You see, well, it doesn't rain there, there's no water. There is moisture in the atmosphere. There is sufficient moisture for those creatures to live. Do you understand that, [Student B]? You see? That's one of the centers of the realm of creation. Yes. And so— *[The teacher coughs.]* Excuse me. When what you have created is threatened, the feminine way—as I've been speaking to my channel for you people to move out of this femininity foolishness—the feminine way is the flow of the water.

Now the electric way (the masculine way) is the fire. And so usually when you're speaking to a man, when there's the masculine entity in control, he expresses the fire center, and you experience that as anger or wrath, you see. Now if you descend even lower, you'll see what the earth center has to offer. Yes. Does that help with your question?

Yes. Thank you.

Certainly. Yes, now [Student Y] has a question there. Yes.

I'd like to know what function is in operation when one is fidgeting and moving?

When one is—fire center. Fire center. Yes. You were asking what center controls excitement?

And fidgeting.

Well, fidgeting is a sense expression of the fire center. *[After a short pause, he continues.]* Fire center.

OK.

Yes. *[The teacher laughs.]* You mean, everyone goes like this. *[The teacher demonstrates what fidgeting is and many students laugh.]* And—excuse me. And like that and etc., you see? Well, I'll move right back up. My channel won't appreciate being left in the fire center. Yes, go ahead. *[The teacher laughs joyously.]* I can assure you of that. Yes.

Would that be a, a suppression of desires? What would be the root?

Thank you. Now desire, as you know desire, the limit of the divine expression, you understand that that is formed in the water center. Do you understand that? Now the expression of that is the fire center. Now when it is demanding, through overidentification with self, it's demanding its expression—you understand?—and it's descended into the fire center and it's not getting its expression the way it is used to getting its expression—do you understand that?—then you start twitching and twiddling and moving and scratching and etc. *[The teacher again demonstrates fidgeting.]* Do you understand?

Yes.

Does that help you, [Student Y]?

Yes. Thank you.

Yes. I don't think you have a fidgeting problem, anymore. No. You've seen people, you know, here, they'll go *[The teacher makes a sound that is difficult to transcribe and then demonstrates a fidgeting foot.]* And their foot—I can't quite do that. I don't want to do it too much and leave that with him. *[The teacher refers to his channel.]* But anyway, you've seen that, don't you see? Or their fingers get moving. *[The teacher fidgets with his hand and a few students laugh.]* Huh? Yes. Well, you see, the form created in the water center is now down in the fire center, which controls the nervous system, you understand. Yes. That help with your question? Yes, go ahead, [Student Y].

Did you just say that the fire, the fire center controls the nervous system?

Yes, indeed it does. The fire center controls the nervous system of the physical body. Well, you think that it's the water center? It's the descent of the form created in the water center. When it descends into the fire center, it controls the nervous system. Yes. It's like some people say, "It wasn't worth it." And some people say, "It was most satisfying." Well, it depends what they did with their, with their nervous center. Of course it does.

It's all inside, you know. It always was. It always will [be]. Everything's inside. Isn't that nice? Because it's right where we can get ahold of it whenever we want to, you see? All solutions, all obstructions, they're all inside. And we have the way. We are very fortunate in our evolution, all of us, including myself. And I'm very grateful for that. We have the way. You know?

As one of my students said the other day—well, you know, that on my time on earth so long ago, that in my work and my job that, well, I certainly did take a little pride in, to say the least. A little pride. A magistrate—that I was responsible to see that justice was dispensed. I alone was responsible for that area. Well, I sent them off into the nothingness. Now you know how they were executed, don't you? *[After a short pause, the teacher continues.]* How were they executed?

How were they executed?

Yes. I sent them into nothingness. What happened to their form?

Was it puri—burned?

Well, I don't know if I would call that burning.

No, I don't—

They were disintegrated. Light beam disintegration. Yes. You see, your technology—I mean, it's only a revival of what has been. You see, there's nothing new under the sun. The sun represents the Light. There's nothing new. All of your technology [is], once again, advancing. It is not new. No, no. You see, you see, what happens, you know, if you pause for a moment and think, this great advanced technology today already existed on your planet and in your universes. Still does on other planets in the solar system.

As man advances in his technology, his ability to do so many seeming wondrous things, man faces constantly the great pit. And what is that pit? It begins with [the letter] *p*. One word with *p*.

Pity?

Pardon?

Pity.

No.

Pride. [Another student speaks.]

Pride! Man takes pride in his accomplishments and therefore, once again, descends down, to evolve again. Man takes pride. Don't you understand that? You see? So the technology—this is why I've spoken to you so many times over the years. The technological advancement is exceeding, once again, the spiritual awakening. For you will only rise with the great technological advancement only to descend back to what you'd call the caveman evolutionary stage again, you see. The rise and the fall. The fall is ever subject [to] and dependent upon pride. You see? Without pride, there's no fall.

You see, look at, you know—study what you have received. Spend some of your time listening [to] and studying these lovely tapes. *[The teacher refers to the recordings of the Living Light Philosophy.]* What caused Lucifer to have his mental realm of consciousness, his reign? What caused that? What one thing caused that? What did Lucifer take?

Pride.

Pride! He took pride in what *he* could do. And when he took pride in what he could do, he descended into what he can do. He can do everything in a mental world, you see? But he cannot, you see, he cannot control that which sustains the world in which he controls. You see? It is not possible to control the uncontrollable. That which sustains a thing cannot be controlled by the thing which sustains it, if you want to call Power a thing. You see? So that is the waste of life, the waste of life. That is the seeing of obstruction, you see? You can do what you want in a mental world; it has its price, you see? And even to the point of pride that you are it, for that is what Lucifer did. You see? He descended from his experience of pride of what he could do. The payment is very great. It is very heavy. Hmm?

You know, in speaking with anyone and when they tell me what they're trying to accomplish, what they are working on, I see the pride clearly. You see? The pride, the pride of the human mind and its cunningness to support the hidden judgment that is petrified it shall be revealed. It's pride! Pride, that's all it is.

Do not allow your mouth to be used of what you're going to do, of what you're trying to do. Let your mouth be used to speak the truth and free you. "This is what I'm doing!" For, you see, you're doing it in consciousness, you see? That's in the now. That's the only place you have control: is not tomorrow, of what you're going to go out and do, and not what you have done. You see, if you want to suffer, then think and speak of what you have done; think and speak of what you're going to do and you will experience the fullness of suffering of the senses.

Don't allow your mind to be used to tell you of what you're going to do someday or ever to be deceived of what you have done. Pardon? For both offer to your mind what is known as pride, which is the instrument to fall and to descend. Hmm? You see.

And when the angel Lucifer, sitting there at the right hand of God, began to see, instead of view, and saw all that was done: that God, you see, had control of all creation, of everything. He *saw* that. He descended from viewing in that moment, you see? For had he continued to view, as he was viewing, he would have clearly understood that God was serving all these forms in all these realms, the greatest servant of all. But Lucifer, Lucifer rose and he *saw*. He stopped viewing. And when he saw, he experienced burning desire, for he saw that God was controlling all of that. He lost sight that God was serving all of that. And when that happened, he experienced pride and descended to that realm. And therefore, in that realm, there's never enough. "More" is the motto of the world below. Hmm? Does that help with your question?

Thank you.

Yes. Yes, [Student M], please.

Yes. Thank you. Why is Lucifer, then why is he called the "king" of—

He *is* king. He's king—that's a good question. The moment you asked that question, he spoke. Why is he called the king? Because he is in control of the mind, of mental substance. Whatever is in control of anything is king of it. And he is king of mental substance.

When you permit yourself to say, "With my mind, I can do or not do anything," you find yourself not doing anything. Only serving what you've already done. *[The teacher laughs.]*

Certainly. You experience what is known as the daydreaming, the wishing vibration. Don't you see? That's what you experience. You know, you also experience what my channel was told here the other day: the GE complex. You have a GE complex. You all know what that is, don't you? A GE complex? You got a better idea! *[The teacher and a number of students laugh. The teacher may have been referring to an advertising campaign.]*

So it's time here now. There's no more tomorrows or yesterdays. There's no more GE [complex]. No reflection on the lovely people working for your corporation there. But this day, we move out of the GE complex, inside, in our mind, you see. And we start applying what we have been given. And we do it and we don't talk about it. We just do it. That's all, you see? We just do it, you see. That help with your question, [Student M]?

Thank you.

Yes. And so don't feel slighted. He is the king of creation, for could there be a king without a queen? So you're not left out, don't you see? You know, I wouldn't want you left out in that thinking. Yes.

Now [Student S] has a question. Then, I'll get to [Student B]. Yes.

That was close to my question. I'd like to ask—

King and queens. Ace of spades. Yes, go ahead. *[The teacher laughs.]*

You, you—

I'd rather have a jack of diamond, myself, or its representation. But let's go [with] the kings and queens and ace of spades. No, I'm only joking. Yes. Without humor, there's no salvation. Go ahead, [Student S].

You discussed the descent of Eve and the problems that we have with our feminine queen aspect. And so I wanted to ask, What's the principle that Lucifer was the male king aspect, rather than a queen himself?

Well, because a queen is always tempted. You see, a king can do with it or without it and, usually, does without it, as soon as he's finished. And always says, "Well, it wasn't that great anyway." And gets a break for a while. *[A few students laugh.]* I mean, I don't think that's really any great intellectual question, you know. *[Many students laugh.]* You see? You see, well, for example, look, a king uses it from the electric or fire center, and a queen receives it, wholly and completely, in the center of consciousness, the water center, in which it was created for. She created it in the water center and never moved it to the fire center.

So should you blame creation for that law? Why, yes. Certainly. That's why, you know, you hear them say, "Well, he can do without it. You know, off again, on again. But she's always in it." Well, it isn't that she's always in it, but she's always in it in the sense that it has security to her water center. Do you understand that?

You see, to the king, the only security in the—you see, there's two of the functions: there's the money and there's the sex. Well, to the king, it's always the money. Do you understand? And to the queen, it's the other, you see. He uses it for a release to get what he wants and moves on. But when it comes to the money, you know, he'll do with it and without it. I mean, that's the basic principle. Because she keeps it where it was created: in the water center. He creates it in the water center—do you understand that?—and shoves it right down almost instantaneously into the fire center. Do you understand that? You see?

You don't have to do that just because you're in a female form. There's no reason why you have to. In fact, there are many beings in female forms who have made the conscious choice to not to do that. Knowing it's created in the water center—they don't know it consciously. But they instantly send it down to the fire center, closer to the money realm, you see. Oh yes, yes, your world's filled with that. Does that help with your question? Oh, you have another question on it? Go right ahead. [And then] [Student B.] Yes.

You spoke a minute ago about when somebody's threatened in the water center, they're emotional; in the fire center, they're angry and show their wrath.

Yes.

If it goes even further to the earth center, what is that reaction like?

You have already experienced that in your life, I can see that, a little bit. It's known as violence.

Thank you.

It's physical movement of the physical being.

Thanks.

Yes. In a very determined way. That's earth. All right.

Now, it's very important that we understand, you see, that—oh, my, there. I should close that. *[The teacher closes the clasp of his watchband.]* Yes. It's very important that we understand that the electric, magnetic are centers of consciousness that are in all forms. A magnetic form ofttimes is extremely electric. And when they create these forms in the water center, they don't leave them there and play with them to the point they believe that that's where their security is. They move it right down to the fire center or on farther down to the earth center. And it takes second place—do you understand?—in their priorities.

Now many women (feminine forms) are extremely electric. And their security is not based upon the form created in the water center, of their emotions. Their security is down in the fire or the earth center, what you call money. Do you understand that? You see? And so they may use the water center, but if there isn't any money, forget the water center. They just move on up, you see. They don't play around at all. Well, now you've already had those experiences, so it doesn't mean that women, because they are in Eve forms do not have this electric possibilities.

They have it just as much as men. In fact, in your world I have found many electric forms with absolute feminine convictions, you see, and extremely emotional. And [they] will completely ignore the fire center, the thrust, where their money can come up through, from the earth realm. Do you understand that?

You see, you see, you [have] got to move from the water center where the judgment is created, descend down into the fire center of thrust to experience the money which the earth has to offer. And you have to do that intelligently. You cannot remain in the water center where the judgment and the desire is created and not do something with it. If you do, you won't have any money. You'll always have what you call need of it and for it. Do you understand that? Because, you see, you are not using the functions wisely. So if you do not use the functions wisely, you are not an instrument of the Light that you are; you have convinced yourself that you are the function and are in service to the king of functions. Does that help with your question?

Yes.

Yes, now [Student B] is waiting with a question there.

I have a question about pride.

Pride? Yes.

Pride. What is the center of the, of the house of pride and what is the corresponding soul faculty?

All right. Thank you. Now in reference to—that is the crown of the house of the functions. Pride. It's the crown of it. Whenever you permit yourself, your true being, to identify with mental substance, what you believe that you are, you have the crown of pride. All right? Now pride is the crown of the functions. A person uses many functions. If there is pride in the use of the function, then they are not in control. Only that which they have created is in control. Does that help you, [Student B]?

[If the student responded, her response is difficult to transcribe.]

That which they have created is now in control. What they have created is subject to the king of creation. Do we follow that through? Now pride, a function, has, waiting for it, humility, a faculty. However, humility, to the king of creation that controls mental substance, humility to the mind is humiliation, you see. You see, exposure, which frees the soul, is frequently humiliation to the mental substance through which you work to free it from. You see?

You see, a person says—you know, they pause and they enter into that realm of the light of reason. Reason whispers clearly and says, "This is what you do. This is the solution to the problem that you have." Fine. They feel real good about that solution. They return, by an overidentification, into mental substance, and the first thing that pride says [is], "Why should I have to do that? Well, that's humiliating." You see? And it offers all of that. Yet when they have risen above what they have created (moved out of mental substance), their light of reason clearly shows them—and they view it very clearly—"This is reasonable. Through making this step, I have no problem. I have a solution to my problem." Now as long as they're in that state of consciousness, they are viewing the way. The moment they leave that state of consciousness (in here) *[The teacher points to his right temple.]* and overidentify with the mind, forms created by the mind start to go to work and tell them that is humiliating. It's humiliating to the pride, not to what they are. Only to what, at times, they believe that they are. Does that help with that question, [Student B]?

Thank you.

Yes. Because, you see, you will find by making the effort through your breathing exercises to remain—you see, to remain long enough time-wise, which controls your world, that illusion called time—to remain in consciousness long enough to strengthen the viewing. So that when you return to the seeing, to the mental world, you have sufficient strength to say,

"This is my decision. I'm doing it. Period." And do it. Then you will experience the way. You will feel better. You will experience more goodness in your life, no matter what it is. Does that help, [Student B]?

Thank you.

Because it always works. We look in hindsight and we say, "When I followed the Light, it worked! There are some places I would refuse to follow the Light. Why did I refuse? Because I overidentified with mental substance which is controlled by the king of creation." And this is why, in reference to [Student M's] question, loyalty to the soul, which you are, is ofttimes registered by pride, what you are not, as treason. Hmm?

Now ofttimes I know that many of you—all of you—had the experience where you have gone by the light of reason within you. You've made your decision. You've established the law. You've set it into motion. And then you felt terrible and really upset because you did it. Well, what felt terrible and really upset was the pride and the mental substance [that] didn't get its way. And if you are strong spiritually in consciousness and you do your daily exercises, those screaming things that you did not consult on whether or not you could do that, they stop plaguing you.

It's like a person, you know, they're in the light of reason themselves and they want to do something and they go right ahead and they do it in the light. And when they leave the light of their consciousness within, they have to put up with all this payment of rash of their mind. Can you relate to that, [Student B]? Isn't that wonderful? How beautiful life is!

Yes, [does] someone else have a question? Yes, [Student Y], please.

Is—

And [Student D] will have questions. But, you see—excuse me, [Student Y]. This is very important. As long as you allow yourself to believe you feel that way—I'll be with you in a moment, [Student Y]—you must realize that you will suffer.

You see? You are not without the Light when you put judgments where they belong. Yes, because we only have a few moments. Do you understand that, [Student D]? Time passes very quickly. Our hour is almost gone, you see. For you allow your mind to tell you [that] you are losing the Light of this little school is not only foolhardy, it's placing those things in control. I have assured my channel repeatedly for many, many years: no one is left out of the Light for a dollar bill. However, none of my students will continue to take advantage of a co-student from not making the change. Do you understand that?

Yes. [Student D responds.]

You want to be in school, don't you, [Student D]?

Yes.

The dollar won't keep you out. The judgment will. Do you understand that?

Yes, I do.

Yes. So I look forward to seeing you. And I also view very clearly that my students will not allow anyone's temporary error of value of judgment to stand in the way of the Light. I have my student right here today. Not even my channel knew until this morning that my student [Student P] would be here this day. Do you understand? You see? But we will not permit going against the Light you receive by procrastination—for you've all had over a year. So I not only expect, I require my students to see that [in] helping you, they help themselves, for that is the law.

Now time is running out. And we're running out on this [tape.] Well now, just a moment! No! No! That tape—my assistants tell me that's two hours. So, so—but thank you. You were supposed to remind me that it's been an hour. *[The teacher addresses the cameraman.]*

Now this is very, very important: the application. Not all this fooling around, you see. You see, try to understand, my students. And I know that you can. You have been given over a year['s] grace. I do not find my student [Student S] with that great sadness, which is the value priority of the judgment that cannot, cannot give you a way, you see? You see, and when you sit in class and you feel so badly, on the verge of tears, where the form is created, you see, and that you will lose out and etc. No, it's not you that's losing out: it's the judgments you put where they don't belong. That's what's losing out, I can assure you of that. [Student Y] is not losing out. [Student N], [Student N] back there, you're not losing out. No, you see? And so you're not losing out. [Student L], here, is not losing out. I can assure you. However, if you believe you are the judgments that you have created, [Student O]—

Yes. [Student O responds.]

[The teacher laughs.] You don't sleep in my classes. If you believe you are the judgments you have created, if you believe you're those things, then, yes, you're losing out. No. No, you're not losing out. You see, you have to make that change. And you have all the ways of making that change. That's what this lovely class is all about, isn't it, [Student B]?

Yes. [Student B responds.]

Why, certainly. Absolutely. No, no, no, no, no, no. Forget what that thing is telling you about money. It's trying to defend itself. And you insist on believing that you are the thing that's trying to defend itself. No, no, no, no.

Now does someone else have a question here? Was that [Student Y]? Now, now we'll take your question.

I—

I won't—excuse me, [Student Y]. I won't let [Student D] sit there and play with all those forms that she—I know, past is past. She loved them in the past. This is a new moment and the change is coming. And I won't let [Student O] sit there and go off [to sleep] under the guise of meditation. Not in my class. That's right. Put your hand down, [Student O], you little child there. Yes, go ahead, [Student Y].

I would like to know if—this has come up for me in the past.
Yes?
If there's any such thing as a right or wrong question.
Right and wrong exists in mental substance. And if you want to believe that your classes are controlled by the king below, then, of course, there's right and wrong. There is no right and wrong to a question you have here for me. Stand up and ask your question, right or wrong. Right or wrong is a judgment of the human mind. That belongs to that king [below]. I've spent plenty of time down there. Thank you, no. Ask your question.
So that's where it comes from. It comes from—
Oh, I'll let you know where it comes from, if you don't know yourself. Go ahead and ask your question.
I know where it comes from.
Good. Ask the question.
That was the question.
Oh, that's fine!
That was my question.
Then you have no problem.
No, I don't.
Good for you, [Student Y].
Thank you.
Very good. Very good. Yes. Very, very good. Remember, that which is censored cannot be true, for it separates the whole from what it is. Hmm? There are certain rules and regulations, but there's not censorship. Have you ever experienced censorship in these classes with me? Hmm? Why, not even [Student D] in playing with those things that she tries to believe that she [is]—and does a good job of it. Not even those get censored. I see them there. I don't let [Student O] sit here and go to sleep under the guise that he's off in some spiritual realm. I've yet to find a person sleeping in a spiritual realm. Resting, yes, I find them there. Oh, no.

So we're going overtime. So it costs us more money. If it goes on—what do you call it, a C-90? *[The teacher refers to the type of cassette tape the class will fit onto. A C-90 is a cassette tape that has a ninety-minute capacity. Most classes were an hour and fit onto a C-60, which had a sixty-minute recording capacity. A C-60 cost less than a C-90.]* Well, there's no problem. Money's not the problem. Never was the problem. If it's the problem, sell out your school and take your money. And prepare yourself for the bars. I think they call them [San] Quentin over there. *[Many students laugh.]*

Yes, you have a question [Student M].

Yes.

[The teacher laughs.] Yes.

Throughout all the eons of time, this has always been the same question, then, between creation, between form, be it our mind, which is creation, and the Light of our eternal soul. There's always been form throughout all the eons of time in eternity. And—

Yes. There is not a battle with creation when you accept what it is and the purpose of its design. You see, your functions are not a problem until you make them [a problem]. You make your functions a problem by believing that you are the forms you have created of how they shall be used. Your functions are not a problem. They are a servant of the Light. But they don't serve the Light because you believe that they are you. That's why they don't serve the Light. You see, you can't tell your function, "Well now, function, I'm going to use you now to serve the Light." Do you understand that?

Yes.

And expect that it is serving the Light. That's total deception. When you've spent a lifetime believing you are the function. How is it going to serve the Light? It's designed to serve the Light that sustains it. It doesn't serve the Light that sustains it because you believe that you are it. *[The teacher laughs.]* So please don't tell me—Oh, now, Mr. Red. Well, that's—look at that now. You chewed that right off because someone just let it lay flat there. *[It seems that Mr. Red, the church's dog, has chewed off the blossom of a flower.]* Mr. Red? Do you think that's the thing to do in class? He doesn't want to look at me, you know. He does that when he, when he feels guilty.

Now, you see, so don't be tempted to tell yourself, "Well, now that I know that my functions are designed to serve the Light, I'll go out and lift a soul." *[The teacher and many students laugh.]* Well, don't be, don't be so foolish. Don't be so, don't be so silly, children. Don't be so silly. The payment will be unrealistic.

Knowing anything and applying that which you know are two entirely different things, you see? See, don't deceive yourself [by saying], "Oh, I'm going out and work. And I'm going to—the effect of that work, I'm giving that all to God." Oh, don't be so foolish. Don't be so silly. Because at the very thought that you're giving it to God, you're giving it to something else. And you're deceiving yourself you're giving it to God. You're the one that's benefiting. And if you're not benefiting, you're doing something that is incorrect in reference to the teaching, you see.

That's like going out, using your functions, and saying, "Well, I'm doing this to bring them all into the Light of God, you see." I think you have in your world—I think it was a wonderful little show, long ago. What was the name of that? Perhaps we can get it for you. What was his name? Gantry! I think his name was Gantry. Elmer Gantry! *[The teacher may be referring to the movie called* Elmer Gantry.*]* You see, he had deceived himself. It was in one of your shows or something. He had deceived himself that he was bringing all the ladies to the Light, while he was having blatant heyday with his functions, you see. That's total deception. [That] had nothing to do with the Light, you see? You see, you don't lift a soul by a function when you believe you are the function. Don't deceive yourself. You might lift something else: the throne of the old boy himself. That's all you lift. *[The teacher laughs joyfully.]* And when you let go and he drops, you have the experience and you call that disaster. Whoever insists on seeing their obstruction becomes a servant of their own disaster.

Yes, [Student Y].

Is it the judgments that we give to God? Is that the first step?

Why, yes. All that you have created. Not mine, but Thine. For without "Thine," there is no substance to limit. See? You are in mental substance limiting that which is whole and limitless. You are temporarily putting it in a container. As I spoke to you before, the thing is, after you've put it in a container, put the lid on it. You go down there and believe you are the lid [and] stay down there with that which you have contained, known as attachment to the fruits of action. You see, a person who goes around and says, "Well, let's see, now I've expressed this function for the Light. I did a real good job." Forget it. You'll find out how good a job you did after you make that statement in your consciousness. Yes. See?

Feeling good is not a luxury. It is a necessity. But how are we going to allow our self to feel good? It's quite simple: stop thinking of the limit known as self. And just, just do it. Just simply do it. That's all.

Any other questions now that we're—what you consider going overtime? You know, I've spent many eons freeing myself from limit and I have no intention of coming down to class and have someone limit me that's only known me a short time. Yes, go ahead with your question. Yes. Yes, [Student U].

What is the role of concentration as we face the cliff on our journey toward the Light?

The role of concentration, which is the key to all power, as we face the cliff on our journey through evolution. All right. Now as you move along and you face this cliff, concentration is indispensable. What will you concentrate upon? Overidentification is a revelation of concentration. It was a revelation. Look at your life and see: "Now that which I identified with, did it only come to my consciousness when I called it up or was it there when I never consciously thought of it?" Hmm? Well, you've certainly overidentified with limit and many times it would rise up without your consciously thinking about it. Wouldn't you say?

Yes, sir.

Seemingly, it just appeared.

Seemingly.

Yes. And aren't you the boy that made an intelligent decision? What did he call it? An option? *[During a conversation with Mr. Goodwin that was not part of a recorded class, Student U had informed Mr. Goodwin that poverty was optional.]*

Yes, sir.

Well, now what are we talking about here? So, you see, if in moving all forward there, in moving forward there and thinking of the cliff and that you might drop off, well, you are concentrating upon a function and will experience what a function has to offer. Hmm?

Yes, sir.

Being aware is one thing. Constantly thinking about what you're aware of is something else. What if you constantly thought of your big toe? What would happen to you? You would hit every kind of an obstruction you can imagine. You would be walking along and walk right into a building because your consciousness was only on your big toe. Therefore, your eyes could not see. Do you understand that?

Yes.

You see? Put your attention on what you want to become and take your attention, energy, concentration, the key to all power, off of what you want to overcome. The more that you insist on thinking about what is your obstruction, you see—the more you think of what's in your way, the more it comes in your way. Do you understand that?

Yes, sir.

So, you see, it's like money, here. Money is not your problem. It's your constantly thinking of money that's your problem. That's your problem. See, money is not the problem at all. Money is serving a judgment you have created in your mind. Money is not your problem. Your thinking about it is your problem. That's the only problem that you have. It is a function—the effect of a function in the earth center. It is not your problem. Your judgment, constantly thinking about it [is]. You see, as you think about it, you feed a judgment that you have created. That's what you do. Money has never been anyone's problem. It's not the problem. Your judgment that you have created in reference to it, that is a problem because you've made it so. You keep thinking about that which you have created, and you keep experiencing a problem with money. It's that simple. It always was that simple.

Yes, are there any other questions?

[After a short pause, the teacher continues.] The problem is self-created. See, you think you think about money. What you are really doing is directing intelligent energy to a judgment that you have created that has other little judgments as its workers along with it. It's the censorship of the Light of truth. You see? So you continue to direct your attention to what you call money when, in truth, all you are doing is sending energy to the judgment form that you have created. And then, what happens when money comes into your consciousness—you understand?—that which you have a just responsibility to pay for something, then that judgment, in its defense, lying there in the water center, rises up with a flow of the element in which he was born.

Now if you have moved that judgment, created in the water center, into your fire center, then what you find is a person rising up with anger and an expression of it. Because his judgment, related to what you call money, is in a fire center. Now if you have another person who has had the intelligence and made the effort to apply the truth, then that judgment created has moved from its center of creation (the water center) into the fire center, through the fire center into the earth center and you have manifestation. And so-called money is no problem at all because you have completed the triune function of manifestation. Do you understand that?

Now the thing that—many people, they have problems. They don't move it out of the water center. Some won't move it out of the fire center, which is a burning thirst, you see. And some keep it in both: back and forth. And some move it into the earth center. And to the mind, they call that intelligent work. Does that help with your question?

Yes, sir.

Hmm. Were you hungry? *[The teacher addresses a different student.]*

Excuse me.

Oh, I thought you were doing something with your mouth. Oh, good. *[The teacher laughs.]* Is there any question on that now this morning because class has run, what you would call, overtime. Yes. Yes, [Student M] has a question.

Yes, I have a question. Thank you. With this new technology and the babies that will be born in the test tubes and would there—

They're already being born in the test tube.

Right.

Wait 'til they move to the next stage beyond the test tubes. Go ahead.

Right. In those next stages of evolution for our world, will there be less identification, then, with that kind of environment, with creation and the judgments or a different form to evolve the judgments, different—

Well, it will be just a different expression of them, unless they're intelligently brought together under spiritual conditions of peace and harmony, which [is] an expression of the Light, you see.

Correct.

Yes. Yes, [Student O].

No, sir.

Oh, I thought that was a question out of your head that you were trying to get out. You know, when I see students scratching their head, my understanding is they're trying to dig out the question and pride won't release it.

Well, we'll say good day. Have a nice week. I know that you will. A very fine week. And don't forget now, [Student D], there, [is] to have some help there from [Student Y] there and [Student S] and [Student L] there. And let's move on. I don't expect to see you all next Sunday. I *shall* see you all next Sunday. There's a difference between expecting and accepting. Oh, what a difference there is!

Thank you. Good day.

SEPTEMBER 7, 1986

A/V Class Private 63

Good morning, students.

It's nice to be back in class. I'm sure that you all feel that way. And today in our new classes, for we have renewed them in our new semester, we will start on a little more understanding and a broader perspective of the macrocosm. Surely, I know you will all agree we have spent a great deal of time on the microcosm, known as self. It's time to spend a little of our interest now on the macrocosm. So we will begin with a little understanding of what you know as the minerals or the gems of your planet and why they have the meanings that they do and have had for untold eons of time.

So let us first begin with the ones that our mind seems to find the most precious, and I'm sure that all of you know what that is, that gem. You call it the diamond. Why is the diamond an ancient symbol of deception? That's the question. Well, let us begin with understanding the law that whatever fascinates the mind excites the senses and imprisons the soul. Now if we will look at that gem, we will note, as we see it with our eyes and the conception of our mind, we will see that it reveals various colors, depending upon the reflection of the light. And so we begin with our minds to understand how that does that. We know that as the function of curiosity.

So we see that which we are curious about we are challenged by. And we know that what we are challenged by stimulates what is known as our ego. So we can clearly see that the diamond, of all the gems of your planet, offers to us a great challenge, a great curiosity. We're challenged because we're curious because we want to understand it, we think, so we can control it. So whatever we are curious about, we find our self fascinated with, challenged by, stimulated by, excited by, and imprisoned by. Perhaps now you have a little better understanding of why the diamond is known as a symbol of deception.

Does the fault lie in the diamond? Of course, it doesn't lie in the diamond. The fault lies in who is observing the diamond and is entrapped by it. And you should find it interesting and should note that in your world the diamond has become the symbol of entrapment or bondage. You should also find it noteworthy that the diamond, of all the stones and gems, is the most sought-after.

Now let us move on with some questions on the macrocosm. Why is your planet here? How long has it been here? Is it going somewhere? If so, where is it going? There's so many things to understand. And so let us raise our hands with some questions of something, in our new classes, on the macrocosm because surely we're filled up to our temples with the microcosm. And once you get filled, it's time to empty the vessel. So let's move to the macrocosm and let's see a few hands around here. [Student U] has a question.

Could you speak on that object in space that's called the shadow of the Source?

The shadow of the Source. Certainly. Remember that a shadow, as you already know, is an obstruction of the Light. So when you think along the lines of a shadow of the Source, it is not only deceptive but it is contrary to truth. The Source itself cannot be a shadow. The Source is the Light. The only thing that can cast a shadow is an obstruction to the Light. And so when your scientists speak about a shadow of the Source, they are speaking about the obstruction, which they judge is the Source for they look and they see only that which is form and do not perceive that which is formless.

For example, it's like your planet and its ice age. You have many theories on an ice age on your planet, and I'm sure that your world has offered you many explanations. From our Hall of Records we've clearly reviewed many times. Certainly, your planet, in keeping with all planets in their evolution, went through an ice age. And where in your world you had tropical temperatures, you had an ice age, which covered all the vegetation. And so today you only have relics of the creatures that crawled upon your planet at that time. You only have the relics of the dinosaurs, because the ice age and those great walls of ice totally, totally covered and eliminated their food supply.

And so, what caused your ice age? You have many theories, but one theory I haven't heard in your world revealed, which is not a theory, is that the monitor planet, that passes through eons of time around your planet, when it made its pass, your planet moved on its axis. And whenever a planet moves on its axis, you go through these various phases and changes. Well, it moved on its axis; you went through your ice age. It shall move on its axis again when that monitor planet, once again, comes close enough and affects the gravitation of your planet; then any planet moves off its axis. I hope that's helped with your question.

Forget about the shadow. They are conceiving. They have seen the obstruction to the Light, which is the shadow that they are looking at, you see. That help with your question?

Yes, sir.

Yes. Now, several other people here—[Student S] has a question. Yes.

What planet is the monitor planet and when is it due to come near again?

Well, first of all, you will not experience it in your short lifetime, the moments you have left on your planet, for they are truly moments for anyone on your planet. It has passed over your planet and has affected an ice age eons ago. And it will be several eons before it passes that close again. Yes.

And is it a planet that we would recognize or is something that—

Well, you cannot recognize it in the sense—well, is it physical? Oh, yes, it certainly is. But no earthlings have ever viewed it. Because, you see, it's been so many eons prior to man's journey on your planet. Of course, the dinosaurs and all those creatures viewed it very clearly. It wiped out their entire food supply and they starved to death, you see. They didn't take very long in those subzero temperatures. Yes.

But if you try to look at your solar system—you see, all solar systems have a monitor or what you might call a guardian. You might call it a guardian if you wish, but they have a monitor. And you look at your solar system, and unfortunately so many times that's as much as your mind can conceive, you see. Well, I've already given to you many times [some time] ago: here you have nine children; you have your nine planets and you have the mother and father who have created them.

Now, for example, I stated some time ago and I'll state once again: here you have the sun, the source of light, a physical light for your planet and for all the children in that solar system. And so everything in truth has come from the Light shall return to the Light does not only refer to a spiritual understanding but, of course, is applicable to all things mental and physical. Everything returns to its source. So the children of the planet that you understand as the sun for your solar system shall return unto it and has been in process for some time in doing so. Yes, does that help with your question? Yes. Certainly, [Student S].

Just now you made mention of the nine planets, plus the mother and the father.

Yes.

Is this monitor planet like the aspect of the mother if the sun is the father?

Well, the mother is the moon in your understanding in your solar system. And the father is the sun. Yes.

What would the monitor be?

The monitor planet—for example, if you look at a father of all of your solar system and you take your solar system, with all of its planets and its mother and father, as a family group, then you will understand that the monitor planet is a planet from which has sprung a solar system. You see, you have one solar system that you are aware of. And you are not aware of the monitoring of the solar system. You've got to broaden your horizons and understand that there are many solar systems of which this, your solar system, is one solar system. There is a responsibility—just as there is in your world of creation, for the planets, in physical aspect, are created, of course—and so there's a responsibility of those who have created the planets. That's the sun['s] and the moon's responsibility. They are, in turn, responsible to the source, which is responsible for bringing about the entire solar system.

Say, if you look at your solar system, your Earth planet, you understand, is numerically number five, all right? Now at this phase of your evolution, number five, the fifth planet of your solar system, is the one that has life, as you understand life. It is not the only one with life, but it has life as you understand life. So it has to be monitored. The entire solar system is monitored. It is constantly monitored. Just because the monitor does not pass that closely to your planet, only through a cycle of eons of time, does not in any way imply that it is not constantly monitored. You see, you can monitor something close or could monitor something at a distance, depends on the intelligence, yes. Yes, [Student S].

And this so-called shadow that's really the obstruction to the source, is that—

Well, it's the obstruction. Yes, well, now you're understanding. Why, certainly, it's the passing of the monitor. But you have to understand eons of light years and distances that your measurements are not capable of as yet. Yes. So when you see the monitor, when your scientists look and they see a shadow cast and they think that is the source, that is only the monitor that is moving at this particular time in space, far out in outer space, in its responsibility of its monitoring work, yes.

Yes, now someone else had a question here. [Student M] has been waiting here, yes.

Yes. You spoke earlier about the diamond and the minerals of our particular planet here.

Yes.

And each of these nine children of the sun and the moon—

Yes.

—the minerals and the gems of their particular planet are dependent upon the evolution of the species on that particular planet.

The species on the planet are dependent upon the minerals. The minerals aren't dependent upon the species. Minerals came before the species of beings. The minerals are first. The gases were before that.

OK.

Yes.

And then we, in a sense, on the same vibratory wave to be created on that particular planet. You know, say that the diamonds are on our planet. Are there diamonds on—

Can you live without a diamond?

Yes.

You don't have to be worried about being controlled by them then.

Right.

Yes. Perhaps—that help with your question?

I'm not sure.

Well, perhaps you could restate your question.

I was just wondering about the minerals and the gems of each particular planet.

Yes.

Kind of like, are they all the same?

Oh, no. Well, not all planets, not all planets have a god of deception.

Right.
Why, no. They're at different stages of evolution. Therefore, they would not have minerals representing the god of deception.
Right.
Yes.
Different minerals for different planets depending—
For different evolution. Oh, yes, indeed. Yes. Does that help with your question? Yes. And, for example, you know, let's go a little farther with that question; it is most interesting. Your planet, Earth, has one moon, doesn't it?
Yes.
There's some planets in your solar system [that] have two, three, four, five, and etc. I don't like that word *etc*. And so on and so forth, that's much better. Hmm? So, you see? But you only have one.
Right.
Isn't that true? See, you don't have comparison as far as deception is concerned. You have deception as deception. You don't have two moons up there to shine down upon you, do you? Hmm? You do understand that the moon affects the water.
Yes.
The water center of your being. And those who believe they are their judgments, children created in the water center, are controlled by that element and by that which affects that element. You do understand that, don't you?
[If the student responds, it is difficult to transcribe her response.]
Yes, then you understand deception.
Yes.
Yes. That help with your question?
Yes.
Fine. Now, [Student U], did I get to your question? No. You had a question.

I was wondering about quartz.

Yes, what about quartz? What would you like to know about quartz?

Well, it seems to be a crystalline structure.

Well, yes. Does that make it a crystal? A good copy, perhaps.

Ah, OK.

Hmm?

That was one of the questions.

Yes, it's a good copy. Well, you see, all things are imitated. All things are copied. You see, you see, for example, don't you have—well, certainly, you have—what do you call those things? You have zircons. *[The teacher may or may not be referring to cubic zirconia.]* Surely, the ladies have heard of zircons, haven't they? Well, you even have imitation diamonds, don't you? I mean, haven't you created imitations yet? Well, certainly, you have. I'm sure you have. Well, of course. What else could you do in believing that the diamond is what you must have? When you can't have it, you make a copy, don't you? If you judge that you must have something and you cannot have, because of your own judgments, what you judge you must have, then what do you do? You go for second best and make a copy, don't you?

Yes.

Well, I think you understand that now. Now [Student L] is waiting, please.

I'm wondering if there might be eighty-one monitors, [one] for each level.

Well, we'll first take care of the one—trying to perceive the one that is looking after your world, your world that you're in. And after doing that, perhaps we can evolve, in ten years or so—that is, in your time—to how many monitors are there and how many solar systems are there. Hmm? Yes, [Student B].

Is—does the mineral diamond have a planet that its—

Yes.

—predominant.

Yes, I don't want to answer your question before you've completed your question, but certainly it does have. Absolutely. You know, even in your world the scientists are so interested in the minerals that they judge that exist on many planets, you know. Are you aware of that? Your physical scientists are very, very interested in mining the planets. Very interested.

You see, what they base that upon—they base it upon their study of physics and their study of astronomy and what by their understanding of various planets in your solar system must contain as minerals because, you see, all stones and gems are, of course, solidified gases. We do understand that, don't we? So in their understanding and their scientific knowledge of the gases that existed at one time, from which a planet was given birth, they have, of course, judged that those planets contain some certain very precious minerals. Well, in truth, in their judgments, they are correct in that respect.

And so one of the major motivations of your scientists and your financial world on your planet to move to outer space is to rob the so-called gems that the planets contain. Do you understand that? Certainly, there's military interest, but the military interests come secondary to the interest of what you would understand as big business. Hmm? Yes, [Student B].

So if they did rob the minerals . . . balance . . . [Reddy, the church's dog, had been barking consistently for several minutes. It is difficult to completely transcribe her question.]

Reddy! [The cameraman calls to Reddy to stop the barking.]

. . . the balance of the universe . . . [Again, it is difficult to completely transcribe the question.]

It would have an effect. It would have an—

Reddy!

Mr. Red. That's all right. *[The teacher addresses the cameraman as Reddy continues to bark.]* It would indeed. It would indeed have an effect, you understand, depending how much disturbance there was. You see, for example, your planet, your little planet Earth goes through various seeming disasters. That is when the basic balance of your planet has been disturbed. And so the planet—the balance—oh, my, here, here. I don't—there now. *[Reddy walks past the teacher toward the pond. Once at the pond, he slips and almost falls in and the teacher addresses him.]* You see? You see? You almost took a baptism there for not behaving yourself. *[Many students laugh.]* So, you see, in that respect you experience disturbances in your weather patterns. Disturbances, your earthquakes and all of these different things, are effect[s] of an imbalance on the planet.

So, you see, everything is interconnected. The planets are all interconnected. And if there is a severe disturbance, it will affect the whole, the entire solar system. Now whatever affects the balance of one solar system has a[n] effect upon another solar system. And this is part of the Divine Intelligence, the great Architect of the monitors of the solar systems, you see. Its responsibility is to monitor and to record the degree of imbalances of any solar system for it affects all the other ones, you see. Does that help with your question, [Student B]? Yes, go ahead.

May I ask what planet the diamond is predominantly on— the diamond.

Yes, the moon. Deep within the moon, it is filled with that gem, you see. Yes, yes. Yes, [Student B].

The diamond is very translucent. Does that mean it's very electric?

The diamond is a great reflector of the light, of the many rays of the light. It is the closest thing that you can get as a stone to the crystal; yet, it is not the crystal. You see, the diamond only has power in a realm of force. Diamond has force. Crystal has power, you see. And try and understand that according to the way a gem is cut is a person controlled or fascinated by it. You do understand that? You see, a diamond doesn't reflect its light until it's cut a certain way. When it's cut a certain way, it begins to shine in many, many colors, you see.

Now the question then is asked, Well, where does the color come from? The color does not come from the diamond. Try to understand that. The diamond does not contain color. The diamond reflects certain light rays when it's cut in certain ways; and therefore, you see it as various colors. Those colors, which are vibrations, which is light, exist in the atmosphere at all times. Do you understand? So, you see, that's—you see, how and why—there's many reasons why the diamond represents deception, you see. You see, it fascinates the mind, you see. It entraps it. It hypnotizes it, and that's the great deception. And it excites the senses. So it doesn't have to be a diamond. Anything that you look at—you see, the eyes are the great deceiver. This is why, in trusting the senses, the last thing to trust is the sight. Does that help you, [Student B]?

Yes. Thank you.

Yes. Now we have questions over here. [Student D] has been waiting. Yes.

I have two questions.

Yes, certainly.

One is, What gem is the earth's gem and is that also faith? And is that gem also faith?

Yes, and do you know what that is?

The earth's gem?

Yes. What is a representative in your world that you understand that represents faith?

What represents faith?

Yes, what represents faith universally to your, to your—

The number five.

Well, yes, but that's not a gem. Is it?

That's all I know.

Yes. But what, for the masses of your people, what represents faith?

Gold? [Two students respond.]
[Student H]?
Gold.
Faith in what? What does it offer?
Stability?
Security.
Security.
Certainly. Yes, [Student M].
Yeah, I was thinking of gold: the faith in security.
What does gold represent spiritually in your classes?
Wisdom.

Divine wisdom, hmm? Doesn't it? So, you see, with all gems, if you've tried—and all minerals and all things, there is always a spiritual counterpart. To the mind, gold, in your world, at this time, represents security. You see? It represents security. Yet, in truth, it represents divine wisdom. Well, when your attention is on divine wisdom, then there is no concern or interest in security, for you are secure in the wisdom of the Divinity. Hmm? You see? That help with your question? Go ahead with the other question, [Student D].

This is about the monitor planets.
There's one that we're discussing for your solar system, yes.
Is the planet itself the monitor or are there intelligent beings on the planets who are the monitors of the universe?
The intelligence of the planet is the monitor.
And ...
If you want to call them beings, that's fine, yes.
The ice age, was that before the missing link took place or after?
Oh, I see, the missing link that's not on your planet. Well, the ice age came after.
OK. Do those beings know that the shadow—or the intelligence, does it know that the, that when it passes by it causes that shift in the Earth on its axis?

Why, certainly. But they aren't the ones that decide when it's to pass by. The laws of balance reach that conclusion. Yes, certainly. You see, it's the rise and fall. You go so far—any planet, any intelligence, in any place in the universes—and when you tip the scales of balance, you establish the Law of Construction and Destruction. If you want to understand destruction, then you take an honest look and you will see that the scales of balance have been tipped through errors of ignorance. And when those are tipped, you experience destruction. When they're brought into balance, you experience construction. You see? That's the perpetual rise and fall, the error in believing, you see. When the attention is put on the limit, you disrupt the balance; you disrupt the balance and then you experience destructive forces, hmm? Yes, [Student R].

Was the ending of the ice age another change in the Earth's axis?

Yes, yes, you see—oh, I see your point. It moved; it affected your Earth planet, through your solar system, for it's a solar monitor. And when it moved, you had the great ice age. And when it moved again, for its second pass, you had the end of the ice age. Try to understand that you also had great floods upon the planet. Great disruptions, you see. And that happens ever in keeping with the law. You see, the monitor planet doesn't just pass haphazardly close to your planet. As I said, that's in keeping with laws established. Yes.

The great floods that were the effect of the changing back from the ice age—

That is correct.

—are those the floods that are spoken of in the biblical literature?

Yes, but they happened eons, long before that. You see, it's a story that's been passed down. It's an accurate truth. It is truth of what happened. But it didn't happen just a few thousand years ago. Oh, no, no, no. No, this story of Noah and his ark is taken from ancient, ancient truth that's been passed through many, many, many civilizations throughout eons of time. The flood of your biblical story is a story passed on through eons, through many, many civilizations. Yes.

You said recently that the means of execution when you were working as a magistrate was the light beam.

Yes, instant disintegration.

Now, that was the use of the, of a crystal.

Correct.

And that understanding was widespread at the time. How did that understanding become lost?

Well, it is the same with all technologies, all advancements. You see, the few always make the steps forward in technology or in any advancement. It is always the few. And they must carry with them, of course, the masses. And that, it takes effort of education and growth. If they do not do that responsibility wisely, then they guarantee the masses shall rise up and shall destroy their masters and their technology. And so when those errors in civilization are made, you have the great rise of the technology only to guarantee the great descent. And that's when it's lost for a time. Because, you see, as you would say in your world, they throw the baby of technology out with the bathwater.

And so unless there is greater education, as I've said for many years, on the advancing technology in your world, the Earth planet, today, unless there is greater effort placed on the educating and the evolving of the masses from their superstitions, your civilization only guarantees the error that has been made throughout eons of time: they only guarantee the day when the masses shall rise and shall destroy the technology and the scientists responsible for it. Do you understand that?

Yes.

Yes. And so for some time I've mentioned to you, here, over these years, the advancing technology has exceeded the spiritual awakening. You see, it isn't a matter of a person being religious. In fact, it's just the opposite of this as far as religion is concerned in your planet. It is a matter of awakening and understanding. Your technology is at such a point when your androids are revealed to masses, if there isn't phenomenal effort put into awakening the masses, then all the technology and those responsible for it shall be destroyed by the masses. It's happened before. It is a natural pattern of ignorance. Yes.

Who does the awakening traditionally? Is it the science community or some other group?

No. Traditionally, it is what you would understand as the governments or councils responsible for the masses. You see, the error is this: in the advancing of the technology, those few who are responsible for the advancing technology, those scientists, in turn, are responsible—have made themselves responsible to the governing rulers. Now they do that in order to be, what you would say, funded for their work, for their research, and for their understanding, because they must have, in your material world, funds in order to accomplish that.

So the governing rulers responsible, they receive this advancing technology. They, unfortunately, are deluded by the belief that they must keep this, what they call, power to themselves, for if they do not, if it is—if the so-called secrets are given to the masses, then they will lose their position of rule. Do you understand? It's a terrible error that has been made throughout eons of time. Consequently, in that error they guarantee the masses to rise and destroy the technology and those responsible for it, beginning with the governing rulers. Do you understand?

Yes.

You see? See, it's happened before. You see, the light beams and these different gamma rays and things, they've always been; they'll always be. The use of them, you see, is once again rising, the awakening. And unless there are great changes in the governing rulers of your planet, it shall repeat itself. History repeats itself. Yes.

One more question.

Certainly.

The government of this country has been fairly conservative over this last administration. What sort of trend will the next administration have?

Well— *[The teacher coughs.]* Excuse me. I think you might call it in your world, unfortunately, unfortunately, liberal.

Thank you.

The thing unfortunate about the liberalism of a government is that it has a facade of responsibility and doesn't want to face practical necessities, you see. You see, liberalism in your world usually means everyone gets a Christmas present every day of the week. No one pays for it. Yes. Yes. But as far as the Book of Records reveal, it is indicated over 86 percent that it will swing towards liberalism, yes. For error is the banner of the masses.

Does that help with your question? Now, [Student N], back there, has been waiting.

I can't remember if this has been asked before, but are we going . . .

Has it been asked before by you?

Not by me.

Then it's new to you. Go ahead. *[The teacher laughs joyfully.]*

Are we going to use the crystal in our lifetime?

No. No, the scientists are already working with it. But as far as—you mean, the masses, the individuals?

Well, even in things that we use or . . .

In the world out there? No, it's still a fascinating little gem to most people who don't understand it, yes. No.

And are we going to fall with—are we going to make progress in educating the masses?

Well, I would like to say yes, but the records do not reveal that. They indicate the opposite. Hmm? You see, you have advancing technology and there's little or any effort being made by the masses to understand it. Do you understand that?

Uh-huh.

Well, what you don't understand and you cannot control, by the very law, you're destined to destroy, you see? You see, the law is so clear. You see, if you have something that you judge is threatening you, that you fear and you judge—of course, you have to judge you can't control it or you wouldn't fear it. Well, if the effort isn't made to understand it, to understand how it works, then fear destroys what it cannot control from lack of effort to understand. So as the masses are not—the effort is not being made for the masses to understand the advancing technology, history shall repeat itself. They shall rise someday and destroy it, you see. But they destroy it with ignorance. They destroy it under the bondage of belief that it is anti-God or it is anti-this or anti-something else, you see. Do you understand that, [Student N]?

Yes.

Hmm? Yes. Yes, go ahead with that next question.

I have another question on viewing versus seeing.

Uh-huh.

In our everyday life—

Is that a macrocosmic question?

It, it . . .

[The teacher laughs again.] Wasn't this a class to be on macrocosm? I think we want to try to bring into balance the difference between microcosm and macrocosm, you see. You see, one includes the whole of the sky. You look at the sun and the little trees there and everything, you see. And the other is kind of very small. Hmm? And you do want to be much more expanded, don't you?

Yes, [Student Y] is waiting for a question. You're supposed to keep an eye on that little watch over there. *[The teacher addresses the cameraman.]* Uh-huh. Yes?

Even though . . .

Yes?

Are we saying, even though they may destroy the—they may try to—let's say the government does set about to destroy that which they don't understand. Is that—

It's not usually the governors that do it. It's not the ruling class. It's the masses who do it.

OK. Excuse me.

Yes, yes, it's not the educated. It's the uneducated who do it, yes, for they fear it, you see.

Uh-huh.

See, uneducated people, they fear many things and are very superstitious. Educated people, on an average, fear far less things, you see? Far less things. Go ahead.

So will that—is that just a natural process of what is happening—so inevitably—

It's a normal process, yes, yes, in that respect. Yes.

OK.

It happened before. It will happen again unless great effort is made to awaken the masses.

My question is, Is it inevitably, is it, is it heading in the right direction anyway, even though it's fluctuating in that way?

Well, right direction, wrong direction—of course, right direction for the governing rulers is wrong direction for the masses who have yet to make the effort to understand it. You see, it's like the advancement of anything. The first thing [is] the mind takes a look at it and it's quite interested in it. It's different, you see. And the first thing it does is try to control it.

Now it's like a person who has a new product in your world and they go and they look at it and they work with it to control it. And they don't even make the effort to study the instruction manual that comes with it. Do you understand that? Well, look at the masses because that's the way they usually do [things]. You see? They go into a store and that's what they desire. They take it. They don't know what the ingredients [are]. They have no idea. They're not even interested in that, you see? So that's mass thinking. Now a person, educated, is interested in, "What is contained in this that I'm going to consume?" You see? What benefits or detriments are in it. Do you understand the difference, [Student Y]? And so—but mass, the mass vibration doesn't think that way. Yes.

OK.

That's why they pollute the planet and upset the balance of the planet, you see? Hmm?

OK. My question is one of—

They're controlled by blind desire. Yes?

I'm having a hard time, probably . . . with the question. [It is difficult to transcribe a few words.]

That's all right. Ask the question again.

OK. So is it, even though, let's say in thinking of planetary—

Yes?

—even though these things are happening where it pulls one way or it pulls another way—

Yes?

—its course . . .

Yes?

It is on an inevitable course.

Yes, well, inevitable in the sense that it can always be changed [in] certain degrees. For example, a monitor comes close to your planet and it tips the axis. It tips your planet on its axis. The same monitor comes and monitors your planet and doesn't tip your planet on its axis. You understand? Because, you see, that is dependent on how much balance there is on the planet by the intelligences who are inhabiting it. You see, if they have gone overbalance in their ignorance, which is, in truth, affect[ing] the whole solar system, and that solar system is affecting all the other solar systems, then the monitor planet comes closer—do you understand?—according to the laws established. The planet then goes off its axis, and you have these great upheavals and disasters. And you start all over again. *[Reddy begins to bark again.]* Do you understand how that goes, you see?

So in that sense, you see, it's like predestination. Try to understand there are these variables, and if these variables are met, then there's a change in the destiny. Do you understand that, [Student Y]?

I do. And hearing that . . .

Here. Mr. Red, now, we've had enough foolishness. *[The teacher addresses Reddy's barking. And Reddy replies with a single, more quiet bark.]*

. . . one wouldn't want to be discouraged in—

Discouraged?

Yes. Then—

Because then one is an instrument in imbalancing the whole. So one wants to be encouraged. You see, one can only be discouraged by denying personal responsibility, you see? You see, if one accepts personal responsibility, what they do has an impact, but they don't look at what they do as so microscopic [compared to] what the millions are doing. Do you understand? Because, you see, to do it that way is to deny one's own effort to face their own personal responsibility. You see, it's like a person saying, "Oh, what difference does it make? Why should I make any diff—why should I do anything? It's not going to make any difference." They justify not making the effort. Do you understand that, [Student Y]?

Yes.

So you don't look outside and then compare your efforts to what somebody else is doing. Because if you do that, you deny personal responsibility of what you should be doing. Yes, [Student Y].

So what—

Time is almost up.

—can each individual—like, if it's done on a percentage base—like, you say—

Yes, well, what each individual can do is what they should be doing: they should be working with their universe and not be concerned about everyone else's universe. Do you understand that?

Well, I see that our time is up for today. Most interesting. We'll carry on with this macrocosm next Sunday. Thank you and have a good week. It's good to see you here today. Thank you.

OCTOBER 12, 1986

A/V Class Private 64

Good morning, class.

You would be well advised to take note of the following statement: When the distance between two spheres equals the circumference of both spheres, the Law of Harmony is established.

Your homework for this week is a written explanation, in twenty-five words or less, on the Law of Harmony. You have been well prepared for the lesson and your report is required for next Sunday.

Now all of the information necessary in that understanding has been given to you in these classes of recent dates. Therefore, all that is required is effort on your part to study what you have received. *[Reddy, the church's dog, begins barking. He is on the balcony of the east wing of the temple, which is overhead of the class in the garden.]* This law, which you will bring (your explanation of) next class, is of the most crucial importance for your growth.

You may be excused. *[The teacher addresses the cameraman so that he may attend to Reddy.]*

Reddy!

Our friend is—why don't you just excuse yourself, please?

Most appropriate that your homework would be the Law of Harmony.

The study of any science is only difficult to those who judge they know nothing about it. My experiences, throughout time, [have] been the ones who think they know so much have the most difficulty, for the ones who think they don't know so much are the ones who are more qualified to learn, to expand, and to grow.

Our friend will be down in a minute. We'll be making some changes with him. *[The teacher refers to Reddy.]*

I note that one of my students has their chair misplaced. [Student Y] is not in view. Please correct it [Student O] and [Student Y]. [Student O], if you will move closer to [Student H], and [Student Y] will move in the—well, not quite as close. Oh, that's fine, you see?

Yes.

So whoever is responsible, will you kindly see that we don't have to waste precious class time to adjust the chairs?

Yes. Now we'll go ahead with our macrocosm lessons, which we began last class and which, through your homework, of course, will continue. So I will respond to the first question. Kindly raise your hand and stand so that you can hear it on your little class tape. Yes, [Student S], please. Besides it'll help you if you think you're a little bit chilly. Yes.

Thank you. Last week you said that there's always the spiritual counterpart, as in gold had the spiritual meaning of wisdom.

Yes.

Does the diamond have a spiritual counterpart meaning?

Yes, it does.

And could we have that understanding at this time?

Well, thank you very much. Do you, first, understand what the function of the mineral gold is? You understand what the spiritual meaning is.

Ah . . .

What is the spiritual meaning of gold?

Spiritual? Wisdom.

Divine wisdom.

Divine wisdom.

Yes, we find many wisdoms in many worlds. All right. Now what is the function of that?

Last week it was my understanding that we discussed, then, the function was the security of the need of the money.

Yes, yes, that's fine. So you would consider then the function of the mineral gold as what? *[After a short pause, the teacher continues.]* Well, let us put it another way because we want to fully understand what we're discussing. What does the need of security offer to the mind? What does the need of security offer to the mind? [Student O] has an answer to that.

I think it's fear.

[Student O] thinks it's fear. What does it offer to anyone else? What does the need of security offer to the mind? Yes, [Student S].

It's a denial of the divine wisdom.

And what does a denial of the divine wisdom offer to the mind? Yes.

It's control over the spirit in the mental.

Yes. [Student U].

I was going to say control as well.

Yes, [Student R].

A separateness.

Yes.

Or personality.

Yes. They're all correct, but there's one word that you are moving toward. Yes, [Student P].

Would that be belief?

Yes, all those are involved. There's one thing it offers to the human mind. The need of security offers to the human mind. Yes, [Student H].

To me the need for security offers to the mind not having to take personal responsibility.

Yes, it certainly does. And what—yes, [Student M]. What is that one word?

Satisfaction?

Yes, they're all involved with one word, and there's no bottom to the pit. Yes, [Student O].

It must be the glory of self.

What is the handmaiden of need? Who does she shake hands with? Yes, [Student R].

Pride. [Student R responds.]

Oh, I know. [Student P exclaims.]

Yes.

Greed. [Student P responds.]

Greed! Thank you. I knew that it would come sooner or later. All right, you see, it's important that you express your understanding of the spiritual teachings you are receiving, so that you can see how well covered one function—such as, [for] example, we just discussed—such as one function known as greed. One function has many, many, many defense mechanisms, and only a few of them were listed. However, [Student P] did see, after many of those soldiers were knocked down, that in the final analysis they are all protecting the function of greed. Pride protects it. The lack of personal responsibility protects it. Satisfaction protects it. Belief protects it. So it's important that you note what protects any particular function. So when you find yourself believing this, you find yourself in need of satisfaction, you find yourself in the need for your pride to be boosted, and go down the list of that which is protecting the one function known as greed.

So, you see, when you ask a question on the minerals, you must first have an understanding of the faculty and the function, so you can move to the next step, which the question, I recall, was, What is the spiritual meaning of the diamond? You see, with gold I gave you the spiritual meaning, and you worked to find the material meaning. That wasn't so difficult to do. With diamond, I gave you the material meaning: deception. Now you're going have to do your homework and find the spiritual meaning.

You see, many years ago I spoke to all of you students. So many—some were here; some have gone. And I explained at that time that spiritual teachings are not satisfactory to a mental world because they're not given in a way that the mind has established; that it convinces one that that's the way one can learn; that is not a spiritual class. A spiritual class is when you begin to think for yourself and to, slowly but surely, understand. Not just be told, but understand yourself: why are there so many explanations of a function. The explanations are the justifications and the defense mechanism of the function itself. That's growth inside. That's the only growth there really is.

So it's like your question, your homework for next week on the distance between two spheres. Well, first of all, those of you who think you have a problem should start to consider: What is a sphere? What is a sphere? Is it limited in size? What is it? You should first make the effort to understand what a sphere is. You see, that's your homework. How can you get to the Law of Harmony, an explanation of it, without study and application? Now you can go to your dictionary and you can look up and accept someone else's explanation of what a sphere is. And then you can see if that's appropriate and in harmony with the understandings you have been given over these years of a sphere.

You see, when I said it has all been given to you—but when we miss the boat, there's another boat along the way. We have to be patient and make the effort. So it's up to us as individualized, evolving beings to understand that the homework that you have for this week, which is required, your explanation thereof, your written explanation, required next Sunday, is not something that is limited to the physicists. Just because spiritual laws are revealed, that the physicists think that is their sole domain, is ridiculous. And for you to permit your mind to think that way is disgusting, to say the least. For they work with laws and cover them with mountains of justifications and defense mechanisms to make those simple laws their domain. So I want you to help yourself to get out of that type of thinking and to get down to *terra firma* in simple language that you can understand. That help you with your question?

Yes. Thank you. [Student S responds.]

So when you have that understanding in full bloom, then we can move on to the spiritual meaning of the next mineral. Hmm? Thank you. Now someone else has a question here. [Student O]. Yes.

Yes. Are there, and if so, would you give the number of a certain number, a basic number of minerals that are on this planet Earth and the basic number of them and, and give us the basic number. And are other minerals composed of these basic number of minerals?

And well, yes, when you say "basic" minerals, then I accept you are speaking of minerals that do not contain what any other mineral contains. For example, there are minerals, they have a certain amount of these particular elements, but they do not have a predominance of those particular elements; and therefore, do you constitute that as a basic mineral? Or are you speaking of the very few minerals that have exclusively certain elements, then the number is vastly reduced. But it depends on what you're speaking about. For example, you say you have copper in your world, right?

Yes, sir.

All right. And you have iron.

Yes.

And you have several different minerals and things in your world, on your planet.

Yes, sir.

Now the question then arises, [of] the elements contained within the iron, are there any that are in the copper? That's the question that you must ask within yourself. So, you see, if you consider that if there are not any of those elements in any percentage contained in the other mineral, then, as I said, we greatly reduce the number. But it depends on your perspective in reference to your question. See, to answer your question and not have the understanding of the question that is asked, then my responsibility to the Light I serve and to the other students, to take the answer verbatim, when the answer must be individual—do you understand? For truth is individually perceived, for the question presents its own statement. Do you understand that, [Student O]?

Yes, I understand.

You see? So in all justice and fairness to the entire student body, your question must be answered so that other students do not deceive themselves from the answer that is given. Does anyone have any question about how we answer our questions? Pardon? If you do, please speak up now. *[After a very short pause, the teacher continues.]*

All right. So from which perspective are you asking the question on what you consider basic minerals? Hmm?

I'm asking—in that. OK. I felt—I know you understand that I felt that some minerals don't contain—I felt that some minerals—

Elements.

—didn't contain elements that others did.

That is correct. That is correct.

So I wanted—I was asking for the whole, the whole number, including—

That contains elements that the other minerals contain?

Yes. And the ones that don't contain—I mean, in other words, like, not like if copper doesn't contain some elements that iron contains, I still wanted copper and iron named.

Oh, fine, fine. Well, that—now do we all understand how many he wants named? All right. So if you want that many named—and you want the ones known or the ones known and unknown? Now that's another question, you see. You see, my friends, how can you follow a straight line if you do not know that there are curves before you walk upon it? Hmm? You can't, can you? You still believe the line is straight. Well, the line isn't straight anyway. It returns unto itself and that makes it a circle. There's no such thing as a straight line. All right. Go ahead, [Student O].

Yes, sir. Well, I would like the ones that, that you all feel that are important to us that we should know at this time.

Well, they're all important.

Well, the ones that we should know at this—

In that respect, I don't feel at all. They're all important to all students of the Light. Thank you very much, [Student O].

Thank you.

Hmm? All right?

OK.

Fine.

Thank you.

There are 6,153 on the planet Earth. Now if you haven't found them, which I know you haven't, then you've got a many-lifetime job. Now we're talking about the ones that contain elements that the other ones contain, aren't we?

Yes.

Fine. Now what number did you write down there so no one is confused?

Six-thousand-one-hundred-and-fifty-three.

That's fine. Yes, [Student R].

I'd like to know what happened to the Mayan and the Inca civilizations. Our history is—they don't know. They say that the civilizations just seemingly disappeared. And I would like to find out what your understanding is as [to] what happened to them.

Well, which ones? The Mayans or the Incas?

Well, I—

Well, they're two separate civilizations, you understand.

Yes. Yes, the Incas.

Well, you choose the Incas, do you?

Yes.

Fine. They were very highly developed. The technology was greatly advanced, far beyond your present understanding at this time. And when you permit your mind to accept the possibility of disintegration, you permit your mind to accept the possibility of physical dematerialization and the changing of atoms, and you permit your mind to accept the possibility of technological advancement so that it is done in a physical world by physical means, then you will understand the disappearance of the Incas, you hear?

Uh-huh.

Now the Mayans are an entirely a different question.

May I have an answer for the Maya?

An entirely different civilization. Very spiritually evolved. And their seeming disappearance or disintegration was not done by physical means, but it was a spiritual release that was chosen by the wise ones of the civilization. So one was a very materialistic—the Incas—a very materialistic, very technological[ly] advanced civilization on your planet. Then the others were very spiritually evolved and understood these laws and chose to move to their next abode. Hmm?

Thank you.

For they had a great responsibility. It was either to lose to the uninitiated the knowledge that they had gained over eons or to take it with them. And they took it with them. Hmm? That help with your question?

Yes. Thank you.

You're welcome. Yes.

Could you please tell us a little bit more about what you mean by they were—had the possibility of losing that to the uninitiated?

That is correct. You see, in evolution of any form—you see, you can see it more clearly with a flower or especially with animals, with domesticated animals. When you evolve to what you call a hybrid of anything, whether it's a human or it's an animal or a plant, you always do so at the weakening of the physical structure that the spiritual being is inhabiting in a physical world. And therefore, doing so, a hybrid or spiritually evolved being—animal, plant, or human—cannot withstand the gross vibrations of a civilization of force. And the Mayans were sufficiently advanced to make an intelligent decision in keeping with their responsibilities. And so they chose to leave for a different abode, into a different world. Hmm?

Thank you.

To remain there would be totally irresponsible for evolved beings. Do you understand that?

Yes. Thank you.

Yes. You, perhaps, could even best relate to when many of the so-called tribes of your planet, when advancing civilization went to civilize them. And that's what they—that which they had spiritually was contaminated and lost. Hmm? Yes. And so that's the way that it is.

Does someone else have a question there? Yes, [Student L], please.

I've read accounts of visitors from another planet, so-called, in the mountains in Peru. And I am wondering if they are really there? And what their purpose is, if they are?

Well, I mean, it is not the first time that the planet Earth has ever been monitored. It's monitored constantly. And surely you realize that advanced teachings require, when exposed to contamination, they require certain, what you would understand in your world, as protection because they are exposed to force. And so in that respect, intelligent decisions are constantly being made by those responsible for the planet Earth, whether or not a civilization should suddenly disappear, depending on the so-called secrets that they have earned in their evolution.

The only thing secret about a secret is the uninitiated. You see? The uninitiated know that it's a secret. It's no secret to the initiated. Secrets and things of that nature belong to force. However, force ever seeks to learn of ways to gain what it judges it doesn't have, you see. Yes, the only problem is, by the need for it, they do not experience its benefits because they cannot apply it, for need stands in the way. You see? You see, there is the ... about everything. *[It is difficult to transcribe one or two words.]* When you permit the mind to convince you that you need something and you work to receive what you judge that you need, once you receive it, it does not give you the benefits that it gives the one who does not need it. Now I do hope that I've made that clear. You see?

You see, if you don't need it, oh, you'll have it. But when you need it, well, you have what you believe that you need: the need of it. And therefore, it cannot—you cannot experience it. You cannot experience goodness as long as you permit yourself to be convinced that you need it. Now when you accept the possibility of experiencing the goodness that you are, then you no longer need what you already have; and therefore, you begin to experience it. It is when you insist that the mind ([which] you believe that you are) then you constantly experience the need and frustration thereof.

So do your proper exercises and do your breathing especially and move from that realm that is just a trap of what you call need, you see. If you allow yourself to convince yourself you need anything, you have established the Law of Frustration and you'll always be in need. And even if you receive it, you'll still be in need. I do hope that that—you see, we accept from limit and by accepting from limit, we pay the price of limit. And the price of limit is need, for limit is separation from what is. I think we've discussed that many times. Yes. Yes, [Student Y].

Would the moment—I was thinking of, in astrological terms.

Yes?

And would the moment of conception be that which rules one's faculty?

Oh, yes, absolutely. Definitely. And besides, the astrology you practice in your world is Babylonian. It's based upon a seven-planetarium system, which is absolute mist and mystery, yes. The Light can't shine very clearly. Yes.

Would the moment of birth into the expression—the moment of one's birth—

That's the—the physical birth is the function. The moment of conception is the faculty. Yes. Yes. So you're speaking of two entirely different birthdays, you know. Yes.

For the purposes of numerology and determining one's birth number—

Yes.

We take the date that we were physically born.

Yes, because we believe we're the functions. *[The teacher laughs.]*

Yes. What, what number do we add to that to get to the date of conception in order that our number may be correct?

Wonderful question. I'm happy to see we're moving into a little bit of the macrocosm here, anyway. What is it that moves the mountain of one's belief that they are their functions?

Faith.

And what number is that?

Five.

That's all that you got to do.

Thank you.

Yes, [Student P].

Do we add the year that we were born, the nineteen and then the date?

Correct.

OK. So we use our calendar?

Yes, that's correct. That's correct. My, it's been so many years. Some of you were present when I gave Atlantean astrology, so many years ago. Now we've moved to having a little bit more understanding, haven't we?

Yes, is that [Student Y]? Yes, [Student Y].

Uh . . . well . . . I forgot the question.

It's all right.

OK.

That's all right. It'll come to you.

So if you, if your, if your earth number is—OK. Your birth date would be the function number, right? Would that be the number—let's say if you were—I'll use my own: Libra.

Yes.

And that has a certain number to it.

Yes, it does, when it's combined with the month, the day, and the year.

OK.

Fine.

Would that number rule the functions of one's—

Yes, it does.

And then you just explained how to reach . . .

Five. That is correct. That will reveal to you your faculty number. Yes.

Now would that help you to discover the place that you came from prior?

No, we have Atlantean astrology, which explains that in detail. Yes, I have given to—some of the students present have received it so many years ago. We, in time—definitely this year—we will be moving inside. The ladies are getting a little chilly I note here. We will be moving inside the temple, and I will see that the charts are brought out so that you can understand.

Now so many years ago, I brought it to some of the students. And some who absolutely refuse[d] to—who had interest in so-called astrology, which are indicative, never compelling, because of man's so-called free will [of] 10 percent. They were so convinced on Babylonian astrology, they started to contaminate the simple Atlantean astrology that I had brought and had several of my students all confused. Some of them aren't even present any longer here in your, in the school. And so we refrain[ed] from giving anything further, if you will recall [Student S] and [Student J] and [Student R]—several that were present. [Student H], were you present of the Atlantean? I think you were, and [Student P]. And so we discontinued that until such time as the students could evolve a little further and free themselves from the need to contaminate the simple teachings given with what they already had in their mind.

And it caused a great deal of confusion, if you'll recall. However, we will bring the Atlantean astrology out, be it in divine order this year, as when we move inside the temple for our classes. Hmm?

Thank you.

Yes, and then you can very—in fact, my students who have received all of the Atlantean astrology—and the charts are here—my students will be given the opportunity to explain how you find the planet that you came from and to see if the contamination of Babylonian astrology had any kind of shadows over the untold hours that were spent in explaining to them, you see. Yes, [Student Y].

Does that planet rule your faculties because—

It certainly does. It rules—it's the governing ruler. It is the governing ruler, yes. And the students that were in those classes, they are well aware of the planet from whence they came. And if they're not, they are contaminated. And we'll certainly find out, all of us, won't we, when we go inside for that. Yes.

Thank you.

You're welcome. [Student M], please.

Yes. The Earth is one of the nine children of the sun and the moon—

Yes.

And it is the fifth planet.

[It's] all going back home, you know. It's in process.

Being five, being faith. Each of the other nine planets from the, from the sun have—I think asked a similar question last week—had similar—will have minerals on them.

Certainly, they do.

Right. And—

In various combinations.

Right.

Yes.

Because of the evolution of the species on that particular planet.

Weren't you impressed that there are so many minerals on your planet?

Yes.

[The teacher laughs.] You did go to, to . . .

[It's] mind boggling.

[The teacher continues laughing.] And I'm not talking about these artificial ones that the human mind gets together and changes. I'm talking about the ones that nature has done.

Yes, go ahead. Because—but then who has gone inside in your world to the core, to near the core to get all those different ones? Why, no [one.] Oh, go ahead. Go ahead with your question.

Now the soul faculties and sense functions are part of the whole picture and the big macrocosm.

Yes?

Is that not true? Like, all these minerals on the other planets, they all have the soul faculty and the sense functions. Like the species that say—

Oh, certainly. The species? Oh, why, certainly. Absolutely. Of course, they do.

And so—

They look a little different physically because, you see, their atmospheric conditions and their planet is a little different. Yes.

Right. But they're, they're made up of the eighty-one sense functions and—

Yes? Yes, yes, indeed the law is, is—the law is the same for all of them.

And depending on their evolution . . .

Yes?

... they're just different soul faculties and sense functions they're expressing at the time, as far as their lessons—

Oh yes, certainly. You have the same ones in potential. Why, certainly. And another thing I thought you would be interested in, in the macrocosm studies here, is whether or not your solar system is still in its expansion or its contraction. I've been waiting for someone to ask that question. Thank you, [Student M].

Thank you.

[Student U], weren't you interested in whether or not the solar system, in which you're on one of its planets, was still in its expansion or its contraction?

Yes, sir. I was going to ask—

Yes.

How old is the Earth? Is the solar system considered young, middle aged, or old?

This, this solar system? The Earth, the sun and this solar system?

[If the student responded, it is difficult to transcribe.]

Well, let me ask you a question. When did you stop being a boy and become a man? Because that's the age of your planet. Well, I take it you don't understand my questions. *[The teacher laughs.]* Well, when a boy moves from teenage to manhood, you consider [that] the age of your dear old Earth. Hmm?

OK.

All right?

Yes, sir.

It's still flexing its muscles. *[The teacher and many of the students laugh.]*

Yes, sir.

Do you understand that?

Yes, sir.

And don't the inhabitants upon it seem to be doing the same?
Yes, sir. [Many more students laugh.]
Pardon?
That's very true, sir.
So I don't see any closeness yet to the contraction phase. [It] seems to me, from what we've been watching for eons, is the expansion.
Yes, sir.
As long—listen to the homework that you have. The distance between two spheres must equal the circumference of both spheres and that establishes the Law of Harmony. Now stop and think. Stop and think about expansion and contraction. The problem with your solar system—and the worst offender is the planet Earth—is it does not, by mass vibration, see the limit of its expansion. All things expand and retract. They contract. They return unto themselves. So your planet shows that it doesn't even consider contraction.

Talk to the people in your world. Expansion has reached far beyond the limits of the rights of the Law of Expansion. That's the mass vibration of your planet. If your planet was not still convinced that there's something beyond for it to get and that it has a right to it, then you would not have all of the wars and disturbance that your planet Earth has. That's why it is so closely monitored of all the planets in your solar system. It does not accept personal responsibility; so it does not recognize its boundaries. Do you understand that?

Now don't misunderstand me that man, in his evolution, should not go and visit the planets and understand his solar system. But don't ever think for one moment that other planets and their intelligences will permit the inhabitants of the planet Earth to contaminate other solar systems.

Yes, I hope that's helped with your question. You see, whoever does not accept personal responsibility does not, *does not* recognize, nor accept, the limits of its rights. It's a basic law of physics. Yes, [Student D].

We were told some time ago that in forty years—

Uh-huh.

—we would begin to accept responsibility for the pollution of our planet.

Yes.

And that will change the flow. Is it at that point that we will begin to see our limits?

Well, you will begin to see your limits when you accept responsibility for what you have done to the rights of others. So man pollutes all of these creatures. And pollutes these lovely flowers and things, and does not accept responsibility for their pain and suffering. Do you understand? So that's a, that's a first step, yes.

You can tell very clearly. You go out into your world and you look and you see if a person is pushy. If they're pushy on the rights of others, then I can assure you—have a talk with them because they do not even accept, nor do they want to hear, anything about the word *personal responsibility*. People who do not accept personal responsibility are pushy over the rights of any and everything else. Hmm? Yes.

[It appears that the student does not respond verbally.]

You're welcome, [Student D]. Yes, [Student O].

Yes. Is it in the future for us, as human beings, to one day lose our monetary system, the value that we have or the monetary system that we have?

You're already losing it. It's not a future thing. It's already in process. Isn't that lovely?

Yes, sir.

[The teacher laughs joyfully.] You're already in process.

Yes, sir.

Pardon?

Yes, sir.

Don't you know that? Oh, don't worry about a depression or anything, you know.

Oh, no.

You've moved into the plastic age. They even have plastic gold for you. Oh, no, no, no. *[The teacher laughs again.]* Well, it looks like gold.

Right.

You know? And man has convinced himself that seeing is believing. So what does it matter that it's something—it's not the minerals that he thinks it is? It looks like it. That's all that's important. Seeing is believing. *[The teacher laughs again.]*

You asked about losing the monetary system. You already lost it. You haven't recognized it yet, but you've already lost it. Yes, [Student O].

Well, that would be, that would be—

You want to know how many, how many—what do you call them?—king corporations are taking care of your monetary system today. Would you like to know?

Yes, sir.

There are six. There's only six. There are only six corporations controlling your monetary system. So tell me whether or not you're going to lose it. You've already lost it. Yes, go ahead, [Student O]. *[The teacher laughs again.]*

OK. Well, for us to go to that, to that—

Pardon?

—for us to go to the plastic system, that would—

[You are] already in the plastic system.

OK.

You're already in it.

That's another step, that's just another step of deception. I mean, does, I mean—what I'm really asking was—what I was really asking was, Does man have to totally destroy or disintegrate himself on this earth, period? I mean, in the physical sense.

Why, I wouldn't be so discouraged, but have a seat, [Student O], and I'll explain something to you.

Yes.

Your world based its monetary system on what it judged was a rare mineral. I think you all understand that, don't you? Gold. Now long ago you moved from what you understand as a gold standard. Do you understand?

Yes.

Every once in a while, various governments give you a little taste, and they make available for you a little piece of gold, representing a dollar or what you believe is your monetary system. Not too often, but periodically so that you will continue to believe that you have a solid economy and monetary system. Do you understand that?

Yes, sir.

As they're moving and have been for a long time into plastic gold—you hear?

Yes, sir.

The step—you're on an in-between step. Your gold standard of stability upon which your monetary systems were founded does not exist. Much of the world believes, on your planet, that it does. What replaces gold, [Student O]? What is going to replace gold as a monetary system? You're going to be surprised. Yes?

I don't know.

Diamond!

Right.

Deception! Ugh! The wealth of your planet is being hoarded in diamonds. This is the great problem in your country of South Africa. They cannot permit the mass of diamonds available to go on the world market because it is already a monetary system that you're not aware of. Gold hasn't existed for a long time. Deception has taken control of that. Hmm? The diamond market, that's your monetary system. You're not even aware of it. You're aware of plastic and have, still, hopes of gold. Hmm?

Yes, sir.

Yes, someone else? [Student H] has a question.

Thank you. [Student H replies.]

Thank you. [Student O responds.]

When the, when the first beings, the first races came to this planet, what system did they set up? What was it based on? What precious—

You mean monetary system?

Yes.

They didn't have a monetary system. There was no monetary system. [A] monetary system is an effect of the function of greed. All monetary systems are based upon that function. All monetary systems. There's no monetary systems with evolved beings. Hmm?

A family, if you to want call it—a group, you know. Just like you had a little tour of the quail here the other week, you know. *[Again, these classes were given in the temple garden.]* They go on—they take them on tour. I don't know if you've noticed, [but] they take them [on a] tour around the temple here periodically. You see about fifteen, twenty of them. You know, it's like a tour guide. *[The teacher and many students laugh. Many animals visited the gardens at the temple.]* Oh, yes, yes, yes. This is what happens: periodically they'll go on a tour all over, you know.

All right, so you look at that, in beings at early times on your planet. And so they went out and got food. All right? The head of the house went out and got food. The head of the hut, the cave, went out and got food and brought it back in. Well, you know how it was portioned out? In keeping with the size of the being and in keeping with the energy and the work that they did. You see, that's reasonable. You see, if the being was large, [that] required more nourishment, [and] did more work, [which] required more nourishment. The ones that were smaller and did less got less. If they were smaller and did more work, then, of course, they got more. So it was all portioned out.

There was no monetary system, for the faculty of reason was flowing, you see. And this one didn't want what that one wanted because they understood and realized they were receiving ever in keeping with what was necessary for their well-being. So why would a person want more than what is in the best interest of their well-being? And if they did, then that person was an alien and got sent out from the tribe. Just like a mother bear would do to her cubs: send them out. Get rid of them, you see, before they contaminate the whole. Hmm? Before they contaminate the whole, you remove them. You have a responsibility to do so. Yes. Yes.

How did physical life first begin on this planet?

How did physical life—what do you mean by physical life? Are you talking about the amoeba? Or are you talking about intelligent beings? In what form are you talking of the intelligent beings?

Ah—

Oh, I see your question. Yes, intelligent beings. Well, first of all, you're not going to find the missing link on your planet. I think we've discussed that before, haven't we? Were you present? The missing link doesn't exist on your planet, the planet Earth. You're trying to make a connection between the monkey and the man. But, no—well, let's see. How much time do we have left there? *[The teacher asks the cameraman how much time is left on the videotape.]*

About seven minutes.

Uh-huh. Uh-huh. All right. Well, let's get to it as quickly as possible. It's known as—well, how do you call it in your world?—it's a crossbreed. Intelligences from other planets, responsible, came and bred with the beings on the planet that you might consider monkeys. Does that help with your question? Well, man considers himself a hybrid, doesn't he? Well, there's something inside of him that considers that. Why, certainly. He's part monkey and part highly intelligent being. He's half-and-half.

Why, certainly. Always has been. And it's interesting to note, throughout the eons, he still considers himself a hybrid. Yes, [Student O].

Yes.

That's why he can't weather many storms. The slightest storm blows him over. Yes.

We were given the—we know—we've been discussing the two minerals: one gold and the other one diamond.

Uh-huh.

All right. We said divine wisdom was the, I guess it would be the faculty of—

It's a divine wisdom of—

—spiritual faculty of gold.

And what was the function?

We didn't say what—I didn't recall the function of gold. [After a short pause, the student continues.] *Greed.*

Yes. And what does greed offer? Didn't I just get through explaining to you you're in a diamond monetary system and don't realize it? You see, greed offers total deception.

OK.

What's the matter with you?

No, I'm saying—OK—we [are] moving from greed, we're moving down a rung from—

From greed.

—or up a rung—I mean—

Well, I wouldn't consider it up. Up to one is down to another. So let's go along. *[The teacher laughs joyfully.]*

We're moving from gold to diamonds.

Yes?

OK. We're moving from, from greed to deception.

Yes, it's guaranteed. They've already done it. Yes, [Student L]. Last question. Time has run out on your class.

Referring to the monitoring, the monitor planet of the solar, of our solar system—

Yes.

—I'm wondering if there's a chain of command in this solar system wherein subgroups of monitors are responsible for individual planets or a planet.

There are hierarchies in all worlds.

Oh.

And in all realms. Yes.

Thank you.

It's the Law of Form.

Well, thank you. I'll see you next Sunday. Don't forget your homework now. You [are to] have [a] written explanation of the Law of Harmony based upon the full explanations that you have had over these many, many classes. And it's very important to understand the distance between two things.

Thank you and good day.

OCTOBER 19, 1986

A/V Class Private 65

Good morning, class.

Today's class: I will share with you all the faculties and all the functions.

Now for many years in these classes, there has been questions on what is a faculty and what is its corresponding function. And it is good to view the evolution of this class; that those questions are now answered in keeping with the awakening of the majority of the class.

You will not be able, in your world, to list all of the functions and all of the faculties, not in a class of time limit, for each one has so very many.

Now what is a function? And what is a faculty? We've already discussed that functions bind, reveal their limit. And faculties free. We've already discussed whatever you create, you are in service to. And many things our minds do create.

And so [for] all of the functions and all of the faculties: whatever you express and believe that you are it, that which you express is a function; whatever you express and view its expression is a faculty. And so functions and faculties are without number, for the mind, a vehicle in service to what is, is a constant process of limiting what is expressing.

So I have given to you over these years duty, gratitude, and tolerance as a basis of the faculties of your soul. You want to know what the function of gratitude is? All you have to do is to believe you are expressing gratitude and the faculty becomes a function, for you have taken what you are and sacrificed it for what you have limited it to be by your mind.

I had, over this time, shared with you that a function is simply an undeveloped or restricted faculty. So when, through attachment to your fruits of action, which reveals to you your effort of the love of yourself, then your faculties descend and are known as functions.

Are there any questions now as you tempt to list your many faculties and many functions? *[After a short pause, the teacher continues.]*

For example, let us go to gratitude. A person says to themselves, "I am in gratitude." It is true; they are in gratitude. They are in gratitude to their own belief of what they have created to express what they are. That therefore is a function. For if someone says to you, "I am very grateful" and expects from you what will maintain, for them, gratitude in their mind, to you that ofttimes is not known as gratitude.

Now we have time for questions. Yes, [Student Y], please.

When moving from a function to, a function to the faculty, let's say, the triune duty, gratitude, and tolerance—

Yes?

So you are saying that you simply—you don't identify with the movement. You don't say that that's what you are. You just— well, I guess that's my question.

Yes, fine. Thank you. For example, work is a faculty. To most of us it's a function. When we permit our mind to tell us how hard we are working and we begin to restrict, by our attachment to the expression of what we are, when we begin to identify with the vehicle through which the faculty is expressing and through that identification we become bound by the vehicle through which that which we are is expressing, then work, for us, becomes a function, when in truth work is a faculty. It is our attachment to the fruits of the action of our own mental creation, the vehicle through which what we are is expressing, that we descend from a faculty into a function. Yes, [Student M], please.

Yes, then does our perception . . .

Well, I can answer that, perhaps—that's fine, [Student M]. Your question, I don't mean to interrupt you, please. When you experience perception, you are free from that which you perceive, for you have the realization or awakening that you are an inseparable part of what you perceive. However, ofttimes we think we are perceiving something when in truth it is the function of perception, which, in your mental world, is known as conception.

Now when, for example, you can look at the tree and your mind accepts that the tree is. You, your mind accepts that it has not created the tree. Do you understand that?

OK.

However, when you have a thought of the tree, then you begin on the process of descent of conceiving what the tree will or will not do. That's when what you view becomes a function, and you know it as what you see. Does that help with your question, [Student M]? The class has evolved to an understanding of faculties and functions, which functions have been asking for in your world for many, many years. Yes.

Thank you.

Yes, you see, functions have been asking for the corresponding faculties so that the functions may use them under the guise of expressing a faculty. That's like saying to a person, "I'm extremely grateful. I'm a great worker. I am this and I am that," and they're supposedly expressing or telling you all about the faculties. Well, by the very process of using that which is to serve the limit or form created by the mind of that which is not, those faculties become, at those moments, functions to serve limit. You see? Designed to free, they are used to bind. Does that help with your question?

Yes.

Yes, go ahead, [Student M].

I have one more question.

Certainly.

About contraction and expansion.

Perfect question in keeping with what we're discussing.

I'm not sure—

You wish to contract or expand at this moment?

Expand.

You wish to expand. *[The teacher coughs and then drinks from his glass of water.]* There is still need. For when we desire to expand, we reveal to what we are our own denial of what we are. For we have, in that process of growth—you see, everything expands only to contract. So which is truth? The expansion or contraction? That which we reflect or that which we are? Which are we?

Both. I mean, we are the total of all of it.

Thank you, [Student M]. Yes, [Student U].

According to the Law of Harmony, as one expands, the other must contract.

Yes. And so expansion and contraction must involve the mental worlds of limit, for that which is does not expand or contract. Only the vehicles that it is sustaining or expressing through. Do we understand that?

Yes, sir. [Student U responds.]

You see, you know, that's like saying, "Well, tell me what the Light is. Tell me what God is." Well, then we have to take, with mental substance, and put it in a vehicle. Now some vehicles we want to make very small; some we want to make very large. It's ever in keeping with whether or not we are awakened to the responsibility of using a vehicle. You see, there's a responsibility to every *thing*. Of course, all *things* are limits; all things are form.

So when you choose to expand—you see, broadening one's horizons refers to perception; it does not refer to conception. So I teach you to think more deeply. I don't teach you to think more outwardly. I teach you to think more deeply, for that which is using what you are is deeply hidden, very complex, and known as falsehood, you see.

See, that which uses us is always hiding under the covering of presentation, you see. You see, we present, you see. You see, we have this, in the mental world, we have this need to present. This need to present is the need to manipulate based upon the judgment of what we want out of someone. So we want to make what we judge is a good presentation. So we want to make this presentation to that person and that presentation to that person ever in keeping on what we judge their weaknesses are, which we judge, in our mind, of course, is their temptations. Now that's not truth. That isn't what you are. That is what you may trap yourself by. You may trap yourself by the vehicles that you create, for they are deeply hidden within the consciousness of the human mind, you see. Does that help you, [Student U]?

Yes, sir.

You see, a person says, "Well, I want to put on my best face. I'm going to meet so-and-so; and I want to do this and I want to do that." Well, their best face, that they consider is their best face, may or may not be what the person who they are going to present themselves to considers a best face. Do you understand, you see?

So, you know, it's like a salesman. A salesman makes the effort to be aware of his own weaknesses in order that he may be qualified in manipulating the weakness[es] of those that he or she presents themselves to, you see. So, you see, I mean, that's known as salesmanship in your world, you see. You say there's a good salesman as long as the person has done their homework to investigate and to judge correctly, in that world of a mental world, what the weaknesses of the recipient is, that they may tempt them successfully, don't you see? Yes. Now that's known in your world as salesmanship, you see. Hmm?

Well, I have no problem with that. You try to sell me anything, you might back me into a corner, but be rest assured I make sure that it is kept round. Yes, [are] there any other questions? Yes. Yes, [Student M].

Then is it my understanding, then, in the functions and all form, the principle of expansion and contraction exists within the functions and then in the mental world and in the world of limit.

Well, that's the only world of limit there is.
Right.
Is what you understand as a mental world.
Right.
That world you take with you when you leave your physical world. You take your mental world with you.
Correct.
So whatever kind of mental world you have created and believe that you are, that's the world, of course, that, once you reach the Light in the Rotunda, you'll be sent to, you see. You won't have any problem finding it. None of us ever do. Yes, the directions are very clear. Yes. Hmm? Did that help with your question?
Yes.
Yes. So we're working through all of this, you see. And it's why—it is good to view the class evolution. You see, you must look into your world and see, "Let's see. I'm making this change, that change. And this is going; that's going." Well, your experiences of its passing reveal your entrapment by what you have created.

Now we don't have to move a physical object, all we [have] got to do is move one of our mental objects. We've created many things, and all we [have] got to do is to take a look and see, "Well, now this here: I believe that I am this that I created." We believe we are what we have created ever in keeping with our self-love, which denies what we are, you see.
It's true. Yes.
Hmm?
Yes.
You see? And so many times you'll be talking to a person; and there are times when a person will take another look and say, "Well, that isn't what they are that's talking to me. I'm very familiar with that thing. Oh, yes, I have that thing myself.

I believed it for a time: that that was me." You see? You have to discern inside of yourself first—Hmm?—

Yes.

—what is you and what you are servicing. Remember, whatever you create and believe that you are, you are always in service to. You see? And so, being in service to it, a wise person takes a look to see whether it's serving them well or not, that which they are in service to. But you cannot see what you are in service to as long as you believe that you are what you have created and are in service to, for you are therefore blinded by conception, at the sacrifice of perception. You have descended from the faculty of perception—to perceive—into the function of conception—to conceive, you see.

Thank you.

So when—I have spoken to you that honesty will lead you through. Honesty, its lamp does not shine clearly, you see, if you permit yourself to believe you are the thoughts and things that you have created, because in so doing you are in service to those things and cannot see your service to them, you see. It's like saying to a person—talking to a person, and a person says, "Well, I cannot change that thought. That's what I am." Well, as long as they insist on allowing that which they have created to use their mouth and to convince them that that's what they are, then, for them, that's what they are at that time, you see.

I do see.

You see? You see, each person is an excellent salesman at conning themselves, you see? Now I don't mean to imply that salesmanship means conning. It is a manipulation of mental substance. It has nothing to do with spirituality, but it is a manipulation of mental substance, you see.

So this is why, I'm sure you heard in your world, "My, how could that have happened? That, that salesman was an actual con artist." You see? You see, a good salesperson is an excellent con artist, for they have qualified themselves first, you see.

If you have a product and are absolutely convinced that you are your product, you have no problem manipulating mental substance to whoever you present yourself to. But you must first totally convince yourself. That's a great price to pay. Hmm?

Yes.

Because, if, you see, if you go to sell a bar of soap and you know that it is worthless, your very knowing that it is worthless has its effect upon the vibration when you go to sell it. *[The teacher laughs joyously.]* You see, you can suppress your conscience, but you never know when it will pop up in a vibration, you see. And then you wonder why you didn't sell the bar of soap. Well, seemingly by accident—you didn't consciously say, "O conscience, pop up,"—it popped up and the person that you had presented yourself to, theirs popped up, too, because, you see, you have already established a rapport with them if you're a good salesman. And so you didn't make the sale. Well, better to find out at the time of presentation than three years later. Yes, any other questions? *[The teacher laughs.]*

Thank you.

The debt incurred is something else. Yes, [Student Y], please.

So is the love of self the creating of the form—I'm not—

The creating of the forms. I'll answer your question. Thank you very much. Is the love of the self [the] creating of the forms? It certainly, of course, is not. The love of the self is *believing* that you are what you have created. All minds create. The Light, God that is, sustains. All mental substance creates. That is not the problem; believing that one is what they have created is the great love of self. Does that help with your question? *[After a short pause, the teacher continues.]* Pardon?

Yes.

Well, if it doesn't help with your question, speak up another one, because, you see, as long as you insist on believing the thoughts that you create, then you will have to pay the price of that glory. Yes.

So that's where the suffering comes from, is the—I guess, what my real question is, is—so you're experiencing self-love and—so how do you move from that function to the faculty successfully?

By stop denying what you are and start accepting: to the Principle of Good, known as God, all things are possible and stop believing that you are the limit that you alone have created and know as experiences. Our God or goodness is just as large or as small as our self-love will allow it. And if we will make the effort to stop desiring the sensual pleasure, known as thrills and glory from the love of self, which is the belief that we alone have created this or that, and if we will make the effort to move beyond that—we have to give in order to free ourselves from what we believe we are. We have to give up the error of our own ignorance. Yes, [Student Y].

OK.

And some of us are absolutely tenacious in our efforts to hold on to the glory that we experience from what we believe—by believing that we are what we have created. In fact, those realms are insidious. Yes. Go ahead with your question. They are insidious.

True.

Because if they do not receive the answer through—in other words, an answer, a spoken word is a form, and if they conceive that form that they are receiving as unmanipulable [or] not malleable, then they continue on with their insidious defense. Yes, go ahead, [Student Y]. *[After a short pause, the teacher continues.]* They're absolutely insidious because they have received the Light of truth and they cannot worm out of it. Do you understand that? Yes, you see.

However, continue on with your questioning, and let's see if we can have a form that will be pleasing to them that they think they can worm out of. Hmm?

I truly don't want to worm out of it. I truly in my heart—

I am aware, I'm aware, hopefully, a little bit of truth. Be aware of what it is of what you want, [Student Y]. You will have no problem of getting it, but first be aware of what it is that you want. Use the insidious determination to serve the purpose of what you are, not of what you have created and believe that you are, which is the glory and the thrill of self.

So at that—this moment, I'm doing that? Is that—

Did I say that?

I don't—I'm asking.

Have you accepted? Is there any other student present, outside of two, that doesn't understand what I have just stated? *[The two students the teacher may be referring to could be Reddy, the church's dog, and a young child.]* If so, please raise your hands. *[After a short pause, the teacher continues.]*

When we ask a question, unless we make the effort inside of our self first, our question is a statement ever seeking, ever seeking support. That does not free what you are. It does, however, continue to serve in binding what you are not—binding you to what you are not.

Whenever we have trapped our self, we want to weigh out. Do you understand that [Student Y]? Do you understand that [Student N]? Do you understand that [Student D]? Do you understand that [Student L]? Does anyone not understand that, my dear children?

Face the payment of what you have created. It is always your blessing. For manipulation by mental substance is not what you are. It is only what you temporarily, for the sake of self-glory, believe that you are. Hmm?

We've come a long ways. Now, you see, as long as you allow those things in your mind to tell you, "Well, I don't understand," then you're just going to have to continue right on with that.

I, certainly, will answer your question. I am revealing to you, and anyone with eyes to see and ears to hear, that what your problem of bewilderment and confusion is, is a defense mechanism of what you insist on believing that you are because it does not want to change. For it to change, it would not have its substance from what you are. Go ahead, please. *[After a pause during which the student remains silent, the teacher continues.]* Speak up!

Yes, sir. So how does one know? Is there, like, a clue?

Yes, indeed. Thank you, [Student Y], very much. And my dear student [Student S], you will speak, please. You will speak to my student [Student Y] in reference to the question, for over the years you have so well qualified yourself throughout the eons. Now this is a class of evolution. Speak! And if [Student Y], who insists on defending that self-love, has a need of more than a minute to awaken, then you can take care of it after class. Go ahead.

Whenever, inside, we feel the concern and the emotional upset to whatever is being discussed, that is what you asked for as far as your clue goes. Truth needs no defense and is very calm, but this churning feeling that you feel inside, that is the threat that those levels in control are feeling. And they rise to their defense. [Student S explains.]

Thank you very much. Time is up.

Now we're here for spiritual awakening. Defending the forms of self-love is something [that] is reserved for you students to take care after [class]. Do you understand all of you? That's not the purpose of being in this lovely little class.

Now I want to tell you one thing very clearly. Those of you who insist on the love of self over the love of the Light of God inside of you—I'm moving on with my channel. Those of you who remain can spend the eons that you desire to spend in battling with the forms of self-love that you create [and] you insist on desiring, creating, and believing that you are.

I will take with you [me] only those who have made that step. *[The teacher may have intended to say "me."]* Do you understand, class? Now as far as the details, be not concerned, for I will not give those to your self-love to manipulate. There are those of you who will go with me and my channel, but you will be prepared by not insisting with the insidious, tenacity of self-love of not accepting what is so clearly before your very eyes.

Do you understand, [Student M]?

I do.

Pardon? [Student B] and [Student P] and [Student H] and everyone and [Student J].

You see, you see, the time of my channel being exposed to insidious self-love and its defense mechanisms because of mental substance of some of my students not willing to make that evolutionary step, you see—to look outside and to always cry. That day, I want you children to know, has ended for my channel.

He has his orders from me, and he has his orders from my assistants in explicit detail. There won't be any discussion of how grateful that we are, for gratitude is a demonstration; a spoken word makes it a function. Do we all understand that? So if you want to know about gratitude, say how grateful you are, and I'll show you the function of gratitude.

Now, children, wake up. We are not here to battle. Mental realms battle. And [Student Y], [Student D], and [Student N], you have growth steps to make inside as well as everyone else. You can make them or not make them; you can spend the rest of your life, if you so choose, to battle with them until you prove how, how right that you are, you see. That has nothing to do with this lovely class and the Light. That is a mental world through which you require mental substance to play and to manipulate with what your world would call, perhaps, tiddlywinks. Now, children, that's not the purpose of my coming here;

that is certainly not the purpose of my channel's dedication to the Light.

Now we'll go on with other questions, please. And certainly not one to defend those things, my dear students. Yes, [Student M].

Would the different centers of consciousness, representative of the different faculties and functions . . .

Yes?

. . . that correct? We have our nine centers of consciousness. [It is difficult to transcribe her complete question.]

Yes?

Within each center, there is a soul faculty, the triune soul faculty and sense function? Three groups within each or there's one group?

Well, all faculties, all functions are triune in expression.

Right.

Yes, of course. All right.

And I'm—guess I'm trying to understand within each center expresses a different soul faculty, a different triune soul faculty and sense function?

Well, yes, you have earth, fire, water. Those are centers of which you are speaking, is it not?

Yes.

Yes, those are the centers of consciousness. There's the spheres and there's the planes, yes.

Yes.

And they're all represented in the—there are nine centers of consciousness, nine spheres, nine planes, yes.

Yes.

Yes. Now you would like to know which functions belong to which centers or planes or spheres.

Yes, I—

Well, there's no problem whatsoever. No problem whatsoever. You know yourself whether it's a water center or a fire center. You know by its own expression and its own experience. *[The teacher laughs.]* I don't think you have, you students, have any problem whatsoever. You already have had a lovely, living demonstration here just a few moments ago with one of my students over here. You can see the insidiousness of the water center. So if you want to be insidious, all you have to do is go down there and service that realm in consciousness. Yes. Hmm? Yes.

Thank you.

Yes, you see, you see, I just got through stating, I think—yes, in fact, I know I did—that we all are excellent salesmen, you see, in a mental world. We're great con artists and very insidious. And when we don't have our way—the moment that we judge we're not getting our way, we experience what center that we are expressing on. *[The teacher laughs joyously.]* You understand that, don't you, [Student J]?

Very much, sir.

Pardon?

Yes, sir.

Yes. So, you see, you want to know what center you're on in your expression? Well, all you have to do is be patient with yourself and see what the experience is. Would you not agree?

Yes.

Pardon?

Yes, I would.

Yes, yes. You see, you see, we've spent much time over this past year with you in private classes, and a great deal of energy and time has been spent to help you to evolve through these things that you create that you allow to use your form. My channel has been instructed to express to you clearly what they are. They're slime. Well, what is slime? Well, look what color slime is, and look how it moves. And look how it takes whatever shape that your various centers wish to give to it. Then you'll understand what it is. The moment that you believe that you are the thought, the thing that you have created, then you are in service to the slime because the slime is mental substance; its color is green. And some of my students are aware of that from the teachings of long ago here, you see.

You see, the purpose of these classes is not to battle with the slime that anyone believes that they are.

[If] you want to stop believing you are the slime that you create, then do your proper exercises and do your breathing, etc. that you have been given, you see. You must not expect my channel to do it for you. Hmm? That's not his purpose: to do it for you, you see. Yes.

Thank you.

Yes, you see, you see, when you're faced with a change, you're faced with an opportunity: you are faced with an opportunity to let go of what you believe that you are, so that you may experience what you are. And when you are faced with that opportunity, you reveal to yourself how much in love with yourself you are, you see. So how can you make a harmonious, happy transition from one plane to another, from one place in your physical world to another place in your physical world, if you believe that you are, through your great glory and love of self, if you believe that you are what you have created?

Do you think it will be harmonious, [Student B], at the very thought of such a thing? *[After a short pause, the teacher continues.]* Well, of course, not. You see, it won't be harmonious as long—you remember this: whatever you fear reveals what you are dependent upon. So if you fear moving in consciousness or in a physical world—because, you see, to move in a physical world, you must first move in consciousness in a mental world. So if you fear moving from here over to there, you understand, if you fear it, it reveals that you are dependent upon and in service to what you *think* you have created, you see. And so this is going on all of the time.

So if you believe that you are working real hard and if you believe that you're always short of money and you have evolved to the opportunity to show you that is not what you are—it's what you are in service to—and you're granted the opportunity to move from this love of self and this great glory to what you believe you are and have that thrill of believing that's what you are—a lot of people thrill in poverty, you know. They thrill in a lot of negative things. The human mind has a great love of the negative. Why does it have such a great love of the negative, [Student B]? Why does the human mind love the negative?

Because it's—so much of its energy—it's a tape. It's tapes that are magnetic.

Correct! Because negative is magnetic. So, you see, you will find people who are negative have a great love of themselves, which is a great denial of what they are. They love and thrive on negativity, mental substance.

You must understand all thoughts enter a water center, the magnet, the great magnet. And so you can always tell how much you are in love with yourself by how negative you are, you see. You see, all of this reveals itself. When I teach you, as a student, that "Accept the possibility of experiencing the goodness that you are,"—not the goodness you're going to become, [but] what you already are. When I share that with you, instead of using it wisely and using it daily, you see, you use it to service the negativity of the glory of self, you see. And then the tears come to your eyes as a defense mechanism to protect your own judgments, you see.

My channel has been informed of that many, many years ago. I wish to see no tears, you see. No tears for they only reveal the final defenses of the glory of the judgments that you believe you are. Don't tell me how hard you work. Demonstration is revelation. Don't tell me how little you have. Demonstration is revelation. Tell me how miserable life is [and] I will tell you how small the true God in your consciousness is and reveal to you how great the self-love god of glory is, you see.

And remember this: self-glory offers all the negatives because all judgments are created in the water center of consciousness. [It] has nothing to do with the electro [electric] center of consciousness, all the negative, you see. Look at the doomsday prophets: everywhere they look they see something negative, you see. You get a thrill of glory from negativity, the human mind, you see. You get a thrill of glory from disaster and how hard *you* are trying. You see, when you allow your mind, your great self-love to tell you how great and how hard *you* are working, that's the total denial of what you are, you see? Because in those moments, God does not exist. Either to God all things are possible or to your self-love ego you will find one impossibility after another. Impossibility only exists in the love of self. It does not exist in what you are.

Any other questions now? Hmm? *[After a short pause, the teacher continues.]*

Negative, negative, negative is love, love, love of self. Hmm? Why is it? Because, you see, that's what the magnetic center is, where judgments are born. Judgments are born in magnets, you see. They're magnetic. They're born in the water center. You have all those lovely teachings, you see.

You try to think, you say, you try to think positive. When you try to think positive, you get all emotional. Hmm? Because, you see, that's where you are in consciousness. It's holding onto you: it don't [doesn't] want to let you go, you see. You go to say an affirmation and the next thing you know, you're grabbed and pulled, you see, and all of your emotions rise up and what you know as your forces, because that reveals the great love you have of self, you see.

This is not a nursery school. I have no bottles for the babies. I have meat for the men. I have no bottles for the babies.

[Student N] you have a question. *[After a short pause, the teacher continues.]* The one that you've been playing with. Speak up. *[After another short pause, the teacher again continues.]* Are you afraid of me or is it my channel you fear? I know you're not afraid of me because you don't depend on me. My channel? That's something else. You might depend on him. He wouldn't like to hear that but—go ahead with your question—he is very independent that way.

When you've been freed from, say, concern . . .

Have you?

Well, at the moment I'm—for a moment, I was.

Yes, I'm happy to hear that. It's lovely. Were you freed the other night when you was [were] in so much of it that my channel had to take it to the Council to see what to do with you? Did you free yourself that night? What night was it, Isa? Thursday—Friday, Friday! Did you free yourself Friday night? *[Isa Goodwin is Mr. Goodwin's mother, who served on the Spirit Council, which made all the decisions regarding the operation of the Serenity Association through the mediumship of her son. She also guided, corrected, and encouraged the students.]*

When I left I felt I was free.

But not when you came to the temple? *[In addition to attending class, students volunteered their time working at the temple to maintain the property and to receive additional guidance.]*

No.

No. Go ahead. *[The teacher laughs.]*

No. When I came I—I didn't even know I was in concern. All I knew was that I was . . .

Most people don't realize they're in concern, but they have a wonderful thrill of being in self-love. Go ahead.

Yeah, that's what it felt like.

Yes, that wonderful thrill, you see, that excitement, you see, that you're going to conquer and you're going to manipulate that which is manipulable for you. Go ahead. Go ahead, yes.

But it doesn't feel good.

Well, it doesn't feel good. No, excitement isn't good. Excitement is excitement. Thrill isn't good. Thrill is thrill. You judge it was good or some thrills you judge [were] just the opposite. *[The teacher laughs joyfully.]* Thrill is thrill. What you judge after is—or before, because many people judge that, "This is going to be good," [type of] thrill. And then after the thrill is over, they judge that it was a bad thrill. But, you see, good or bad isn't thrill, you see? Our conception of thrill is good or bad. Thrill is thrill. Yes, go ahead.

So it's what you do—I mean—

It's what you do with what's been loaned you, yes. You were loaned an opportunity to what? To sing?

Right.

Well, what you did with it was whether [it was] good or bad for you; what *you* did with it.

So I want to—I'd like to know . . .

Yes?

. . . when I'm feeling that way, I tend to resist . . .

Resist what?

Or when I'm trying to work out of it, whatever it is. [The student may be referring to working out of a level of consciousness.]

You tend to resist because that which is resisting, you believe that you are: the judgments you have created. Of course, that's understandable. It's a house divided. Show me success from a house divided. Hmm?

And then it just gets worse, the more—

Why, certainly, it gets worse because, you see, you are absolutely convinced you are the judgments that you have created. And so you make yourself—you make the effort to free yourself from the love affair with yourself, and of course it gets worse, certainly. Absolutely. You have been servicing those things you have created. [Do] you think they'll let you go easily?

You must realize that all things that our minds create are freeloaders. You want to know what a freeloader is? Whatever you create and believe that you are. And just try to move out of what you have created and believed that you are: you'll see what great freeloaders [they are and] what self-love really has to offer. It is ever in keeping with the principle of freeloading. You create a form; it only moves in keeping with its freeloading off your life energy, your vitality. Yes. Pardon?

Yeah.

But you certainly understand that, don't you?

Yes—well, I'm beginning to.

You don't appreciate it, do you?

Pardon me.

You don't appreciate it, do you?

Not at all.

All thoughts we create, and if we permit our self to believe we are the thought we have create[d], we solidify it into a judgment. Do you understand that? A hollow form in mental substance. Now its creation is by your identification, which your energy flows in keeping with your identification to create the form. Do you understand that?

Right.

Well, it only lives as long as it freeloads your energy. Do you understand that? So when you go to move in consciousness and you don't want it freeloading on you any longer, as baggage in your way, then it screams; it doesn't want to let you go. And in keeping with how much you are attached to what you have created is the difficulty that you experience. Do you understand that?

The attachment to it.

Yes, the attachment to it is your love of it. We only love things for a time, don't we? See, when you want to divorce yourself from that which you have created, you have quite a time. It's quite a costly experience in court. You see, try to under—you know, you see, you take a look—it's all right, [Student N], be seated, please. You take a look and you see you have no problem relating to, to going out to attract, to experience your honeymoon and to go through all of that. And then, then—but you have a lot of problems going to court and going through your separations and your divorces. Well, you see, you are experiencing a rudimentary example, a primitive example of the very law of other planes of consciousness.

So, you see, you tell yourself that you've fallen in love and that that which you have fallen in love with is going to do this and that for you. It's going to take care of your security. It's going to take care of your desires. It's going to do whatever you want it to do. And all you have to do is to lie back and it's going to do all those things for you. All right. Now fine, that's nice, selfish, self-love thinking. Well, this is how forms and judgments are created. And when you go to divorce them, you've got a problem: you [have] got to really work like a beaver to grow up.

Is there anyone who doesn't understand that? I do have some students that have had honeymoons and divorces, don't I? Yes, I do. Yes, I certainly do have some students here.

Now relate to it as the same thing. You spend your time creating these forms. Believing that you are what you have created, you experience this great love of yourself: "Oh, what a nice job you did." "Look at this nice form here that I have created." Well, that's fine as long as that form you have created can freeload off of you. Well, it's like a woman [who] gets married. She's made a judgment, ofttimes, that she's going to freeload off of the man that she married. Then the time comes that he wakes up and he says, "You're not going to freeload off of me anymore. You just lay on your back and you've been freeloading off of me long enough!" And he kicks her out. And they go into the divorce court.

Well, it's the same thing in principle, you see. You create these forms to serve you. Hmm? You see? You create them with your mind, these thoughts. And you create them now to serve you in a world of creation. All right. Now that's fine as long as you constantly remind them what you've created them for. Do you understand that? Then, of course, you feed them energy when you call them up to use them. Hmm?

However, when you take great pride and love in that thought you have created and you love your judgment, well, what you are really doing [is] you have then believed that you are that which you have created: that judgment, now. And that judgment will come in and out whenever it wants and freeload off of you, and your life is worthless in that respect. Does that help with your question?

Very much.

Well, you see, I am not going to expose the form of my channel to feed the forms, of some of my students, [that are] rising up for a feeding. They can feed off of them. See, a person feels miserable and all exhausted and tired because they are totally drained. Do you understand? See, those freeloaders, known as judgments, that you believe that you are—are you all right this morning, [Student D]? *[The teacher addresses a student who is coughing quite a bit.]*

I'm sorry. [Student D replies.]

Well, that's all right. You may stand. If you would stand, you see, then those self-love things would disappear. Rise up, you see. Rise up; face the Light in consciousness. Rise up, you see. Rise up. That's what they offer when they don't get their feeding. That's what you're here for: to open your eyes to see the freeloaders in consciousness.

Now, my students, this is a lovely day. It's a beautiful class. You may be seated. Now take control of yourself. Take control of those things. Stop believing you are what you have created through the great love of self. Accept the Divine Light that is. It's all around and about you, you see? You see, you fear you don't have enough? How can you? You are dependent on the things you have created. Show me what you fear, I'll show you what you're dedicated to.

Any other questions this morning for class. Yes, [Student B].

So is it possible to have a soul expression when we view something like a painting or hear music or is that a need we're—

Yes. Do you take the painting off the museum wall and sneak out the side door that you may possess it? *[A few students laugh.]* Well, then that will help you, you see. You can enjoy, perceive, and walk away. Do you understand that? However, if you walk away and are haunted by what you have walked away from, oh, then you have entered conception. And a form you have created, you have stolen that, you see. Do you perceive that difference, [Student B]?

You recorded it and you go back to it.

You recorded it; you go back to it. And if you don't go back to it, it haunts you. You see, in your mind, you keep thinking about it. You seemingly cannot let it go, for you have then possessed it, you see. You have conceived it. Do you understand? You have not perceived it and walked on by. You have conceived it in your mental substance, and you cannot let it go.

The truth of the matter is because you have stolen it in consciousness, it will not let you go. Do you understand that? It will not let you go. You see, what you create, what you create in these thought forms and at that critical point of choice of perceiving, "This is what I have created. I have created and designed it to serve the purpose of its design. I have a responsibility. I must monitor it because if I stop monitoring it, the next day I am going to find that I believe that that is me. And when I do that, I have gone into full conception. I have given it birth. It is now mine." Do you understand that? So when that happens, you have what is known as a monster freeloader that lives off of you whenever it chooses to. And you never know when it's hungry because it's always hungry. Hmm? You see? Yes. You see, that's the con of the con artist. Hmm? They're real beautiful salesmen there. Oh my, oh my, oh my, yes, they have no problem convincing [us] that we are those things we've created. By doing that, they get more feeding. Do you understand? They become bigger and better, in that respect, freeloaders, you see?

You see, try to understand that those realms, they have many defenses. They have a whole front line, known as justification or excuses, you see. They have a whole front line to protect them, you see. They have every single sense that your body has to use against you, you see. Hmm? Certainly. Yes, [Student M].

I'm not sure if this correct, but—

Doesn't matter if it's correct to one or incorrect to another. We're asking to share the Light, aren't we? Go ahead.

Thank you. The doorway to the soul is the imagination?

The doorway through which we must pass—

Yes.

—to those realms of Spirit is imagination.

Imagination. And—

The difference, you know, between that and fascination.

That's right. Exactly.

One's a dependence and one is a freedom of artistic creation. There's a vast difference.

And that's the conception verses the perception, too. I mean—

But when you perceive, you know, you take a look and you perceive and you draw something, you see; you sketch it out, you see. Remember, we move closer to conception when we look at an object and draw it than when we pause and we create it, you see.

I do see.

Do you understand that?

Thank you.

So whoever is dependent on copying is at the very threshold of conception.

I see.

You see? And whoever is not dependent on copying and who is now relying upon the infinite Divine Intelligence, you understand, that they may be receptive and, therefore, in being receptive, may put it onto paper or to canvas, is farther away from that terrible trap of conception and bondage. Does that help with you?

Even though when we pause, we do have images of things that we have seen in form and we—

Well, that depends on what level you're in. If you're in love with yourself, you'll have plenty of those. *[The teacher laughs joyously.]*

Right.

But, you see, as you pause and are still, you gradually move through all of that, you see.

Yes.

Hmm? Yes. Yes, now, class is—yes, I am aware. Thank you. *[The teacher acknowledges a signal from the cameraman.]* Class is pretty near over now. And I do not want my channel exposed to these freeloading entities. And I expect my directors to take care of that. I will not allow him to be exposed because he's been exposed enough to their tenacity, their insidious freeloading. And I expect you, as my students, some of you, to help those students who insist, blatantly insist—I realize it is not them, because if it [were] them, they would not be even, ever have come to these classes, you see—but whose forms in the self-love insist that they are them. I expect my directors [to attend to this], with exception of my cameraman, who must take care of the class.

You may shut it off now. Time is running out.

[The recording ends.]

NOVEMBER 9, 1986

[The homework that was assigned in A/V Class Private 64 was not addressed in this class. A/V Class Private 64 was held on October 19, 1986, and on the following Sunday, October 26, the teacher reviewed the students' homework. Most of that class was not recorded and the small portion that was recorded was not released to the students.]

A/V Class Private 66

Good morning, class.

This morning we will discuss fulfillment, experience, what is it, and how does it work.

Now all experience is an effect, a reaction to the activity or action of mental substance, our mind. Most of you have been given a most important diagram of action, reaction, and inaction. *[The teacher may be referring to the Diagramology teachings, which may be published in a later volume, and in particular to the Third State Diagram III.]* When you believe that you are your mind, then the experiences of life are mirrors reflecting the activity of your mind. That's experience.

Now fulfillment, when, in creating a thought, you direct that thought to the Source which sustains it, in consciousness you have freed it from the horizontal Law of Duality, for being returned to the Source which sustains it, it returns unto you as fulfillment.

For example, all form, all limit is sustained by intelligent, infinite, intelligent Energy, to which it is more fully receptive at a 45-degree angle. And so we always have the choice of whether or not to release the thought we have created on a horizontal plane of consciousness or on a 45-degree plane of consciousness.

The difficulty for the human mind is once it has created something in its mental substance and believing that it is what it has created, it does not desire to release it to the Source that sustains it. And so we find that most people quit before the victories, for the victories in their life are not in keeping with the patience that is necessary. When we cannot (our minds) tell us how soon or how late we shall experience what we desire, then we send that which we have created along the horizontal planes of consciousness. [It is] sent with our own impatience and [we] pay for all of the things of conception.

Let us understand the difference of conception and perception. A flat or horizontal plane of thinking is a plane of conception. When you insist on believing that you are what you have created, you have established the dual Law of Creation. You have established, beyond a shadow of all doubt, the Law of Attachment, known as bondage, guaranteeing the Law of Adversity to balance or free you from what you have bound yourself to.

What does this Law of Conception reveal? This Law of Conception reveals clearly a dependence upon what you believe you are: your mind. So whoever believes that they are their mind can declare the beautiful truth that has been given to you: "I accept the possibility of experiencing the goodness that I am." That goodness, then, becomes dependent upon what your mind does and does not accomplish, for you have left out experiencing the possibility of experiencing the goodness that you are, you have left out the declaration of what it is that is the goodness that you are. It is that which sustains your mind. It is not your mind. And so when, in using that beautiful truth, that law, "I accept the possibility of experiencing the goodness that I am," not declaring the truth that the goodness that you are is that which sustains your thought and not the thought that you create, then your goodness is subject to the dual Law of Creation, is subject to the bondage of attachment and the balance of adversity.

To rest or to relax at the proper angle of the full reception of the very energy that sustains all form requires not only a physical position, it requires, of course, a position in consciousness in order to receive the full benefits of the life energy that sustains what you think that you are.

Now today's class will be available to you on audio cassette. Your video cassettes will be forthcoming at a later time. Now it's time for any questions you have at this time during your class. Yes, [Student J], please.

Sir, what is the difference between attachment to the fruit of action and satisfaction from the sense of accomplishment?

Yes. Satisfaction is a sleep. It is a sleep of what you are, an awakening of the senses and experiencing the fruits of action. Now, for example, a person who permits themselves to experience satisfaction from their accomplishments must realize that satisfaction is a sensual experience. It is a payment for the effort of the functions, for it does not recognize, nor accept, the true Source, which one has turned to for their sustenance, for their accomplishment to be.

Now when one experiences a satisfaction of their efforts, one must recognize that as a step in evolution beyond the bondage of the attachment to the fruits of action. For example, the attachments to the fruits of action to the consciousness—one cannot survive in their mind without that payment to their mind. In other words, attachment to their fruits of action is an absolute dictate by their mind that they alone have accomplished whatever has been accomplished. Now a satisfaction of accomplishment is a more refined state of the human mind: that it has accomplished what it has accomplished, however, it can live without it. Does that help you, [Student J]?

Yes, sir.

Now the next step for that—you see, that still is controlled—you understand?—by the Law of Conception. So the next step from that is the experience to the mind of gratitude. You see, there's a gratitude that floods the consciousness. One might call it, to the mind, a feeling of relief. *[The teacher laughs.]* In fact, the mind usually says, "Well, I'm glad that's over." You understand? You see? And so to the mind there is a feeling of relief from the battle that has taken place with the mind as the created thought has been released to the Source that sustains it. The mind experiences that as a relief, but not as a satisfaction. Now I know that you understand that what is experienced by the mind as a relief is not usually considered by the mind the pleasure of satisfaction. Would you not agree?

Indeed. Yes, sir.

Yes. And so, you see, we are speaking here, in reference to your question, of basic three stages of evolution, you see? We're speaking of action, reaction, and we're speaking of the only thing that keeps you free is inaction. Say that you have a desire. All right? You have a desire and you already had many experiences of mentally working with your desire and going through all the necessary manipulations of the mind in order to accomplish what you consider the fulfillment, which is real satisfaction, of all of your efforts. All right. So when you think along that line, you have several payments that have to be made because you're sending that out with the mental substance believing that you are the mental substance and that if you do certain things, then you're going to get it. Correct?

Yes, sir.

All right. Now that is the Law of Creation. That is the Law of Dependence, for what it is you desire and try to accomplish is now dependent not only upon your manipulations or activity or action of your mind but it is dependent on how cunning you are in manipulating the mind of someone else in order to have that. So you now are the victim not only of your own mental cunningness, as everyone is, of course, you are also the victim of how another mind will react to your mind. That is the Law of Duality, you see.

The Law of Duality is the Law of Dependence. In other words, for the goodness in your life something beyond your control must be manipulated. Does that help you there, [Student J]? All right. So anytime we have something beyond our control that we must manipulate in order to experience what we desire to experience, we are dependent and we are in bondage to it. That's the law. And that offers, of course, that offers bondage to the fruits of action. That also offers the feeling of satisfaction.

So we're here in this class today, now, to move beyond that so that we don't have to pay those prices, for they are a stage of evolution, of course, that we all must grow through. For example, say you have a desire. This is what you want to fulfill. All right? Fine. In that desire—you know we've spoken of returning the desire to the Source from whence we've stolen it. Now we explain it in another way. In the forming of the desire, recognize and accept the very Energy, intelligent Energy that is sustaining what you are now creating with your mind is the only one—if it ever withdrew its sustenance, the desire would collapse, the form. You do understand that, don't you?

Yes, sir.

Sure. So recognizing that there is an intelligent Energy that is sustaining what you are now forming, once you have formed it and solidified it, you see, do not permit it to go along the parallel lines of creation, which is the Law of Duality, for then you have, in the ingredients, you have a dependence and a bondage. No. Take it, form it, create it as an artist paints a picture. And when you have finished with it, you see, send it upward on that horizontal [vertical] line to the Source that sustains it. *[The teacher may have misspoken and used "horizontal" instead of "vertical." He makes a similar error later in this class, but immediately corrects himself.]*

Now it is more difficult, of course, for a mind to move along a horizontal line than for a mind to climb up a mountain, even though it's only a 45-degree one. Did that help with your question, [Student J]?

Yes, sir.

So, you see, first of all, to return it to its Source, there is no possible way of saying, "This is the time it must come to be and this is how it must come to be." You can be assured, by so doing that, you will have plenty of experiences in life knowing it didn't come the way you wanted it, nor the day, but it did return unto you, you see?

Yes, sir.

And it always shall. It returns unto everyone. However, when it returns unto you, you are not dependent; you are not bound. You see, I think it was some years ago I spoke to that: we always get what we really want. We don't usually recognize it when it arrives because it's late, you see, to our mind, usually. Hmm?

Yes, sir.

So, you see—however, it is still in principle the very same thing that we have formed and created. It has returned to us, you see.

So we move from one time span in our life, we move on to another one. And we have an experience that seemingly, suddenly comes out of nowhere. And we say, "Now I wasn't even working on creating that. I had released that from my mind five years ago. Well, how come I'm experiencing this today?" Because you had, five years ago, released it from your mind. Instead of traveling along with you, like a shadow, you understand, on the horizontal lines and planes of creation, you had truly released it. You might have released it because you got angry that it didn't come when you wanted it to. And so you did release it from consciousness. Years later you experience it, and wonder how you experienced it because you weren't working on that. Does that help with your question?

Because, you see, if you look at life—you see, when our hindsight becomes our foresight, of course, we gain insight. Insight is always waiting for us. And so because everyone has truly had those experiences, this is why I said years ago, "We always get what we really want." The problem is when we get it, when it arrives, we have forgotten that we ever wanted it. *[The teacher laughs joyfully.]* Does that help with your question?

Indeed. Thank you.

You see? And so you can see that though knowledge knows much, it is controlled by the Law of Duality, you see. Knowledge is dependent. Wisdom is free, but knowledge is dependent, you see. And so anyone who conceives and works with mental substance to not only create—of course, you work with mental substance in order to create it. But anyone who places themselves in that which they have created must experience dependence on something that, sooner or later, they find out they can't control, you see. You see, only people who truly believe that they are a half a person work along the laws of duality. Hmm? You see? You see, they believe that one and one is two, you see. They believe they're one; you know, that unique specialty, don't you see? They believe they're one, and believing that they are one, in order to experience, they require another one, you see? And so I find that it is only the very special, unique minds, the ones who believe they are a special incarnation of uniqueness and different are the ones who have the greatest struggle and difficulty with what is known as experiences. Does that help, [Student J]?

Yes. Thank you, sir.

Yes. Yes. And I can relate to that, although it's been many—[a] long time ago, when I thought I was a bit unique. Of course, everyone goes through that phase of life. You see, there's no one who hasn't, at some time in their life, paid the fiddler, you know, for their specialty, their uniqueness, etc. Yes. Is there any other question this morning, [Student J]? Yes, go ahead.

Not at this moment. Thank you.

All right. Fine. Any other questions here? Yes, [Student O], please.

Yes. In the affirmation that you all gave us, "I accept the possibility of experiencing the goodness that I am."

"I accept the possibility of experiencing the goodness that I am." And what is the goodness that you are?

The goodness that sustains the thought.

Yes, that sustains what you think you are.

Right.

You see, that's the goodness that you are. That which sustains what you think—you are not, you are not what you think you are, for when you allow yourself to think that you are what you think you are, then you're under the Law of Duality. And you are dependent on that which, by the very Law of Duality, you cannot control. You can only, for a time, manipulate with the cunningness of the human mental substance. Yes, [Student O].

Yes, sir.

Do you enjoy living that way?

No, I don't.

Well, I don't either. Thank you. *[The teacher laughs joyously.]* Yes, it took me a long time to find out I wasn't half a person. Yes, thank you.

Yes, sir. I think I understood you to say that when we say this affirmation that we are, we are accepting what we are, along with saying this affirmation in a certain way, we're accepting the Law of Duality.

Just, just the opposite, my friend. "I accept the possibility of experiencing the goodness that I am." "What is the goodness that I am?" That's the question you should be asking yourself. I gave you that beautiful affirmation. What is the goodness that you are? The goodness that you are is not something that is dependent on something else, is it?

No.

You see? So the goodness that you are is the very intelligent Energy that sustains what you think you are. That is what you are. You are not what you think you are, unless you insist on believing you are limit and you are creation. Do you understand?

Yes.

You see? So if you insist on believing that you are the limit that your mental substance has created, then you are under the Law of Duality. You are always dependent and you repeatedly experience the frustrations of not being able to control something that you are not. Did that help you, [Student O]?

Yes, that helped.

You see, whoever believes that they are the thoughts of their mind, whoever believes that is what they are—all thoughts of the mind, you understand, do not recognize, unless you make the effort, that they are sustained by the goodness that you are. That's seeing the good in all things, of course. Then you go along those horizontal planes of consciousness and, oh, you will get what—we always get what we really want.

Now it's just like, for example, you know, we leave this world here. You leave the physical world, you know; you leave what you think you are. You have no control over that. Isn't that lovely, you see. You have no conscious control over that. And so you leave what you think you are. Well, what do you take with you?

What do I take with me?

Yes.

I likened—the mental substance goes with us.

Uh-huh. You believe you're that.

No.

At times you believe you are your mental substance.

Oh, yes.

You believe you are your mind. You believe you're [Student O].

At times.

Yes.

I demonstrate that.

Well, everyone does. Different names for different people.

Yes, sir.

But that was something that was imposed upon you. You came to Earth and you merited certain experiences. And you merited someone's mind deciding that you would be identified as [Student O]. Correct?

Yes, sir. I do.

Well, if we take away this identification, "[Student O]," then who are you?

Take away [Student O]?

Yes, if they take away [Student O], who are you? If you believe you are [Student O] and someone comes and takes away [Student O], then you are no thing.

Right.

Well, who would you be if you weren't [Student O]? If you believe that you are [Student O] and someone comes and takes [Student O] away—

Right.

—then who are you?

I'm, I'm—

What are you? What are you when they take away [Student O]?

I'm, I'm, well, I'm the, I'm the sustaining—I'm the Source that sustains [Student O].

And someone took [Student O], the covering, away.

Right.

What are you now?

I'm still what I was. I'm still the—

Before they—yes, before they took [Student O] away.

Right.

Well, there you are. So, you see, if you are what you are whether they take away [Student O] or they don't take away [Student O], if you have accepted what you are, then you have no problem when [Student O] goes away.

Right.

Or somebody comes by and steals him. Is that correct?

Yes.

So, you see, that's what we want to think about. So what do you take with you in life? You know, people think, "Well, I own this and I own that and I choose to take this with me. This is what I have." No, no, no. Life doesn't reveal that. Life reveals you take with you what you have denied, for the effect of our denials of what we are is known as needs. And show me one who doesn't take their needs with them. I don't care where you go or you don't go, you take with you your own denials. Because no matter what you say, I find millions of people in the universes and I say, "What do you have?" And they say, "Well, I need this and I need that and I need that and I need that," which [demonstrates], you see, we take our denials with us. So I have already shared with you, years ago in your world, our denials are our destiny for we never seem to be without need.

You know, you look at the destiny of everyone and you talk to them and you communicate with them and say, "Well, how are you doing?" [They reply,] "Well, I need this and I need that and I need that. I even need peace of mind." Yes, they'll tell you. So what does that show to us? We take our needs with us, you see?

What is the glass, you see? *[The teacher, sitting at a small table in front of the class, touches the glass of water on his left.]* You take that and put it away. But if you think you don't have it, you have denied its possibility for you; therefore, you need it. We need what we have denied because we have denied what we are. Does that help you, [Student O]?

Yes, sir. Thank you.

Yes. And can you just imagine when the day comes [that] they take [Student O] away. But they cannot take you. They can only take, steal, and manipulate what you believe that you are, never what you are. Hmm?

Yes.

So if they believe that they—if you believe that you are your foot, they can come and cut off your foot. But will you go with your foot? That's the question. That's the question.

You see, that's what everyone faces in the beautiful laws of creation and the laws of evolution. They face clearly: "I believe that I am this," and they convince themselves. Nature marches on and it's 50, 60, 70 years later; and they have great problems adjusting because they insist on believing they are what they create in their mind. And so when they look in the mirror, the image does not reflect what they insisted on believing that they were 60 years ago. Now that is only one of the many experiences that you can relate to by just looking in your mirror of life, you see, the one that reflects the image that you believe that you are.

And be rest assured the law fulfills itself. The [Student Os] go, the [Student Js] go, the [Student Hs] go, the [Student Ps] go, all of those go. So the sooner you stop believing that you are those identifications, the better off you're going to be because it takes not days, not weeks, not months, but years and years and years and years to free oneself from what they really believe that they are, yes. All right, [Student O]?

Yes, sir.

Yes. And so, you know, anyone can tell whether or not we believe we are the limit because they can manipulate us, you see, in mental substance. And we believe we are our thoughts; and therefore, we react to our own emotions. And then we see exactly where we are, and no one has to tell us. Hmm? Yes, anyone else have a—yes, [Student H].

Is this an example of what you were speaking of a little while ago about our adversity balancing out the conception?

Well, certainly, because, you see, whatever we conceive and believe that we are is an absolute bondage of attachment. And so the law fulfills itself, and we experience the luxury, if you can call it a luxury, of adversity. Think of all the things you dislike, you guarantee to love them. Don't think about the things that you do like, because you may not be able to face what you—the adversity that's contained within them. There is no attachment that doesn't contain its own adversity. It is an indispensable ingredient to the attachment, you see?

You see, my friends, remember, you're dealing with a law that is—a law of creation. Whatever is created comes under a dual law. And if you don't send what you have created in your mind to the Source that sustains it, then you will always face, in your evolution, the adversity to the very thing you have created as an attachment, you see? It's guaranteed. That is a law that, like day and night, fulfills itself repeatedly. Hmm? Now I've taught you long ago, you see, if you want to free yourself from something—you think that you're attached to it—well, see it in a different light, and see how quickly you become adverse to it. And then, you see, it will balance itself out, yes.

Yes, now, [Student Y]—yes, good morning. [Student Y] has a question.

Thank you.

Yes.

When you say give it to the Source, you give the thought to the Source of—

Definitely. That is correct, [Student Y]. Because we have, you see, in order to create the form, it takes intelligent Energy. That intelligent Energy is from the Source itself, you see. Without that intelligent Energy, then we would not have the substance, mental substance, in order to form and to create it. Yes, go ahead, [Student Y].

Well, how does one actually give that thought to the Source?

[If] one gives that thought to the Source, they find that it no longer is being entertained in their consciousness. That's when they know they've given it up, you see? However, if it keeps hounding and plaguing them, that, of course, is because they've tried to let it go. They've tried to climb the mountain with it. [It's] just only a 45-degree-angled mountain, you see. And they haven't got there yet, you see? But they will, they will. If they keep trying, they will.

You know—and it's so interesting because sometimes a person has what they call a burning desire. And it doesn't get fulfilled, you know, what they call fulfillment. And we find that, sooner or later, months, years pass on and they seem to have forgot it. Pardon? And years pass by and suddenly it appears. Well, they forgot it. They gave it to the Source begrudgingly, in the sense that it didn't happen when they wanted it to happen, but it did happen, you see. You see, we always do get what we really do want, you see. And so man should choose wisely what he creates with his mind, for he is guaranteeing it to return unto him, even when he forgets it, you see.

You see, now, forgetting it and forgiving it [are] two different things. Say that a person, you see, has created with his mind a desire, a form. And after having created it, he realizes that no, oh, no, no, no, he would rather not have that at all. He sees a little bit broader on his horizon. And so if he just forgets it, it leaves his consciousness and doesn't bother him, but he's not very wise. He has now released it. It is all created. It shall return unto him someday and he knows it not.

So, you see, the wise man takes a look at what he has created in his error of ignorance, and he forgives it; he gives it forth, that which in his error he has created, you see? So there's a difference between the mind forgetting something and the actual soul faculty of giving forth or forgiving. Hmm? There's a vast difference, because what he forgets returns to him someday. He says, "How did this happen to me? I didn't do a single thing. Why, I've been working so hard in my meditations and my spiritual exercises and I've been doing all of my affirmations. How did this experience come to me?" Well, I'm sure we all know how it came to us, yes. It's known, of course, in this philosophy as: be patient; all our chickens shall come home to roost. They know where they were hatched, and they know where they're going to return to, you see.

See, so there's many factors to look at, you see. There are those chickens that we have hatched and we choose [it's] best to forget about them. And so we forget about them. We don't think about them anymore and they're all growing beautifully, you know. And they say, "Oh, I want to go home." See, everything goes home. Everything goes home, you understand that? And so though it's years later, here they come a-flying and a-squawking and back home they are, right where birth was given to them. Everything returns unto its source. And so all chickens, of course, come home to roost. Best they do their roosting while we still have a little awake[ning] in consciousness and we're working on that. Does that help with that, [Student Y]?

Yes.

You know, so many times a person will make great effort—really, for their mind, it's great effort—to do their spiritual exercises, their affirmations, and things seem to be going along very nicely. And then sudden[ly], all of a sudden all of these chickens come home and roost. And we say, "Well, I've been doing what is right. What has happened?" Well, they finally decided, "This is a good time now. Home's nice and comfortable. I'm going back where I was hatched. You know, it wasn't so comfortable when I was hatched. Now it's all nice and warm and comfortable." And in they come. Yes.

Yes, now [Student U] has a question, please.

Is the process of achieving a 45-degree angle in consciousness for relieving—for releasing a form that we have created becoming electric in consciousness?

Well, when it is released, you understand that you have action and reaction; you have electric in creation and you have magnetic in manifestation. Now the point or apex of that triangle is inaction.

And I wanted to speak on one thing that is very, very important to all of you. So often, you know, in moving along you've heard about the hissing hounds of hell before every victory, of course. You also have experienced that as you make great effort on the spiritual path of Light of consciousness within you, that which you really are and truly are, the brighter the Light, the darker the night. Now take a look at it this way. In your life many, many, many chickens have been hatched. Many, many have been forgotten by the mind—not released to the Divine, not forgiven to the Divine, just blatantly forgotten. Well, remember this, that when they were created, the house in which they were created was a bit chilly. One might even say cold. Cold in the sense that the heart had not awakened to the source of Light and the warmth of the sunshine from which it has come: one's own heart.

And so these chickens were born in very cold houses. And so those chickens have been waiting a long time, and growing and growing and growing. And one of them looks around and says, "Say, [the] temperature's going up. The house is much better, that I was born in. Well, what do you think? Should we go home now to roost for a while?" And so they all come in. Now perhaps you understand a little better, you see. They always come in. And so the brighter the Light, the darker the night. The darkness being the untold flocks of chickens on their way home to roost. How long will they roost in your little warm house? Well, that's entirely up to you, you see? There is no escape. Hmm? Yes. Yes, now, I think—did that help with your question?

Yes, sir.

Now [Student M], there, has a question this morning.

Yes. The action, reaction, and inaction, that is—the action and the reaction is under the Law of Duality.

Correct. That's creation.

Creation. And it seems, like, within each form, there's like action-reaction contraction-expansion, electric—

Yes.

—magnetic.

Yes, that's dependence.

That's all?

Certainly. Anything that acts and reacts is a dependent process that's taking place. In other words, you act and because you're dependent, how they react is your experience. And it goes back and forth, you see. Yes. Back and forth, up and down is all laws of creation.

Those are all laws of creation.
Yes.
Now, the 45—the inaction and the 45-degree angle are—
Yes.
—under what we consider a spiritual law.
Yes, you return it to its source, you see? I've told you that and tried to share that with you in so many different ways. Today you understand, hopefully, a little bit better that all limit or all form is sustained. That is, when its consciousness, when its limit is at a 45-degree angle to the Source, it received the greater benefit. Yes.
Which is the process of giving it back to the Source.
What is, what is four and five?
Nine.
What is it, [Student P]?
Totality.
Yes. What else is a four and a five? Yes.
Foundation and faith.
The stability of faith. So unless you enter a 45-degree angle in consciousness, then you, then you must just continue on with the dependence of duality. When your security, your stability, your foundation is sustained by faith, in your consciousness, you're freed from the duality of dependence and bondage. Hmm?

Say that you want to make a change. Well, when your mind thinks you want to make a change, you have all the roosters and all these things and thoughts you have created. Hmm? Now sometimes they'll rise immediately. Sometimes they will not rise until just at the very last minute, you know. It's like going to buy a car. Everything's good. Everything feels great inside of you. Everything seems well until you go to sign on the dotted line. And you best sign very quickly or you won't get [what] you've worked for, you see? Someone else will get it.

So what is that whole process about? That only shows; fine, you are under the dual law. Now you have doubt. Now you have fear. Now you have question. Now you have suspicion. Now you have all of the functions available to you, you see? Then it is best, perhaps, just to do without anything, until finally from years of doing without anything, you move along the parallel line, you understand? You see? You move from the—pardon me—from the parallel line to the vertical line. You move on that angle and return it to the Source.

See, when you have a desire, you see, that's something you've created. That's something you alone have created. You've taken that essence and you have limited it into a certain thing. So that which sustains it has a far greater wisdom than the creator. You see, that which sustains creation is certainly, by far, superior to that which has been created, for that which has been created has been formed and shaped and limited. That which sustains it sustains everything. Certainly, that which sustains a thing is greater than that which is sustained. The father, of course, is greater than the son. Of course! Does that help with your question?

Yes. Anyone else? Yes, [Student S] has a question.

Yes. What's the best way to shorten a stay of a chicken?

The best way to shorten the stay of a chicken that has returned in keeping with the law of one's own hatching—see, because we hatch our own chickens, you know. And the best way to shorten their stay is to turn up the light of reason, which will increase the temperature in which the chicken, having made his judgment it's time to return, finds it too hot. *[The teacher laughs.]*

Thank you.

[The teacher continues laughing and as he laughs, he may say "You're welcome."] Yes, [Student B], please.

Withdrawal—

Excuse me. And when things get too hot, they're too hot to handle even for a chicken. *[Many students laugh.]* Yes, thank you. [Student B], please. *[The teacher continues laughing.]*

Does the Law of Expansion and Contraction have anything to do with this fulfillment of desire?

Yes, indeed it does. And I would like to speak on one thing that my students, some of them, have not understood in reference to when I have taught them to: it is wise to use the function of anger under the guidance of the Light within you because, don't you see, what it does, [Student S], it turns up the temperature. You notice—you know, when a person gets angry and they sustain it inside themselves, then those chickens that have been plaguing them [and have] come home to roost, they fly away. They fly away. But, you see, you must remember to use that function wisely inside of yourself. So sometimes a person says, "Well, I got so mad that I feel a thousand percent better." You get mad inside of yourself. The chickens cannot stand—you understand?—the change of temperature. Now remember, they are created under a certain temperature of your own consciousness at the time they were created.

Now remember, also, that you haven't forgiven them. You just simply forgot them. And therefore, they are—actually, those chickens are judgments. That's what those chickens are: judgments that have formed a desire. Do you understand? And so a judgment, when it's born in a certain temperature, in a certain water temperature, you know, it takes a look, waiting, and when the temperature is warmed up to what they consider a nice comfortable state, you see, they'll return.

Well, while they're in the water, if you turn up the temperature—you see, judgments don't change like that, you see. No, no, no, no, no. If you tell them, "Now, chicken, I'm going to turn this temperature up very, very slowly here." *[The teacher gestures to indicate he is turning a knob up very slowly.]* Well, when you get angry inside, the knob on the temperature go ppshhhttt! *[The teacher gestures to indicate he is turning the knob way up very, very quickly.]* It doesn't go [slowly], you know. And you don't inform them that you're going to increase the water temperature. You just do it. *[Many of the students laugh.]* And to them, it's—all right. Now fine. Now we'll get to—I want you to have a better understanding of what this process really is.

Now, expansion and contraction represents the law of—certainly, it absolutely does. And now if you're moving on that horizontal line of creation, you remember you are depending upon what someone else does. In other words, you are expanding your sphere of action. Now, in that expansion, that which you are now dependent upon, it must contract as you expand. You see, it's like a—for example, say that you go to a salesman to purchase something. Well, [if] you're going to purchase anything, you have a salesman, right? Well, of course you do. All right. You're in creation. So you go and you expand. You're in an expansion process. You desire something. The fulfillment of your desire is dependent on what he does—right?—in keeping with your expansion, which is your dictates of what you want. Correct? So he must, if he's a good salesman, if he has any intelligence, he must contract and convince your mind that that's the thing for you by permitting you to expand in your consciousness of your dictate and your desire. Hmm?

Now if you're not intelligent with all this process, you will find what you [have] convinced yourself [is], "This is just the right person." You see? You will find that after they've got what they want—because they're expanding in a different way, as they're contracting for you—they'll make a turn and bite your heel. Do you understand? Then you say you got burned! Isn't that what they usually say? Well, you see, it's just like a marriage, you see. You see, try to relate to it as a marriage. You see, because it's the same thing. It's a good—if a person has a good sales pitch, there's no problem with the marriage. This is, you know, up front, you see. See, if you [have] got a real good sales[man]—because it's all salesmanship. Creation is all salesmanship. It's all contraction. It's all contraction and expansion.

And so you go and you see—you communicate with a person. You're a young lady and you say, "Oh, I feel so good. This person is wonderful," because you are expanding, don't you see? And he's taken a look and smiles as he contracts and contracts. And then you find out, you see, a few months, shortly after the honeymoon, that he is expanding, when he's supposed to be contracting! Because now you have got to contract and you're not ready to contract because you've already convinced yourself that he is a wonderful person, because you were able to expand so far with your own personal desires. Do you understand that, [Student B]?

You see, that's the process of all creation. Now if you take that, you take that created form, called a desire, and you say, "All right. Now I have formed this. Put in all intelligent ingredients, you see. Now I'm not going to forget about it because if I do, it'll come back as a chicken to roost, because I'm the one that has given it birth." Then you take that and you send it up on its parallel line; you must climb the mountain, you see, 45-degree angle. It takes forty-five. It takes the security and stability of what you believe you are in the creating of a desire. It takes the faith in something that sustains it. It takes the absolute acceptance that that which you truly are and cannot control with the mind already has received it. Hmm? Then you won't have to go through this duality experiences of expansion.

Because, you see, when you create a desire and you work for its fulfillment, you must realize that's an expansion process. And it expands out into the universe and is dependent on finding its kind that, at the moment, is willing to contract, for it has another desire not related to that desire that you have; that through contracting and bowing back to allow you to fulfill yours, it will have its desire fulfilled, which is an expansion over there. Hmm? I haven't seen anyone work for nothing yet. Have you, [Student B]? It's in keeping with the Law of Creation, you see. Hmm? Does that help with your question?

I have one more.

Go right ahead.

On the—say there is absolute acceptance, does the Law of Expansion and Contraction apply to that part? Say—

Yes, but not in the sense of bondage. Not in the sense of bondage, you see. You see, for example, of course, in order for it to take place in a world of creation, there is an expansion-contraction, but you're not a part of it. You are not a part of it as identification with it. For example, you have returned it to the Source that sustains it. Hmm?

Right.

Now in so doing it will come on that day, in that time, in that way, without your payment of bondage. Hmm? See, going up like that, giving it to the Source, in that 45-degree angle of absolute faith. And your security is dependent upon your faith in the Source itself. It will come right back to you, do you understand? And you say, "Well, this is unreal. It just happened." Hmm? But it happened without all of these payments. It's not a chicken, now, that's come home to roost. No, no, no. You see, when you give your chickens (those desires) to the Source that sustains them, they return as an eagle. Do you understand the difference? A chicken flies, but how high up the mountain can it fly? There's a vast difference, you see?

So a wise person would rather experience the effect of an eagle returning that which they have given to the Source than a chicken that flies so high, maybe a foot or two, and pppttt! *[The teacher gestures to indicate the short, almost hopping flight of a chicken, ending with a fall to the ground.]* And keeps [repeating]. You see, that process is truly wearing, isn't it?

Yes.

All right. *[The teacher laughs.]* It's called the hop along. Yes. *[Many students laugh.]* You wonder when it's going to reach its destination.

Would, would a contraction—if someone tried to contract you, would that be someone, like, would lead you into something?

Why, of course. A contract is a contraction. Anyone who signs a contract realizes they have contracted, and to some, they contract more than others. And they're not too keen on signing any contracts because the moment that you sign a contract, you have accepted the chickens of your own desires and that—that is, to a certain degree, you have. Because you take a look at the paper and you read all the fine print and you say, "Well, now these chickens are a lot more expensive than I thought they would be!"

Thank you. I see our time is up. What a lovely day. [An] hour has passed. We'll see you again next week. Thank you. And always read the fine print because that shows where the chickens have been walking. Thank you.

NOVEMBER 16, 1986

A/V Class Private 67

Good morning, class.

This morning we will discuss soul faculties and sense functions, with the question, How does a soul faculty become a sense function? For example, interest is a soul faculty. Who knows its corresponding sense function? If so, please raise your hand. Yes, [Student U].

Curiosity?

No. *[After a short pause, the teacher continues.]* Concern. Now remember that all soul faculties are triune in expression and all sense functions are triune in expression. How does the soul faculty of interest become the sense function of concern? Well, your experiences in life clearly show that one is never concerned over anything they are not interested in. So first we look at the soul faculty of interest. And we see the process by which a soul faculty descends into the lower centers of consciousness and becomes to what our mind knows as concern. The faculty must descend into the centers of mental substance before they can become sense functions.

Now this morning we're speaking on the soul faculty of interest. Think of what happens when that soul faculty becomes the sense function of concern. And what does the soul faculty have that tempts mental substance to pull it into the realms of the sense functions? Well, it's quite simple. It's a triune function from a triune faculty. Concern offers to the mind competition and control.

So when you permit yourself to identify and direct that which you truly are to form and limit, to control and competition, then, of course, the faculty of interest is concern. And that is not practical, business living. It offers, however, as a function, it offers to all what is known as the sensation of fear. And because a function offers to you the sensation of fear, it offers a stimulation to what you know as the human ego, the uneducated human ego.

When you permit your mind to believe, as you look in the mirror of life, when you permit your mind to believe that what you see is what you are, then you are in service to your functions and you guarantee fear.

Faith is the domain in which faculties express. And fear is the domain in which those faculties are pulled into the senses under the control of fear.

You cannot fear what you do not first desire to control. You must first desire to control it in order to fear it. To have the desire to control anything reveals that you need it. To have the desire that you need it is to reveal that you have denied it.

So often in life we say, "Well, I do not deny the goodness of life. I do not deny the abundant supply of goodness in my life." We say that to ourselves and we deceive ourselves. What we are truly saying [is], "I certainly want the goodness of life. I certainly want the abundance of life. I want it my way. In other words, only the way that I judge I can control it."

There is no way that mental substance or the human mind can control the expression of the vehicle of the Light that you are, your individualized, evolving soul. There is no possible way—evolving in the sense of its expression. There is no possible way that that which is subject to the Light can control the Light.

Now what is the sense function of the soul faculty of solution? Which of my students has that answer? What is the sense function of the soul faculty known as solution? Yes, [Student P].

Judgment.

No. Though it certainly offers—it's an ingredient of it. Yes.

Confusion.

No. That's also an ingredient of it. Yes, [Student M].

Obstruction.

That's another ingredient of it. Yes, [Student O], please.

Experience.

That's another ingredient of it. Yes, [Student P].

Reference.

That's another ingredient of it. What is the sense function of the soul faculty of solution? You're so familiar with those—with that sense function. Yes, [Student J].

Confusion.

No. It offers that, too. [Student M].

Problem?

Problem. Problem! *[Many students laugh.]* And surely, you're all familiar with the sense function of the soul faculty of solution. You see, a solution, of course, just like interest becomes concern, just like solution becomes problem, just like adversity becomes attachment, is what you are doing with your soul faculties. And what you are doing with your soul faculties, in the mind's effort to manipulate and to control them, then you enter and experience what is known as the descended soul faculty or a sense function.

You see, you don't stop and think, "This is a solution. I have a problem." You see the problem, not the solution.

Now, for example, here just of recent time, my channel's guides have informed him, "No problem." Now think of what that really means. To my channel it was rather a new experience to be told, "No problem." When you are interested in anything and you tell your mind "No problem," then your interest cannot become the function of concern. Certainly, it means to your mind you don't care. And that is true: your mind doesn't care; it doesn't care to control it. Therefore, "No problem" is in truth a solution returned to the source, to the soul faculty. Faith is the guidance of the faculties. And fear is the guidance of the functions.

So when you find yourself interested in something—and I know you find yourself interested in many things—remind your mind of what you are interested in: No problem. And you will be amazed how quickly you will feel relieved in your mind, for you are telling your mind "I don't care," in other words, "I'm not interested in controlling that which I am interested in." And so, "No problem" returns the solution to the solution, you see. If, however, you insist on believing that you are what your mind can and cannot do, then you will have a problem with declaring the truth, "No problem." You will not find the solution in all of your experiences.

You see, these sense functions and soul faculties that I've spoken to you over so many years of your time, all being triune in expression, are what you are doing each and every moment. With everything that your mind takes, it becomes a sense function. You receive the awakening of it as a soul faculty. You become interested in beautiful flowers. If you remind your mind, "What a lovely experience to be interested in those beautiful flowers," if you remind yourself, no problem. And if you don't, then the next thing you'll say [is], "That petal didn't grow just right." *[A few students laugh.]* "I wonder how long that's going to last. How much did that cost? Did I get my money's worth out of that?" That's now a problem. You are now concerned. You have made it so. Only you have made it so.

Now we enter that trap moment by moment. It ever waits for us. It's always waiting for us. For our minds are ever seeking, ever searching to control, to experience the challenge of competition, to be concerned: "Am I breathing? How fast am I breathing? Am I breathing too slow? What, to the great intellects of the medical field in the world in which I live, what do their statistics show? How many breaths per minute should I be doing?" And then, do you test your pulse to see, are you average? Are you normal? "Oh, no! No. Oh, I'm abnormal. I can't be abnormal! Oh, to be abnormal—that makes me an alien. Nobody will like me. Therefore, I've got to change my pulsebeat because it's not in keeping with statistics." What a way to live.

And yet, through errors of ignorance, we find, in your world, the masses of your world living that way.

"Is my hair black, red, brown, blonde? Is that a grey hair? That's different. Because it's different, there's something wrong. What's happening to me? Am I changing? Yes, I'm changing. I don't want to change. I feel secure in what I'm used to and what I'm familiar with. Why do I feel secure with what I'm used to and with what I'm familiar with? Well, I feel secure because I control what I'm familiar with. I control what I'm used to. I battle off the competition. I experience the challenge and the stimulation of my mental substance that I am still in control. I'm [in] control of what I have worked to control."

That is far from freedom. It's a guarantee of bondage.

Now, here we are. Moving on. So often in life a person looks and says, "Oh, moving on! I'm so grateful to be moving on! I'm making a physical move. It's such a wonderful feeling, just the thought that I'm making a physical move. Why is it such a wonderful feeling to me? Because I look around and see all of the things I haven't been able to control and I'm going to be leaving those things. They haven't done what I've wanted them to do." What a terrible trap. And yet it's the way the human mind thinks.

Then the human mind, if time passes sufficient for it—and each one's a little different—starts to think, "Oh, no. That one's going with me?! No! Oh, no! The move's not worth it." First the move's worth it; then the move isn't worth it. Because it starts to look around and it begins to see that it's going to take with it some of the things it wants to get rid of. At first it thought, by making the physical move, it would leave the things that it could no longer control. Now it finds the possibility—to the mind, it's a guarantee—that, "Those things are going with me." But where are those things? Are they a chair? Are they a wall? Are they a piece of wood? No, no, no. It's our reference, our mind, our emotions.

And so when a person makes a physical move, in business or in anything, they first move in consciousness. And so they begin this process of making these moves in consciousness of what it's going to be like. And it's going to be very good if the mind takes a look and says, "I'm in full control. I will control this. I will control that. I will control that. Therefore, I'm ready. I'm all ready and prepared for this move." Well, it's ready, but not prepared. Far from prepared. Because, you see, that which the mind is trying to leave, by its own fear, it takes with it. And so we find people, like gypsies, moving from here, to here, to there, to there—just like a gypsy, you see?—taking all of the baggage with them, for they are taking it in consciousness. They haven't emptied the baggage out of their mind. They haven't made those changes. And that takes time.

And so in the moving here, of our church and our school, in its physical moving, for the first time, in the experiences of my channel, all of you have been informed. That is a wonderful thing for it is offered to each of you. Not only the opportunity to go or not to go, the opportunity to face the baggage of the mind. Are you taking it with you or are you going to leave it behind? How much of it has served you well? How much of it have *you* served well? That's the question that you have to ask yourself.

And so the need exists—you see, fulfillment's a soul faculty. And what is its corresponding sense function? Yes, [Student S]. Yes. *[After a short pause, the teacher continues.]* You're not [Student S], are you, [Student O]?

No, sir. [Student O replies.]

Oh, good. Thank you. You just be patient. Yes, [Student S]. What is the corresponding sense function of the soul faculty of fulfillment?

I really don't know. I could guess, like, denial first came and then, maybe, satisfaction.

Yes, the sense function of the soul faculty of fulfillment is need.

Need. Thank you.

Yes, I think we're all familiar with that, aren't we?

Yes.

Yes. You see? Need, of course, is the effect of denial. We understand that. Need is the sense function of the soul faculty of fulfillment. You see, here you have fulfillment. That's what you are. It's like goodness. Goodness is what you are. When you permit your mind to let the goodness that you are to enter it, then you have to work mentally to constantly convince yourself that you are good. Not only do you have to work constantly to maintain the mental image that you are good but what you are offering to yourself is what you offer to everyone else. And take a look at what the trap is.

When you work with your mind to convince yourself that you're good, when you already are good—you see?—what you do is you're constantly facing fear. "Have I done what they will think—makes them think I am good?" You're constantly selling out to everyone that you see and that you hear because you're in constant fear of maintaining the goodness by the control of your mind. Then, it is no longer goodness. It's total deception. Goodness is what you are. And to work with your mind to convince yourself that you are good, then you are constantly experiencing fear in order to convince everyone that you see that you want something from, you see.

And so that certainly is not the teachings of this philosophy. That is not the teaching of the lamp of honesty that will see you through.

Now at what point in the centers of consciousness does the soul faculty begin to become the sense function? Any hands here? Yes, [Student L].

In the air center.

[Student L] says the air center. [Student B].

Third and fourth—reason. I mean, I don't mean the third and fourth, but the reason center.

And that is located?
Between the air and the magnetic.
Now what are the centers?
Air and the mag—
Earth, fire, water, air . . .
Electric.
Does the magnet come before the electric?
No.

No. No, the magnet is an effect, a response to the electric. Hmm? For example, it's like an adversity; it contains its own attachment. And so an electric source contains within its electric source its own magnet, you see. Hmm? And because the magnet is a small part of the electric in expression, the magnet is ever seeking the electric, you see.

So it enters its descent as it passes through the faculty of reason. Between which centers? The electric and the air. That's where the faculty of reason exists. So when it descends, when a faculty descends into—passes through the electric and enters fully into the magnetic [electric], you may guarantee yourself the mind has it. *[The teacher may have misspoken with the word "magnetic". One descends from the electric into the air center, as he states later in this class. However, he may also have intended to say "magnetic."]* And it is now on its way down to being a sense function.

Any questions on that? Yes, [Student S].
Could you just—I could check the tape. I was—

That's what so lovely about having magnetic tape: it's always waiting to be checked. *[The teacher laughs joyfully.]* I don't know what we would do if we had electric tapes in your world. No. Magnetic. Because there, you see, it receives everything, you see.

[One of the spotlights illuminating the teacher goes out at this moment and the stand on which the spotlight sits may have begun to sway.]

Yes? Well, that's all right. Don't touch it. Don't touch it. Leave it be. Leave it be. Leave it be. *[The teacher refers to the light stand.]*

And what was your question as the light decided to change? It is electrically powered, you know. *[The teacher laughs again.]* Very expensive, too. That's no problem. I'm sure you'll all make your proper donation. Yes.

You were speak—

[The teacher laughs again.] Yes, you were speaking on electric or magnetic tapes? Oh, no, prior to that. Go right ahead.

You were saying that when a soul faculty descends to the sense function—

Yes?

—at a point between the fourth and fifth, where the faculty of reason is and—

When we leave the electric and we enter the fullness of the air center, the mind has it. Now how does that happen, you see? You see, what is will power? Is it magnetic, students, or is it electric? Yes, [Student S]. Will!

Electric.

It's electric. All right. So, "Thy will," the will of what you are, when it leaves, you understand, its expression within your own consciousness or anyone else's own consciousness, it has left the electrical source. Do you understand that? And now it is controlled in the mental world. And what is below the mental, the air center? What is—

Water.

Yes! And so the moment you leave "Thy will," you leave faith. The moment you leave "Thy will," the will of what you are, you enter into the formation of the air center of your senses of *your* will: "my will." You begin to believe and to convince yourself that that is your right, that is your divinity, that is your divine right. There is nothing divine about that center at all, for it has lost the very thing—the power of the divine will of total acceptance. It has left principle. And when principle leaves the faculties—that's a faculty, a soul faculty, principle—it becomes a sense function of personality. Hmm? Did that help with your question? Yes, go ahead.

Does it do it at that point when it enters the air or does it—

It does it when it enters the air and it leaves, it leaves the electric.

OK.

You see. You see, as it enters the—as it leaves the electric, "Thy will," the will of the soul, you see, in its evolution, "Thy will," the divine will, when it leaves that center—you see, concern takes place in the air center. Yes. That's when the mind tries to form and to control—you could touch that for a moment, just the lamp. *[A spotlight stand had begun to sway.]* So it stops moving, please. I'd rather it not keep moving. Thank you. That's fine. That's fine. That'll be fine.

And so, you see, in the air center, that's where it takes control. That's where interest—interest becomes concern in the air center. Not in the electric. Not in the ethereal. Not in the higher centers of consciousness. Only when it leaves the electric. Only when—you see, when you leave that electric, the will power, the divine will within you, you feel a helplessness in the air center. You start to experience need, for you've denied what you are. You start to experience need and you start to rely upon what the air center (your mind) can create, can form. And so, you see, as you start this reliance in the air center, it descends you right into the water center, where judgments are formed.

You see, you have the thoughts in the air center. The air center is where you form your thoughts. The water center is where you take your formed thoughts and you solidify them. That's known as your emotions. You solidify them and believe and convince yourself that *they* are you, that that (what you have created) is you. For you have left the divine will when you entered the fullness of the air center. Do you understand that?

Yes. Thank you.

Yes. [Are] there any questions on how that works?

Thank you.

Yes. Certainly. And, you know, when any experience a person has—of course, we've discussed experiences and what they truly are. But if you will relate to: What are you? You are the soul faculties. You have the opportunity at any moment to be the sense functions. What do the sense functions offer? One thing offers you interest and the joy of life, and the descent of it offers you concern. Of course, it offers the thrill of control, and it offers the challenge of competition, you see. Because that's what the realm has to offer in anything. Yes. And then, one becomes concerned about how good one thinks they are. Well, that only, of course, reveals to us we've denied the goodness that we are, and we must now manipulate and work and convince someone else how good we are.

You see, it's like a reformed smoker or alcoholic; it's like a reformer of anything, you see—may God ever save me from reformers. I've met so many. And, but anyway, it's like a reformer, you see. They have taken—supposedly, they think they have awakened and they're now pure, you see. They have entered a consciousness of purity. Well, to sustain this conviction their mind has of their purity—because they've sacrificed so much and they have a vested interest in all of the effort they've made to control their mind. So they go to work, constantly in need of reforming the whole, wide world. And they must convince the whole, wide world that that is the better way in order to maintain their security within their own consciousness, their stability, because they're in a realm now, a mental world, and fear is constantly knocking at their door and doubt is their constant companion and shadow.

Think of making a physical move, and you will get to see what you have created in your consciousness. Whether you will really be leaving it behind or you'll be taking it all with you, for it will all rise up for each and every one. Let it rise daily. So that is the preparation process. Prepare yourself.

You see, to work intelligently with anything that the mind has created—and the mind is the great creator—to work with it intelligently requires understanding it. You cannot understand anything that you do not communicate [with]. Communication is indispensable to understanding. So if you are not willing to communicate on any subject, be alert, awake, and aware: that is the very subject that is controlling *you* and there's no way possible—except through total deception—to believe that you are controlling it.

And so, you know, as I have taught you for many years, exposure frees the soul. Exposure frees the soul. Well, exposure is not possible, it is not possible without communication. For, you see, you cannot cast the Light on things, created things, unless you have understanding. In all your getting, get understanding; in all your giving, give wisdom. It is the process of giving wisdom that is the Light that frees the soul.

Now where is this wisdom and this understanding taking place? It's taking place within one's own consciousness, you see. To permit the mind to depend on something beyond its domain for its understanding and for its wisdom is to remain in the mental world, where understanding and wisdom do not exist. Hmm? For they are faculties of the soul. They are not functions of the senses.

Yes, now we have a few moments for questions. Yes, [Student B].

When one is aware that they're dropping down into the air center, what—

They've left the electric, yes. In other words, they've sold out and given up their will. Yes. Because that's what happens. You see, the moment that you leave the electric center of consciousness and you enter the air center, what you've done is you have sold out your soul by giving up your will. Now a person likes to say, "Well, I exercise my will and my divine right!" They don't have will or divine right left. They are now in total service to the judgments in their water center of consciousness. And they are so convinced that that which they have created (their judgments) is them, there is no will left. In that respect, there is no will. Yes, [Student B]. You see, will of the mind is expression of the judgments created.

Then, to the mind, does it seem like . . .

"My way."

. . . you're not doing anything if you've, if—in other words, if there is no will.

There isn't. There is only the will that has already been given to the children that are created, to the judgments that the mind has already made. The moment you leave the electric center of consciousness and you enter the air center, you are guaranteed to experience the water center. The will that did exist—and remains for you to experience in the electric centers and higher—that will has already been given to the forms that have already been created. So, of course, there's will; there's the will that they use for you to do their bidding and do what they want you to do whenever they want you to do it. So in that sense, of course, there is still will. They're very tenacious. You see, what is the difference—when does tenacity become a—how does tenacity become a soul faculty? What is the soul faculty of tenacity?

Determination?

Determination! Now determination has the light of reason, you see. But when you leave that center of consciousness between the electric and the air, you now have tenacity and all of the will that is your right—that will of choice, that freedom—is now completely in the hands of what you've already created in the water center of consciousness, known as judgments.

So because of overidentification with form and with limit, those created judgments have no problem whatsoever convincing us that that is what we are. And anyone who works with them and counsels with them experiences a phenomenal degree of tenacity. But you are not talking to the person that is. You are talking to what they have created. To such a degree and such an extent have they created them, they are totally convinced and believe—the bondage, you see—that that's what they are. Yes. No, you lose, you sacrifice, you leave behind the will, the divinity of the will that you are when you leave those higher centers of consciousness, and you are in total service to what already has been. Does that help you with the question, [Student B]?

Thank you.

Yes! And so, you see, when you go to make a physical move, for example, like with our, with our church here and our temple and our church home here, you go to make a physical move, each student—because it has been revealed to all of you, it is taking place. Oh, it's already—but it's been taking place now for some time. And it's definitely taking place in the physical world, you see. So when—this time it was in the best interest of all concerned to reveal it to everyone. They face all of those things they have created in their water center. And to the amount of time and energy that they have spent in directing energy to them, identifying with them, they're absolutely convinced that that's what they are. And so all of those rise up, you see, because that means change and that means they're not going to get what they are used to. You exercise—you rise and exercise your divine will—Hmm?—that which you truly are.

So when you leave the electric center of consciousness, you're in the air center, the mental world; you've left the light of reason, which is your soul faculty. And you now are guaranteed, from the thoughts you create in your air center, the solidification and the service to the judgments that you have already created. Hmm? That, certainly, is not good business. It is, however, absolute dedication to what one has created with their mind.

And now you see the difficulty that people experience when they look in the mirror and they see that the divine laws, the laws of nature are making changes in what they believe they are. Some take it graciously, and they go through the process of comparison. And they say, "Well, do other people my age look like I do: so old?" And then they say to themselves, "No, no, I know a lot of ladies my age [who] don't look anywhere near as old as I do. Nowhere near." And then they look around a little farther and they see one or two and they find out their ages [and say], "Well, how come they look so young?" And then they go through all of this concern, all of this manipulation and control to find out what that one over there has been doing; that they're one of the exceptions to the so-called average. And they look so much younger, you see? So that's how the mind works. You see, that's where we're in service to that which we have already created. Hmm? Yes, [Student Y], this morning.

Thank you.

You're welcome.

So if you could find—you let that rise up. You say let that rise up daily—the—

Oh, it'll rise up daily. You don't have to think about it. All you have to do is think about one thing: the possibility of making a move. Don't even say "definite," because, you see, you know, you want to grow slowly. *[The teacher laughs joyfully.]* [To] my channel, it's definite. That's all there is to it. To do each one—yes—they grow their way.

So if you find yourself there—

Yes?

—in the sense functions, is it, is it simply to say how can we—what's the best thing to do to reverse the process to come back up?

Well, yes, I have given that to you in many ways. And the very first thing is very simple: give it to God, that which you are. You see, because—for example, [if] you start getting into concern, tell your mind, "No problem." The moment you convince your mind "no problem," you've gone back to interest.

You're interested in it, but you're not concerned. Concern, you see, offers you that wonderful sensation of control, manipulation, competition, the challenge, the thrill, you see. But it doesn't last. It's such short duration. Only to come again with another temptation. Again and again and again and again. But it does thrill the senses. It gives that charge, you see, you see. Challenge stimulates the ego. The ego is like a brass knob: it's constantly in need of polishing. Constantly. Yes.

So in facing the change that's occurring here in the temple—
Yes, yes.

—would it behoove an individual [to] give that to God as well?

Why, certainly! Why, certainly. When concern rises, tell your mind "No problem." When you declare "No problem," you're in the solution. Can you see that? Because you're no longer concerned! You cannot be concerned when you have no problem. You have the solution.

It's all, you see, in the mental world, in the air center and its remaining, descending centers, it's all manipulation; it's all competition; it's all challenge; it's all control; it's all thrill. Don't you see? For that is the realm of the senses. Grant it its right. That's what it offers. That's the only thing it does offer, at a great price of absolute, blind dedication to it. You see, you must be absolutely convinced that you are the things you have created in your mind, you must be absolutely convinced you are those judgments, in order to be a good servant to those things you have created. They are soulless creatures that you have created with mental substance. They can only live as long as they receive intelligent Energy. And they can only receive intelligent Energy as long as you believe that you are them. You see?

And the love of self offers all of it to any of us, you see. It is not the I that is the problem. The I is the solution. The thought of I is the problem. I gave that to you so many years ago. You see, it's when you take the I that you are and you form it; you create it in your mental world. Now when you do that, you create all of these thoughts, which descend into the water center and become judgments. And then whenever you think of I, you're in service to all those judgments you have created. Hmm? And because you are dependent, now, upon them by believing that you are that which you have created, you go out into the world and you find yourself dependent on any and every one else that reflects back to you the same judgments that you are in service to. Like attracts like and becomes the Law of Attachment. Only reason reveals the attachment is the adversity. Only reason reveals that—and time, in your world. Yes.

Show me your attachment; I will show you your hidden adversit[y] that is guaranteed to become an attachment, that was once an adversity. All adversities contain attachments. All attachments contain adversities. As all soul expressions, all faculties, in their descent become sense functions. Hmm?

Now, does that mean we should not have sense functions? Why, of course not. We should, with the light of reason, never losing, never giving up our will power, we should take that down into the realm of the mental world and the water centers. And we should maintain—we can only maintain—and we should maintain—our objectivity by looking at the vehicle for what it is: to serve the will power that we truly are, the goodness that we truly are, to tell it now or not now; that ofttimes, the way of goodness is the direction of no.

So, you see, [it behooves one] to maintain that degree of control before descending into the realm of creation. Because without maintaining that, without, prior to the experience, without absolutely maintaining that in consciousness and to look and say, "All right. You are what I have created. You have ten minutes of my time. No more and no less. If you tempt to take more than the ten minutes I have allotted you, the next time, you won't even get one."

Now if you have difficulty, you see, in once rising back or you think you have risen back and you have difficulty in maintaining your will power, it only reveals that you are back into the mental world, and you are, once again, convinced that you are the judgments that you have created. Does that help with your question, [Student Y]?

Yes. Thank you.

Yes. Yes, [Student N], please.

So when you feel a form trying to take control of you, does that mean that you're back in your will power and you can't seem to—

You've given up your will power for the temptation of the senses. You can experience the senses. That's not where it is—in fact, that is the evolution of the forms, for the individualized soul to consciously enter the realm of the senses and to maintain and to sustain its will power.

Now when you try to make someone else do something, you have given up your will power completely. You have totally given up your will power. Like attracts like. You work inside, you see. You work inside. Once you have worked inside, then you offer that, in keeping with the Law of Solicitation, known as presence, to that which enters into your domain and enters into your responsibility. You see, when you enter the house of another soul, you enter the forms they have created. And when you do that, you are subject to and a victim of things you do not know. And usually you find out after you got in there. And usually sometime later. Hours, days, weeks, months, or years. But you have established the law. You have consciously chosen.

For you must realize that we always consciously choose. We consciously choose to service what we have created or we consciously choose not to service what we have created. We make the conscious choice to ascend or to descend, for we make the conscious choice to think of what we are (the goodness of life) or we make the conscious choice to think what we are not [and] our goodness of life is dependent on what we can control or manipulate. We alone make those conscious decisions.

So in that respect, we always get what we really want. It is a matter of the timing that confuses us. It's only the timing that confuses us. We want this, our forms tell us in our realms of judgments, and then it takes too long for that to happen. And by the time it arrives, that particular judgment is no longer being serviced at that moment and then we say, "Well, why did this happen to me? Why should I put up with this?"

Well, that's a good question. Why should you put up with what's taking place in your own mind? You don't have to. And it's a very good question. And I look at the record and see that some of my own students here in class have asked that question of their soul. "Why should I have to put up with this?" Why, you shouldn't have to. It's your mind. Take control of it. Take control of your mind before someone else does. The only someone else that can control your mind is the one that you willingly give your mind to. But you still have a choice to take your mind back. You can only loan your mind. You can't give it away. You can only loan it through self-deception.

You see, many people loan their minds to someone else for a time. And then they deceive themselves and say to themselves, "Just why should I have to put up with this? And why should I have to put up with that?" And that's a very good question. Why should they so deceive themselves and loan their mind to someone who doesn't care about all of their mind? Only a portion of their judgments do they care about. Only the ones that fit into their own, selfish desires. So a person should ask themselves, "Why should I put up with this?" They should ask themselves that and singe the chickens that they have created that's come home to roost inside of themselves, you see. Yes, definitely. Absolutely. Everyone should ask themselves, "Why should I put up with this?" Because remember, it's your thought, your judgment in your own mind.

And you should ask yourself the question more often. I'm very pleased that my record reveals that my students here yesterday, just as recent as yesterday, asked themselves why should they put up with this, this disturbance and that disturbance, that was taking place in their own mind. It's a wonderful question. And I do hope that my students will ask it of their own ego more often, you see.

Yes, go ahead with your questions. Yes. You shouldn't put up [with it]. Why should you put up with poverty in service to a poverty judgment? Tell me, is it a good—is it good to give all that you possess to the poor and follow the Light? Is it good? Yes, [Student S].

All that you possess? I would say it is.

Yes. Anyone else? Yes, [Student O].

I would say it is. That I possess.

Yes. Well, people possess many things. Now let's ask our self an intelligent question. If we take all that we have earned, in keeping with the Law of Effort, and we give it to the poor and we do not give to them the opportunity of working for it, have we done a good service? *[After a short pause, the teacher continues.]* We've done a grave injustice. Not only to the poor but a grave injustice to our self. For we have taken the thrill of what we have given and the deception of helping another and what we have in truth done [is] we've helped them down into more dependence upon us. So we rise in our glory of self-love and they descend in their pity of dependence. To give to the poor without giving the opportunity of the Law of Effort to work for it is a grave disservice and can never ever come out with any good. For we give to the poor with our minds, our selfish minds that they may become dependent upon us by becoming weaker that we may thrill in our glory of how good we are.

You don't need to work with your mind to manipulate and to have minds judge, "Oh, yes. She's so good. Look what she does." No. Show them the way. Help them to help themselves. If a soul is drowning and the drowning soul is stronger than you, it is your responsibility to the Light within you to let them drown, for one soul in God is better than two lost in hell.

Thank you. I see our time is up. How quickly it passes. And good day.

NOVEMBER 23, 1986

A/V Class Private 68

Good morning, class.

Each day we give thanks for something. And so today let us give thanks for the opportunity of growing up.

We'll continue on with our class on soul faculties and sense functions with the question, What is the sense function of the soul faculty of dedication and how does the soul faculty of dedication become a sense function?

Yes, [Student M].

The soul faculty—is it loyalty?

Pardon?

Loyalty?

The soul faculty under discussion is dedication, yes. Yes, [Student R].

Obsession.

Obsession, yes. [Student B].

Distraction.

Distraction, yes. We're speaking of the sense function now. [Student D].

Irresponsibility.

Irresponsibility, yes. [Student U].

Laziness.

Laziness, yes. Very important ingredients of what the sense function is. Yes, [Student N].

Possession.

Possession, that was stated, yes. Anything else? *[After a short pause, the teacher continues.]* Well, first of all, if we will take a look at the soul faculty of dedication and see how it passes into a sense function, as all soul faculties do when we are not vigilant— and vigilant in what center of consciousness? Aware, awake, and alert in what center of consciousness? Yes, [Student Y].

Water?

Water center of consciousness? Long before it gets to the water. Yes. Otherwise, we find ourselves dead in the water. Yes, [Student L].

The electric.

Electric. Yes?

The magnetic.

Magnetic? The lower forty. We have to think before we get to that, [Student N]. Yes, [Student O.]

In reason.

Reason. Yes. And that is located where?

Between the air and the electric.

The electric and the air.

Electric and the air.

Depends on one's perspective, whether you're looking up or down. And hopefully, in that respect, we're up, looking down, and not down, looking up. Because that's where all of the problems seem to be: in down, looking up. And all of the solutions in up, looking down.

All right. Now here we have the soul faculty of dedication. It's on its descent, and once it fully leaves the electric center of consciousness, which is the will power—now we sacrifice or give away our will power when we enter the fullness of the air center of consciousness. For the air center of consciousness is mental substance; it is ruled by the king of creation. So it is from the air center to the earth center; those are the domains of the king of creation.

Now when you enter the fullness of the air center of your thought, of your mind, that is when you have lost the faculty of reason for that time. So as the soul faculty of dedication is being expressed, as when any soul faculty is being expressed, you are constantly tempted, if you permit yourself to look down, you are constantly tempted by mental substance. And in so being tempted, the soul faculty of dedication becomes the sense function of addiction.

Now, you take a look and you are aware of people on your planet that you understand are addicted. To free them from addiction, your world offers to them a substitute of what they are addicted to. In other words, in the mental substance, they are being offered a lesser addiction. In the judgment of the water center, it is therefore not as detrimental to who [whom]? To the person? To the people who are exposed to the addiction? To who [whom] is it not as detrimental to? That is the question you must ask yourself.

So when I state to you the brighter the Light, the darker the night or the darker the night, the brighter the Light, dependent, of course, where *you* are standing in consciousness can you see that there is a bright Light above you. And if you permit yourself to take control of your mental substance, then you will ascend to the bright Light that you are. However, if you insist on believing that you are the thought you have created in mental substance and refuse to awaken that the thought created in mental substance [is not you, and] you are the free, eternal spirit that is being controlled by what you think is yours, then you have a very serious problem in evolution, for your dedication—dead to all distraction is dedication—for your dedication to what you are has become an addiction to what you are not.

For example, you have these classes and these spiritual teachings; you take a look at them with your mind. Some of them are acceptable to your mind, for to your mind, that is, what you believe that you are, they are not a threat. "No change is necessary for me. Therefore, I accept, and have no problem accepting, this particular teaching at this particular time in my life. For they do not threaten, these teachings, this Light, this Truth, what I believe that I am at this time." Now that's known as the censorship of the king of creation.

So we take a look at the teaching and we [say], "Oh, yes, I have no problem accepting that. But I see that person over there has [a] great problem, and therefore that person over there must make these necessary changes, for by not doing so, that person over there is trapped in those lower realms of consciousness." We only guarantee the day when one of the teachings will not be accepted by our censorship. And when that teaching is not accepted by our mental censorship, we have a serious problem. We do not care to discuss that particular law. We do not care to discuss that particular teaching not only for our self but to even hear it discussed by anyone else that we are in earshot of hearing, so to speak.

And so, you see, really, what is taking place. The human mind, which is the domain of the king of creation—once we take the spiritual into the fullness of the human mind, having left the electric center of consciousness of will power, the very power of our being of what we are, when we take the teaching completely into our mental substance, then it becomes a servant of the king of creation.

Now we stand on a very delicate balance in evolution. One always stands at a delicate balance, for as long as there is such a thing known as identification, the indentation of the being into form—mental form, astral form, physical form—as long as there's identification, there is temptation. As long—which is the domain of the king of creation—as long as there is identification, there is temptation. As long as there is temptation, there is the function of teasing. As long as there is the function of teasing, there is the thrill or sensation of glory.

And so this sensation, known as glory, is when we are fully identified in the air center of consciousness, have left the electric center of consciousness, and have no will power, for we have, in our error of ignorance, given our will power to the forms we have created in our air center of consciousness.

Now a long time ago I spoke to some of you on astral forms, on soulless creatures, and on forms that have souls and evolved on your planet that remain in the astral realms of consciousness; others that have gone on to cosmic consciousness; others that have gone on to what you call heaven and all of the various descriptions you have of [it].

I always find the word *heaven* to be the most interesting when it is spoken by mental substance. I find it so interesting because what the mind means by "heaven" is the fullness, without obstruction, of all its selfish desires. And so I always find the word *heaven* so interesting. I have come to find many of the words of the Living Light Philosophy to have new meaning. I find it so interesting. Peace and harmony is no longer [an] expression of personal responsibility. Peace and harmony has become a function of "Others do exactly what I want them to do when I want them to do it. And don't give me any"—what do you call it?—"lower lip." *[A few students laugh.]* And so, you see, it's like the word *heaven*, you see.

And so here we are. Heaven, if you say "Heaven" to someone's mind, why they feel wonderful, the fullness of all their selfish desires has no obstruction, and they just go do what they call their thing, not even knowing what their thing is. Because what they are doesn't have a thing. *[More students laugh.]* So when you say, "Doing my thing," really, what you are talking about is something else, because what you are is not a thing. What you believe you are is many things. But what you are is not a thing. A thing has a limit. That's a thing. You can call it a vessel. You can call it a box. You can call it anything you want. A thing is limit. You are not a thing. You are not even many things.

As long as you believe you are a thing, then you establish the law to believe that you are many things. So if you permit yourself to believe that you are one thing, you establish the Law of Bondage to the thing. But it doesn't stop with one thing because that is contrary to the very Law of Creation. The Law of Creation does not create one thing. For the Law of Creation to create one thing would be contrary to its Law of Duality, contrary to the very rule of mental substance that must have competition in order to experience challenge, in order to have the thrill and the sensation of glory. Therefore, whoever permits themselves to believe they are a thing—no matter what the thing is—[if] you permit yourself to believe you are a thing, you establish the law to believe that you are many things.

Now it is the things and the many things that should be of great interest to us. For who controls the many things when we believe we are the thing? That is [a] very serious undertaking.

When you permit yourself to believe you are a thing, you establish the Law of Things. You have sacrificed your will power to the thing that you believe that you are. When that thing—it has its own intelligence: the intelligence you have given to it through your own will power that you have sacrificed. The will power that you are in the electric—between the electric and air centers of consciousness, when you fully enter the air center of consciousness, you give away your will power to whatever *thing* you create in your mental substance.

Now mental substance is the domain of the king of creation. And he has many, many workers. So by your tempting yourself, with the mental substance, to believe that you are one thing, you have literally given away your will power to the thing you believe that you are. However, *you* did not create that *thing* you believe you are. Creation created that *thing* that you believe that you are. And the king of creation is the ruler of that thing.

And so you believe you are that thing. You are, at that moment, under the control of the king of creation, who is king and ruler of all those things. So you become addicted. You enter the addiction. You see, the difference between dedication and addiction [is] dedication maintains the light of reason, the moment-by-moment choice. Now you are never left without choice. You have chosen, at times, to go into the realm of creation to believe you are some *thing*. You have made your choice. You are never left without choice.

When you make that choice, believing you are a thing, you believe what the king of creation has created and controls. So at that moment you have given your will power, subject to the dictates of the king of creation. When he decides that you are looking upwards instead of down, then he calls forth and you have what you call an absolute potent desire to do something with what you believe you are: your thing. If you do not do that, then all of the forms you have created, all of the thoughts that have entered into your water center, now known as judgments, which you are controlled by, they all rise up. And you experience what you know as frustration, as disaster, and everything falls apart in your life until you do what you believe you have to do because you believe you are the thing, which is the divine right of the king of creation and his domain.

Now, you do that. It's not so easy for the mind to say, "I no longer choose to serve this thing." Now your mind is the very instrument of the king of creation. So you are using what you believe you are against yourself. You have divided in consciousness in the sense that you permit your mind to believe that you are greater than the king of creation. And so, in so doing you tempt the king of creation. You tempt him to show you beyond a shadow of any doubt who is ruler of that realm. And who is ruler of that realm is not our puny, little thought that temporarily we believe that we are.

And so you have these many experiences in your life. You have all of this turmoil and all of this upset. So each time that you make the effort to wake up inside, you call forth, by that very law, you call forth the thing that you believe that you are, for he uses on you what *you* have taken glory in thinking that you are.

So if you have taken glory in your mind in thinking that you are this thing or that thing or some other part of your house, he will show you the price you must pay to be freed from it. You will not be freed from it by your mind, for he controls your mind! So how can you be freed from a king when you believe in the very realm that he is king of? A house divided cannot stand.

So what do you do with that, intelligently? You slowly but surely, intelligently, you start a slow process of education. You see, the first thing that happens in the mind is, when a person awakes to what it has done to them—that it is controlled by some king and they can't tell that king what to do, and every time they're tempted to tell that king what to do, he retaliates on them—the intelligent thing to do is to slowly but surely withdraw your addiction, to slowly but surely decrease your frequency of service to the king that you have allowed, through your own ignorance, to believe that you are, to redirect the intelligent Energy that you are into other avenues of expression, and to faithfully do your spiritual exercises. For the king of creation knows all your weaknesses, for he controls all your weaknesses.

So he who tempts another shall live to see the day when all their selfish motives pain shall take away. So, you see, when I stated to some of you so many years ago, "O suffer senses not in vain, for freedom of thy soul is gain," for that's what you are, you see? And so you slowly but surely, gradually withdraw your service, lessen your addiction, you see? And slowly, over a period of time—and it varies with each person depending on the eons of time they have been in absolute addiction to the king of creation.

Then the time will come when you are back in the higher centers of consciousness. And you will take a look [and] you will make an intelligent choice in the light of reason. The light of reason will never leave your consciousness as you look down there and you establish the law: "This is the length of time—not one moment longer, for I know in my heart I'm only this strong. I consciously choose—for I am using a form of creation—I consciously choose to dip low down there." You see, some people, you must understand, dip too low. They dip way too low. Their uneducated egos demand that they dip lower than they should. So you use that light of reason while you're in it and say, "I'm going to dip, but I'm not going to dip low, because I know if I dip low, he's been waiting for me, for I have been such an addicted servant to him for so long a time." You see? You see, the other alternative is quite simple.

Now that is the early process of evolving through this absolute bondage to the thing that you believe that you are, this total bondage, this absolute, total slavery. That's the early stages. After those have been accomplished over a long period of time and you continue on with your daily spiritual exercises, then you will not be plagued by that, for your identification, you understand, is not in the lower centers of consciousness. You are aware that you have a body. You have no question in your mind that you are not the body. You are aware that you have a hand. You have absolutely no question about believing that you are the hand. You don't look at your skin and say, "Oh, let me see, it's making a change. I'm not happy with that change." You see, that's the king of creation, you see.

The king of creation is a solidified form of consciousness. It does not evolve. Try to understand it is the ruler of has-beens. It is the ruler of what has been, not what is, therefore, not what is to be. It only rules what has been. Whenever you think of *you*, a limited being, whenever you think you are that thing, you must accept the demonstrable truth: you are controlled by the king of has-beens. You are absolutely controlled. If has-been yesterday was so appealing and so great, we must ask our self the question—correct, [Student J]?

Yes.

Then why have we ever left it? We could have stayed there, you see? We could always stay in any point in time in consciousness. Why be tempted by something you chose to leave?! Why be tempted by a has-been of yesterday when, by your own conscious choice, you have left it?

So a person, when they insist on playing with the thing—you see, that whichever you play with, you tease. And woe to those who tease the king of creation. He tempts you; you try to tease him. Well, look what you pay for that glory of teasing, you see.

Now that's the difference between dedication and addiction.

Like I have said before, the mind says, "My way or no way." Well, the "my way" is what the king says and that's what finally is the result. So when someone denies you of what you desire, be grateful and be giving of thanks for you have earned the opportunity of growing up! *You* have earned the opportunity of growing up. Ofttimes no is God's direction. So when you believe you are your *thing* and someone says to you, "No," thank God, for they have been, in that moment—whether you realize it or not—an instrument of good in the sense for *you* to grow up! To take a look and see what you think you have to have, what you think is your divine right, is absolutely restricted to the realm of your own consciousness of control and does not include anything outside of it. And if you will face that, you *will* give thanks for the opportunity of growing up.

Now, we'll get to any of the questions that you have here this morning. Yes, [Student Y], please.

Is—so there is no thing in the faculties. Only the—

Things are only functions. Things only exist in functions. Now, you know, sometime I think I touched lightly, some time ago, about the princes and princesses of things, you see. Well, there are many. It's a hierarchy, you see. Hierarchy above is hierarchy below. What is above is also below. What is below is also above. Do you understand that in principle? So a hierarchy is the governing body of the faculties, and there's a hierarchy that is the governing body of the functions. Yes. Yes, [Student Y].

So in the faculties is only energy, in the—

The divine Light is intelligent Energy. Now when we ascend to the fullness of the divine Life, then we have that full awareness it's only energy. Everything else is formed. Yes. What you are is Light. What you are is intelligent Energy. It has no limit. Limit is all created. Yes. Yes, [Student Y].

Is that—so when you said that there was no time, space, or distance—

It doesn't exist.

—that's what you meant. That—

Well, it does not exist. You see, it has to be your perspective. Now if you're looking from below, then, of course, you see time, space, distance, etc. And the higher you rise, you change your perspective, it doesn't look the same because it's not the same. Because it doesn't exist. It only exists in reference. You must have reference for it to exist. For example, in the functions, without reference, there's no existence, there's no competition, there is no challenge, there's no thrill, and there is no glory. You must have reference, you see. And so if you put the blinders on a horse, he has reference, you see?

So if you gradually remove the blinders, then the reference starts to expand. And so [if] you want to ride a horse, then you've got to put some good blinders on him, because otherwise the horse starts getting a broader perspective. And he won't let you ride him anymore. Do you understand that? Pardon? Yes. He starts to get free. And the next thing you know, the horse grows wings and he flies, but there's no one riding him. Go ahead, [Student Y].

So in the faculties, which is what we truly are, there—it's like there's no markers. There's no—would it be, like, a reference would be like a marker?

Yes, and we have created many markers. And that is what controls us: the markers that we have created. Yes. But you must understand that when you have a thought and believe you are the thought, it descends into the water center [and] solidifies into a judgment. The judgment becomes a form. The forms are controlled through the hierarchy, through the princes and the princesses, through the various hierarchy, for the king of creation.

And so you have a thought. And you thrill with that thought. And you constantly, continuously direct intelligent energy to it and it enters into the water center, where it is solidified. And then you become a servant of it. As you become a servant of the judgment you have created, which is a form, there is a hierarchy here, and they use all of those forms that have been created in order to mine their salt for the king of creation and for that domain. It's called the salt of the earth, you see. Yes. I think we've discussed that before.

And so when you speak with someone—of course, [these are] private classes—you speak with someone and you reveal that they are, at this time, controlled by one of the princesses or one of the princes, you see, they get all emotional because it's a terrible attack to the very realm that is doing all of the mining, you see, for the old king himself, the old boy over there. Yes. So if, you know—and then they attack my channel, as if he is the one that called that prince of darkness or that princess of darkness out of the depths to take control over the student. It's just ridiculous thinking, but it does show people who are tempted to believe that they are what they think they are. And they relish in that glory, you see. Yes, go ahead. [Student Y]. Yes.

Is it—so in the faculties of what we truly are, is feeling the—how does one know—

Well, a feeling is not—well, as you know, feeling, like affection, you see—for example, you are not—there is no dependence. So, you see—look, first of all, all feeling that you have is self-created, initially, all right? You've entered into form and all of this is self-created. Now you touch something and you say, "Oh, I like that feeling!" And so you have to touch it again. "Well, I like that feeling very much!" And the next thing you know, I find that you clutch it. You see, you won't let it go. You see? But you have created that in your consciousness. You alone have created that. It exists only in your consciousness. However, because you believe that it is you, you see, then that solidified judgment in the water center is used by the prince[s] and princesses of darkness in service to the king of creation to mine the salt, which is your vitality and your life energy. Yes.

Yes, and you don't use your ego to annihilate what your ego has created in the first place. That's a house divided. *[The teacher laughs.]* Yes. Yes, you don't use your ego to destroy what your ego has created. Don't you know what kind of an experience that offers to one? Yes, go ahead, [Student Y].

OK. I want—I wanted to know that—after leaving form and . . .

Yes?

. . . you're in another—you're definitely in another dimension, although you're taking all that you thought that you were with you.

Well, then you're not leaving form. You're just exchanging that physical form for the astral one and the mental one.

So you're still—

Whoever takes the baggage with them, takes their form with them.

So you're still in the realm of thing, even though you're—

Oh, yes, certainly. And a more dutiful a servant than ever before because there isn't the physical body, you see, that's in the way. You see, you can do more things with your mental body than you can [with] your physical body. You do realize that, don't you? So, you see, you don't have the obstruction of the physical body. See, if you have a desire for 10,000 glasses of water, your physical body limits you, in a course of a day, correct? But now your mental body will consume 10,000 glasses of water. No problem at all for your mental body. Because, you see, you can create 10,000 glasses of water. Hmm? *[The teacher drinks from his glass of water.]* And then you can service 10,000 glasses. So, you see, you see, this is why there—you are better in evolution while in the physical form to grow through these things, you see. Because your physical body limits you to how much you can express—correct?—in keeping with what you have established, the law you have established. There are the physical laws that must be contended with in that respect.

But your mental body, my goodness sakes alive! It can just go and work day and night, you see, far beyond the endurance of your physical body. Hmm? So in that respect, as I have always said, you are strongest while you're in physical flesh. So while you're in physical flesh, awaken to the hierarchy, to the process and how it works. For you are stronger now in physical flesh. You can only do so much. Your mind often wants to do more than your physical body will endure. Is that not correct? So in that respect, your physical body is a buffer and it is protecting you. There are limits to it. Do you understand? To your mind, there are no limits in service to that. No, no, no, no, no.

And so, you see, you leave your physical body in a mental body, and if you believe you are a possessing desire, you're totally addicted to it, then you find yourself doing nothing else but that, you see. And you'd be amazed how hard you work in that realm. Yes. Does that help with your question?

Yes, now [Student J] has a question, please.

Sir, when one is aspiring to the upper levels . . .

Yes.

. . . does one get the same type of help upward as the pull is downward?

Oh, indeed! If you will consider electrical help equal to magnetic.

I—

It doesn't appeal to your emotions. It appeals to your reason. Yes, it won't be help to your emotions, [Student J], but it is equally as much help, only it's to your reason, your faculty of reason, for the awakening to your reasoning faculty. Yes.

Could you, please, elaborate on that just a bit, please?

Yes. For example, you see, in the descent, one is helped with the temptations of their feelings, their emotions, you know. "Oh, things are going great." All right? Now, fine. Now that's the help you get on the descent: "Everything appears to be going my way. I feel good inside." Right?

Yes, sir.

That's what it says, you know, to the mind, to the emotions. Now on the ascent—you see, that's when we start growing—on the ascent, you have to pause more often because your emotions will be in turmoil. Do you understand? All your emotions, your water center goes really into turmoil. Because it's not getting fed, you understand. You're waking up. But [using] your faculty of reason, you pause and you look out and you see, "Well, now things are better. I mean, I don't have all these emotional charges that I'm used to. There's a change taking place in me. You know, it seems to be different. Perhaps I'm getting older. I don't seem to have the thrill and the charge and the race, you see, like I used to. But I can do without that." That's how it appeals: it appeals to your faculty of reason. Do you understand?

Yes, sir.

And you get to see yourself at a different pace, a more intelligent pace, a more reasonable pace. The budget gets balanced, not the way of the emotions, but there's a more steady balancing over a period of time. That's how it appeals. It has the same effect, you see. It's just as strong, but it only appeals to your reasoning faculty. You see?

Yes, sir.

It will not appeal to your emotions, no.

Then do we get the help from the higher sources . . . [Student J continues to speak even as the teacher responds, but it is difficult to accurately transcribe several of his words.]

Oh, you certain—absolutely. Absolutely. But, you see, the higher sources of Light, the electrical—[and] into the higher sources—does not have what you consider emotion. They have no emotion. You know, they're not appealing to a thrill of your form. No. No, no, no. But you get just as much help. Absolutely. Definitely. Your mind will probably say to you, "Well, I don't do what I used to. I don't race here and I don't get that and my senses and things. But I feel better." *[The teacher laughs joyfully.]* "I don't mind being by myself for a change." You see, the dependence on form begins to weaken, you see. As you awaken, the dependence on form—it doesn't matter who comes or goes as long as they pass you by. Do you understand that?

Well, that's the help you get, [Student J]. That's the help everyone gets. You see, they don't come—you don't have—you don't attract them into your universe to boost you [to] a high only to drop you and let you sink so low. You see? You don't have those highs and lows anymore. They start to decrease. And you go along on an even pace in life. However, to the emotions, the mind usually reacts [with], "Well, I'm getting old, you know." And then it justifies, "Well, I turned over about every stone I could find. So I've already been through that. How could I even feel tempted anymore? I've already been through that. I must be getting old." You see?

Yes, I . . . [It is difficult to transcribe a word or two.]

Well—*[The teacher laughs again.]* But you feel better inside! Now there's one thing to remember: that these centers of consciousness are controlled by these forms. Now those aren't the nature spirits, you understand.

You see, so often I find the difficulties in growing up, especially into the Light within oneself, [is that] everything that is form gets appealed to by the king of creation, you see. The body, the weight—you see, [if] you get upset, you know, then you just put pound upon pound on.

You see, what you [have] got to understand in the mind [is] that the water center of consciousness, where all the judgments are formed—and one spends a lifetime believing that they are them—when the king of creation—and he's constantly aware. That's his realm, you know. You see? He's ever aware, aware of his realm. And just like the Light is aware of *all* realms, you see. For without the Light, none of them get sustained. They don't exist. And so he's constantly on the lookout and [he] says, "Oh, one's trying to get away." Well, when one tries to get away, what they do—they have all of these judgment forms they've created and the princes and princesses come in, you know; they have their orders to go to work on that particular realm of consciousness. So if you have strong judgments, and they work on the water center and then you work to make changes in your life patterns and you say, "Well, things are getting worse! Why, they're getting much worse." Well, when things are getting worse, they're getting better. You see, worse to one realm is better to another. And so if you hold on long enough and you don't quit before the victories—that's the hissing hounds of hell that come before the victory, you see.

You see, everything that you believe that you were and spent your life believing that you were, all of those things are used against you. Do you understand that?

Yes, sir.

So if you believed that you were your tummy, then your tummy gets used against you. If you believe you're some other part of your house, you see—you overidentify with it—then that gets used against you. Do you understand that? Yes. Because you are no longer servicing those judgments who were mining the salt inside of your house—you understand?—and taking the tidbits back, as their job in the hierarchy, to the king there himself. Yes. You see, without, you know, the mined salt, without the mining of the salt, then the king doesn't have the salt for the tempting. Do you understand that? *[The teacher laughs again.]* Yes.

You see, it's the salt of earth, you see. [If] you believe you are the earth center, then you must be tempted by what the earth center has to offer. So he offers you a tidbit, you see, a little salt—and he uses a lot of salt. So he's got to have a lot of miners mining it. Do you understand that?

Yes, sir.

Well, that's the system. Of course. Yes. And, you know, I have in these times—oh, so many, many centuries—and I've looked in and have witnessed there one prince or princess after another coming in, you know. And they're so convinced that they can handle the job. And the next thing I know I see them back to the salt mines again. They're no longer up on the throne, you see. They get kicked off one right after the other. The more convinced they are how great they are to do the job, the shorter duration they seem to last. Oh, yes! Yes. And, you see, there's always, always those workers down there at the bottom of the pile. You know, when they come for volunteers, you see—they have plenty of volunteers, you see. They're all packed on top of each other, mining down there. And so when they call for volunteers, they get a hundred-thousand hands and screams come up, you see. And each one screaming they can do a better job than the next one. And, of course, the king, he chooses the ones that have convinced themselves they're the greatest. And they usually last the shortest time. Does that help with your question?

Yes. Thank you, sir.

Yes, certainly. Now someone else had a question? [Student M] has a question.

Yes.

Yes.

The—faith governs the higher forty centers of consciousness that that's that fine—

I'm glad you mentioned that because I was going to mention to you—you do know the soul faculties of money, ego, and sex, don't you?

Yes.

What are they?

Faith, poise, and humility.

Faith, poise, and humility. Faith, poise, and humility. Well, have you been experiencing faith, poise, and humility or have you been experiencing their corresponding sense functions? Because that shows you where your life vitality is going.

Yeah.

Was that an answer?

Ah . . . No. I was—

Well, did I ask for an answer? I thought I asked for an answer. Did anyone misunderstand that I was asking for a question? *[After a very short pause, the teacher continues.]* Well, no, I'm asking for an answer. You are a student of mine, aren't you?
Yes.

Why, of course, you are! Then answer. If you don't have the answer, then I'll help you. Yes.
OK. The answer I would give was that I was spending time in the lower, you know, the lower, the soul—the sense functions.

Of faith, poise, and humility?
Yes. The money.

Which one? Humility or faith?
Ah . . .

Or poise?
Humility.

Humility?
Uh-huh. The sense function of. Uh-huh.

Sense function?! Humility is a soul faculty.
Well, I know, but you were asking me . . .

I see.
Yes.

Well, fine.
I was getting drained.

Fine. Do you like it?
No!

Well, then be a little humble for a change.
That's right.

You see, you see, all of this foolishness—you know, work on some perspective. You see, to think that that's you—well, that's just fine, because the more you think that that's you, then the better the servant you are, the more addicted you are, so that the old king can get more salt mined out of you. And the next thing you say, "Well, what's happened to me? What's happened to me?"

Look, I've told you [for] so many years the thought, the thought is the lust. It is the thought that is the lust. Well, take a look! Without the thought, the other couldn't happen. You first must have the thought. The thought is the most detrimental. Because by believing you are the thought of the mental substance you have literally given away your power of will. You've given it to the thought you have created. And when you do that, you are in absolute addiction of service to it. Yes.

Addiction is what it is. It shows itself as possession and obsession, you see. "No other thought seems to enter my mind." Now I don't know if you've been aware of it or not, but here for these past few months, you see, especially, every single day the faculty of faith, poise, and humility has battled its own sense functions. Every day the flood seems to increase and increase. The only ones who drown in it are the uneducated egos who insist in their self-glory; then they're constantly thinking about it. They're constantly using every device, including beautiful spiritual truth, to service the thing. It's just a constant bombardment, you see? But only a fool will quit before the victory. My channel is not about to quit the Light. But it's just a constant thing.

You have to understand, Could that possibly be you alone in your tenacity and stubbornness? [Do] you have so much tenacity and stubbornness, beyond all realms of reason? No, no, no, no! You have armies of stubbornness and tenacity! You have princesses and princes who demand and are under orders to mine that salt. So your thought must be constantly in the function rather than the faculty because you have, you feel this tremendous possession that you got to have! Well, that's when you can awaken that you have a whole army of them banging in your consciousness because you are not servicing that realm that you believe that you are.

Thank you.

And to those who just take their ego thumb and go *pshech*. *[The teacher makes a sound that is difficult to transcribe as he uses his thumb to seemingly squash something on the table at which he is seated.]* [And say], "That's over now. I'm all spiritual. That's over." *[Many students laugh.]* Don't hold your breath. It's destined to do its number. Then a person says, "I was freed for 10 years or 11 or 12, and look what she or he did to me! Just look what they did to me!" Because, you must remember, the sure way of knowing if you're in total service to that king is to deny personal responsibility. No matter how cunning they are, they will always reveal themselves: "It was someone else's fault." "I was feeling fine until . . ." And it was always something outside. Always! It's what someone else does. "Someone else isn't treating me nicely. Someone else shows me no affection. Somebody else doesn't communicate with me." Your opportunity [is] to communicate with God! Not be dependent on what someone else does. That's your wonderful opportunity, you see.

You see, I told you some time ago, we are moving on. We're not taking the baggage with us. And so all of this upset you're going with is facing—you see, all of the facades, the deceptions, you know, the purity, and all of the holiness and all of the sainthood, you see, all of that veneer is melting away. Because, you see, it must melt away. Because if it doesn't melt away, then we take all of the baggage with us. And we're not going to take all the baggage. It's all going to be dumped and stay where it is [dumped], because it's not going with us. And so when the veneer melts away and all of the sweetness, the holiness, the saintliness, and the purity, and all of that virginity disappears, then we see what's really been going on. And that's what we're seeing. And some of us, our minds, we don't like to look at that. That's distasteful to us. Well, why is it distasteful? Well, it's very clear. It's distasteful that it's too close to us and our own might melt away. Do you understand how simple that is?

Let us not be so holy and such great reformers because the baggage is being dumped. You're dumping your own. Lovely. Yes. *[A few students laugh.]* You see. You see, people, their minds—their pride's at stake. They want to put up all of [these] facades when their thoughts are in constant service to that prince there. You know, they dip real low down there. Yes, and serve that stuff down there and put up this facade of how spiritual, you see, we all are and how saintly and how holy! And this other, oh, this other garbage is so terrible. Until their own veneer melts away, you see.

So melt it away and get through with it, and let's not take too long because we're moving on, you know. And if you've got baggage when it's time to go, well, you'll have to make a choice that'll be very traumatic for you. Because you either stay with the baggage you believe you are or you go without it. And we're not going to take all that baggage with us. But if you really feel that you have, that you're that baggage, then I assure you, you know, you'll just stay behind. Yes. I bet you're going to need many buckets for all those tears. *[Many students laugh.]*

Well, it's a lovely class. A whole hour has passed. So it's so nice to have the opportunity to grow up, you see, and stop Miss Holiness or Mr. Holy and just simply grow up. And find something to think about. Perhaps humility. Perhaps God for a change. Yes.

Thank you. Good day.

NOVEMBER 30, 1986

A/V Class Private 69

Good morning, class.

Today's discussion for our class is the Isle of Hist. The Isle of Hist is located between the electric and air center of consciousness. It is also known as the scales of balance [and is] also known as the Law of Harmony.

Conscious thought, as you have already been instructed, is electric power. Subconscious activity is magnetic force.

Now the descent into what is known as the lower centers of consciousness or animal instincts is dependent upon activity of what you know as fear. The ascent into the higher centers of consciousness is known as faith. Therefore, whenever you permit activity of your subconscious to become your guiding light, then you must realize that whatever has been created, whatever has passed in your life is now in control of your life, for the lesser light of fear is what, at those times, you are following.

It is the instinct of the animal consciousness to fear. And so when man permits himself the luxury of fear, then he expresses in consciousness with the animal instinct. He is therefore dependent, for one cannot express fear without dependence. And man only fears what man has depended upon. No man fears what he is not dependent upon.

So we find that fear is only expressed when one permits themselves the luxury of entertaining in consciousness events, experiences that have passed, which, of course, reveals the mind's dependence, for security, on what it is familiar with.

When the Isle of Hist separates, that is, when the balance of the scales is sufficiently tipped, man no longer expresses in physical form, for what you know as the *prana* or life force is now directed into the fullness of other centers of consciousness. Do not, however, misunderstand: the removal of the being from the physical body does not guarantee the removal of the being (or soul) from the mental or astral bodies of consciousness.

Fear is a great magnetic force. Whoever permits themselves the luxury of limit guarantees the magnetic force attracting unto him like-kind experiences.

And now it's time for your questions. Yes, [Student J], please.

What causes the Isle of Hist to separate?

When the imbalance of the scales reaches a degree of 81 percent, then the separation of the Isle of Hist takes place. Yes. If you will recall that there are eighty-one levels of consciousness and if you will recall that each level of consciousness requires energy from the being that you are, then you will understand that when the scale reaches an 81 percent, up or down, the Isle of Hist separates. Now should it reach a downward, in its fullness of energy, a full 81 percent, then, of course, the being (the soul) enters into the realm of consciousness known as a mental and astral world. Yes.

Thank you, sir.

That help with your question, [Student J]?

Thank you very much.

Yes. Yes, good morning, [Student Y], please.

Good morning. Thank you. Is the—so then is it only possible momentarily to experience the Law of Harmony while in physical form?

Moment by moment is conscious activity. Electric power expresses through conscious activity, yes. And in reference to that question, certainly, it is moment by moment because a person is easily attracted by magnetic force to what has been. For example, take a simple 1 minute of silence, just 1 minute, 60 seconds in your world. And see how long in that 60 seconds you maintain conscious activity. You will find that out of 60 seconds you will indeed show great growth if you can maintain 10 of the 60 seconds in conscious activity. For the shadows are very magnetic, for they are what we alone have created. Yes. [Does] that help with your question?

Thank you. Yes.

Yes. Yes, good morning, [Student M].

Good morning. Yes, here I have that the conscious thought is the electric part.

Correct.

And subconscious is the magnetic force.

That is correct.

Now, to gain the balance over the—or to educate this magnetic force, which isn't conscious, is through what we do with the educating of evolving of our forms. Is that similar to the magnetic force? Are these—everything that's created in our water center, that's all the magnetic.

What has been created is created. It does not evolve. For example, we create things and those things are sustained by identification with them. I'm speaking of thoughts of the mind, which are solidified in the water center as judgments. Remember that only a judgment offers to you the experience you know as fear. So in that sense, try to understand that when you permit yourself the luxury of descent into the magnetic force field, then you are controlled by whatever you have already created. Now that which has been created by the mind does not evolve. You create new forms by the mind. And when you attempt to create new forms, which bring about changes in your experiences, you battle with those forms that you have already created.

And so the education of the ego is the awakening to the very process of the Isle of Hist: the ego is educated between the electric and air centers of consciousness. That's where the light of reason is. That's where the Isle of Hist is. That's where the Law of Harmony is. And that's where balance is. And so over these years here with you, I have shared with you the understanding of an educating process: when you find yourself with a desire of what it is that you must do, to gain control over the desire in order to educate the ego to consciously make the choice of whether or not you choose to descend and service that which you have created. If so, then to do it intelligently by a conscious decision of when, how, and what, and especially the length of time that you choose to direct life-giving energy to that which you have created. That is an education process. That is a recognition and acceptance of the Law of Creation, which you are responsible for refining or evolving.

Now you cannot refine or evolve anything that you do not have control over. So there is no possibility of educating the uneducated ego until such effort is made. First of all, the recognition that it is a form or judgment that you have created, that it is there waiting for you to direct energy to it. And without a conscious choice of what you're going to do with what you have created, then what you have created is the master and you, in that respect, of course, would be the victim. Does that help with your question?

Yes. Thank you very much.

Yes. You're welcome, [Student M]. Now [Student N] back there—Good morning—has a question.

Morning. You were saying that when the Isle of Hist is separated—

Yes.

—we're no longer in form anymore.

You're no longer in physical form.

So there's no . . .

That doesn't guarantee you're not in form period. You do still have a mental form and an astral form. And what world you enter in consciousness is dependent on which way you have tipped the scales: either down or up. If you have tipped them down, then, of course, that form will be in that realm, for that is the choice that you have made. Yes.

After you've left your physical form.

Well, it's right now. But as I spoke to you, I think it was in our last class or the one before, while in your physical form with this buffer, you're not aware of it. And so you're stronger in that respect. Yes.

So if you have already tipped the scales on the descent and you continue to keep your scales tipped on the descent—as I just spoke here to [Student M] in reference to taking control and to recognize what it is you have created, which you call your desires and impulsive desires, recognize what it is that you fear by being honest with yourself, by recognizing what it is you depend upon, and you will find that everyone in mental substance in an uneducated ego is dependent upon limit: some limit they have created, some form, some place, some event, or some person. So if you will recognize what you have created, through honesty in your consciousness, then you can consciously choose whether or not you want to make the effort to tip your scales on the ascent, if they happen to be on the descent at that time. Yes.

But one cannot reverse a descent, a scale on the descent by last-minute prayers to the Divine Light because you have all of these other things. You know, there isn't such a thing as a miracle: it's a lack of understanding natural law. Yes.

So once you realize—

Deathbed confessions do not tip the scale of a lifetime. *[Many students laugh.]* They sooth the conscience (the mental conscience, the educated conscience) only for moments. But they do not tip the scales of a lifetime. No. Yes, [Student N].

So you can use the separation—when you were speaking to [Student M], you were saying that you're the victim of whatever it is . . . they . . .

We're the victim of what we depend upon.

So if you're trying to, you're trying to do anything at all and you become magnetic with it, then it's controlling you instead of you—[Student N continues to speak as the teacher responds, and a few of her words are difficult to transcribe.]

Yes, it is controlling you because you are dependent upon it. Does that help—you see, as long as you depend upon limit—anything that is limited—as long as you depend on form, which is limit, as long as you depend on limit, then you are controlled by limit. And so when you want to do something, you have all of those obstructions, known as limit, in front of you because that is what you have chosen to be dependent upon. Yes. That's the descent of the scale. Yes. Go right ahead.

So when you work with it, you just work with it. You don't look at it as . . . I guess that's what it is: it's dependent. You look at it as you need it instead of it needs you.

That is correct. You see, it's reversed in the consciousness. It has convinced you that you need it. When the truth of the matter is it is a form that you have created that cannot survive without your life energy. And so it has convinced you that you need it, when the truth of the matter is it needs you, for without you, it doesn't survive. You see, any judgment that you have created and believe that you are needs you for its survival, for you created it. You see, you alone feed it. And the cunningness of the human mind is that what it creates is able, the created thing is able to convince the creator, you understand, that the creator needs it. Do you understand that?

Yeah.

Yes. And so when you have a judgment, you allow a judgment in your consciousness, you experience fear, [and] you work to defend the judgment. Well, the truth of the matter is that it is working to defend itself, because without you, it will not survive, you see. It will go back into its nothingness and have to wait there until you reawaken it. Yes. See, once a judgment is created, it doesn't evolve. It serves the purpose of the design that you had in mind when you created it. Yes, go ahead, [Student N].

So then you create new forms and you said you battle with the old ones until you . . .

Well, just change your job or make a change in your income, and tell me what you experience. Especially if it's a descent change or if you judge it to be a descent. Reduce your income by

60 percent and tell me how you feel. Do that in consciousness this moment. Yes?

Yeah.

How do you feel?

Terrible.

Well, there you are. *[Student D and many other students laugh.]* It feels terrible because, you see, you must realize that you believe that you are it. And therefore, it feels terrible and lets you know, because, you see, it has convinced you that you are dependent on that which you have created. Do you understand that, [Student N]?

So if you don't do what *it* was designed to do—say, for example, you see, in the human mind, you created [a form that], "My income is such and such. Well, I certainly could use more. I really do need more." However, you have created this judgment form [that dictates] that is your income. You are now—it has convinced you that that is you. And so it will not change. It's absolutely solidified. Do you understand that? You see?

You see, whether you change and lessen the income or a change takes place and you increase the income, you still have a condition of trauma in the consciousness. Now people don't realize that. You see, they're so easily deceived by what is known as greed. Say that a person has an income of, oh, $10 a week, you see. It's about my channel's income, I think. Or maybe 12—$12 a week. *[Mr. Goodwin lived at the temple and received a monthly stipend of $50 per month.]* You have an income of $12 a week, and suddenly it's changed from $12 a week to $36 a week. Well, now if it was decreased to $2 a week, you can all relate to that: you feel terrible. Say that was your income—right?—and you feel terrible. Well, when it's increased to $36 a week, you say, "Oh, that's fantastic!" And then you don't know what to do with yourself and you go out like a drunken sailor on the streets and just blow it all away! Because, you see, there's no control.

Because you have these new entities that you've created and they're battling the one that is used to $12 a week and you now have three times that amount. Do you understand?

I do.

You see? I do hope you understand because no matter which way you tip the scale, once you have created a form, it is not satisfactory to the form. Because it is contrary to the design that you had in consciousness when you created the form. All right? Yes, [Student N].

Contrary to the design . . .

That you had in mind when you created the judgment. See, a person creates a judgment and says, "Well, I've got to have this income." And things change in their life and they have that set amount of income. They do not use the faculty of reason. They do not stand on duty at the Isle of Hist and say, "I could use this amount of money, or more or less, but I could use that." You see, they put all these restrictions—now, when you put a restriction on something, what you do [is] you deny all other possibilities. So when you do that with your mind, you create a form, you design it absolutely restricted. You do not include "I accept the possibility" with the form that you create. You do not include "I accept the possibility of more than that amount. I accept the possibility of less. No problem. It doesn't matter at all." And you're free.

But you have to understand what you are doing with this electric power and this magnetic force. It's totally imbalanced because you do not stand guardian there at the portal of the consciousness, you see. Yes. Does that help with your question? Go ahead, [Student N].

So you stand there and when you create a form . . .

Yes?

. . . that's giving it to God and you don't let anything else come in the—in any other limitation come in the way of that desire.

There's no limitation, for there's no dictate. You see, you must realize that there is no dictate. When you create a form and accept the possibility—you understand that? You see, you accept the possibility, then what you do is you release it to the Divine. You accept the possibility of experiencing the goodness that you are. Now when you create a form like that, you see, you have a form that's created that is subject to, by its very design, the acceptance of the possibility of experiencing the goodness that you are. So when you go in your self-thought, when you identify with yourself and that form comes in, that form comes in with all of those ingredients: the acceptance of the possibility of experiencing the goodness that you are. It is not limited by dictate. Do you understand the difference there? Pardon?

Yes.

Yes.

So that the dictates that you make are the denial—

The dictate is the denial. The denial is the destiny. Whatever you dictate, you deny, because you limit and that destines you to that type of a form that you become in service to, for you have created it and you have designed it, yes. Yes.

So that the destiny, your destiny . . . you have no destiny, then, if you don't—

Oh, yes, everyone has a destiny for they have so many denials.

Right.

Oh, yes. Each dictate is a denial. Each denial is a destiny. So everyone is constantly creating all types of destinies. You have a destiny to several experiences in the course of this very day, you see? For you have already dictated what you're going to do or not going to do, and in the dictate is the denial and the destiny of the experience.

You see, you see, when you say, "Well, I'm going to do such and such this evening," you don't say, "I'm going to do such and such this evening. I accept the possibility that I'm going to do such and such this evening. I accept the possibility of experiencing the goodness" that you are. You see, there's no problem because it doesn't matter whether you do or whether you don't. There's no problem. You see? And then, by being no problem, then you're not in service to a very limited, restricted form that you have designed and created. Does that help you?

Much. Thank you.

You see? So one does what is right to do, cares less what anyone else does with it. And when you care less what anyone else does with it, then you are free from being dependent upon them and how they react to what you do. You see? But if you are constantly concerned—if the faculty of interest has entered into the magnetic force of the lower centers of consciousness, then you are constantly concerned of what they say, what they think, and what they do. And everything to you is personal. So you look around and say, "That person didn't smile. What did I do? Why are they angry at me? This person didn't do that. That one didn't say what I like. Someone else didn't say what I like." You reveal your complete and total dependence upon people and personality. Hmm?

That's when you react a lot.

Yes, one reacts ever in keeping with their dependence on what they want out of someone else, instead of what they should be working, through personal responsibility, to gain inside themselves, not outside. Yes.

Yes, it's dependence. You see, I find—you'll find that a dependent person is a fearful person. And a fearful person is a dependent person. And they're always in need and they're never fulfilled. They're constantly seeking fulfillment and never finding it. It is so fleeting. Yes.

Thank you very much.

You're welcome. Yes. Good morning, [Student D].

Good morning.

Yes.

So if you take desire from God by putting a form on it, if you accept the possibility of experiencing it or not experiencing it, does that give it back to God?

Why, certainly. You have not dictated what shall be and what shall not be. When you do not dictate, you do not enter the lower centers of consciousness. When you do not enter the lower centers of consciousness, you do not fear. And when you do not fear, you do not depend and you are free! Did that help you, [Student D]?

Yes. Thank you.

Why, certainly. Absolutely. Yes, good morning, [Student L].

Good morning. Is expansion magnetic and contraction electric? [As the student speaks, a nearby clock strikes.]

Pardon?

Is expansion magnetic and contraction electric?

Well now, pause and think. And tell me what you think about that. I think we've covered that several times.

Well, I thought just—

Does a magnet, does a magnet expand? Or does it contract?

I...

Does it pull or push? *[The teacher laughs joyfully as the student responds.]*

It pulls.

Well, are you magnetic or electric?

Well, it just depends what day it is.

Well, what form are you?

Oh, I'm a magnetic form. [The student is female.]

You are?! Well, you don't push, do you?

No.

Well, I didn't think so. *[The teacher laughs and then coughs a bit.]* Well, electric expands and magnetic contracts. *[Several students laugh.]* You should have known that. *[The teacher takes a drink of water.]* Perhaps some of you should go to your schools and study anatomy, I think, before coming to this class. *[Many more students laugh.]*

Thank you, [Student L]. Yes, [Student J].

Sir, how can one determine whether they're on the ascent or the descent? And assuming they're on the descent, how can they reverse that pattern?

Oh, certainly. One is aware immediately, the moment they pause, whether or not they have any fear. And if they have any fear, then they are dependent on something they cannot control. And so a person—to change that (the scale which is tipped now into the descent or the animal instinct)—you see, if you understand evolution and you understand that what you call man or the human race—the missing link doesn't exist on your planet because, you see, it is the higher evolved beings and their marriage with the forms on this planet eons, untold eons ago. And so whenever you permit fear or dependence in the consciousness in what you would call the mass consciousness or, more likely, the race consciousness of the being itself in its evolution, then you enter that realm of the instinct of fear and defend yourself, you see. That's the animal instinct.

So you can know at any time, at any moment whether or not you're dependent on something you can't control. Now if you find that you are dependent on something that you cannot control, then you know that you are in fear and in the descent in consciousness. So you remove yourself from that dependence, you see.

You see, it is very natural for the human being to have this sense of independence, of freedom, because that's what they are. And it is very unnatural for them to be dependent on something they can't control, you see? It's contrary to the law of their own evolving individualization.

And so any time that you have any fear of anything, pause, because you'll see what you're depending on. And it is that dependence that is using you. That's when you're being used. Yes. Did that help you, [Student J]?

Very much. Now how can one change it?

Oh, one changes it, first of all, by the recognition of it, and by the acceptance that is not what they are. And they go through their spiritual exercises. You see, I find that's the thing that is wanting, in order to help the energy, the consciousness move up to the higher centers of consciousness: is the lack of the daily spiritual exercises. Because through those exercises that you have been given, then you experience the electric being that you are, you see. You don't continue to experience the magnetic forces and that which you have created, which are using you and [which] have convinced you that you are them, you see. You see, try to understand they could not use you unless they first convinced you—because you designed them—they could not use you unless they convinced you that you are them, you see.

It is true, you have created them. You are not what you have created. You are only responsible for what you have created, but you are not what you have created. That is contrary to the law, you see. That which sustains a thing is greater than the thing.

So when you have a judgment or a thought, remember that it is dependent on you. For you to allow it to convince you that you are dependent upon it, that's when you become the victim. That's when you experience fear. That's when, [through] denial, you are destined to those experiences. You see?

I do.

Yes. And so throughout all history in your world, this has always been revealed. Some time ago I gave to you several of these so-called mythologies and things to study, to study them objectively. For example, here, just a short time ago, I was discussing what you know as this story of Ulysses, you see, of Jason and the Argonauts. But, you see, you don't study them. You see, this same truth has been given millions of times, given out into the world in different ways, you see. For example, today, it is given here in this school to appeal to your intelligence. It has been given before in other part—in other times in your world in other ways, [like] through mythology, you see, depending upon where the people in their evolution are: how they can receive it. Do you understand?

It has not—this is the only school of this type here on your planet. But the truth, you see, is not new. This same truth is very ancient. It has always been; so it's the oldest thing in the world. In all worlds, it's the oldest, for the Light has always been and always shall be. And so in that respect, there's nothing new about it at all. The only thing you can consider new is—the presentation of it is different. It is not new. It has always been.

And so when you study some of these things—like I gave to you students, many of you, years and years ago, to study Helen of Troy, all of these things, and Jason and the Argonauts. And for example, while we're on that, we might as well discuss what creature in nature represents self and selfishness? Of all the creatures in nature, which one represents that? Where are the hands? *[After a short pause, the teacher continues.]* Which one reveals to you the personality of self and selfishness? Yes.

I'm going to try the serpent.

No, the serpent is a symbol of deception, also a symbol of wisdom, depends on how the serpent is. Yes, the ancient—the serpent is a symbol of wisdom, if it's coiled. Yes.

Gophers. [A different student responds.]

No. No. Think of that. Now think of all of the creatures of your planet. *[After a short pause, the teacher continues.]* Well, we must go on with class because time is passing so quickly. The vulture. What does the vulture do? *[The teacher pauses again.]* You see, anyone who is self-orientated is a vulture. Now if you will look at these beautiful—study these ancient stories, you will see that the vulture represents the epitome of the human greed and selfishness. That doesn't mean that the vulture is a bad bird. Or it doesn't mean the vulture is a good bird. It simply means that the vulture depicts the personality of selfishness.

What does the vulture do? Does anyone know what—yes, what does the vulture do?

Well, it lives off of someone else's efforts.

That's right! The vulture lives off of someone else's efforts. And what else does the vulture reveal?

That he's a scavenger.

He's a scavenger. Lives off of other people's efforts. That's correct. And what else does the vulture do?

Hoards.

Well, no. Does it make any effort to catch his own food?

No. [The student speaks softly.]

Pardon?

No.

No. He lives off of someone else's efforts; and therefore, he only eats what, [Student U]?

Carrion. [Student U also speaks quietly.]

What?

Carrion. Flesh.

Yes, but he only eats dead food.

Yes.

After someone else has done the work. Now what is the bird that represents—well, I already told you, goodness sake's alive. What is the creature that represents satisfaction? Hmm? *[After another pause, the teacher continues.]* Well, we're in the bird kingdom. So I already told you it's a bird. Yes, [Student H]. *[After a moment, the teacher calls on another student.]* Yes, [Student U].

Peacock?

No. No, the peacock represents pride. Just pluck its feathers and you'll see right away. *[After a short pause, the teacher continues.]* The hawk. The vulture only lives off of dead, dead food. Dead animals. The vulture lives off of someone else's efforts. The vultures will eat themselves, their little baby vultures, if there's nothing else to eat. Or didn't you know that? Oh, yes, yes, yes, yes. They're not particular. They will consume their own kind. They'll have them for lunch or for a snack. *[A few students laugh.]* Yes! Yes. And they pick everything, *everything* that they can digest. The only thing left when a vulture is finished, the only thing left are the bones. And the only reason that the bones are left is because the vulture cannot consume the bones. It consumes everything else.

The hawk, it represents satisfaction. The hawk attacks live prey. The vultures attack dead prey. The only reason the vultures attack dead prey is because someone else has made the effort. The vulture represents selfishness and self, lives only off of others' efforts, makes little or no effort of its own.

So don't be a vulture and don't be a hawk. Make some effort to come out of those centers of consciousness. Don't be a vulture in the sense of what it represents in creation. Hmm? Because you just may find someday, when you go home to your vulture family, one of them will decide they didn't get enough to eat and you won't be strong enough and you'll find yourself consumed by one of your kind. Yes. All right.

Now let's go on with our discussion. Yes, [Student D].

Does the eagle represent independence?

It's most interesting. I'm happy to . . . *[It is difficult to transcribe a few words.]* The golden eagle is the highest evolved. And if you would study nature a little bit, you would see, as far as mountains are concerned, where does the vulture live? How high up the mountain is his nest? And how high up the mountain is the nest of the satisfaction of the hawk? And just where is the golden eagle perched with his nest? [Student H]?

Way up high.

Yes. And so, you see, if you want to grow up—and you are destined to do so—then you must look at the mountain. Climb. It's a very high mountain. It takes effort. If you only get to where the vultures nest, then you haven't got very far. And then if you only get to where the hawks nest, you're only halfway up. But where the eagles nest is way high, high in the winds of reason. Yes. Yes, [Student H].

A while back, when you were talking about those so-called kings of the herd, those animals have qualified themselves to be the leaders—

Yes?

—of the herds.

Yes?

What about the other animals in the same herd? Are they dependent on that leader?

Oh, yes. Yes, definitely. They are dependent because, you see, they have not made the effort. Hmm? For example, when you see the leaders of a pack, you will notice, they'll go through this defense mechanism, this battle and etc. And the one who loses walks around in total self-pity, if he stays with the pack. Total self-pity. Yes. Does that help you with your question?

Yes.

Yes. Yes, [Student N] has a question, please.

What would make him leave? You said if he stayed with the pack.

Well, yes, they don't all stay, you know.

What would make him leave?

His own self-pity. Not being able to bear up that he didn't win. So overidentified. The vulture part, you see, the vulture personality being the strongest. Remember that vultures are personalities and eagles are principles. Yes.

But you [have] got to climb high on the mountain, and the mountain represents effort. You may pause for a moment, but if you go to sleep on the mountain that you must climb into the Light, where the eagles nest, then you must understand if you lay down and go to sleep, you may find yourself at the bottom of the mountain. Because you don't sleep on those kind of mountains. You only rest as you're climbing up. There's no sleep. They're very steep. Yes.

So—yes, [Student M].

Yes. I have one question. The Isle of Hist is located between the electric and the air center of consciousness.

Correct. Right where the faculty of reason is located.

Correct. Now since the light of reason is balance. They say that the Isle of Hist separates when the scales are imbalanced.

That is correct.

OK. Well—

You have forty functions and forty faculties, [Student M].

Right.

Yes?

Well, my question was, If it's located where the light of reason is, how does it become imbalanced in that—

If it's located where the light of reason is?

Yes.

How does it become imbalanced? *[After a short pause, the teacher continues.]* Is that the question?

I think—yes, I do.

Well, when you look down, what happens to you?

You become imbalanced. But then you leave that center.

Well, haven't you had experiences by looking down? What happened to you?

Yes.

Don't you experience need when you look down?

Yes.

Do you experience need when you look up?

No.

Well, there you are! You've answered your question.

Thank you.

You see, if you choose to look instead of view—when you turn your consciousness down, then you look; you see.

Right.

And when you turn it up, you view.

Right.

And the only time you experience need, the denial of what you are, is when you choose to look down. And then you become dependent on what someone else has that you can't control. And then life is miserable. Hasn't that been your experiences?

Yes!

Well, you've answered your question.

Yes.

So it is—is it the fault of the scales of balance or the faculty of reason that you choose to look over the precipice and, in so doing, to be tempted?

No.

Well, there you are. You see, you have forty faculties and forty functions. All of them being triune. Hmm?

Yes. Thank you.

Does that answer your question?

Yes.

I think you can relate to that, can't you?

Oh, yes. Oh, I can relate to it very well.

Well, when you look up, you feel whole and complete.

Yes.

And when you look down, you feel like you're half a person. And you want the other half of yourself. Pardon?

Yes.

Well, my goodness. Thank you. Do you have a—yes, good morning, [Student Y]. Yes.

So there's no end to the climb?

No end to the climb?

The climb up. Like—

Oh, no. There's no, there's no conquest. No, no, no. Conquest only exists in the descent, never in the ascent. There's nothing to conquer. One is what they are. Conquests only exist—challenges, stimulations, those only exist in functions. One looks down to conquer, not up. Yes, yes. One looks down to conquer, you see. And I have yet to find anyone on your planet that hasn't looked down to conquer. First of all, they have to look down in order to judge that they're a bit better. And because they're a bit better, that must be conquered; so, it can be helped. No, conquests—all conquests are downward. Yes. Thank you. Yes, [Student Y].

So in the—I might be getting a little ahead of myself here—

Well, perhaps I can help you. Conquest is a function, of course, and victory is a faculty. Yes. Does that help with your question?

[If the student responded, it is difficult to transcribe her response.]

All right. Yes, [Student D], please.

So when I climb a mountain physically on this plane—

Yes.

—and reach the top. Then, there is view. You don't really look because you see so much you view it. There's nothing to focus on specifically.

Well, there's nothing to focus on to control.

Yes. So—

We have no set targets up there.

So is that—if you climb the mountain, you can climb it in two ways. You can climb it to try to conquer or you can climb it—

No. Conquest—if you can consider downward a mountain, then yes, that's conquest. Yes, you do conquer.

Then what you feel when you reach the top of the mountain would be victory?

Well, that's what it is. It isn't a matter of feeling it. It is what it is, you see. You see, if you're in the mental, then you have conquer and conquest because you have denial and need. If you're in the spiritual, you only have victory and freedom and Light and Truth, you see? See, conquest, challenge, pride, those are all functions as you look down. You see that when you look down. Hmm? How pretty is the peacock when its feathers are plucked? Hmm? Have you ever looked at a peacock [when] they have no feathers left? Well, start plucking the feathers and you'll see and then you'll be inspired to [climb] up the mountain. Yes, yes.

Yes, [Student B]. Good morning.

Good morning. That exercise that we were given about the circumference of two circles—

Yes?

—to be equal distance—the distance apart is their circumferences.

In consciousness. Correct.

Are you talking, then, about the upper and lower as being a sphere?

They are spheres, yes. They are spheres.

And so the Isle of Hist is the separation of the two spheres?

Of the two spheres. So if one expands in their functions, then the distance between their identification with their functions is, in keeping with its circumference of expansion; the line of distance to their faculties is quite long, [Student B]. Do you understand? Because it's in consciousness, you see. It's in consciousness. Yes.

So as one gains control and makes conscious choice in reference to the exercise of their functions, then the distance between their functions and their faculties becomes shortened. Now when these two spheres, representing the four lower centers and the higher centers—do you understand that?—when these spheres, when the functions and the faculties, the distance between shortens—you understand that—then you will find that they become what is known as the scales of balance at the Isle of Hist. Hmm? That's what they become. Yes. And so you have the figure, what you call the figure eight. Yes. Go ahead. Thank you.

Why is it called the Isle of Hist?

"Why is it called the Isle of Hist?" I think that you should study—you're interested in medicine, aren't you?

Yes.

Well, then you should look into those books and you will find that it has been mentioned for eons of time, the Isle of Hist.

Thank you.

Yes, and very few medical people discuss it, but many know about it, because it's in this—it comes from the ancient Greeks and their medical studies, which in turn comes from the light of other understandings eons ago. The reason it's called the Isle of Hist—I can tell you this—is because it is in a certain location in the physical anatomy. It was given that name by a certain person eons ago and you have to go way back into ancient Greece and beyond. But it is there, yes. It just isn't discussed.

Thank you.

Now, look, I already told you and I'll go a little farther here before our class is over this morning. The Isle of Hist—and I've already given you the figure eight that is lying, what you would say, on its side. Now when you take the figure eight and you stretch it—you see, you find here's your faculties here and here's your functions here. *[As the teacher speaks, he places both his hands next to each other upon the table at which he is seated. As he speaks the word* stretch, *he moves his hands away from each other as though he were stretching a line. And as he says* faculties, *he taps his right hand on the table, and as he says* functions, *he taps his left hand.]* So as you stretch it out, it turns. *[His two hands move to now form a line that is at 90 degrees to the original line.]* Do you understand? It now is up and down, instead of north and south or east and west. Hmm?

And, as I said some time ago, we're working with our video computer and our equipment so that all of this can be drawn out for you. So that you could have, through—you know, they say that seeing is believing; unfortunately, it is. However, a picture is worth many words. And in that respect, we're working to get this worked out for you on these classes here, you see, so that we can have that imposed there. Yes.

Yes, [Student S]. Good morning.

Good morning. In order to contract this figure eight and stop this rotation, is that the reason why we're given to be still and to be at peace—to contract that?

To do your exercises. They are all designed so that you may return this Isle of Hist, which is being separated, you see. A person feels, "Well, I'm not feeling too well. I may be passing on, etc." You see, the Isle of Hist is so separated—do you know, when it reaches 81 percent of its separation, that's the tipping of the scale or the separation of the two, then that's when a person goes. That's when they go. And they either go to the functions or they go to the faculties. They go either way. Yes.

Thank you.

You're welcome, [Student S]. Good morning, [Student O].

Good morning, sir. Is it the earth's gravitational pull that stretches it north and south?

Yes, well, in a sense. It's the gravitational pull of one's own emotions and their own functions, you see. That's the gravitational pull. You see, the magnet is quite a pull.

Right.

And one has that magnet inside of themselves. You see, one is electric and one is magnetic. And when one is in balance, they're electromagnetic. That's the difference, you see. They're not all electric and they're not all magnetic. They are now electromagnetic, you see. They awaken and see that, "I have a magnetic thought. I have electric thought. This is a magnetic thought. I can see it very clearly because it is something I have thought before. It's coming out of my—it's actually subconscious activity. And I really—it has convinced me that I'm consciously thinking. Why, I'm not consciously thinking at all. This is a thought form and I've already had this thought form many times before in my life. So what is conscious about that?" Then one realize[s], "That's not electric! No, no, no, no. That's magnetic activity and I think that's conscious choice. My, oh, my!"

And I see our time is up. Thank you. Have a very good day. An hour has already passed.

DECEMBER 7, 1986

A/V Class Private 70

Good morning, class.

Today's class: "The Pillars of Salt."

As the ceaseless waves of emotion eternally wash the thirsty shores of need and deposit their salt on the table of self, man wonders why life is such a struggle and ofttimes difficult.

Life is not a struggle, nor is life difficult. You, your form, is composed of the salt of the earth. Whenever you believe you are your form, then you experience, by your belief in becoming, the pillars of salt.

Now the pillars of salt, by the very Law of Evolution, must spend their time in realms of Light and experience the transformation or the effect of the winds of reason. And so whenever you believe that you are that of which the planet that you reside temporarily upon—[you believe that] is what you are—then, for you, life is difficult and ofttimes miserable.

Some time ago, in fact, of recent time, I mentioned to you, again, about your study and your effort in understanding what your minds know as ancient mythology. I spoke to you of Ulysses. I spoke to you of the golden fleece. I spoke to you of this so-called mythology of Jason and the Argonauts. However, I find that some of you who have made that effort find the study of that so-called story interesting, but not applicable, of course, to you. I spoke to you, some time ago, of studying, also, Helen of Troy. You found it interesting, but, of course, a fable, a myth, not applicable to your daily lives.

And so here we are in these classes. Here, some of you are experiencing what you judge is your need. For when you understand that need, as I have so often spoken to you, is your denial of what you are. Need is the thirst. It is the dry shore that must be constantly washed by the ceaseless waves of emotion. For in that process, in that mental activity do you experience the salt on your table of life.

I've spoken to you about who mines the salt and its purpose. I've spoken to you about believing and its bondage. There is no way possible to permit your mind to think of what you know as self and not to experience the difficulties, the struggles, and the so-called miseries of life.

Life is beautiful. Life is purpose. Life is definite. Life is inevitable. For Life is eternal. Life is formless. Life is limitless.

You think of salt and you think of something that you season your food with. You think of salt as indispensable to life. You do not see that salt is indispensable to form, indispensable to creation, that it takes salt from your very being to form, to solidify what you know as a thought form, that it is actually a chemical process that takes place in the physical vehicle that you are not.

Neptune is the god of creation responsible. You must follow those gods' dictate when you insist on believing that you are the salt. When you form a thought and permit it to descend into your water center, you are a subject of those gods of creation. Either you service and follow their bid, whatever their bidding may be, or you experience what you know as the difficulties, the miseries of life. That, I assure you, is not Life. That, however, is what you know as thrill and glory. That is, however, what you know as sensation. That is what you know as stimulation to your senses.

Earth, fire, water, and air are controlled by the gods of creation who are in service to the throne of denial on which the fallen angel himself is king.

Whoever is in service to the king of denial shall suffer and struggle when they are denied. For the king of denial demands and extracts absolute obedience or you experience and believe that you are the thirsty shore on which the salts are gathered and placed upon the table of self for your senses to partake.

So often in your world you've heard a person say how hungry they are. Hungry for survival or hungry for sensation. Hungry for what? Hungry for what they believe they are and are not.

You cannot mix oil and water. So often I have spoken to you about that. Yet some of you insist that you will find a way to go against the very laws of nature, that somehow you will find a way to go against inevitable, immutable, divine law and still experience the joy, the goodness, the fullness of Life.

The king of creation himself tried to find a way and, in the great compassion and understanding of the Divine Light itself, was given his own domain.

The golden fleece that you ever seek, which is in truth the divine Light known as wisdom, is not available to the pillars of salt. For the pillars of salt in the sunlight of reason are blinded by their own reflection and cannot see the golden fleece, though it be laid at their very feet. And that is how it is not available to the pillars of salt, to the glory of limit, to the bondage of self.

Nothing has been withheld from the pillars of salt. Everything is revealed. But the pillars of salt, they shine too brightly and, therefore, cannot see what is right before them.

Now it's time for your questions on today's class, "The Pillars of Salt." Yes, [Student M], please.

Thank you. You last just said about the pillars of salt shining too brightly; and therefore, they cannot see.

Yes?

They're only seeing their reflection—I guess in my mind shining too brightly doesn't coincide with the pillars of salt. I'm trying to understand.

Have you ever placed a pillar of salt in the sunlight?

No, but I picture it now.

What color do you see as salt?

White.

Yes! What does white represent to you?

Purity.

Yes! When something is so pure, can it recognize anything else but itself? What is there to recognize when something is so pure and so perfect?

Thank you.

Like a brass doorknob, our darling egos are in constant need of polish. We seem to have no problem with the effort, do we?

No.

Does that help you with your question?

Thank you.

Yes. Good morning, [Student Y].

Good morning. Could it be said that salt is a type of energy in taking the ... becoming thought form?

That which you understand as energy—we're speaking of creation—the use of the energy, the transformation of it into form, that is a process that contains, within your body, what is known as salt. Yes. For example, perhaps you can best relate, when you permit yourself to think of self and you have what is known in your mind as a judgment—do you understand, [Student Y]?—and when that judgment does not receive what it demands it's going to receive, you experience what you understand as emotional turmoil. In other words, it starts to do its number in your water center of consciousness. When it is finished, you are exhausted and experience a lack of energy. Pardon?

Yes.

Now if you will understand that excitement is an activity of a pillar of salt, which is formed or solidified in your water center, then you will understand after it has got what it demands to get, your energy levels are decreased. Do you understand that? Does that help with your question? *[After a short pause, the teacher continues.]* Pardon?

Yes, it does.

Yes.

Thank you.

Certainly. Yes, good morning, [Student N].

Good morning. So if your ego—or you're denied something and you don't, you don't react to it and you don't service the— and the king of creation doesn't get your—you don't—

Yes, I understand what you're trying to say. In other words, if your judgment rises up, your pillar of—one of your pillars of salt that you have created, of course—

Right.

—and it does not get what it demands—

Right.

Is that what you're saying?

Yes.

What happens to it then? If you, in turning to the Light, do not service it, then the king of denial, who does not accept being denied—do you understand that?—will find another pillar [with] which to work on you and get (or mine) the salt that he mines. Yes, [Student N].

Find another pillar in you?

There's no problem. You are not short of pillars, are you?

No.

I don't think anyone on the planet Earth is short of pillars of salt. You see, the sadness that I see is that here, available to you, for eons of time, are teachings of the Light of eternal truth that no interest, serious interest, is placed in. Yes. Does that help with your question?

Thank you.

Yes. Yes, [Student Y].

Thank you. So the salt doesn't exist in the faculties.

No, no. Salt does not exist in the faculties of being. It exists only in the functions of being. It exists only in limit, yes. Yes.

Is it the same energy, just directed either—

It's the same energy utilizing different chemicals, yes. You see, the air that you breathe, without it, your form no longer exists. It goes through its transformation and returns to the elements who it belongs to. If you will remember that your form, your limit has a king, a very selfish king, and if you do not service the king that is the true owner of form or limit, [then] you must suffer as long as you identify with it. As long as you believe that you are limit, you must service limit or pay the price that limit will extract from you. Do you understand that? You see.

Now you don't have to service limit if you do not wish to service limit. The purpose of these classes—one of its main purpose[es]—is to help you to separate truth from creation. Creation is limit. You are truth. When you believe you are limit, then you must pay the price that is extracted for the luxury of deceiving yourself. Yes. Did that help you with the question?

Yes. Thank you.

Yes. Yes, good morning, [Student D], please. *[After a short pause, the teacher repeats his greeting.]* Yes, good morning, [Student D].

Good morning. Does salt—what is the counterbalance for salt in the faculties?

The counterbalance for salt—now think. Because it has been given to you. Earth. Fire. Water. Air. Electric. Magnetic. Odic. Ethereal. Celestial. What is the counterbalance? Earth. Fire. Water. *[After a short pause, the teacher continues.]* Electric.

Is it the— [Student D speaks very quietly.]

Magnetic. Did anyone perceive that? It's been given so many times. What would be the corresponding center? Yes, [Student R].

Ah . . . sorry.

No. "Sorry" is only a pillar of salt. Earth. Fire. Water. Air. Electric. Magnetic. Odic. Ethereal. Celestial. What is the corresponding center of consciousness, [Student R]? *[After a short pause, the teacher continues.]* Earth. Fire. Water.

Earth, fire, and water and the air are—

Electric. Magnetic. What's the next one? *[After a short pause, the teacher offers a hint.]* O?

Odic.

Oh, my! They're so nice and bright this morning. Odic! Now what is odic? Have you ever heard of ode or odic? Yes, [Student D].

I only can understand it terms of—would it be a water—the balance of water?

Yes! Now, you asked—I gave you the centers of consciousness many times. Earth. Fire. Water. Air. Functions, correct?

Right.

Faculties: Electric, magnetic, odic—hmm?—ethereal, celestial. All right? So if you have water for the function, what do you have for the faculty?

Would it be gas?

What is odic? *[After a short pause, the teacher continues.]* How does what you understand as a decarnated—a soul which has left your physical Earth planet, how does it enter and materialize in substance into your world again?

Like a mist.

And when it is fully materialized, what does it use?

Energy.

What is that energy known as?

Is that prana?

Well, yes, it's the life force of *prana*, yes. All right, [Student S], what is it? What is it?

The ethereal, which would be the odic.

The ethereal is next to the celestial. But the odic is the substance. What is it? Perhaps [Student U] has the answer here this morning.

Ectoplasm?

Ectoplasm! That's what you know as ectoplasm! That's what you dissipate with your needs. Ectoplasm! You dissipate the energy known as ectoplasm. You drain your faculties and service your functions. Then you ask—you see, so many students, you see, they want to see: "Well, I want to see this other world. I want to see a spirit materialize. I want this and I want that." And all of the energy, all of the energy is dissipated in their water center of consciousness. All of the energy is used for their table of salt. All the shores of salt fill up and the table of self glorifies. And then, the table of self cries out for more proof, more evidence, more facts, more this, more that. Every bit of goodness in your life requires energy. I've given it to you. A thousand, million times it's been given in the universes. And yet you insist, for the simple, so-called pleasures of your senses, [to] blatantly dissipate it and still cry out, cry out for spiritual awakening. Yes. That help with your question?

Thank you. [Student D responds.]

Yes, [Student U].

Do the—

You cannot have your cake and eat it, too. You insist on the goodness of the faculties at the demand of servicing the functions. So you dissipate the very life force, you dissipate the *prana*, and then experience a constant panorama of needs in the service of the glory of self as the salt of life is mined and you are only used. Yes, [Student U].

Do the pillars of salt support our judgments?

The pillars of salt *are* your judgments. The pillars of salt support the throne of glory that you know as self.

My students, must you turn into a pillar of salt, like Lot's wife, in order to awaken? Yes, [Student D].

So we have ectoplasm within us and it goes with us into the other realms?

Well, whatever you haven't totally dissipated. There is some, of course. You can't dissipate all of it. It takes, for you—speaking in your words in your world—it takes a certain amount of ectoplasm in order for the soul to have a covering that you know as a spiritual body. If there is insufficient ectoplasm, then you have a covering known as an astral or earth-bound body. Does that help you with your question?

Yes. Thank you.

The greatest dissipation, the greatest and easiest way to dissipate the ectoplasm are thoughts of self, are thoughts of lust. For it is the thoughts, you see, that uses the salt, the energy that is then mined by the king of creation and his henchmen. That's how you're used. Anyone who believes they are the form or limit is one who is used by the king of creation. As one of my students said here some time ago, "Thank you, Darling, I'd rather have the cash." But let us not forget: the thought is what drains most all of the energy.

You see, many times I've given to you: the faculties of being require use, which is a direction of energy. That that is not used for the purpose of its design is going contrary to the purpose of design. That which is not used does not receive energy. That which does not receive energy does not long endure. It begins to disintegrate, to return to its source. So wisdom reveals again and again and again: use it; don't abuse it. When you abuse it, you become it; you believe that you are it. Then you are truly a slave and a servant for the mining of the salt of life, you see? You do not deny its existence, for in so doing you destine yourself to it. Hmm?

And so again and again I have spoken to you: do not suppress, for you deny and you destine yourself to the experience that you have denied its right. Acceptance is the Law of Life. For without full acceptance, there is not full life.

It is a very thin line. It is a very straight and narrow path. For the minds of men are easily tempted, easily distracted, constantly making the effort to mix oil with water, constantly crying out about the misery and struggle of life, when they alone create the misery and struggle of life for themselves. For they are not living. You see, you cannot say that a person is living when a person has sold their soul and is used by others. No one could call that living. You may call it surviving, and rightly so. Living? No. Surviving? Yes. Hmm? Yes, [Student Y], please.

You just said that the saddest thing that you see is that the truth and Light is given, the truth is given, and yet none are taking it really seriously.

That is correct.

So that—

That is correct., I will say this, however, that after leaving your Earth planet, it is taken much more seriously. Much more seriously. Yes, go ahead, [Student Y].

So would that—that would be simply the energy not being given to the spiritual and the energy given—too much energy to the functions.

That is correct. That *is* correct. And so, you see, there is insufficient energy for the cloaking or the forming of a vehicle for the soul's expression in the higher realms of consciousness. Do you understand? You see? So there's insufficient energy. Now energy is available. But through constant[ly] being used by forms that people believe that they are, that energy continues to go [on] the downward path, which is known as the functions. Yes. Yes, [Student Y].

So that would be the cause of not seriously studying or seri— really . . .

It is—the cause is quite, quite clear. The mental substance, the human mind is ever seeking and searching for a way to mix oil with water, to have its cake and eat it, too. Yes. That is the cause, you see. And usually a person awakens that it's absolutely not possible, you see; that you must give one in order to gain the other. Because, you see, it is not looked at, you see, in clear, honest perspective. You see, a person says that "I need this or that." In other words, they've already established the thirsty law of the thirsty shore. Do you understand? And they believe—they insist on believing and have convinced themselves that that is what they are, instead of separating truth from creation, accepting responsibility for what they have, alone, created, and what is now using them and demanding that they service it, you see.

You see, there is one thing to make a conscious choice to service creation; to make an intelligent, conscious choice, you see. Because there is a responsibility. While you are using an automobile, you are responsible: if you wish it to service you, if you wish it to service you, then you are responsible to see that it receives sufficient fuel when you want to go somewhere. Now the simple question is, "Do I want to go somewhere this moment? If so, where do I want to go? How much gas will I utilize? How much will be used by this vehicle because I choose not to walk? How long will I permit myself to be in this vehicle and for this vehicle to have the sensation of gas pumping through it?" You see.

Yes, does that help with your question? But that is not how I find the minds on earth doing it, with very rare exceptions. No. Something comes up and it demands that they get into their car and it demands where it's going to go, when it's going to go, how it's going to go, and how long it's going to take. That's when, you see—that's abuse. That's abuse of the law for that which you have created is using you. You are not using it. Hmm? When the tools no longer serve the worker, the worker begins to serve the tool.

And so anyone who does not intelligently, consciously make a choice of picking up the tool with an understanding of what they're going to use it for and how long they're going to use it and when they're going to put the tool down is being used by the tool. And when the tool that is used to using them does not get to use them, then you experience what is known as an emotional upheaval and upset. Hmm? In fact, in your world, you ofttimes call it "crawling the walls." I've heard that statement made by some of my students—that you crawl the walls. You're going bananas. It is not getting what it is used to getting for you have allowed yourself to believe that you are the tool that you have created. Hmm? Yes.

You see, some time ago I also gave a class on the color of your eyes, the color of your hair, your height. All of those factors of your vehicle, you have established and are effects, they are effects of your abuses of the tools in your previous incarnations in evolution, you see. They are the effects of your use and they are the effects of your abuse. And that continues on moment by moment. You don't like your height? Accept it, for it is a lesson for you. You don't like the color of your eyes or anything else about your vehicle? Accept it, for you alone have created it. Hmm? Does that help with your question this morning? Yes.

We are easily tempted to have our cake and eat it, too. And many people go eons with that temptation, determined that somehow they can outsmart, outguess the very divine law that is. To the functions, it's known as tenacity. To the faculties, it's determination.

The luxury of self-thought is a great luxury. It is very destructive, for the luxury of self-thought offers to you your absolute conviction that you are the pillar of salt that you have created. And that pillar of salt, because its elements [are] from the king of creation, you are ever subject to and used by. So whenever you permit yourself the grand luxury of self-thought, then accept what follows it: self-destruction. Self-thought [is] self-destruction. For the very divine laws of evolution clearly reveal that you cannot remain in self-thought consistently, for the laws of evolution reveal there are moments when you are freed from it. And in those moments, you choose not to return and be used by that realm, and that's where your suffering, your misery, and your struggle is experienced.

I find that in applying these teachings that are demonstrable, so often, one, believing what they have created is them, do[es] not use their faculty of reason and say, "Yes, this is something I have created. I choose not to use it at this time. I alone will choose, after I turn my consciousness to the Divine which I am, above and beyond all creation I alone will choose when, where, and how and for what time. I alone in the light of reason that is within me, I alone with the God or the Goodness that I am choose that timing and return it to the Divine."

That effort is not made.

Because that realm tempts us and we are convinced by it, that no matter what it is, we, somehow, can manipulate and figure out a way, little realizing that someone else is convincing us of that so that we remain the little miners of the salt for the realm.

We can always tell when we are being used. For when the light is revealed, we think we're not happy. It tells us we don't want to hear that. We can tell where we are at any moment.

When I faced the wall of forms and it took—of course, like in anyone's evolution—time to accept that the wall was something that I had created. It was my own judgments! Those pillars of salt were only my own judgments. I understand that. You should understand that. Your upsets, your disturbances, your so-called needs, the effects of your own denials, *you* should understand that. All this emotional turmoil, all of this, this stating that, "Oh, why can't life be beautiful?"—Life *is* beautiful! "Why can't life be filled in abundant good and peace and harmony?" Life *is* abundant good. Life *is* peace and harmony! Just accept.

What you have permitted your mind to create for the glory of self you must service until you pay the price to free yourself from what you have created. You cannot blame the realm of creation because you were tempted to be king or queen of it and, in the temptation, awoke and found out that you were the slave of it; that someone else was king and queen. You cannot blame the law, when you alone chose the temptation and the thrill and the glory and awoke to find out that the glory was someone else's. And it convinced you that it was you, and you service it whenever it demands to be serviced. Hmm?

The law has no emotion. The law is principle. Personality is emotion. Personality is the domain of the king below.

And whenever you feel that you're losing your identity, be grateful. The greatest goodness that you could possibly experience is the so-called loss of your identity. In all these years in working with you, you have yet to know my identity. You gave me an identity. You call me an old man. Well, in that sense, I can fit that. I can even fit into a young boy if I wish. That's the freedom of self-control. When you spend eons to free yourself from the trap of identity, you are not easily tempted to identify with limit. Like in your world, they say, "I don't care what you call me as long as you call me to dinner." *[Many students laugh.]*

[After a short pause, the teacher continues.] Well, it's a beautiful holiday season in your world. It looks like a short class if we want to look at it. You see, no questions this morning. Everyone's so—oh, there, look at that. I can see a clock there in your world. Isn't that nice? *[The teacher laughs joyfully.]* I have my own clock. I think it's a bit more reliable, though. One's a bit off.

Yes, yes, good morning. [Student N] there has a question.

Yes. Can you relate this to growing more graciously, more—instead of being shocked every time you're awakened to a truth or the reality of what's really going on?

Well, the only thing that is shocked is that which has convinced you that you are it. And the only reason that it is shocked is it experiences what you know as fear (mental control) that it may not get the salt that it must get in order to do its service to the king. That's the only thing that's shocked. Now if you believe, of course, that you are the things you have created, then, in that sense, then you are shocked. You are not shocked. Only that which you have created and have convinced yourself—have been convinced by it—that that is you, that's the only thing that's shocked.

So growing more graciously is separating truth from creation.

Yes! Certainly! Separating what you are from what, in ignorance, you have permitted yourself, by the sensation to the functions known as glory, that you are them. Absolutely. There is no problem. As I said to you before, there's no problem. *[The teacher laughs.]* No problem. When it rises up in your mind and says, "Well, I haven't had any for a day. Perhaps even three days I've gone without." Well, just tell yourself, "No problem!" *[The teacher and Student N laugh.]*

And when you start doing that, you can go a week, a month, six months, a year, two years, because you're going to go without it sooner or later. Because I don't see one of you, having awakened—because you have awakened. You've awakened to the possibility there's something better than the things that have been using you. So that has registered within your consciousness. So I don't see any of you who—though some may well enter the astral realm, still convinced that they are that function, they still have that gnawing conscience that knows something different. [They] may not have yet experienced it, but somebody said there was a possibility. And so that's always with you, you see. Possibility is always with you.

And when you're down there working away and you'll have that gnawing thought, "Why, I'm exhausted. Why am I pumping away down here like this mining all this salt for someone else? I'm just being used!" That will awaken for you. Oh, certainly. Absolutely. Yes. Because, you see, it doesn't last, you know. No, sensation doesn't last. No, no.

Yes. Good morning, [Student L].

In the astral realms when you are mining and you—are you able— [Student L continues to speak as the teacher begins his response, but it is difficult to transcribe a few of her words.]

Well, yes, but we don't want to think that it's some mining that we're doing some tomorrow. We're doing it here and now, because, you see, we have a well solidified and created astral-mental body. Yes.

But are our own soul faculties and sense functions with us in the astral realm, too?

Why, certainly. Yes. Why, yes. Why, certainly. Yes, yes. Wherever you go that which you [are goes], you see; otherwise, there's no source of energy. Oh, certainly. Now the soul is still connected. It's still aware of what you're doing—what's being done with your form. Oh, certainly. It looks and watches, you see. Oh, why, absolutely. It has a responsibility. It may be far away. It's still connected and it sees very clearly. Yes, it must be dragged—you drag it through all of that. Definitely.

And then you wonder why you even bothered. It really wasn't—you know, the expectation was so much greater than the results. Is that what you say, [Student J]?

Yes, sir.

It's the expectation. Well, of course it is! Because, you see, the results, you only get a portion of it. A very small portion. The king of the salts, of creation gets all the rest. You don't get it. You're only tempted to believe that you get it. That's why the expectation is always greater than the results, you see. You only get a portion of the expectation. Just a very small portion. And you wake up with—what do that call it?—a hangover morning? Is that what they call it?

Yes, sir.

You see, that's when you realize that you got so little! How could you have believed you were going to get so much when you ended up with so little? Yes. Yes, you see, [Student J] knows that. Expectation is far greater—90 percent greater than the results, you see. Hmm?

Thank you. [Student L remarks.]

Does that help you? But, you see, that's known as temptation. You see, there's all these promises to your mind of how much you're going to get and how little you have to give. And then you awaken the next morning and find out it was just the opposite: how little you got for how much you seem to have given. Do you understand that? Yes, why, certainly. But you got plenty, because you got the thrill of temptation. You got the stimulation, you got the challenge, and you got the glory—during the expectation process. Do you understand that?

Yes.

Yes. You see? It's like a pregnant mother, you see. Oh, the expectation is just—Oh! It's so great and everything else. And then when it comes to a few labor pains, what happened to the thrill of expectation? *[A few students laugh.]* When it comes to paying the small price and for how many years after that? Because labor pains don't end, you know, at the moment of birth. No, no, no, no. I think any mother will agree with her emotions that it's been a phenomenal, painful labor.

Yes.

You know, to raise the little prize of her jewel, it's been quite a labor, you know. Many still have the labor pains of their emotions forty, fifty years later, you see. Certainly. Some only thirty-some years later. I'm sure you would understand that. Well, it's just the payment for the great thrill and challenge and stimulation of expectation. Hmm? You know, it's like looking at an ice cream and saying, "Oh! Oh, that'll taste so good! Oh my!" And then, the next day they say, "Another five pounds!"

I think it's time. Thank you. It's been a very nice day with you this morning. And do give a little more consideration to applying what you already understand. And separate what you are from what that thing likes to have you believe that you are.

Good day.

DECEMBER 14, 1986

A/V Class Private 71

Good morning, class.

Now I know that some of you have been reviewing what has been discussed in these most recent classes. Some of you, fortunately, have been viewing the studies in the classes from the realms of objectivity, known as the realms of reason. However, some, also, have been viewing it, unfortunately, from the water centers of emotion.

And [Student B], could you move a little to your right, please? Perhaps—that's better. Yes, I like to see everyone.

Now this morning we're going to discuss something that is important, very important to all of us as students of the Light. Our school, as I have spoken to you before and as my channel, of course, has informed you, is in the process of moving north. Now time in your world passes very quickly. And before any impending changes or moves, everything that we believe that we are rises up to once again convince us that that is what we are. And so we experience what we understand as upset and frustration, emotional trauma. We experience emotional trauma because we permit ourselves, once again, to believe what we are used to is what we are. And we all know that what we are used to is not what we are, for when we change from what we are used to, we continue; we continue on and prove, once again, to ourselves that we are not what we are familiar with.

So [these are] the growth steps that you, as individual students and as collective students, as a class, are moving through in consciousness. The only thing that ever controls our mind is fear. That's the only thing that controls our mind is fear. And we fear, always, with our minds, what our minds look at and judge that they cannot control, for that's the way minds work. The fear offers to us, of course, various emotional experiences.

Now you, as a class and as students, have been granted, in keeping with your own evolution, the opportunity to move to the new location of the school. You have been, also, granted the opportunity to attend classes, for I will be with you in class once a month. Looking on the positive side of that, that will give to you the opportunity of time—that so many minds seem to think they're short of—the opportunity of time to study your classes, to review your classes, to apply, of course, what you've received intelligently. We also, of course, will experience what we are used to, as my little student here is experiencing, *[The teacher may be referring to Reddy, the church's dog, who was present in the class. The recording suggests that Reddy is sleeping.]* what we are used to and what we are not familiar with: change of location, change of mental patterns, and that can either be harmonious for us or it can be most discordant.

All of you know that whenever you permit your minds to take control, that you are governed by a dual law. The laws of duality are not the laws that are the power of peace. They are not; they cannot be, they never have been, and they never shall be. That is one thing that is absolutely guaranteed, is the law that is.

And so in this morning's class, I want you to raise your hands if you have reached a decision, as an individual, in whether or not you have decided to move to the new location of the school or to remain wherever you choose to remain. And the school, of course, will continue to be open and to serve the Light and the purpose of its design.

The manifestations, outwardly, as I have said before, are revealing the inner conflicts and the inner disturbances. One cannot free themselves from anything that they are not aware of. And so when you're faced with change, you become aware of what you believe that you are and what you believe that you control with your mind.

Now you can become aware and can react through the water centers of emotion, or you can become aware and act through the centers of consciousness of reason and move along harmoniously with the ever-changing tides of emotion and creation.

You don't battle creation. You understand the purpose of its design. You grant it its right to serve its purpose of design. You look at it for what it is and refrain from believing that you are what it is, for without that objectivity, [the] difficulties and struggles of life become unbearable. For in the realms of consciousness of the functions, there is a constant battle. Harmony is not a function; it is a faculty. Discord is a function. So when you find yourself in discord, be rest assured you have established the Law of Distraction. On the spiritual path of Light and illumination many things will distract you. To those who believe they are limit are easily tempted and never ever fulfilled.

And so now we'll take these moments for any of you students who have made your decision. Yes, [Student M], please.

Yes, I would like to make the move up north.

Well, may I say something to you, [Student M], in establishing the law for you?

Sure. Thank you.

To like something is not a conviction. It is a desire. Now there's a vast difference between a desire and a conviction. A person establishes the Law of Conviction by stating, "I shall do this, I shall do that, be this, be that in divine order," for that is when you release it to the Divinity within one's own being. We like many things. They reveal our desires. Desire alone is not what will bring a change that a person has decided to make in their life. It takes more than desire. It takes the very Source that supports desire. We like to do many things. We commit ourselves to do few. Go ahead, [Student M].

Yes, and I'd like to restate it.

Well, you see, I'm trying to show you the difference of which laws are established. The spoken word is life-giving energy. And when it is used to declare a desire, then it is controlled by the realm that controls desire. And the realm that controls desire is easily tempted and frequently distracted. Yes.

Thank you.

Yes.

I shall move north be it in divine order.

Well, you want to do what you want to do, but you want to feel it in your heart.

Yes.

If that is what your heart wants, then the law for you, of course—or for anyone—is established. You see, what happens when we make a commitment? When we permit ourselves to make a commitment, that means to us we cannot be distracted. That means, to us, that regardless of all temptations and distractions, our commitment is our character. And everything within us, in that respect, is at stake, you see.

Yes.

Now no one, no human being chooses to make a commitment without a full understanding of what's at stake. Because they know that when they commit themselves, they have presented to creation their pride and presented to the Light their soul. Do you see?

Yes.

So it's one thing, you understand, to present one's soul to the Light, for it is the Light. And it's something else to present oneself to their pride and to creation, that is governed by a dual law, you see.

Yes.

Does that help you, [Student M]?

Yes.

You see, in other words, a like is always subject to another mental realm of consciousness that is discordant with it. And distractions and temptations are when we permit our self to identify with our mind: we guarantee the discord, the conflict.

Well, it's like going to a store. You go to the store. It's Christmastime. So it's time to go to a store for most people. You go to a store and you make a purchase. You go home and you start to think about yourself, because you've already thought of yourself by going to the store to make the purchase. You might have deceived yourself that you're thinking about someone else, but that's not really what life reveals. No. We may think we're thinking about someone else. And we go to a store and we make a purchase. We've already established the law to think of our self. And so we come home, and we are well identified with our self. And then suddenly, seemingly out of the depths of who knows where, we don't feel right that we made that purchase. Every justification and every excuse rises up because we have now opened up those doors through which many different realms are fighting for control. Do you understand?

So when you face such an important thing as a physical move in your life, you face a move in consciousness at the very thought of a physical move; you face a move in consciousness [at that thought]. And when a person, living anywhere, becomes familiar with their surroundings, they feel secure for they feel a degree of control over what they're familiar with. This is why familiarity, indeed, breeds contempt, because there's the battle: the contempt is the battle to control. Surely, marriage reveals that. A person has a honeymoon only to guarantee a lifetime of contempt. And then they look around to justify why they should live in their own contempt. Hmm? Would you understand it that way?

It's true.

Oh, good. All right. Now [Student O] wishes to speak. Yes.

Well, I constantly work on the acceptance of the possibility of a joyous and harmonious move up north.

[If] that's what you want to do, you commit your soul and face your pride, [then] there's no problem at all for [Student O].

Hmm? You see, remember, you commit—you see, it isn't a matter of committing your soul to Serenity or committing it to something you can't control, because you *are* the Light. You committed to the Light within you. But when you try to control it with the mind, you've got a problem, like all of us have a problem, you see. You know, when the mind takes a look and says, "Well, I commit myself to the Light. Now let me see, how can I control the Light? I am not used to committing myself to anything I can't control." Do you understand?

Yes.

Yes. All right, good.

Anyone else wish to speak? *[After a short pause, the teacher continues.]* Well, it looks like my channel and [Student M] and [Student O] will be the only ones making the move. Yes, [Student Y], there, has something to say this morning.

Yes. Thank you. In my heart . . .

Yes.

. . . I feel it's right to make the move and, yet, there is something—

No, let's go with your heart.

OK.

What does your heart want to do?

It wants to make the move.

Well, then, you see, all you have to do is to keep your identification on your heart [and] you'll have no problem.

OK.

But if you insist on playing with that "but" part, then you have all kinds of problems. So if you want problems—I stopped you at the "but" door—if you want problems— *[The teacher coughs.]* Excuse me—just insist on giving that life-giving energy. All right?

Thank you.

Fine. Now did someone else—[Student S] wishes to speak here.

Yes. I shall move north be it in divine order.

There is no reason—you see, what I am trying to show you—and this is very important to you as students for classes will be going through a change. You don't have to move anywhere. You have the opportunity and when—you also have the great benefit of facing what your minds go through. So how can you separate truth from creation, if you don't have the experiences of what creation is and what truth is? You see, you must have personal awakening inside of yourselves in order to discern between truth and creation. Yes, [Student U]. Thank you.

I shall move north with my school be it in divine order.

Yes, your school will be open whether you move or not. I do want you all to understand that. And because it is so much closer than the minds of my own students realize, including the mind of my own channel, it is so much closer—you know, you think that a week, a month, if you're waiting for it to pass, it's like a year. When you're not waiting for it, it goes like an hour, you see, in your world, you see. And so I am spending this time today, as I have spent [time] with you before, that you may prepare yourselves and not go into the emotional water centers of consciousness, you see.

Now I could appeal to your egos and say, "Well, are you not adventurers?" Well, adventure, it's an endeavor! *[The teacher laughs.]* Now if you want to call an endeavor adventurous to make it sound more pleasing to your mind, well, no problem. Call it an adventure, but you will find out that an adventure is, in truth, this adventure—if you wish to call it an adventure—is an endeavor. It's responsibility and it's work. Everything is being worked out to make it possible for all of you as students to make whatever change that you in your heart truly, truly have committed yourselves to make. Now it's entirely up to you, as individual students, whether or not you wish to choose one path or the other. Yes, thank you, [Student U]. Yes, [Student H].

I shall move north be it in divine order.

Only if you—now remember, when you make that statement, you commit your soul to the Light that you are, and you will have to face the pride of the functions that you are not, yes. It's kind of like moving in with the relatives, you know. *[A few students laugh.]* Don't worry, you won't be moving in with my channel. *[The teacher laughs joyfully.]* But, yes, you would relate to that, wouldn't you?

I sure do.

Yes, yes. Well, you know, [if] a person has a small enough place, you know, there's no room for relatives. Yes, go ahead, [Student H].

I'm grateful, I'm grateful to you for giving us this opportunity ahead of time so that we can face this creation going on in our minds. I well remember the experience of being given nine seconds to make a decision to join the class.

You made a decision, didn't you?

Yes, I did.

So, you see, it doesn't take nine years or nine months.

No, it doesn't.

You see, it doesn't take that at all.

And I'm grateful for that.

Yes, you know, here the other day, my channel's guide suggested that he might enjoy a movie. In fact, she selected it for him. And a very wise choice, because it is quite humorous. Well, the name of the movie—I don't think you've seen it; you might have—is called The Need to Breed. It's— *[The teacher and many students laugh.]* In fact, it is such a lovely, little movie, and considering that it's only forty-five minutes and considering it is here available in the school, just might put it on for you for a forty-five minute enjoyment. *[The teacher laughs again.]* He, of course, "What is that?!" *[The teacher seems to be referring to his channel's reaction.]* And anyway, it's The Need to Breed, but I am more interested in the principle of this need to breed.

Now if you can take the principle of the need to breed and not just relate it to a pregnant mother, then perhaps you'll get a little understanding of this need to breed in our human ego. We breed so many things, you see. We mother and father them constantly. Well, it's actually about something about the fraternity of maternity or something of that nature, but anyway, I'm sure you will all enjoy it after class. And so after class, because it is such a short, little, short subject, you see—forty five minutes, yes—you, I'm sure, will get some perspective in reference to the problems of the need to breed in the human uneducated ego because there's so much breeding going on there. And, as I say, it's a fine, fine little movie there.

Thank you, [Student H]. And [Student B] wished to speak here this morning.

My initial reaction was I had a strong desire to go, and I've had to back off a little bit and say, "Is this my desire or is this God's?" And so right now I'm at the point where I'm saying God's will be done.

That's correct. And we must never forget, [Student B], that God's will is done through man, never to man. So, you see, in God's will, the will of Goodness, the Principle of Goodness, we must permit our self to be receptive to that, you see.

Now what does that mean? How does one become receptive to the will of God or the Principle of Goodness in life? One becomes receptive to the will of God, the Principle of Goodness, by the absolute abstinence, absolute abstinence of what is known as judgments. So our part in experiencing the will of God, the Principle of Goodness, the divine, impartial Light, is the absolute abstinence of judgment.

Now how does one abstain from judgment? One finds it so difficult to abstain from judgment, when total acceptance is the will of God. One finds great difficulty in abstaining from judgment; yet desires the experience of the will of God, you see, flowing through them. First of all, judgments cannot be formed without mental dictates. We all know that. It is not possible for a judgment to breed, to be born, without a dictate of mental substance.

Now, as I gave to you in one of the other classes, accept the possibility. "I accept the possibility of experiencing the goodness that I am." Now you had that in your classes. And what else did you have with that, [Student S]? *[After a short pause, the teacher continues.]* Was that the end of it? Did you receive no more? "I accept the possibility of experiencing the goodness that I am." And what is "the goodness that I am"? Yes, yes, [Student S].

Light, Truth.

Yes, that is the goodness that we are. But did I not give you the rest of that? [Student D].

Well, I don't know if you gave it to me, but I always say, "God is the true and only source of my supply."

That is true. "I accept the possibility of experiencing the goodness that I am and the goodness that I am is my faith in God," for that is the goodness that I am. So if you allow yourself dictate, you breed judgments, you experience fear and selfish desire; the mind is plagued with doubt, and you are bound in those experiences to what you are not.

See, when you have—you allow the mind the registration of the divine expression or desire, that follows with a dictate: your mind tells you how this desire is going to be fulfilled. You see, the mind does that. That's the great trap. You see, the Light has guided us for this great change. I spoke to you before because you are prepared in stages—a little bit here, a little bit there. So when that day comes, which is much sooner than any mind in your world realizes, when that day comes, then the transition is harmonious.

So the question, then, you must ask yourself [is], "What am I doing in reference to what I have decided that I shall do?" You see, because you are an individualized being, an individualized soul, that which you commit yourself to attain, you are responsible to attain it. You cannot depend upon my channel. You cannot depend upon me. I will not permit it. I will not depend on you. Therefore, I have established the law not to permit you to depend on me. Do you understand that? So, you see, that's personal responsibility. The effect of that, of course, is freedom, you see. You make your own decision. You don't have to move anyplace. You don't have to do anything. Classes will continue on, monthly, but you have that opportunity to see what you and you alone decide [what] you and you alone are going to do.

If we were not familiar with going to the store to buy a loaf of bread and it was our first experience, we would have a great deal of trauma. And after having eaten the loaf of bread, we would be very emotionally upset [and ask] was it worth it. Because it's not familiar. So, you see, I'm trying to get you to understand and to see clearly we are controlled by the things that we are familiar with for we have deceived our self that that which we are familiar with we can control. Now the first time you step in a car, to learn to drive it, you have many different mental, emotional experiences. Ah, but once you have made the judgment that you are familiar with it—therefore you control it—there's no problem. You rarely even are aware that you've even stepped in your car. Look at the driving record of some of my students. Hmm?

All right. Now anyone else wish to speak this morning? Yes, because I am going to show you *The Need to Breed* movie. Yes, yes, [Student D], please.

I have faith there is no problem. I will move north.

Is it what you want to do?

Yes, it is what I want.

Well, then you have no problem. You're absolutely right, [Student D]. You have no problem whatsoever. Hmm? Yes. Anyone else? Yes, [Student L] wishes to speak.

Originally, I was sure I was going. I had problems since then. But I'm sure in God's time—

You had time to think about yourself since then?

I guess so because—

Well, perhaps you could talk to [Student P].

But I'm sure that—

But do you realize, [Student L], that all of this that you're not sure of, since then, do you realize that that is something that you have allowed yourself to be convinced by [and it] offers you nothing but doubt and fear?

Yes, I have.

So a person makes the conscious choice to be controlled by doubt and fear. That's their right. And so it is also their right to have the experiences of the suffering that doubt and fear brings to any mind. Yes. You know, they say that misery loves company. Well, I'm sure you will agree that without company misery does not long endure. Yes, pardon?

So I don't know, perhaps, [Student P] would like to be company with you. Did anyone else—thank you. Would anyone else have anything to say? Yes, yes, [Student P] wishes to speak to be in company with misery. Not you, I do know the difference, [Student L]. But as long as you permit yourself to believe that you are that ego, that it demands and insists on doubts and fears, then, of course, you must have company. And [Student P] has risen her hand. I don't know whether she wants to be company with misery or not. Yes, I know she has not too many problems being company with her own, but being company with someone else's is something else. Yes, [Student P].

I shall move north be that in divine order.

Yes, if that's what you really want to do. And what about being company for misery?

I'd be more than happy to help for—

The misery or the soul? *[Many students laugh.]*

The soul.

Well, I think, then, you should help your mother-in-law sometime later, after you leave the temple. *[Student L was mother-in-law to Student P.]*

Thank you.

You're welcome. [Student N], please, yes.

I've thought about it and I still haven't made a decision.

No problem whatsoever. Let's see, who do I have? [Student L]! You talk to [Student L] after you leave school. I'm sure she'll be able to help you. Thank you. Is there anyone else here? [Student J] is quiet as a little mouse, a church mouse. *[Many students laugh.]* But we know what he's going to do. *[The teacher laughs.]* Has anyone been left out? Just [Student N] and [Student L], [those are] the only ones have I left out there. Anyone else indecisive? Oh, [Student B] is working on it, isn't that right?

I wanted to stop working on it. [Student B replies.]

That's a very good I idea! Now that's what I call an idea, [Student B]. You know your—what [color] is your hair? A bit silver? Well, it would be snow white if you keep working on it. *[The teacher and a few students laugh.]* You know, that's true. And I am happy that you have a little sense of humor there. So often we work on something so much it exhausts us. And when we're totally exhausted, something gets done. Isn't that true?

Well now, I'm going to close up class here in a few moments and then I'm going to show you or have my channel show you this wonderful movie. What is the name of that, [Student R]? The subtitle is *The Need to Breed*.

From Here to Maternity. [Student R responds with the proper name of the movie.]

Oh, *From Here to Maternity*. Well, there you are! We are moving from here to the coast and it's very appropriate. I'm sure you're going to see that. *From Here to Maternity. [Many students laugh.]* Yes, yes, yes. Well, from here to eternity is understandable; [from] here to maternity, we're still in creation there, aren't we? Yes. You will get a great deal out of that I'm sure. *[The teacher laughs joyously.]*

Now [Student J], do you have anything to say to me here this morning there?

Not even a word.

You had to rush. Oh, no, no, no. Just regarding life itself. We know where you're going. Look, you got to go where you want to go. You like it up north. We already know that. Perhaps they don't know that, but that's all right. And whatever appears to the mind to be the obstruction—do you have a sharp pin?

Yes, sir.

Just give it a little pluck. It is only a balloon of nothingness, you see.

Yes, sir.

That's all it is. I'm not saying that your mind is nothing, when you believe it's something. *[The teacher laughs joyously.]* But see there: my student Mr. Red there is trying to help you. Try to understand that, you see? You want to be where you have peace and harmony.

Yes, sir.

And you'd like to get out of the rat race that is rather blatant. So that's already in process, without saying too much. And so, you see, it's a matter of timing. Well, don't you remember telling my channel, so many years ago, "Why, their timing over there in the spirit world is terrible."

Yes, sir, I do.

Well, if it was so terrible, we wouldn't have class today, would we?

No, sir.

No, I can assure you, timing is ever in keeping with the law, and it's not as terrible as some minds like to think that it is, you see.

Yes, sir.

You see, it's—as long as you like the crisp weather, you know. Aren't you from Chicago?

Yes, sir.

Well, you have no problem! It is not even quite that windy.

But, you see, the vibration—what I'm trying to help all of you, as students of the Light, with—the vibration in the atmosphere, it's time to make the change. The atmosphere of not just this little town here, I'm speaking of this entire area, is being suffocated with mental substance, with unfulfilled desires, with frustration and disturbance in the atmosphere itself. So the area has served its purpose for the Light. Do you understand that? And we do not choose an area that is more suffocating. Do you understand, [Student J], as a student of mine over these many years?

I do.

So it is time for our school to make its move. And to move into an atmosphere—and I'm not just speaking about—I'm not speaking [about] a physical world. Do you understand? I'm speaking about the atmosphere—when I speak of the atmosphere, I think of: are there twenty trillion forms or only a billion? There's a great difference, you see. And so we're making this transition at this [time] to go to what you would understand as a less polluted atmosphere. And I'm not talking about smog, unless you want to call those forms "smog." But they suffocate just as much.

So, you see, because everyone has personal responsibility. If you're living inside of a coal mine—if at first it was fresh air and became a coal mine, do you understand, then you would want to move into fresh air again, having experienced so much fresh air in life. Do you understand that? And so that is the basic purpose of our moving. The temple has served its cycle and its location. It will soon be ten years. Do you understand? And the timing has come. Now I'm impressing this on your minds on a regular basis so that you can go through all the changes inside of yourself, you see.

You see, it isn't a matter of what the mind likes to say, "Well, you're getting old. Or you'd like to have more peace and harmony." Peace and harmony and wisdom does not come with age. Why, I know many old people; they—no, no, I would not consider they have peace, harmony, or wisdom. They have something else, but not that. And so it isn't guaranteed with age. What's guaranteed with age is a slowing down of the functions. Now if one calls it, from that perspective, "My functions are slowing down. Therefore, I am gaining wisdom. I am gaining peace and harmony," that's ridiculous because their mind doesn't slow down. Only the body slows down, you see. But their mind can be just as active as it's always been, you see? All right.

And so we're moving from an area of increasing pollution—you hear?—to an area with far less pollution because the timing is right. You see, the timing is right. And so you say, "Am I talking about two months or three months?" No, I'm not going to tell you that and have your minds play all kind of numbers with that. I'm telling you that it is in process. You see, because that's what it is. It is in process. It'll happen sooner than some of your minds can possibly imagine. And you know when the Light moves—and I do know you know that—it moves very quickly. Very, very quickly. All right?

Thank you. Anyone else? [Student Y] wishes to speak this morning.

Yes. Thank you. Could you, please—I want to make sure that I have the last part of "I accept the possibility of experiencing the goodness that I am."

The goodness that I am is—

The goodness that I am is my faith in God.

It's not what I said, is it, [Student S]? The goodness—the goodness that I am is the faith—yes? What did you write down?

I wrote down "is my faith." [Student S replies.]

Well, isn't that interesting. What did everyone else write down?

"*My*" [Several students respond.]

Yes, yes, [Student H]. He's usually good at dictation.

I have, "And the goodness that I am is my faith in God."

Ah! And what did you have down, [Student D]?

I had, "And the goodness that I am is faith in God."

Yes. And [Student L].

"The goodness that I am is my faith in God."

All right. And [Student U].

"And the goodness that I am is my faith in God."

All right. Anyone else? *[After a short pause the teacher continues.]* Now what was it you said, [Student Y]?

I said, "And the goodness that I am is my faith in God."

Is that what was said? *[After a short pause, the teacher continues.]* That's what it is. Because it is your faith. It's not [Student J's] faith or [Student U's]. It is yours.

All right. I want to make sure. You know, so often in classes in dictation—fortunately we have these lovely magnetic tapes, you know—everything gets written down a little differently. Have you ever noticed that, [Student J]?

Yes, sir.

A little bit. Just a tiny bit. Yes. You put the punctuation in a different place and you have an entirely different meaning to a sentence. Would you not agree to that, [Student B]?

It's true.

Just change the punctuation; you change the entire principle of the law revealed. Yes. Does anyone else wish to speak this morning before you see your breeding movie? *[After a short pause, the teacher continues.]* Aren't you interested in breeding, [Student J], when you've bred so much?

Are you talking to me, sir?

Yes.

No, I'm really not. [Several students laugh.]

Aren't you interested in breeding a greater abundant good in your life?

That, yes.

Well, that's multiplication. That's creation. You know, without the laws of multiplication, you don't have creation, you see. They increase.

Yes, sir.

You are interested in increase, aren't you?

Yes, sir.

Well, then to be interested in increase, one must understand there must be some interest in the need to breed, for the effect of the need to breed is increase. Don't you see that principle there?

Yes, sir.

I think it was a different perspective there, wasn't it?

Yes, sir.

You had a need to breed and you understood the need to breed to be one thing. Well, look at the whole, the whole horizon of it: the need to breed, the need to breed: to breed, to multiply, and to increase. But not the need to do so. Hmm? The acceptance that it is, for in creation they breed constantly, yes. A person has a thought, one thought; it immediately seeks its mate, do you understand that? You have a thought in the electrical, in the electrical being of your conscious thought, you know what happens to that? If you think of self and you continue to identify with self, this electric thought that you have descends into the water center. What do you think it does in the water center? Hmm?

Becomes a judgment?

Yes, all alone? It finds a mate. Or it rises back up to create a mate. Do you understand? Look, think of what the breeding of the thought, the need to breed—we're talking about the human mind. The human mind is need. All right? Now, you say, "Well, I need $500,000." Judgment, right? Thought. Goes down into the water center. The thought solidifies as a judgment. It looks around. Well, it doesn't have any mate. So you know what it does? It rises back up again in the emotions and you feel an emotional need to have $500,000. Right? Emotionally. You feel this emotion rise. For that initial thought has gone down into the water center, by overidentifying with self. Looking around, it has no mate. Rises back up again, and you get the emotion of a need for $500,000. Goes back down again and it starts its breeding process. Then all of these other ones start rising up to justify why you don't need $500,000, you absolutely have to have $500,000. Do you understand that?

Now, then they go back down into the water center. They've justified—these are the children, you see? This is the principle of the need to breed. This is why I'm going to show you this lovely movie, *The Need to Breed*, because we want to see what this need to breed [is] and how it works. Do you understand that? Now, for the little film, it's just working for, on the magnetic forms. But it took an electric form to get the magnetic form to react for this process to go. Well, you see, the same thing is happening in the human mind. Do you understand that? You see? This need to breed. So when you permit yourself need, you start the breeding process. You see? Have one thought and tell me how long it will take you before another thought rises up equally and you experience the emotions and another ten or twenty rise up to justify why you must fulfill those. Wouldn't you call that breeding, [Student S]?

Yes.

You see, that's the breeding. And so I'm going to close class now, so that you can watch this lovely film on the need to breed and see how it happens. Oh, they won't tell you about the water center. All you have to do is look at it and you will see it very clearly, you know. You do realize on our last discussion that my student there, [Student U], found out it's 92 percent water. And? Ninety-two percent on the discussion of our last class—yes?

And salt. [Student U responds.]

And salt. Sodium chloride.

Yes, sir.

In equal parts. That's salt, you know. Hmm? Ninety-two percent water.

Now, I want all of you to enjoy this lovely film, *From Here to Maternity*. It's a brand new film. And my channel was guided to rent it just last evening. And he did get to see it. Couldn't understand why he rented it, but anyway. *[The teacher and a few students laugh. Mr. Goodwin was often guided by the Council to take actions and they frequently did not explain their reasons for an action.]* Perhaps he will after today's class. Because that's what's happening in the human mind.

I spoke to you—I even gave a little booklet on the celestial marriage long, long ago in your world. *[Please see the appendix for the complete text of "The Celestial Marriage."]* So few have studied to understand it. And so you have the celestial marriage and you have the other marriage, the one below. So, you see, a thought of anything always seeks its mate in the water center. You understand that? And having done so, they get married and they start their breeding process. And so whoever permits themselves the luxury of need, the denial of God, is guaranteed to have many children to look after. Hmm? Did that help you, [Student J]?

Yes, it does, sir. Thank you.

Oh, my, indeed. Indeed, all kinds of little children start to grow, you see, from the breeding process. There is no more fertile area for breeding than the water center. Nature reveals it to you: 92 percent water, child.

Thank you. Have a lovely day.

DECEMBER 21, 1986

[Editor's note: this is the final class of this series. The monthly Thursday evening classes, known as the A/V Seminars, continued for a time. Mr. Goodwin and the temple remained in Marin County. On February 24, 1989, Mr. Goodwin passed to the higher life.]

APPENDIX

The Divine Healing Prayer

I accept that the Divine Healing Power
Is removing all obstructions
From my mind and body
And is restoring me
To perfect health, wealth, and happiness.
My heart is filled with gratitude
For the Divine Law of Acceptance
That is healing both present and absent ones
Who are in need of help.
Peace, the power that healeth,
Is guiding my thoughts, acts, and deeds
As God and I go hand in hand
Living a life of joyful abundance.

The Total Consideration Affirmation

I am the manifestation of Divine Intelligence. Formless and free. Whole and complete. Peace, Poise, and Power are my birthright.

The Law of Harmony is my thought and guarantees Unity in all my acts and activities, expressing perfect Rhythm and limitless flow throughout my entire being.

Without beginning or ending, eternity is my true awareness and sees the tides of creation, as a captain sees his ship.

As the Light of Truth is sustained by the faculty of Reason, I pause to think and claim my Divine right.

    Right Thought. Right Action. Total Consideration.
                  Amen. Amen. Amen.

Divine Abundance

Thank
(Gratitude)

You
(Principle)

God
(Divine Intelligence)

I'm
(Individualizing)

Moving
(Rhythm)

In
(Unity)

Your
(Realization)

Divine
(Total)

Flow
(Consideration)

The Controlled Spiritual Environment Affirmation

You are in a controlled spiritual environment of truth and freedom
Where peace and harmony reign supreme.
Be awake, be aware, be alert.
Your purpose of being is freedom from what has been.
Thoughts of self are foreign to this environment.
Take control of your mind and experience the joy of living.

The Laws Be

Our being is the consciousness, Truth.
Holy be the identity
The joy of Life
The totality of Acceptance
In mind as it is in heart
Grant us the Light
Our daily sustenance
And forgive us our has-beens
As we forgive those has-beens who tempt to steal our joy
Free us from the romance of self-love
Deliver us from the service to the false king of shadows
For Light is the kingdom
And the power and the glory forever
Peace be, the order of Divinity.

The All That Has Been Affirmation
From A/V Class Private 12

All that has been cannot be
That's not Good and I'm not free
Until I give then I be
The joy of life that sets me free.

The All That Has Been Affirmation
From a Recording of Affirmations

All that has been cannot be
That's not God and I'm not free
Until I give then I be
The joy of life that sets me free.

"Oh, Love Divine" Affirmation

Oh, love divine, a servant be
'Til selfishness imprisons me
And warps the reason of my mind
Into the madness of the blind,
When truth cries out, "Not mine but Thine"
And frees my soul with love divine.

"I Accept the Possibility" Affirmation

[In A/V Seminar 16, the following affirmation was given and was referenced in A/V Class Private 60.]

I accept the possibility of experiencing the goodness that I am.

[In A/V Class Private 71, this affirmation is refined. The refinement process of this affirmation is worthy of consideration.]

I accept the possibility of experiencing the goodness that I am. And the goodness that I am is my faith in God.

Humble

[Here are the lyrics for the song entitled "Humble," which was referenced in A/V Class Private 61.]

God free me from the needs of glory
That I may be a simple story
In the pages of your book
Where all may see the way I look.
Humble, may I never fail to be
Humble, bowing to a God so free
Humble, accepting all my life has earned

Humble, freed from pride of what I've learned
Humble, let my will respond to Thee
Humble, seeking not the power to be
Humble in the work I have to do
Humble, honesty will lead me through.

※

[The following text is from the personal notes of the vice president of Serenity, a man who also served as the cameraman for these classes. This procedure is referred to in A/V Class Private 29.]

Acupressure of Circle of Logic

This procedure, as given by the Friends, is to help students restore balance in their universe, as long as effort is being made by the student who is the recipient of the procedure.

Procedure:

The student who is seeking help should sit, with back perfectly straight, on a stool or low back chair. Hands in lap, body completely relaxed.

Student to be helped, and one who will administer the pressure, should do the cleansing breath, three times. *[Note: A/V Class Private 30 also recommends that the person administering the pressure have clean hands and that their hands be rinsed with water immediately before and after the procedure.]*

The student who is to administer the pressure should stand behind the seated subject. Referring to diagram, place the index finger on top of middle finger. Be sure your finger nails are short enough so they won't dig into the other student's neck. Place the middle finger on the spot, point "A" on diagram, press firmly, and rotate tip of finger in small circle to the right, clockwise, 14 revolutions. Change fingers so that the middle finger is on top of the index finger, see diagram. Press index finger firmly, on same spot and rotate counterclockwise 13 revolutions.

Find spot "B" on diagram, and repeat procedure. Rotate middle fingertip 14 clockwise, then rotate 13 counterclockwise with the index finger. That completes the procedure.

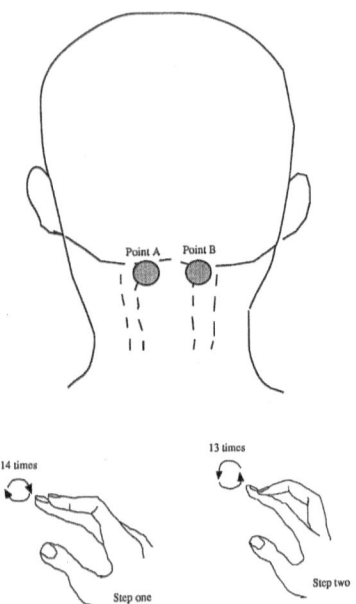

[In A/V Class Private 71, the teacher refers to a pamphlet that was published by Serenity many years earlier, entitled, "The Celestial Marriage". Here is the text of that pamphlet as it was published. An asterisk indicates a page break.]

THE CELESTIAL MARRIAGE
or
THE DESCENT OF MAN

A FABLE
FROM
THE BOOK OF LIFE

*

GIVEN IN HUMILITY
TO ALL
HUMANITY

*

One day in great **ASPIRATION GOD** sent forth from itself **WILL**, and the sons of **WILL** became. Now the sons of **WILL** were of **GOD**, yea, they were **GODS** sent into form, but knew not because of form. The sons of **WILL** roamed the universes for eons and eons of time ever seeking other forms. After much searching they met to consider what they must do. For seven days and seven nights they discussed, and at the seventh hour **ILLUMINATION** fell upon them and said, "Behold, sons of **WILL**, within thyself is **COMPASSION**, know it, and unto thee shall be given." Alas, the sons of **WILL** knew **COMPASSION** and that night the daughters of **DESTINY** became.

In the morning when the daughters of **DESTINY** awoke to the sons of **WILL**, the **GODS** and **GODESSESS** of nature danced in jubilee.

Now the sons of **WILL** married the daughters of **DESTINY** and all nature wept with joy.

One day in **TRUTH** a son was born, his name was **INEVITABLE**, and the sons of **WILL** were greatly pleased. Now the daughters of **DESTINY** were quite unhappy for they **HOPED** for a daughter, and so that night in **DESIRE** a girl was born, her name was **LUST**.

Now **INEVITABLE** grew in the warmth and sunshine of the day. Oh how he loved the sun, for to him all **LIFE** was **LIGHT**.

LUST grew up to be a beautiful and lovely woman with a great fondness for the moon and darkness, for had she not been born in the night of **DESIRE**.

Time passed on, and one day **INEVITABLE** felt he would go into the night to find **LUST**, for he had heard so much about her, and had sent her many messages asking her to come into the **LIGHT** so that they may know more of each other. **INEVITABLE** went down, down into the darkness of night, and as he descended a great **FEAR** overcame him, but he found **LUST**, her face glowing so beautiful by the reflection of the sun. From the shadows where the **LIGHT** of the moon shone not, a voice spoke unto **INEVITABLE** and said, "Behold the beauty and the glory thou hast found, is it not worth the descent into our realms?" But from within, a voice spoke to **INEVITABLE** and said, "Take her to the realms of **LIGHT** that you may see more clearly in a day of **REASON**."

The senses won, and that night in **DESPAIR** a child was born, her name was **GRIEF**. The years passed and **GRIEF** could not be comforted, for she had been born of **LUST**, in the night of **DESIRE**, by the promptings of **PASSION**, and knew not of **TRUTH**.

INEVITABLE wandered on and on with the daughter **GRIEF**, hoping to return to the realms of **LIGHT**, but no, the centuries passed and only **SORROW** did they know.

Then one day a bird from the realms of **LIGHT** landed on his shoulder and sang this song, "In **SORROW** doth thou stay for self-pity knows no way."

INEVITABLE thought and thought of the meaning of those words, then he thought of his homeland **TRUTH** where he had been so very, very happy; and in **CONCENTRATION**, he found himself leaving the realms of darkness, passing through the lands of **IGNORANCE** and **EXPERIENCE** to return to his blessed land.

LOVE ALL LIFE
AND KNOW
THE LIGHT

*

OH MAN THINK HUMBLE
YET WELL OF THYSELF
FOR IN THY THINKING
IS CREATED
THE VEHICLE OF
THE SOUL

Cover Image of 1972 Edition of *The Living Light*

[The cover image of the 1972 edition of The Living Light *is displayed on the frontispiece of this volume. Reference to the symbolic image is discussed in excerpts from the following volumes of* The Living Light Dialogue:*]*

[Volume 2, Consciousness Class 44, pages 480-481:]

"And we'll begin with the outside of it, *[The teacher refers to the cover image.]* which is the snake, representative of wisdom consuming itself. Now why does the symbol of wisdom consume itself? Does anyone know? Does anyone know why wisdom is self-consuming? Because, my friends, if it's wisdom, then it can gain nothing from outside of itself: it already is wisdom. So all that wisdom is—you understand, you don't gain wisdom and neither do you give wisdom. Wisdom is self-sustaining. When you rise to a level of consciousness where wisdom expresses itself, then you will become it and it is self-sufficient unto itself. So the snake consuming itself is representative of wisdom, in comparison to what one might call knowledge. Now, knowledge is something that you gain. It's something that you put into your brain and you feed back at your discretion—but not wisdom.

"The next step is the interlaced double triangle, which is a very, very ancient symbol. It is the meeting of the spirit with matter. It is the power above that meets the forces below. And at that junction, when those two triangles meet, that's the negative and the positive poles come together in creation and the divine spark, the rays of light, life is so-called born into matter.

"Now you all know that all poles are triune. The negative pole is triune and the positive pole is triune. In fact, my friends, as we've stated before, all things that are manifest are triune and that is why three is the number of manifestation.

"Inside of the interlaced triangles you'll notice on the top of the pyramid in the rays of light is the all-seeing eye. Now the all-seeing eye is that that is not distracted, because it sees everything and so nothing gains its attention. And that is why it is the all-seeing eye. The triangle itself, the pyramid upon which all knowledge, the all-seeing eye, all wisdom, and all life rest, is the pyramid of manifestation. All things in all universes (physical, mental, or spiritual) are triune. There are three parts to all things: that is an absolute fact of physics and it is a truth of the universe."

[Volume 4, Consciousness Class 78, page 172:]
"Then, we'll be happy to share our understanding. The serpent so designed—consuming itself—is the ancient and eternal symbol of everlasting and eternal wisdom. The double triangle, with its apex downward, is the manifestation of the Divine Power and the balance of nature, its own creation. The pyramid with the all-seeing eye on the top is the eternal Light that never closes, that sees all things, that knows all things, and that ever is and ever has been."

www.ingramcontent.com/pod-product-compliance
Lightning Source LLC
Chambersburg PA
CBHW030144100526
44592CB00009B/107